POPULARITY IN THE PEER SYSTEM

POPULARITY
IN THE
PEER SYSTEM

edited by
ANTONIUS H. N. CILLESSEN
DAVID SCHWARTZ
LARA MAYEUX

THE GUILFORD PRESS
New York   London

© 2011 The Guilford Press
A Division of Guilford Publications, Inc.
72 Spring Street, New York, NY 10012
www.guilford.com

All rights reserved

No part of this book may be reproduced, translated, stored in
a retrieval system, or transmitted, in any form or by any means,
electronic, mechanical, photocopying, microfilming, recording,
or otherwise, without written permission from the Publisher.

Printed in the United States of America

This book is printed on acid-free paper.

Last digit is print number: 9 8 7 6 5 4 3 2 1

Library of Congress Cataloging-in-Publication Data

Popularity in the peer system / edited by Antonius H. N. Cillessen,
David Schwartz, and Lara Mayeux.
   p. cm.
 Includes bibliographical references and index.
 ISBN 978-1-60918-066-9 (hbk. : alk. paper)
 1. Popularity. 2. Peer pressure. 3. Social acceptance. 4. Social interaction
in children. 5. Social interaction in adolescence. 6. Social status.
I. Cillessen, Antonius H. N. II. Schwartz, David, 1962– III. Mayeux, Lara.
 HQ784.P43P67 2011
 303.3′27—dc22
                             2010045001

*To our wonderful nieces and nephews,
the young lights in our lives
who have taught us so much:*

Maaike, Jop, Aafke, Susanne, and Yvonne
—A. H. N. C.

Jessica, Lucas, and Sadie
—D. S.

Nathan and Taylor
—L. M.

About the Editors

Antonius H. N. Cillessen, PhD, is Professor and Chair of Developmental Psychology in the Behavioural Science Institute and Vice Dean of the Faculty of Social Science at Radboud University in Nijmegen, The Netherlands. Dr. Cillessen's research interests include peer relationships in childhood and adolescence, popularity, aggression and antisocial behavior, the development of social cognition, and research methods for developmental psychology (sociometric methods, social network analysis, observational research, and longitudinal design and analysis). He has served on the editorial boards of *Developmental Psychology*, the *Merrill-Palmer Quarterly*, and the *International Journal of Behavioral Development*.

David Schwartz, PhD, is Associate Professor in the Department of Psychology at the University of Southern California in Los Angeles. Dr. Schwartz's research is broadly concerned with the links between social problems in the peer group during childhood and adolescence and the development of psychopathology. He has published widely on topics related to bully/victim problems in school peer groups, community violence exposure, peer relationships across cultural contexts, friendship, aggression, and popularity. Dr. Schwartz has also served on the editorial boards of *Child Development, Developmental Psychology,* and the *Journal of Abnormal Child Psychology*.

Lara Mayeux, PhD, is Associate Professor in the Department of Psychology at the University of Oklahoma in Norman. Dr. Mayeux's primary research interests are peer relationships and the development of peer status in middle childhood and adolescence, with a particular focus on popularity. Her work, funded by the National Science Foundation, has focused on behavioral, social-cognitive, and gender issues in popularity.

Contributors

Julie Wargo Aikins, PhD, Department of Psychology, University of Connecticut, Storrs, Connecticut

Amy Bellmore, PhD, Department of Educational Psychology, University of Wisconsin–Madison, Madison, Wisconsin

B. Bradford Brown, PhD, Department of Educational Psychology, University of Wisconsin–Madison, Madison, Wisconsin

William M. Bukowski, PhD, Department of Psychology and Centre for Research in Human Development, Concordia University, Montreal, Quebec, Canada

Antonius H. N. Cillessen, PhD, Behavioural Science Institute, Radboud University, Nijmegen, The Netherlands

Karmon D. Dyches, MS, Department of Psychology, University of Oklahoma, Norman, Oklahoma

Gary C. Glick, BS, Department of Psychological Sciences, University of Missouri, Columbia, Missouri

Andrea Hopmeyer Gorman, PhD, Department of Psychology, Occidental College, Los Angeles, California

Sandra Graham, PhD, Department of Education, University of California, Los Angeles, Los Angeles, California

John J. Houser, MS, Department of Psychology, University of Oklahoma, Norman, Oklahoma

Scott D. Litwack, MA, Department of Psychology, University of Connecticut, Storrs, Connecticut

Peter E. L. Marks, MA, Institute of Child Development, University of Minnesota, Minneapolis, Minnesota

Lara Mayeux, PhD, Department of Psychology, University of Oklahoma, Norman, Oklahoma

Don E. Merten, PhD, Department of Anthropology, Ball State University, Muncie, Indiana

Adrienne Nishina, PhD, Department of Human and Community Development, University of California, Davis, Davis, California

Anthony D. Pellegrini, PhD, Department of Educational Psychology, University of Minnesota, Minneapolis, Minnesota

Amanda J. Rose, PhD, Department of Psychological Sciences, University of Missouri, Columbia, Missouri

Cary J. Roseth, PhD, Department of Counseling, Educational Psychology, and Special Education, Michigan State University, East Lansing, Michigan

Marlene J. Sandstrom, PhD, Department of Psychology, Williams College, Williamstown, Massachusetts

David Schwartz, PhD, Department of Psychology, University of Southern California, Los Angeles, California

Rhiannon L. Smith, MA, Department of Psychological Sciences, University of Missouri, Columbia, Missouri

David W. Solberg, BA, Department of Educational Psychology, University of Minnesota, Minneapolis, Minnesota

Mark J. Van Ryzin, PhD, Oregon Social Learning Center, Eugene, Oregon

Preface

An 11-year-old girl cries to her parents one day that the popular crowd at school made fun of her, and then days later asks if she may invite those same peers to her birthday party. A well-known high school athlete is involved in a fistfight with a less popular peer, and the athlete is reprimanded and sent back to class, while the peer's parents are called and he is removed from the school. The news that an admired "supercouple" has engaged in sexual intercourse for the first time spreads quickly across the high school campus, and the boy receives pats on the back while his girlfriend is covertly called a "slut" by other students.

The often paradoxical dynamics of high-status children and adolescents and their peers are puzzling yet fascinating to parents, educators, and researchers. Feature films of the last 20 years and recent nonfiction books such as *Queen Bees and Wannabes* (Wiseman, 2002) attest to the popular interest in "the cool kids." Although there has been a recent surge of interest in popularity and the behaviors of the "in" crowd, social and scientific interest in this topic is not a recent phenomenon. The first empirical study on popularity among children actually appeared in *Child Development* in the 1930s (Koch, 1933), and Moreno's classic book *Who Shall Survive?* was published just a year later. In his book, Moreno (1934) described what he called "sociometric stars"—those individuals who were looked upon favorably by the majority of their peers and stood out as highly accepted members of the classroom. These early investigations of high-status children conceptualized popularity as a combination of acceptance, liking, and positive feelings toward a child on the part of the social group. It was considered a universally desirable characteristic in children, thought to be associated with all kinds of positive attributes.

A long tradition of studying well-liked children, called "popular" children (or "sociometrically popular" children), was born, and hundreds of studies on the topic were published in the decades following Koch's and Moreno's writings.

Developmental psychologists continued their interest in so-called popular children well into the 1980s and 1990s, developing unique and highly technical methods of measuring status and behavior in the peer culture. These researchers broadened our understanding of these high-status children in many ways, describing their typical peer-directed behaviors, social cognitions, and emotional development, and "popularity" came to be understood as an indicator of any number of socially competent behaviors and positive outcomes.

Over time, however, researchers began to question what exactly they were measuring when they assessed "peer popularity," particularly among adolescents. Research findings that did not fit the traditional pattern began to emerge. Consider the experience of this volume's first editor. Along with a colleague, he conducted an investigation of children's perceptions of what makes a peer popular. Children were asked directly to list characteristics of popular children, and the researchers expected to hear responses such as "kind," "funny," "helps others out," and the like. Although those responses did appear, so too did other responses of a very different nature: "mean," "snobby," "hurts other people"—not at all the traditional understanding of popular children.

It became clear over time that the term *popularity* meant something very different to children than it did to the developmental psychologists studying them. (Researchers in other fields, such as sociology of education, had already been conducting ethnographic studies of popular adolescents for some years with much success; the results of their investigations are also discussed in this book.) To children and adolescents, "being popular" suggests a complex interplay of social behaviors, attitudes, and benefits, not all of which are positive, easily understood, or even fair. The scenarios described in the first paragraph of this preface are representative of the often confusing and frustrating nature of social status dynamics, but they are certainly not exhaustive. Since the 1990s, a growing number of studies from a variety of fields have illuminated the distinction between being liked (our old definition of *popularity*) and being socially powerful. Our understanding of the various forms of high status, how they are alike and different, and how they fit into the ecology of the social group has been greatly improved by the efforts of these researchers.

This book describes that body of work. Drawing from developmental psychology, sociology of education, social psychology, and other fields, we present here a summary of the empirical research on popularity as a social developmental phenomenon. To clarify the terminology we use in this volume, the term *social acceptance* is used to refer to social preference or peer liking—peer relations researchers' classic definition of "sociometric popularity." The word *popularity* is used to refer to status derived from social prestige, social power, or social visibility—often called "perceived popularity" or "social network centrality" by researchers. Part I is a review of the methods used to study popularity in the peer system. We begin in Chapter 1 with William M. Bukowski's discussion of the history of the study of popularity. In Chapter 2, Antonius H. N. Cillessen and Peter E. L. Marks then critically analyze the most common methods used to measure peer status during a variety of developmental periods and summarize the strengths and weaknesses of each one. In Chapter 3, Don E. Merten presents the sociological perspective on the study of popularity, highlighting the ethnographic method of studying peer status and summarizing the sociological findings.

Part II discusses the development of popularity, including the development of behaviors that are strongly associated with it. In Chapter 4, Lara Mayeux, John J. Houser, and Karmon D. Dyches tackle a conceptual and empirical question that researchers have faced from the first published studies of popularity: Is popularity any different from peer acceptance? They argue that popularity and social acceptance are indeed two distinct constructs and review the evidence in support of this argument. Amanda J. Rose, Gary C. Glick, and Rhiannon L. Smith then present in Chapter 5 a critical review of how our notions of gender differences in popularity map onto actual observed gender differences. In Chapter 6, Anthony D. Pellegrini, Cary J. Roseth, Mark J. Van Ryzin, and David W. Solberg discuss the important role of aggression and highlight the similarities between social dominance and popularity. In Chapter 7, Julie Wargo Aikins and Scott D. Litwack summarize the research on the role of social competence and prosocial behavior in the development of peer status.

Part III focuses on contextual influences on popularity among children and adolescents. In Chapter 8, B. Bradford Brown discusses the developmental context of adolescence and situates the study of status within the dynamics of adolescent cliques and crowds. In Chapter 9, Amy Bellmore, Adrienne Nishina, and Sandra Graham review the literature on the role of ethnicity in popularity and highlight the need for more careful consideration of the cultural context in which status develops.

Part IV tackles the complicated issues of influence and risk. In Chapter 10, Marlene J. Sandstrom draws from social and developmental psychology to review the literature on peer influence and then discusses the role of popularity in social influence among youth. In Chapter 11, David Schwartz and Andrea Hopmeyer Gorman summarize the research linking popularity with negative outcomes such as substance use and poor academic functioning and present some possible mechanisms to explain the link between high status and risk. Finally, Part V concludes with Chapter 12 by Antonius H. N. Cillessen, which presents a theory of popularity, an integrative account of the development of high status in youth and its implications for long-term outcomes.

REFERENCES

Koch, H. L. (1933). Popularity in preschool children: Some related factors and a technique for its measurement. *Child Development, 4,* 164–175.

Moreno, J. L. (1934). *Who shall survive?: A new approach to the problem of human interrelations.* Washington, DC: Nervous and Mental Disease Publishing Co.

Wiseman, R. (2002). *Queen bees and wannabes: Helping your daughter survive cliques, gossip, boyfriends, and other realities of adolescence.* New York: Crown.

Contents

I. METHODS OF STUDYING POPULARITY

Chapter 1   Popularity as a Social Concept: 3
Meanings and Significance
William M. Bukowski

Chapter 2   Conceptualizing and Measuring Popularity   25
Antonius H. N. Cillessen and Peter E. L. Marks

Chapter 3   Being There Awhile: An Ethnographic Perspective   57
on Popularity
Don E. Merten

II. DEVELOPMENT OF POPULARITY

Chapter 4   Social Acceptance and Popularity: Two Distinct   79
Forms of Peer Status
Lara Mayeux, John J. Houser, and Karmon D. Dyches

Chapter 5   Popularity and Gender: The Two Cultures   103
of Boys and Girls
Amanda J. Rose, Gary C. Glick, and Rhiannon L. Smith

Chapter 6   Popularity as a Form of Social Dominance: 123
An Evolutionary Perspective
Anthony D. Pellegrini, Cary J. Roseth, Mark J. Van Ryzin, and David W. Solberg

| Chapter 7 | Prosocial Skills, Social Competence, and Popularity
Julie Wargo Aikins and Scott D. Litwack | 140 |

III. POPULARITY IN CONTEXT

| Chapter 8 | Popularity in Peer Group Perspective: The Role of Status in Adolescent Peer Systems
B. Bradford Brown | 165 |
| Chapter 9 | Peer Popularity in the Context of Ethnicity
Amy Bellmore, Adrienne Nishina, and Sandra Graham | 193 |

IV. POPULARITY AND ADJUSTMENT

| Chapter 10 | The Power of Popularity: Influence Processes in Childhood and Adolescence
Marlene J. Sandstrom | 219 |
| Chapter 11 | The High Price of High Status: Popularity as a Mechanism of Risk
David Schwartz and Andrea Hopmeyer Gorman | 245 |

V. INTEGRATION

| Chapter 12 | Toward a Theory of Popularity
Antonius H. N. Cillessen | 273 |

| Index | | 300 |

Part I
METHODS OF STUDYING POPULARITY

Chapter 1

Popularity as a Social Concept
Meanings and Significance

WILLIAM M. BUKOWSKI

Popularity is a ubiquitous concept. In Western consumer-oriented cultures, the word *popular* is used to describe a wide range of entities and activities, including music, consumer products, services, foods, types of art, ideas, fashion and modes of dress, hairstyles, forms of dancing, politicians and their platforms, and commercial enterprises. "Pop" music has been part of Western culture for at least 60 years and is a mainstay of our collective consciousness. The major figures from the artistic genre known as "pop art" are among the best known of the 20th century. (Everybody knows Andy Warhol!) In Francophone nations, one can't walk through a community larger than a village without seeing the word *populaire* in the name of banks that primarily serve the needs of individuals and small businesses (e.g., La Banque Populaire in France, La Banque Centrale Populaire in Morocco, and La Caisse Populaire in Quebec). A Google search of the word *popularity* turns up more than 132 million sites, about twice as many as found when *friendship* is used as a key word. Popularity, it seems, is everywhere.

If there is any traditional domain of scholarly study in which the term *popularity* is used frequently to refer to an important construct, it is the study of children's and adolescents' peer relations. Although the word *popularity* was not used in the earliest studies on peer relations (e.g., Monroe, 1898), it appears in all seminal handbook chapters of the past 60 years (e.g., Anderson & Anderson, 1954; Hartup, 1970, 1983;

Thompson, 1960). It appears also, in one form or another (as *popularity, popular,* or *populars*), in a large number of empirical studies from the 1930s to the present day. Bibliographic search techniques such as PsychInfo and Google Scholar turn up thousands of hits when one looks for studies of children and adolescents with the key word *popularity.* Avoiding the concept of popularity is nearly impossible for anyone with an interest in peer relations.

Given its frequent use in everyday life and in research, one would expect that the meaning of popularity is well known. The breadth of its use, however, exceeds the specificity of the meanings attached to it. The word *popularity* has been used in at least two ways. First, in a collective manner, it is used to refer to measures indicating how much a person is liked or disliked by peers and how much status or notoriety the person has in the group (see Bukowski & Hoza, 1989). In this way, popularity is not a particular construct or variable but is instead the name for a set of variables that index a child's general liking-, disliking-, and status-based experiences with peers.

Second, the word *popularity* has been used to refer to a particular aspect of general functioning among peers that is distinct from other fundamental variables such as acceptance and rejection. Whereas acceptance and rejection refer to the overall amounts of liking and disliking a child experiences, popularity is an index of the child's position in the group's dynamics. Popularity is typically measured via peer assessments that assign a "popularity" score to children according to how often they are chosen for items such as "someone who is popular" or "someone who is liked by everyone" (see Cillessen & Marks, Chapter 2, this volume).

Although it is easy to accept the generality or lack of specificity in the first usage of popularity, it is more difficult to do so with the second. In spite of the large number of studies that use a measure of popularity, the meaning of the construct remains elusive. Basic questions about the meaning of the words *popular* and *popularity* have been addressed rarely. These questions include what these words mean, where they come from, how they are used, and how the phenomena they represent fit into our theories about the features and effects of peer relations.[1] The goal of this chapter is to provide some answers to these questions. The particular concerns of this chapter are to examine where the word *popularity* comes from, how the concept of popularity has been used in the study of

---

[1] Two exceptions to this lack of attention are Cillessen and Rose (2005) and Lease, Kennedy, and Axelrod (2002).

social relations, how it has been linked to other concepts in the social sciences, and how popularity intersects with youth development. Particular attention is given to the problems associated with the empirical study of popularity with school-age and adolescent samples. Solutions to resolve these problems are proposed.

WORDS AND THINGS

It is not too much of a simplification to say that this chapter, and perhaps the rest of this book, is about a word and the phenomena it represents. Words, terms, and expressions are the common currency of social processes, including scholarly activities. One does not need to be Benjamin Whorf, Lev Vygotsky, or Michel Foucault to know that the value and power associated with a word depends on the meanings attached to it. The meaning ascribed to a word determines the role and impact that it has in human discourse, thought, and behavior. For these reasons, a discussion of popularity as a social concept needs to begin with a consideration of where this word comes from and how it became introduced into general usage and the more particular literature on peer relations.

Why Go to a Dictionary?

Efforts to trace where a word comes from and to identify its meaning often start with large archival dictionaries of the world's major languages (Krappmann, 1996). The archival dictionary tells us the roots of a word, what it has been known to mean, and when it made its first appearance. This dry but rich information about a word's developmental history can be instructive. One does not need to be a developmental psychologist to know that the past can tell us about the present. A dictionary is one route to knowing the meanings of a word and where these meanings came from.

Where Did It Start?

According to the *Oxford English Dictionary* (OED; Simpson & Weiner, 1989), the words *popular* and *popularity* have multiple interrelated meanings. The adjective first came into English in the 15th century to describe laws and regulations for the common person rather than the aristocracy. In about the mid-16th century, it took on a broader meaning and was used to describe entities of the common people as a whole rather then any group within it. Central to its meaning was the notion of being ordinary or common. Something that was popular was "intended for or suited to ordinary people" (p. 124), had found "favour with or approved by the people" (p. 125), or was "prevalent or current among or accepted by the people generally" (p. 125). In a similar way, the noun form was first used in the 16th century to refer to political movements of the common people rather than the upper classes. By the 18th century, it referred to "actions or practices of ... trying to win favour" among the common people or "condition of being approved, beloved, and admired" (p. 126). Even as a noun, *popularity* has a largely descriptive meaning. Definitions of popularity do not tell us what it is as a particular entity; instead, they tell us that popularity refers to a characteristic that is ascribed to an entity (i.e., that it has general favor or approval).

Liberté, Égalité, Popularité?

The descriptiveness of these words is not an accident. The *OED* also indicates that the words *popular* and *popularity* came into English from the French words *populaire* and *popularité*. The *Dictionnaire Historique de la Langue Française* (Rey, Tomi, Hordé, & Tanet, 1994) shows the links between the two languages with French preceding English. According to the *Dictionnaire Historique*, *populaire* and *popularité* have had a largely descriptive purpose. The adjective *populaire* entered French in the 14th century with an apparently simple meaning. It was used to describe an entity as belonging to the people rather than the clergy or the ruling class. The first uses of *popularité* were also descriptive and quasi-political. It referred initially (16th century) to "membership in or belonging to the same people or nation" and later (18th century) to "having the favor of the largest number of the people" (p. 1580). It is difficult to imagine that it is a coincidence that this latter meaning entered French just before the events of 1789. Noteworthy are the chronological, historical, and substantive parallels between the paths of these words in French and English.

The French words *populaire* and *popularité* worked their way into languages other than English. The words for popularity in each of the other Romance languages demonstrate their common origin: *popularitat* in Catalan, *popolarità* in Italian, *popularidade* in Portuguese, *popularitáte* in Romanian, and *popularidad* in Spanish. Beyond the languages with immediate Latin origins, similar words can be found in Danish and Swedish (*popularitet*), Filiipino (*pagiging popular*), German (*popularität*), Turkish (*popülerlik*), Russian (*Популярность*, roughly *popuyjarnost*), and even Welsh (*poblogrwydd*). The archival dictionaries of these languages indicate that the immediate roots of these words are French.

Importantly, the definitions of these words parallel those found in the *OED* and in the *Grand Larousse*, the archival dictionary for French. For example, the dictionary of Spanish produced by the *Real Academia Española* defines the word *popular* as "belonging or related to the people." According to the *Türk Dil Kurumu*, the archival Turkish dictionary, *popülerlik* means "to be supported by the public." The German dictionary *Duden für Etymologie* tells us that *popularität* refers to something that is "an essential product of the public opinion."

The generality of these definitions is expected given the meaning of the Latin word (*popularitas*) that is the root of the original French word. *Popularitas* is a noun in the genitive case indicating possession. The root of *popularitas* is the noun *populous*, meaning "the people." Accordingly, *popularitas* means "belonging to the people." This definition tells us that something that is popular belongs to the people, but it does not tell us what this "something" is.

Voids of Vagueness

This definition (i.e., "of the people") includes two forms of vagueness. It is vague in the sense that it does not specify what popularity is and instead defines it as something that belongs to something else. And the something else it belongs to also lacks specification. (Who are "the people"?) So vagueness is compounded by vagueness. If vagueness is the enemy of meaning, and if meaning is the engine of utility, then *popularity* as a word and a concept should have sputtered centuries ago. Nevertheless, *popularity* has thrived and claims a prominent place in our daily social (and research) consciousness.

How can a word laden with so much vagueness be so successful? One reason might be found in current theory of jurisprudence. A legal concept known as the *void of vagueness* states that if a law is written so imprecisely or with so much scope ("overbreadth") that one cannot know what it means, then a person cannot be expected to obey it (Bienvenu, 1992). According to this concept, when vagueness is high, meaning is necessarily low and, as a result, humans will find it to have very little value. In the case of *popularity*, however, the extent of its use implies that humans have found it to be valuable in spite of its vagueness. It may be that in some cases a bit of vagueness can be a positive factor because it increases a concept's flexibility. Constitutional scholars have noted that when laws are drafted some vagueness may be tolerable, assuming that it can be reduced via judicial review and interpretation (Hogg, 2007). Bienvenu pointed out that imprecision in a law may be less problematic than imprecision in enforcement. In the case of popularity, an important task for a group of people, such as the students in a particular school grade, is to act as enforcers of what it means to be a popular peer.

The lack of a rigid formula for the concept of popularity means that a group can engage in this enforcement according to its own needs and circumstances. By being able to define the standards or criteria that constitute popularity in a particular context, a group has the flexibility and breadth to promote its own well-being in a way that suits the immediate context. In this way, the flexibility that results from the vagueness in the concept of popularity may be a positive factor because it facilitates the likelihood that the "something" that belongs to a group will suit the group's needs. When these needs change, flexibility, even if based on vagueness, can enhance adaptation to new conditions. A further repercussion of the flexibility of vagueness is that popularity can adapt to cultural variation in group needs and possibilities.

Another reason for the remarkably enduring traction of the words *popular* and *popularity* in spite of their vagueness may be related to the atavistic tribal heritage of the human species. It may be that as social animals humans are instinctively aware of the dynamics that regulate their immediate group structures. Socially oriented animals, from bees to baboons, need to possess a within-group sensitivity to what belongs to the group and to what does not if the group is going to function and survive. This instinctual feel for group processes may be a basic component of our nature as social beings. If human beings are by nature sensitive to the presence of a hierarchical group structure, then the absence of a well-articulated definition for a basic feature of the group–person interface may not be problematic.

A Reversal of Fortune

Just as one can examine how a word entered a language, one can consider how it entered a scholarly vocabulary. Words have typically entered the literature on peer relations via three routes. The best-known route is followed when one uses a word or expression that has been defined already. The words *acceptance* and *rejection*, for example, have been used as well-defined terms for how much a child is liked and disliked by peers ever since the 1930s (Cillessen, 2009). A second route is followed when a new expression refers to a newly developed construct. For example, when researchers wished to distinguish between provoked and unprovoked aggression (e.g., Dodge & Coie, 1987), they chose new words for these constructs (*reactive* and *proactive*, respectively). In both the first and second routes, a word is tightly linked to a well-defined construct. Each of these routes has worked well; squabbling over terms has been typically kept to a minimum in peer relations research.

A third route is more problematic. In this route, a word is brought into the scholarly literature from the outside without being assigned a clear definition. This route is a reversal of the other two. A word without a specific meaning is imported without an accompanying definition, perhaps because it is assumed that the meaning of the word has been established already. The word *popularity* appears to have come into peer relations via this third route. It was taken from common usage and inserted into the vocabulary of peer relations without much thought about the construct it was meant to represent. This practice of using a word without knowing what it means poses obvious problems. Not knowing what we are studying when we say we are studying popularity is not likely to be a royal route to theoretical or empirical clarity.

Summary

Popularity is a ubiquitous social construct. For many people, perhaps especially early adolescents, it is a part of daily experience within the peer group. The word *populaire* came into the French language about 600 years ago at the time of the breakdown of the medieval synthesis between religion and government, and referred to the laws that governed the activities of common persons rather than the clergy or the aristocracy. The root of this French word spread to other languages including, but not limited to, other Romance languages. By the late 1700s at a time of revolutions against monarchical and aristocratic rule, the words *popularite* and *popularity* took on the meaning of "having the favour of the largest number of the people." Contemporary definitions of the words *popular* and *popularity* do not treat them as particular things. Instead, they define them as referents to any phenomena whose value comes from "the people." This vagueness is not surprising given that the Latin word (*popularitas*) that gave way to the French is itself somewhat vague. Not knowing what a word means would appear to impede its use among persons in general and its appeal to social scientists concerned with measuring phenomena and studying them fruitfully. Not so with *popularity*. It may be that its vagueness has given it an adaptive flexibility. The wide spread recognition of popularity as a social construct likely derives from its basic but vague meaning in conjunction with its capacity to respond to the needs and circumstances of a particular group or context. Flexibility also presents challenges. Among them is the need to see how the concept of popularity functions and fits with other social constructs and processes. I turn to these issues in the next section.

POPULARITY: SELF AND OTHER; INDIVIDUALS AND GROUPS

Although the definition of popularity may be vague and elusive, its general meaning might be clear enough so that one can think about how it functions within the dynamics of social systems. A critical feature of the concept of popularity is that it refers to the status of an individual entity within a group. A particular item or person cannot be popular without the presence of a group to give it this status. In this section, I try to show how popularity functions within social processes that wake up individuals and groups.

Solving a Dialectic

One fundamental social process is the dialectic between self and other. This process refers to the need to find a balance between individuality and group participation. Resolving this dialectic is a challenge for individuals and for groups. The individual needs to balance two complementary but contradictory processes: differentiation and assimilation. *Differentiation* refers to a individuals' efforts to show how they are different from others and to assert their own goals. *Assimilation* refers to the process of fitting in. To assimilate means to adopt the practices and traditions of a group and to comply with its values and norms. The group needs to balance group-focused processes with the activities and needs of the individual members. Groups need to promote internal cohesion and harmony while also promoting and accommodating the aspirations of its individual members. The challenge of the self–other dialectic is succinct: A person needs to be an individual and a member of a group at the same time; groups need to be concerned with their collective dynamics and processes and with the value of their individual members.

Popularity: Self, Other, and Individuals

Popularity plays a role in the resolution of the self–other dialectic for individuals and groups. At the level of the individual, the solution consists of a neat trick: The popular person manages to be a distinct individual and a central group member at the same time. In this way, popular persons are simultaneously differentiated and assimilated; they are both part of the group and apart from it. The popular person helps promote the group's dynamics and is given special status at the same time. In this way, a group can promote itself by giving a special status to one of its members.

One way to consider the self–other status of the popular person is to contrast it with that of the elitist. Popular people and elitists both stand out from other group members. There is, however, a critical difference. The popular person stands out from the group but remains inextricably linked to it and wishes to foster both of these conditions. In contrast, the elite person stands out from the group but is distinct from it rather than linked to it. The elitist wishes to foster this distinction but does not wish to foster a link to the group. The distinctiveness of the elite person comes not from the group itself but instead from an external criterion, such as being a champion athlete, a successful student, an extremely privileged, wealthy, or good-looking person, or a certified expert in something. The distinctiveness of the popular person, however, does come from the group itself. The group recognizes the popular person as distinct (differentiated) but also as a key member (assimilated). In this way, the popular person stands out and fits in the same time.

Popularity: Self, Other, and Groups

Popularity also contributes to the resolution of the self–other dialectic at the level of the group. Here's how: In order to function effectively and to survive, a group needs to achieve the goals of cohesion, homogeneity, and change (see Bukowski & Sippola, 2001). *Cohesion* refers to the extent and strength of the links between group members; *harmony* refers to the degree of agreeableness and shared sense of purpose within the group; *change* refers to the orderly evolution of the group that is needed to combat habituation (groups also need to change and evolve in order to be continually interesting to members and nonmembers; Martindale, 1990). Ascribing popularity to someone may be one way in which a group can reward members who help the group achieve these goals. How would this process work? It is likely that popular persons help a group by increasing cohesion and homogeneity among its members and by promoting regulated change. Cohesion can come from several sources, including mutual liking and a shared sense of purpose and outlook. One powerful source of group cohesion is homogeneity. In a group there needs to be agreement about the group's practices, norms for acceptable behavior, and goals. Homogeneity can be seen in styles of dress, language, values, habits, and preferences. It is known already that persons in a group who are popular are those who are trendsetters and who bring group members together.

By exerting influence and making decisions, popular individuals promote standards and bring others together to be cohesive and homogeneous. They also help the group change in organized ways.

We have seen already that at the level of the individual a popular person is capable of standing out from the group and being part of it at the same time. At the level of the group, there is a need to reward the efforts of individual members who promote the group's goals (i.e., cohesion, homogeneity, and evolution) while maintaining the person's status as a member of the group. By rewarding some members with the status of popularity, a group can find a balance between group goals and individual behavior. Remember that popularity means "belonging to the people." Giving this special status of popularity to some members (i.e., valuing a person as a prominent group possession) promotes the group by rewarding people who help the group achieve its goals. It does not necessarily reward someone for being an individual; it promotes the actions of individuals that happen to help the group. It has been known for a long time (see Collins & Raven, 1968) that groups ascribe power to members who achieve its objectives. This power can come explicitly in legitimate forms of leadership. Leaders are given the power to make decisions and control the flow of information within and between groups. Implicit power is less obvious. It has to do with setting standards and expectations for behavior, distributing social rewards and opportunities, and affecting fashions or styles of behavior in the group (Levine & Moreland, 1998). Central to this conceptualization of popularity is that it is about power.

Populism: Popularity in the Political Sphere

A parallel to popularity in the peer group can be found in the political domain. Given the prior conceptualization that popularity is linked to power, and considering that "popularity" first entered the English and French languages via politics, it is not surprising that political movements and the parties, leaders, and governments associated with them are sometimes designated as "populist." The features of populist governments and leaders bear some resemblance to the features of popular adolescents. The central feature of populist governments and leaders is the claim that they derive their power and inspiration from the concerns, needs, and support of the common person. The central ideology of populism is that democracy should be a manifestation of the will of the people. The vagueness of this conception is not surprising given everything I have already discussed regarding the basic vagueness of the concepts popular and popularity.

Three characteristics of populist politicians (Walker, 2008) have similarities to the concept of popularity in the peer group. First, they have strong charismatic personalities, often authoritarian. Like popular early adolescents, they are fashion conscious, prominent, and gregarious and see themselves as serving positive ends. Of course, once in a while, like popular teenagers, they have to throw their weight around to keep the group/country under control. Second, populist leaders are opposed to elitist or entrenched ruling structures. They claim to prefer homogenous milk to elitist cream even though they see themselves as the cream within the milk. Third, they have an ambiguous relationship with equality. They claim to embrace equality, but this belief is not so inviolable that they feel the need to regulate their behavior and lifestyle so that it equals that of the common person.

There has been no shortage of populist leaders either past or present. Populist leaders like to think that they ask for little in return except, of course, power and attention. Eva Peron claimed she did not want tears from the citizens of Argentina, only their admiration and obedience. In addition to Eva Peron and her husband in Argentina, the list of populist leaders includes, among others, Fidel Castro, former president of Cuba; Sarah Palin, former governor of Alaska and former vice presidential candidate; Hugo Chavez, the long-winded president of Venezuela; and Jean-Marie LePen in France. They claim that they are leaders of the people and that their power is derived from the simple will of the people. Some of them have used their power in less than noble ways, justified by the claim that their actions were needed to help the people to whom they belong. A little aggression now and then is simply the cost of doing business in the world of popularity. Populist leaders are often fond of adopting external means of demonstrating their status as being "of the people." Fidel Castro, who used his charismatic personality to wield a strong grip over Cuba for more than 40 years, wore the clothes of a humble foot soldier. Eva Peron wore clothes that were flattering but simple. Diana Spencer, the "people's princess," was portrayed as someone whose instincts, joys, and problems (especially the latter) were the same as those of a common person. Like popular adolescents, populist leaders are capable of casting themselves as above the people and as part of them at the same time.

Summary

The concept of popularity provides a particular resolution to the dialectic between self and other. The popular person is a strong individual and a key component of a group at the same time. They serve the group by promoting basic goals such as cohesion, harmony, and evolution. Given its implicit associations with power, it is not surprising that popularity is a feature of one form of politics. Populist governments derive their strength from common persons rather than from the traditional elitist ruling classes. Populist leaders are often charismatic and concerned with short-term results based on simple principles. They do not all wear the same political stripes; some favor leftist ideals while others are on the right. Like popular early adolescents, some populist leaders assert themselves when a bit of muscle is needed to maintain their power in the group. The popular person and the group that ascribed this significance to the person are strongly intertwined.

WHAT IS IT GOOD FOR: LOVE OR POWER?

So far the discussion has addressed questions regarding the meaning of the construct of popularity. As I have tried to show, this question seeks a definition that may not be possible. It might be useful to free ourselves from definitional concerns and instead take a pragmatic stance that asks "What does popularity do?" and "What is it good for?" (Rorty, 1979, 1991). This approach considers the features and affordances that are ascribed to the popular. It recognizes the benefits and the burdens or risks that come from being popular. The general absence of this sort of examination in the prior literature may be due to the unique position of this question at the fuzzy frontier between two disciplinary domains: the interest of psychology in the individual and the interest of sociology in the group.

Provisions of Popularity

There have been efforts to identify the provisions of different forms of peer experience. Most notable is Furman and Robbins's (1985) description of the primary functions of acceptance and friendship. Based on Weiss's (1974) framework, they proposed four provisions offered by both friendship and peer acceptance: help, comfort, companionship, and enhancement of one's sense of worth or esteem. Acceptance provides a sense of inclusion and belonging; friendship offers affection, intimacy, and loyalty. A possible starting point for a discussion of the provisions of popularity is the well-established view that although we may not know what popularity is, we know what it is not (Cillessen & Rose, 2005; Parkhurst & Hopmeyer, 1998). For more than 60 years, peer researchers

(Northway, 1946) have known that popularity is not the same as acceptance. These two constructs are correlated, but they differ in basic ways. Acceptance is a measure of how much a child is liked by peers. It is measured directly by asking children to nominate their friends or rate how much they like each of their peers. Knowing that one child likes a peer or sees the peer as a friend tells us something about a link between the child and the peer (i.e., that affection flows from one child to the other).

In contrast, popularity is a perceptual phenomenon. Measures of popularity tell us how a child is seen by others. Popularity is typically measured with peer-assessment techniques in which children identify which peers fit particular characteristics. It has been pointed out that popularity is often measured with a single item (e.g., "Someone who is popular"), and that no specific definition is provided to indicate what this word means (Cillessen & Rose, 2005). Knowing that one child has identified another as popular on the basis of a single item tells us how this child sees the other rather than indicating something about the association or relationship between the child and the target peer. The number of times a child is nominated for a "popularity" item is an index of how the child is seen by the group. In this way, a measure of popularity tells us about a child's place in the group rather than the child's association with other children. Therefore, efforts to map the provisions of popularity are more likely to benefit from understanding group processes rather than processes that occur at the level of the individual. To put it another way, one needs to think like a sociologist rather than a psychologist.

The sociological concept associated with popularity is that of status. The concept of status is predicated on the view that groups are stratified into a hierarchy. According to Max Weber's (1968) well-known and enduring theory of group processes, *status* refers to someone's place within this stratified hierarchy. A societal hierarchy is important because it is a structure for assigning duties and rewards to persons within the group. Popular persons have a position of high status in the group. As I indicated earlier, some popular persons achieve this position via their efforts to promote group functioning (cohesion, harmony, and evolution). In return, the group gives them power and claims the popular person as their own. (It has been argued that victimization is the flip side of this process; see Bukowski & Sippola, 2001.) It is likely that popular people are given this power because they need to promote the group's functioning. Without the power to command attention and make decisions, even unwittingly, popular persons would lack the social resources to promote the group's functioning. By giving popular children status and power, they are simultaneously assigned a special position, thus reinforcing their individuality and ties to the group. Without the group, the popular person has no power. In this way, if acceptance is about affection and liking, popularity is about status and power.

Risks and Burdens

Even though it is desired, popularity is not without costs. According to the view I have presented, the popular person is not valued for his or her characteristics per se but is valued for what he or she does for the group. Instead of being a relationship, popularity is a value. It refers to the association between a mass market—the peer group—and an entity that does something for the group. Popular children have been successful in the marketplace of peer group attention. To maintain this condition, they need to be oriented toward sustaining their status in the group. Maintaining this position can be stressful. Castro did not hang on to power by acquiescing in the face of stress. The demands of being popular might be a form of stress that many teenagers cannot manage.

Another burden of popularity may be the opportunities it offers for individual power. This condition presents two subtle but powerful dangers. First, the experience of having the power to be a trendsetting agent of change may have the insidious effect of promoting deviance. Once a popular person is allowed to flex his or her proverbial muscles and to "kick over the traces" in the service of group goals, the boundary between acceptable self-assertion and risky deviance may be blurred. Fuzzy boundaries can be dangerous because it is hard to know which side one is on. The second danger may have more serious consequences. Focusing on status and power at the group level will, at best, distract the popular person's attention from dyadic experiences such as friendship. At worst, it will impede or disrupt these experiences. Nearly everything we know about the positive affective consequences of peer experiences indicates that the lion's share of these effects occur at the level of the dyad (Bukowski, Brendgen, & Vitaro, 2007). Pursuing popularity may preclude these opportunities.

So, what do you want: love or power?

Summary

Popularity is a form of status. As a form of status, it is a form of power. Popular children are valued by the group, presumably for their contributions to group functioning. In return, popular persons are given some leeway by group members. The provision of power might have short-term benefits for popular children. Over the longer term, popularity may be a form of risk because it blurs the distinction between tolerable self-assertion and deviance and it distracts attention from friendship relations and their benefits.

POPULARITY AS A SOCIAL CONSTRUCT: WHAT DO WE DO WITH IT?

Social construction refers to the process in which the meaning ascribed to an idea or concept is shaped by contextual factors (Berger & Luckmann, 1966). Although there have been erroneous applications of this idea (see Sokal, 1996), even the critics of social constructivism recognize that some social concepts vary from one context to another (Hacking, 2000). Given that group contexts vary in their goals and characteristics and that some social concepts lack a precise definition, it is likely that they will be conceived of in different ways in different places. Popularity appears to be an especially ripe concept for contextual variation in meaning. If, as I have argued, popularity means "of the people" and if there is variability in whom "the people" are, then it can be expected that what the people accept as their own varies also. As groups differ in norms, structure, and goals, the group's decisions, however unwittingly, about who will be valued as popular will differ as well.

Earlier in this chapter, it was claimed that the lack of precision in the meaning of a word can impede the clear interpretation of findings from empirical research. Not knowing what one is studying makes research and the interpretation of findings difficult. In the case of *popularity*, however, the lack of precision in the word's meaning and value should not be merely accepted as an insurmountable difficulty that makes research impossible. Instead of throwing up our hands in surrender to this annoying fuzziness, it may be more enlightening to sort out what the variability in the concept of popularity means. For the most part, research has not bothered to recognize popularity as a social construct that is situated in particular circumstances. Recognizing this contextual variability and examining the contextual forces that explain it should be a goal, if not a priority, for research on popularity.

What would such a research program look like? Consistent with the two major sections of this chapter and the explicit goals of assessing the "features and effects" of experiences with peers (Berndt, 1982), research on contextual variability would want to look at what popularity is and what it is good for. Although the study of cultural variations is often seen as what one does after all the basic questions in a research domain have been answered, in the case of the social construct of popularity, questions about variability in meanings and consequences are the basic questions. Given that popularity is, by definition, "group dependent," it is difficult to conclude what it is, what it means, and how it affects individual and group functioning without knowing the context in which it is situated.

Given the many calls for understanding development in context, one would expect that quantitative contextual analyses would be frequent. Nevertheless, they have been rare. Developmental psychologists love to teach their undergraduate students Uri Bronfenbrenner's (1979) model with its concentric spheres of effects, but they have rarely gone "the full monty" by actually bringing him into their studies. The study of popularity, as much or more than any other domain of developmental psychology, is likely to benefit from this form of contextual analysis. What would this kind of analysis look like, and what kinds of hypotheses might be tested? Five questions could easily be addressed and would help us understand what popularity is and what it does. Two have to do with the features of popularity and three with the effects.

Features: A Contextual Approach

One question about which features are associated with popularity and how these associations might vary across contexts can be profitably stated as follows: What contextual or group characteristics influence how popularity is ascribed to different members of a group? The search for an answer to this question could be guided by how groups have been studied already. Two traditions could help us. One concerns the use of dimensions that distinguish between the contextual emphasis on the individual and the emphasis on the group per se (Hofstede, 1980; Oysherman, Coon, & Kemmelmeier 2000). Whereas *individualistic* contexts stress individual achievement, self-reliance, and autonomy, *collectivism* emphasizes the value of cohesion, respect for others, and a sensitivity to the needs of others. Who might be valued in a group that is high in individualism? One can hypothesize that individuals who excel at achievement-related tasks, especially at tasks that put their own group up against another, who are self-assertive but not harmful, who help others in their own strivings for achievement, and who are just and believe in equality are likely to be valued by a group as popular. Aggression may be more strongly associated with popularity in groups that value individualism than in groups that do not. As for collectivism, it is likely that in groups that are high in collectivism popularity is likely to be ascribed to persons who promote cohesion by being caring and trustworthy leaders with good ideas for the group. The moral domains that promote popularity in a collectivistic group would value nurturance more than equality.

Another approach to the study of group differences emphasizes normativeness. It distinguishes between groups according to the activities and values they favor. Norms can refer to many phenomena—preferences for activities, goals, and lifestyle issues (e.g., types of dress). Presumably, individuals who are the most prominent examples of the features that define a group's norms might be those who are most likely to be distinguished as popular.

A second question that can be asked about variations in the features of popularity concerns the link between popularity and acceptance or liking. The correlation between these constructs is neither 1 nor 0; how close it is to either extreme appears to vary from one context to another. How can one understand what might account for these variations? Again, let me fall back on the dimensions of individualism and collectivism. On the one hand, the distinction between what goes on at the level of the mass market (popularity) and what goes on between individuals (acceptance) is likely to be sharper in groups that are high in individualism and that understand social experiences according to a presumed independence between persons. On the other hand, in groups that value cohesion and the inextricable links between group members, being liked and being popular may be seen as more "simpatico" phenomena. These hypotheses that (1) individualism will minimize the correlation between popularity and acceptance, whereas (2) collectivism will increase it deserve empirical scrutiny.

Effects: Place, Popularity, and Value

There are also three reasoned questions to be asked about contextual variations in the effects of popularity. Each of these questions is concerned with the value of being valued. They ask whether and why the experience of popularity may have more significance in some contexts than in others. As with the two prior questions, these questions are based on ideas about the factors that can meaningfully differentiate contexts. In this case, two factors are on a different scale than what we have considered already, whereas the third factor has been considered before. The two new factors are socioeconomic status (SES) and secularization. The third factor is concerned with individualism and collectivism.

SES is an index of resources. Resources satisfy material and esteem needs and those who have more resources can satisfy more needs. According to Maslow, needs are satisfied in a hierarchical manner in which material and security needs must be satisfied before psychological and esteem needs. Although this model has met some criticisms, its general claim is hard to dismiss. If resources in a particular context are sufficiently low so as to prevent the satisfaction of basic material and security needs, the value of higher level needs may be less than in contexts where resources are abundant. Accordingly, it is reasonable to ask whether popularity will have less psychological significance in low-SES contexts than in middle-class contexts.

According to Marx's model of society's class-based structure, people in the middle class are concerned—if not obsessed—with status. Some have claimed that this is truer now than ever before (de Botton, 2004; James, 2007). The argument is that middle-class people need status to confirm the legitimacy of the material- and power-based resources they have or strive for. Apparently, lower SES individuals have other worries. If status is a middle-class concept, and if popularity is a form of status, this provides another reason why popularity should have more significance to middle-class children than to children from lower SES families.

A second question is whether popularity is more important in secular societies. The roots of this question are also found in sociological ideas about the origins of value. Societies have been ascribed the responsibility of creating value and of conveying the sources of this value to its members. For better or worse, cohesion in a society can be strengthened by a shared belief system about what is important. Some societies achieve this goal via strong meaning-making systems such as religion or political philosophies. When these systems are absent, as they tend to be in modern pluralistic secular societies, value needs to come from other sources (Taylor, 1991). Popularity may be one value-making system whose significance may be stronger in secular societies than in societies dominated by powerful dogmatic value systems. That is, popularity will be most meaningful when other types of meaning are weak. The question derived from this line of thinking is whether popularity is more strongly associated with well-being in secular societies than in societies dominated by religious concepts. This question can be posed in several ways. One could ask whether popularity is more strongly related to well-being in secular schools than in religious schools or whether these effects differ in places where religious views are strong rather than weak. One could take a historical perspective and ask whether the significance of popularity has increased in societies that have become more secular.

The third and final question about variations in the effect of popularity is based on the idea that popularity is an achievement. It is possible to regard popularity as the accumulation of a group-based resource, specifically the group's attention and acquiescence. If popularity is an achievement and contexts that emphasize individualism ascribe value to individual achievement, then the significance of popularity may be highest in groups high in individualism. In other words, the question is whether the association between popularity and well-being is stronger when individualism as a characteristic of a context is strong.

Summary

Insofar as popularity is a social construct, its meaning and significance are likely to vary across contexts. The factors that are antecedent to popularity are likely to vary according to the needs and dynamics of particular groups. Groups ascribe the value associated with popularity to individuals who best serve the group's needs. These variations may be linked to contextual or cultural characteristics such as individualism and collectivism and group norms. These and other characteristics of context, such as SES and modernist secularism, may affect the meaning that popularity has and its associations with measures of well-being.

Conclusion

This chapter tells a story about a word. Typically, the definition of words is less important than the discussion of ideas, theories, and processes. In the case of *popularity*, however, the word represents an idea, specifically what it means to be "of the people." In many ways popularity is a perfect modernist concept. It stands between nothing and meaning something precise (Howe, 1993). In spite of its vagueness, its use is widespread and even powerful. As a phenomenon, it stands at the interface between the individual and the group. Its meaning appears to have arisen from historical circumstances in which the common person was empowered vis-à-vis the elitist ruling classes. To be popular means that one is a part of the group and apart from it at the same time. The popular person is valued by the group for what she or he does for basic group functioning. Groups give power to popular children. Ironically, this access to power may be a source of the risk. As a social construct, the meaning and significance of popularity are likely to vary across contexts. Understanding this variability is a challenge for peer researchers. By trying to understand how contextual factors influence what popularity means and how it affects well-being, peer researchers will obtain a richer view of how individuals and groups fit together. In doing so, we will have achieved one of the most critical goals of social science.

ACKNOWLEDGMENTS

My work was supported by grants from the Social Sciences and Humanities Research Council of Canada and by a Concordia University Research Chair. I am grateful to several friends and colleagues, including AMV, LMS, CD, FM, JBS, AES, AMHB, NWHB, CM, PB, and NH, for their constructive feedback and suggestions. I am grateful also to three bibliographic buddies, Angela Ittel, Figen Cok, and Lina Maria Lopez, for looking into dictionaries for me.

REFERENCES

Anderson, H., & Anderson, G. (1954). Social development. In L. Carmichael (Ed.), *Manual of child psychology* (pp. 1162-1215). New York: Wiley.

Berger, P. L., & Luckmann, T. (1966). *The social construction of reality: A treatise in the sociology of knowledge.* Garden City, NY: Anchor Books.

Berndt, T. J. (1982). The features and effects of friendship in early adolescence. *Child Development, 53,* 1447–1460.

Bienvenu, P. (1992). La nullité pour imprécision: Émergence et perspectives d'avenir en droit constitutionnel Canadien [Nullity for vagueness: Emergence and prospects in Canadian constitutional law]. *Développements Récents en Droit Administratif, 67,* 93–119.

Bronfenbrenner, U. (1979). *The ecology of human development: Experiments by nature and design.* (Cambridge, MA: Harvard University Press.

Bukowski, W. M., Brendgen, M., & Vitaro, F. (2007). Peers and socialization: Effects on externalizing and internalizing problems. In J. E. Grusec & P. D. Hastings (Eds.), *Handbook of socialization: Theory and research* (pp. 355–381). New York: Guilford Press.

Bukowski, W. M., & Hoza, B. (1989). Popularity and friendship: Issues in theory, measurement, and outcomes. In T. J. Berndt & G. W. Ladd (Eds.), *Peer relations in child development* (pp. 15-45). New York: Wiley.

Bukowski, W. M., & Sippola, L. K. (2001). Groups, individuals, and victimization: A view of the peer system. In J. Juvonen & S. Graham (Eds.), *Peer harassment in school: The plight of the vulnerable and victimized* (pp. 355–377). New York: Guilford Press.

Cillessen, A. H. N. (2009). Sociometric methods. In K. H. Rubin, W. M. Bukowski, & B. Laursen (Eds.), *Handbook of peer interactions, relationships, and groups* (pp. 82–99). New York: Guilford Press.

Cillessen, A. H. N., & Rose, A. J. (2005). Understanding popularity in the peer system. *Current Directions in Psychological Science, 14,* 102.

Collins, B., & Raven, B. (1968). Group structure: Attraction, coalitions, communication, and power. In G. Indzey & E. Aronson (Eds.), *The handbook*

of social psychology (2nd ed., Vol. 4, pp. 102–204). New York: McGraw Hill.
de Botton, A. (2004). *Status anxiety*. London: Penguin.
Dodge, K. A., & Coie, J. D. (1987). Social-information-processing factors in reactive and proactive aggression in children's peer groups. *Journal of Personality and Social Psychology, 53,* 1146–1158.
Furman, W., & Robbins, P. (1985). What's the point: Selection of treatment objectives. In B. Schneider, K. H. Rubin, & J. E. Ledingham (Eds.), *Children's peer relations: Issues in assessment and intervention* (pp. 41–54). New York: Springer.
Hacking, I. (2000). *The social construction of what?* Cambridge, MA: Harvard University Press.
Hartup, W. W. (1970). Peer interaction and social organization. In P. H. Mussen (Ed.), *Carmichael's manual of child psychology* (Vol. 2, pp. 361–456). New York: Wiley.
Hartup, W. W. (1983). Peer relations. In P. H. Mussen (Ed.), *Handbook of child psychology: Vol. 4. Socialization, personality, and social development* (pp. 103–196). New York: Wiley.
Hofstede, G. (1980). *Culture's consequences: International differences in work-related values*. Beverly Hills, CA: Sage.
Hogg, P. W. (2007). *Constitutional law of Canada (fifth ed. Suppl., Vol. 2)*. Scarborough, Ontario, Canada: Thomson Carswell.
Howe, I. (1993). Two cheers for utopia. *Dissent, 40,* 131–133.
James, O. (2007). *Affluenza*. London: Vermillion.
Krappmann, L. (1996). Amicitia, drujba, shin-yu, philia, Freundschaft, friendship: On the cultural diversity of a human relationship. In W. M. Bukowski, A. F. Newcomb, & W. W. Hartup (Eds.), *The company they keep: Friendship in childhood and adolescence* (pp. 19–40). New York: Cambridge University Press.
Lease, A. M., Kennedy, C. A., & Axelrod, J. L. (2002). Children's social constructions of popularity. *Social Development, 11,* 87–109.
Levine, J. M., & Moreland, R. L. (1998). Small groups. In D. Gilbert, S. Fiske, & G. Lindzey (Eds.), *Handbook of social psychology* (4th ed., Vol. 2, pp. 415–469). New York: McGraw-Hill.
Martindale, C. (1990). *The clockwork muse*. New York: Basic Books.
Monroe, W. S. (1898). Social consciousness in children. *Psychological Review, 5,* 68–70.
Northway, M. L (1946). Sociometry and some challenging problems of social relations. *Sociometry, 9,* 187–198.
Oyserman, D., Coon, H. M., & Kemmelmeier, M. (2002). Rethinking individualism and collectivism: Evaluation of theoretical assumptions and meta-analyses. *Psychological Bulletin, 128,* 3–72.
Parkhurst, J. T., & Hopmeyer, A. (1998). Sociometric popularity and peer-perceived popularity: Two distinct dimensions of peer status. *Journal of Early Adolescence, 18,* 125–144.
Rey, A., Tomi, M., Hordé, T., & Tanet, C. (1994). *Dictionnaire historique de la langue Française*. Paris: Dictionnaires Le Robert.

Rorty, R. (1979). *Philosophy and the mirror of nature*. Princeton, NJ: Princeton University Press.
Rorty, R. (1991). *Objectivity, relativism, and truth: Philosophical papers I*. Cambridge, UK: Cambridge University Press.
Simpson, J., & Weiner, E. (1989). *The Oxford English dictionary*. Oxford, UK: Oxford University Press.
Sokal, A. (1996). Transgressing the boundaries: An afterword. *Dissent, 43,* 93–99.
Taylor, C. (1991). *The malaise of modernity*. Concord, Ontario, Canada: Anansi.
Thompson, G. (1960). Children's groups. In L. Carmichael (Ed.), *Handbook of research methods in child development* (pp. 821–853). New York: Wiley.
Walker, I. (2008). The three lefts of Latin America. *Dissent, 57,* 5–12.
Weber, M. (1968). *Economy and society: An outline of interpretive sociology* (G. Roth & C. Wittich, Eds.). New York: Bedminster Press.
Weiss, R. S. (1974). The provisions of social relationships. In Z. Rubin (Ed.), *Doing unto others* (pp. 17–26). Englewood Cliffs, NJ: Prentice Hall.

Chapter 2

Conceptualizing and Measuring Popularity

ANTONIUS H. N. CILLESSEN
PETER E. L. MARKS

This chapter reviews the measurement of popularity in research with children and adolescents. As indicated in the previous chapter, the study of popularity has roots in both quantitative and qualitative approaches. This chapter focuses on quantitative methods, but qualitative approaches are also briefly reviewed. Specifically, we discuss sociometric measures (peer nominations or ratings) of popularity but also address alternative measures, such as self-ratings, teacher ratings, and observational methods. In addition, some researchers have used mixed-methods approaches—for example, LaFontana and Cillessen (2002) collected answers to open-ended essay questions that were later content coded for quantitative analyses (see also de Bruyn & Cillessen, 2006b; Xie, Li, Boucher, Hutchins, & Cairns, 2006)—and we discuss these studies here as well.

As popularity is becoming a more popular topic (an unavoidable expression) in the peer relations literature, there is a clear need for consistent terminology. A recurrent observation in this book is that researchers have used inconsistent terms for popularity and related constructs. An important goal of this chapter is to propose a clear and consistent use of terms. Toward this end, we review the distinction between two forms of high status in the peer group—likeability and popularity—and the labels used for them. We then propose a standardized terminology for use by researchers.

WHAT IS POPULARITY?

Bukowski (Chapter 1, this volume) presented a broad conceptual analysis of the origin of the word *popularity*. This analysis shows that the roots of the term *popularity* are diverse and its meanings complex. The goal of the current chapter is narrower and limited to the measurement practices across the empirical literature. We focus on the practice of measuring popularity as a psychological construct in the child and adolescent peer relationships literature.

As indicated by Bukowski (Chapter 1, this volume), popularity in this narrow sense in the developmental literature has typically referred to the rank ordering of children or adolescents in their peer groups (classroom or grade) according to a criterion of hierarchy or status (a positive criterion or desirable trait). Those at the top of the rank ordering have been labeled "popular." This practice has been followed for the past 75 years in a large number of studies. Many of these studies dealt directly with popularity; in others, the identification of popular students was a by-product of a focus on other dimensions of peer status, usually peer rejection. This body of research, and especially the data collected over the past 10 years, reveals multiple ways of measuring popularity that are indicators of different underlying constructs.

The heterogeneity of the empirical construct of popularity can be illustrated by a comparison to the construct of attractiveness. Research in social psychology has shown consistently that people who are considered physically attractive or beautiful are evaluated positively, even when their behavior is not positive. A favorite expression summarizing this body of research is "What is beautiful is good" (see Webster & Driskell, 1983). Does this also apply to popularity? Is what is popular also always good? Both anecdotal expressions and research evidence indicate that the positivity bias that exists for attractiveness does not necessarily exist for popularity. Unlike for beauty, what is popular is not always good.

In the anecdotal domain, Abraham Lincoln is quoted to have said "Avoid popularity if you will have peace," already pointing to the fact that popularity is a mixed blessing. Perhaps Lincoln was referring to the heavy responsibilities that came with his position of high (elected) status or to the envies and enmities that came along with it. Oscar Wilde said, "Whatever is popular is wrong." He referred to art, taking the elitist stand that what is liked by everyone cannot necessarily be good. More recently, Yogi Berra has said, "Whoever is popular is bound to be disliked"— wisdom with a close connection to the child and especially adolescent peer group, as we will discuss later. This mixed nature of popularity as a psychological construct is also illustrated by several movies that have shown the dark side of adolescent popularity, particularly among girls (see, e.g., *Mean Girls* and *Heathers*).

Taking these anecdotal illustrations into the empirical domain, studies with children and adolescents have shown that popularity is associated with some negative behaviors and outcomes. Whereas being liked by peers is negatively associated with being aggressive, popularity has a consistent positive association with measures of aggression, in particular social or relational aggression, that is, aggression that is manipulative or excluding (e.g., Cillessen & Mayeux, 2004; Cillessen & Rose, 2005; Rose, Swenson, & Waller, 2004; see also Mayeux, Houser, & Dyches, Chapter 4, this volume). Furthermore, popularity is positively associated with health risk behaviors such as smoking, drinking, and early sexual activity in adolescence (Mayeux, Sandstrom, & Cillessen, 2008; see also Schwartz & Gorman, Chapter 11, this volume). Thus, the anecdotal perception of popularity as a mixed bag is confirmed by empirical data in the child and adolescent literature. This chapter considers the measures of this dual-natured construct.

TWO TYPES OF POPULARITY

Sociometric methods are the methods used to assess peer status in classrooms and schools. Sociometric methods have a long and varied history (see, for reviews, Cillessen, 2009; Cillessen & Bukowski, 2000; Moreno, 1960) dating back originally to Moreno (1934). In the 1980s, Coie and colleagues developed a standard sociometric procedure and a method of classifying children into sociometric status groups. This procedure was subsequently used rather consistently in research for over two decades. Often referred to as the Coie, Dodge, and Coppotelli (1982) method, it is generally used as described in their article.

In the Coie et al. (1982) procedure, participants are asked to nominate peers in the reference group (classroom or grade) who they like most and like least. Nominations received for both categories are then counted for each participant, resulting in scores on four continuous sociometric dimensions: acceptance, rejection, (social) preference, and (social) impact. *Acceptance* is the number of "liked most" nominations received.

Rejection is the number of "liked least" nominations received. *Preference* is the acceptance score minus the rejection score. *Impact* is the sum of the acceptance and rejection scores. As part of the procedure, these scores are standardized within the reference group to control for differences in classroom or grade size. Using specific cutoffs (often ± 1 SD), each participant is then assigned to one of five sociometric status types: *"popular"* (high preference; liked by many, disliked by few), *rejected* (low preference; disliked by many, liked by few), *neglected* (low impact; neither liked nor disliked), *controversial* (high impact; liked by some and disliked by others), and *average* (average on all four dimensions). In this chapter, we refer to these groups as the "traditional sociometric status categories."

This classification system formed the basis of much research in the 1980s and 1990s. The majority of this research focused on children or adolescents with problematic peer relations, in particular those who were classified as rejected. From these investigations, much was learned about the correlates, precursors, and consequences of peer rejection (see, for reviews, Asher & Coie, 1990; Bierman, 2004). There was not much interest in popularity during this time; the major interest of developmental and child clinical researchers was aggression and rejection. The zeitgeist was to focus on children with problems in the behavioral and relationship domains and to design and test successful methods of preventing these problems. There was an anecdotal awareness that the sociometric "popular" classification, especially among elementary schoolchildren, was not the same as one's personal experiences with adolescent popularity in high school, but this was not the focus of systematic research interest.

This changed in the late 1990s, when researchers began to include "most popular" and "least popular" nominations in sociometric data collections in addition to the traditional "liked most" and "liked least" nominations (e.g., LaFontana & Cillessen, 1999; Parkhurst & Hopmeyer, 1998), thereby adding *popularity* as a fifth sociometric dimension to the already existing four (acceptance, rejection, preference, impact). Popularity is determined as the (standardized) number of "most popular" nominations received, or the difference between the number of "most popular" and "least popular" nominations (popularity minus unpopularity nominations). It is important to emphasize that popularity is a different dimension than acceptance or preference. Acceptance and preference are dimensions of likeability, derived from peer nominations of who is most and least liked. Popularity is a dimension of power, prestige, or visibility, derived from nominations of who is most and least popular. In that sense, popularity is conceptually closer to the traditional sociometric dimension of social impact defined previously as the sum of "liked most" and "liked least" nominations received, which is also an indicator of how socially visible someone is in a group, irrespective of the valence of the behavior that attracts others' attention.

TERMINOLOGICAL CLARIFICATION

Historical Perspective: Acceptance as Popularity

In the early sociometric literature, the terms *popularity* and *acceptance* were often used interchangeably. For example, in her classic study in the first volume of *Child Development*, Koch (1933) used the term *popularity* but measured acceptance. Indeed, a general difficulty in considering popularity research from a historical perspective is the use of the term *popularity* as a synonym for *acceptance* or *social preference*. The confounding of these terms actually began before the introduction of sociometry itself (e.g., Koch, 1933; Voigt, 1933; Watson, 1927), despite contemporary accounts indicating that popular children were not necessarily the best liked (Boorman, 1931; Hermans, 1931; Jennings, 1937; Tryon, 1939). By the second half of the 20th century, researchers regularly used *popularity* for acceptance nominations (Polansky, Lippitt, & Redl, 1950; see also Coleman, 1961; Dunnington, 1957). The mixing of terms continued after the introduction of the traditional sociometric status types, in which the label *popular* became a synonym for the highly accepted group.

Toward Terminological Clarification

As indicated previously, status in the peer group can be measured in one of two ways. One is by means of the traditional sociometric categories: popular (meaning highly accepted or preferred in the peer group), rejected, neglected, controversial, and average (Coie et al., 1982). This classification was most frequently used in the peer relations literature in the 1980s and 1990s. The second involves using continuous scores for acceptance, preference, impact, and, more recently, (perceived) popularity. Terminological confusion has emerged because the term *popularity* appears in both systems but has a different meaning in each. In the traditional sociometric status types, the term refers to children or adolescents who are particularly well liked in the peer group. Because this system was originally designed for elementary school samples in which popularity and likeability are positively correlated, using the term *popular* for this group seemed logical (Coie et al., 1982; Newcomb & Bukowski, 1983). However, popularity (usually obtained by asking students to name who is most and least popular) is not a measure of likeability or preference but rather a measure of prestige or visibility.

Parkhurst and Hopmeyer (1998) proposed the terms *sociometric* or *perceived popularity* as the solution to this problem. There are, however, disadvantages to this proposal. First, these terms are somewhat clumsy to use. It is awkward to always have to qualify the term *popular* with either the "sociometric" or "perceived" prefix, although it has been done now in a number of studies. Second, perceived popularity is also most commonly assessed with a sociometric method (peer nominations or ratings). To suggest that "perceived" is not "sociometric" is confusing as well, when sociometric methods are used to assess both. Alternative terms for perceived popularity have also been proposed, such as *judgmental popularity* (Babad, 2001), *reputational popularity* (Prinstein & Cillessen, 2003), and *consensual popularity* (de Bruyn & Cillessen, 2006a). Such terms, however, do not solve the somewhat problematic use of the term *sociometric popularity*. Thus, a clarification of terms is still needed.

The implications of the terminological confusion between both forms of popularity are larger for the study of adolescent peer relationships than for the study of children because the distinction between likeability and popularity is clearer in adolescence than in childhood (Cillessen & Borch, 2006; Cillessen & Mayeux, 2004). One might roughly think of "sociometric" popularity, or *popular as accepted,* as the childhood definition of popularity and "perceived" popularity, or *popular as popular,* as the adolescent definition of popularity. In children's elementary school classrooms, *popular* generally means "well liked by peers." In adolescents' middle and high school grades, *popular* refers to being visible and prestigious.

Thus, the term *popular* can have two different meanings. It can refer to being well liked and accepted ("sociometrically" popular) or to high status as a result of *being seen as* popular and high ranking ("perceived" popular). Sociometric popularity is the result of individual judgments of likeability. Moreno (1934) called them "emotional" judgments: an individual's private sentiments of attraction or repulsion about another that are not necessarily shared with the group or by the group. The resulting likeability scores (acceptance or preference) in a sociometric assessment are composites of these sentiments. If many participants in a classroom or grade nominate a certain peer as someone they like (and not as someone they dislike), this person is well accepted or highly preferred in this group. This is a summary or composite of individual liking and disliking judgments rather than a consensus that is explicitly communicated or discussed in the group. "Perceived" popularity, on the other hand, is a reputation. Popularity judgments are not private sentiments but rather reputational judgments. They are not summaries of personal attractions or repulsions; they are a general consensus of who is most popular and least popular as seen by everyone in the peer group.

Because acceptance and popularity have such different meanings, they should be discussed carefully by researchers. In particular, referring to accepted children and adolescents as popular is problematic. Therefore, we propose a system of clear, unambiguous terminology. The construct that has sometimes been referred to as *sociometric popularity* should be called *acceptance* or *preference* (depending on how it is measured) and could be referred to as *likeability*. Likewise, the dimension of social standing that has been labeled *perceived popularity* should simply be called *popularity*, measured by either "most popular" nominations, "most popular" minus "least popular" nominations, or popularity ratings. The chapters in this book consistently use this nomenclature. Additionally, we propose that the "popular" group in the traditional sociometric classification system should be relabeled as "accepted" or "preferred" when discussing past findings of this system or when using it in future research.

THE MEASUREMENT OF POPULARITY

The uniqueness of the popularity construct can be further illustrated and strengthened by reviewing its measurement in research. Both qualitative and quantitative research is discussed.

Qualitative Research

Qualitative researchers have a long history of studying adolescent status (e.g., Folsom, 1934; Waller, 1937) and related constructs (e.g., cliques and subcultural peer groupings; see Buff, 1970; Gordon, 1957; Hollingshead, 1949; Larkin, 1979). James Coleman's 1961 "The Adolescent Society," which married questionnaire-derived quantitative information with qualitative interview data, was a particularly notable study of peer status, and it set the stage for a sociological focus on adolescent culture over the subsequent two decades. It was not until the mid-1980s, however, that researchers began to focus explicitly on popularity itself. Early reports by Eder (1985) and Canaan (1987) gave rise to detailed ethnographic explorations of the place of status and popularity within childhood and adolescent peer groups (e.g., Adler & Adler, 1998; Eder, 1995; Milner,

2004), supplemented by more focused reports considering popularity in relation to such topics as cigarette smoking (Michell & Amos, 1997), linguistic construction of identity (Eckert, 2000), and relational aggression (Currie, Kelly, & Pomerantz, 2007). As popularity has become central in quantitative research on peer relationships, the past decade has also seen an upswing in the number of qualitative studies on the impact and construction of popularity among children and adolescents. It would be inaccurate to say, however, that qualitative research *followed* quantitative research. Indeed, the qualitative literature has often anticipated findings of the quantitative literature, the most notable example being Eder's (1985, 1995) observation that the popular students in her sample were not at all the best liked, a claim that was later supported by quantitative research.

Quantitative Research

Most recent studies on popularity have used peer nominations or ratings as the measures of popularity. As with research on peer relationships in general, the peer perspective is considered the gold standard for assessments of popularity. Alternative measures that do not use the peer group are discussed separately next.

Popularity Nominations

The most common method of measuring popularity is simply to ask members of a school classroom or grade to nominate their peers who are most and least popular. Nominations received are then counted and standardized as indicated previously. Several studies have used this approach in determining both popularity and acceptance (e.g., Cillessen & Mayeux, 2004). An implication of this approach is that four peer nominations should be used: liked most, liked least, most popular, and least popular. The inclusion of all four nominations is ideal for sociometric studies on popularity, primarily because it allows researchers to control for the statistical overlap between the two forms of status (which can be substantial, particularly in childhood) in the analysis of their data. The reasons to include both positive (most popular) and negative (least popular) nominations in this research are discussed next.

Popularity Ratings

In sociometric studies conducted in the 1970s and 1980s, the use of likeability ratings instead of nominations, or in combination with nominations, was common (e.g., Asher, Singleton, Tinsley, & Hymel, 1979). Nominations are a method of partial rank ordering in which the participant only identifies her or his top choices for a criterion and leaves all other (unnamed) peers unranked. Ratings have the advantage that each peer is evaluated explicitly (rated) rather than given no rating by default if not named. Ratings, however, are more time consuming to collect.

A few recent studies in the peer relations literature have used peer ratings of popularity (instead of or in addition to likeability ratings). In these studies, the classroom was the reference group. For example, van den Berg (2009) and Pennings (2009) collected popularity ratings, as well as most and least popular nominations, in grades 5 and 6 at three times during one school year. Peer ratings of popularity were highly stable in this study and positively correlated with popularity nominations. An advantage of ratings is that they can be used to divide the variance in peer judgments into actor, partner, and dyadic components (Malloy, Albright, & Scarpati, 2007; van den Berg, 2009), which is more difficult with nominations (see also Kenny, Kashy, & Cook, 2006). The balance between the longer time needed to collect peer ratings and their additional analytic possibilities will vary by study, but in general popularity ratings are a useful complement to nominations (see, e.g., Schwartz, Gorman, Nakamoto, & McKay, 2006).

Subsets of the Voter Population

Cillessen (2009) defined the voter population in a sociometric study as the collection of children or adolescents in a classroom or grade who participate as voters in a sociometric assessment. In general, the percentage of students in a classroom or grade who participate as voters should be high. Ideally, all students who can be voted for also participate as voters (i.e., the voter population is 100% of the votee population), but in practice this is seldom the case because of absenteeism or lack of parental consent. If the goal of a study is to determine social acceptance or preference or to classify students into the traditional sociometric status types, voter participation should be high (60–70%, with higher participation rates more important in studies using limited nominations). If the goal of a study is to assess popularity, the situation is slightly different. Popularity is a reputation, and reputations can be reliably assessed by subsets of the entire peer group.

Capitalizing on this principle, some researchers have assessed popularity using sociometric procedures with a subset of the peer group acting as voters. For example, Gorman, Kim, and Schimmelbusch (2002) collected popularity judgments from random subsets of the peer group in middle school. Prinstein (2007) used teacher-identified "sociometric experts" (i.e., students who were very aware of classroom social processes) to approximate judgments of the entire group (see also Angold et al., 1990). Given that the results of such studies are very similar to those of studies using full-group assessments, using subsets of the peer group appears to be a reliable method of measuring popularity.

Group Classifications

Peer nominations or ratings yield continuous scores for popularity. However, some researchers prefer to work with subgroups or classifications for analytic or applied purposes. As indicated previously, in traditional sociometric research, there are agreed-upon decision rules to classify students into the sociometric status types *accepted* (formerly known as *popular*), *rejected, neglected, controversial,* and *average,* as derived from "liked most" and "liked least" nominations. However, there is no analogous procedure to classify children or adolescents as popular, based on "most popular" and "least popular" nominations. The simplest approach so far has been to classify students as popular when they score 1 SD above the mean on a continuous score for popularity and to classify all other students as "not popular" (e.g., de Bruyn & Cillessen, 2006a). Others have created subgroups based on teacher ratings (e.g., Rodkin, Farmer, Pearl, & Van Acker, 2000) or derived groups empirically using cluster analysis (e.g., Lease, Musgrove, & Axelrod, 2002). One challenge is to develop a standard way of creating popularity subgroups, so that classifications can be compared between studies.

Alternative Peer (Sociometric) Measures

There are two sources of terminological confusion surrounding the popularity construct. The first is the use of *popularity* for measures of likeability such as acceptance, preference, or desired peer affiliation. The second is the use of *popularity* for constructs that tap into some aspect of social visibility or power, such as admiration, attractiveness, coolness, dominance, network centrality, or perceived peer affiliation. These latter constructs have a theoretical connection to popularity but are not measures of popularity themselves. In each of these cases, only peer nominations or ratings that directly assess popularity should be called "popularity." Measures of other constructs should be carefully labeled to best represent the constructs that they tap into. Doing otherwise would perpetuate unclarity regarding the popularity construct.

Acceptance, Preference, Likeability

In part because of the historical labeling of social acceptance as "popularity," a number of studies of social acceptance have been published in recent years that contain the misleading use of the term *popularity*. Consumers of peer status research must take care not to interpret the results of a study of acceptance as having implications for popularity. Similarly, some studies have used alternative peer nomination items that have not always been labeled clearly as measures of acceptance or popularity. For example, Franzoi, Davis, and Vasquez-Suson (1994) asked high school students to identify the peers in their school "they wanted to hang out with on a Saturday night" and those "they did not want to hang out with on a Saturday night." Because this item asks participants to indicate a personal choice, or *preference,* for a peer, it falls into the category of what Moreno (1934) calls an affiliative or emotional judgment and thus is a measure of acceptance, preference, or likeability. Franzoi et al. (1994) used the nominations received for both questions to classify students into the five traditional sociometric status groups using the exact criteria of Coie et al. (1982). The popular group in their study thus consisted of students who were highly preferred by their peers and should be called "accepted" instead of "popular."

Similar confounds between acceptance and popularity are frequent in the peer relationships literature and highlight the need to be very clear about measures and terms. It should also be noted that researchers might be tempted to use the Coie et al. (1982) controversial classification as a proxy for popularity nominations. This makes some conceptual sense; controversial individuals, like popular individuals, are liked by some peers and disliked by others and show a combination of positive and negative behaviors and traits (Cillessen, 2009). However, research comparing controversial adolescents with those high in popularity has shown only moderate overlap between these categories (e.g., LaFontana & Cillessen, 1999).

Social Network Centrality

Peer nominations for "best friend," "who you hang around with," and even "like most" can be used as the input for a social network analysis. Common methods use a matrix of dyadic best friend choices to determine the centrality of each member of the social network as well as information about particular group structures and subgroup memberships. For popularity research, network data are highly valuable in identifying subgroups of popular peers and in fully understanding an individual's place within the social network. For example, a common measure of individual centrality in the social network, the Bonacich (1987) index, depends on the number of other network members one is connected to as well as on the centrality of those peers. A child or adolescent with ties to many peers who are themselves highly connected is considered socially central.

Conceptually, the construct of social network centrality has much overlap with the construct of popularity. Popular adolescents, for example, are often described as influential or socially central in their peer group or grade. Indeed, Cillessen and Borch (2006) found a high correlation between popularity derived from "most popular" and "least popular" nominations and the Bonacich centrality index based on best friend choices in middle and high school grades.

The conceptual and empirical overlap may lead researchers to use network centrality as an alternative or proxy for popularity or even to simply equate one with the other. We caution against this practice. Although the correlation between centrality and popularity is high, the difference between both constructs becomes clearly visible when their stabilities over time are considered. Specifically, whereas popularity is highly stable, even across school transitions (e.g., Cillessen & Mayeux, 2004), centrality is much more dependent on the consistency of the reference group (because it is based on dyadic ties) and, therefore, shows much lower stability (Cillessen & Borch, 2006). Thus, although social network centrality and popularity are related theoretically and empirically, they are not identical. Indices of social network centrality should not be called measures of popularity.

Other Alternative Constructs

Still other approaches to measuring status have been used in the peer relations literature, further muddying the waters and making straightforward conclusions difficult. For example, some researchers have asked students to name peers in their classroom for the sociometric criterion "someone who everyone wants to hang out with" (see LaFontana & Cillessen, 1998). This is a measure of perceived peer affiliation and not a direct measure of popularity. A key distinction between measures of acceptance and popularity is that the former is based on individual feelings, whereas the latter is measuring an individual's assessment of the group consensus.

Although such a question is not an assessment of popularity, it is also not a direct measure of preference because it is asking participants to report on group attitudes. LaFontana and Cillessen (1998) examined the overlap of direct measures of acceptance and popularity with such indirect measures as "liked by everyone" and showed that these are related, but not identical, constructs.

In other examples, researchers have used peer nominations of admiration or coolness as stand-ins for measures of popularity. Indeed, being admired and being cool have been named as characteristics of popularity in open-ended studies in which adolescents were asked to describe popular peers (LaFontana & Cillessen, 2002; Xie et al., 2006), and being seen as cool and dressing "hip" are correlates of popularity (de Bruyn & Cillessen, 2006b). Yet care should be taken to equate single indicators of popularity, such as admiration, coolness, or being fashionable, with the overall construct itself. Similarly, popularity has sometimes been equated with membership in crowds or cliques with certain characteristics (see Brown, Chapter 8, this volume). Here, too, membership to a certain group is not the same as the popularity status of the individual.

ADDITIONAL METHODOLOGICAL ISSUES

In addition to making sure that one is indeed measuring popularity and not another (albeit related) construct, several other methodological issues are worth discussing. In this section, we address four methodological issues relevant to peer-based measures of popularity. The first is whether a definition of popularity should be provided to participants when peer nominations or ratings of popularity are solicited. The second is whether positive nominations should be used alone or in combination with negative nominations (e.g., "least popular"). The third issue is whether nominations should be collected within gender or also across gender. The fourth point addresses limited versus unlimited nominations.

Definition of Popularity

Occasionally, researchers question whether children or adolescents should be given a standard definition of popularity when making popularity nominations. The situation is sometimes compared with research on bullying, where giving a standard definition of bullying is a requirement for the use of certain instruments, such as the Olweus (1996) Bully/Victim Questionnaire. In sociometric research using peer nominations, elaborate descriptions of the terms are typically not given. Coie et al. (1982) provided short descriptive labels of some of the constructs they measured (e.g., "Leaders and good to have in charge," "Starts fights and picks on other people"), but in most sociometric studies descriptors of behaviors are usually short or absent altogether, capitalizing on the idea that students should be free to nominate the peers who they personally believe best fit the relatively simple criteria that they have been given (e.g., "best friend," "someone you like," "someone who plays alone a lot").

In this tradition, elaborate descriptions are usually not provided for the term *popular* (in the same way as they are not for "best friend" or "someone you like"). Participants are typically only primed with the term *popularity* as part of the question ("Name the peers in your grade who are popular"). This strategy makes sense because *popularity* is a term that has an immediate meaning among adolescents. This makes it an ecologically valid measure of status, but this validity may be lost or diluted when adults impose a meaning on the term. Evidence in favor of this strategy comes from studies that have used open-ended question formats (e.g., "What makes someone popular?") to determine what children and adolescents understand the meaning of this construct to be within their own school, cultural, or subcultural context (e.g., LaFontana & Cillessen, 2002; Xie et al., 2006).

We also strongly recommend that no descriptive labels of popularity are given when collecting popularity nominations. In addition to adhering to the sociometric tradition, this procedure allows for variability in the meaning of popularity by age, gender, ethnicity, or culture. In the same way that children of different age groups have different definitions of friendship, the meaning and importance of popularity also vary across development (LaFontana & Cillessen, 2010). One of the most interesting recent developments in popularity research is the examination of cross-cultural differences in the definitions and meanings of popularity (see Marks et al., 2010). This research builds on the idea that children's and adolescents' definitions of popularity vary by cultural context. Providing a standard definition of popularity to accompany peer nomination items would prevent researchers from developing a richer understanding of cross-cultural variation in what popularity means to youth.

Positive and Negative Nominations

An issue already addressed is whether positive nominations ("most popular") alone are sufficient or whether negative nominations ("least popular") should also be collected. In the sociometric literature measuring acceptance, there is a strong consensus that both positive ("liked most") and negative ("liked least") nominations are necessary. Researchers generally agree that it is essential to make a distinction between two types of children or adolescents who do not receive many acceptance nominations: those who are actively rejected (as indicated by many "liked least" nominations) and those who are neglected (as indicated by a lack of both rejection and acceptance nominations; e.g., Thompson & Powell, 1951).

For research on popularity, the issue is not to make a distinction between two groups at the low end of the status continuum but rather to make a distinction at the high end. In that sense, it is almost more critical to accompany "most popular" nominations with "liked most" nominations than with "least popular" nominations. Yet there are two reasons to include "least popular" nominations. First, a composite popularity score can then be derived from two items ("most popular" minus "least popular") in the same way that acceptance is derived from two items ("liked most" minus "liked least"), and that makes the two scores more comparable when they are used in the same study. Thus, it is recommended to collect "most popular" and "least popular" nominations as well as "liked most" and "liked least" nominations. The advantage of using both "most popular" and "least popular" nominations is that a composite popularity score is created ("most popular" minus "least popular" nominations received), which is the equivalent of social preference as derived from "liked most" minus "liked least" nominations.

Second, the associations of unpopularity with popularity, acceptance, and rejection are insufficiently known. Low to moderate negative correlations have been found between popularity and unpopularity (Košir & Pečjak, 2005; Lease, Kennedy, & Axelrod, 2002). Just as acceptance and rejection may be seen as being separable constructs with unique behavioral correlates (Graham & Juvonen, 2002; Pakaslahti & Keltikangas-Järvinen, 2001; Parkhurst & Asher, 1992), the sparse research on the relationship between popularity and unpopularity indicates that these constructs also may be separable (Gorman, Schwartz, Nakamoto, & McKay, 2007; Košir & Pečjak, 2005; Lease, Musgrove et al., 2002). To date, however, most studies either have collected popularity nominations without including unpopularity at all (e.g., Babad, 2001; Parkhurst & Hopmeyer, 1998) or have created composite measurements of popularity (e.g., de Bruyn & van den Boom, 2005; Prinstein & Cillessen, 2003). This inconsistency has created two conceptual problems for popularity research. First, we do not yet know the implications of including unpopularity either as a separate status measure or as part of a composite measure. Second, the use of single-item versus composite measures in different analyses makes it difficult to compare findings across studies. Given both these two issues, it is recommended to add "least popular" nominations to the data collection if practical and if ethical considerations allow it.

Same-Sex and Cross-Sex Nominations

There is also some debate in the popularity literature regarding whether nominations should be collected within gender only or whether cross-sex nominations should also be allowed. In the older sociometric literature of the 1970s and 1980s, some researchers collected same-sex peer nominations or ratings only (e.g., Asher et al., 1979). These studies were conducted with young elementary schoolchildren or even children in preschool groups in which play interactions are primarily between same-sex peers. Thus, it made good sense to limit nominations to within gender, because young children have more experience with their same-gender peers. However, numerous studies in the older sociometric literature collected both same-sex and other-sex nominations (e.g., Coie et al., 1982), and there are good reasons to assume that the cross-sex perspective adds to the reliability and ecological validity of status assessed.

Including cross-sex nominations is particularly important in popularity research, which is often conducted with preadolescent and adolescent youth. In early adolescence and beyond, interactions with members of the opposite sex become increasingly frequent. Peer cliques are no longer exclusively same sex in nature (see Brown, Chapter 8, this volume). In addition, status within one's own gender may also depend on or be influenced by the frequency and nature of cross-sex interactions (see Carlson & Rose, 2007; Sebald, 1984).

Limited and Unlimited Nominations

An additional methodological issue regards the use of limited or unlimited nominations. Although limited nominations (typically three) were the standard in older sociometric studies, there are now compelling reasons to recommend the use of unlimited nominations under certain circumstances. The preference for unlimited nominations in modern sociometric research emerged in response to a very practical issue. Respondents in sociometric field studies complained that they wished to name more than three peers but were limited to three or that they did not know anyone who fit the sociometric item but were forced to come up with three names anyway. Researchers became aware that the ecological validity of participants' choices would improve if they were allowed to name as many or as few peers as they wanted in response to each question on the sociometric assessment.

Limited nominations have been used in both older studies (e.g., Coie et al., 1982) and newer studies (e.g., Rose et al., 2004). This method can be advantageous because participants are encouraged to select classmates who most clearly fit the sociometric items (Rose et al., 2004). However, limited nominations also reduce the number of choices each child receives; in some studies, as many as half of the participants were eliminated from analyses because they simply did not receive enough nominations to make any inferences about their status or behaviors (e.g., Babad, 2001). In addition, with limited nominations, each student is nominated on the basis of whether other students are nominated. Once the most obvious peers are chosen, the remaining peers will not be considered (Parkhurst & Asher, 1992). This conditional process may contribute to a skewed distribution of sociometric scores. One possible solution is to use multiple nominations for the same behavior and then compute aggregated scores across these multiple nominations. Another solution is to use unlimited nominations.

In recent studies on popularity, there is preference for unlimited nominations (as well as allowing both same-sex and other-sex choices). This preference is driven by the aforementioned improved ecological validity of unlimited nominations and by the need to obtain a more optimal distribution of nominations received among participants. Two confounded factors that play a role in the decision to use limited or unlimited nominations are participant age and the nature and size of the reference group. For older participants (adolescents), the freedom of choice to deviate from three nominations becomes particularly important. These participants are also in larger reference groups (middle or high school grades instead of elementary school classrooms), where limited nominations lead to more skew in the data and unlimited nominations contribute to a more normal spread of scores across all participants. Thus, unlimited nominations are particularly important when sociometric data are collected with older age groups and in larger grades. In popularity research in middle and high school grades, unlimited nominations are strongly recommended. It matters less whether limited or unlimited nominations are used when sociometric data are collected with younger children in elementary school classrooms or in secondary school settings that are highly structured by classroom groups, as in some countries outside of North America (see, e.g., de Bruyn & Cillessen, 2006a, 2006b).

PSYCHOMETRIC PROPERTIES OF SOCIOMETRIC MEASURES OF POPULARITY

This section reviews the psychometric properties of quantitative (sociometric) measures of popularity, as far as they are available. Four psychometric properties are examined: reliability, stability, discriminant validity, and construct validity. This section focuses on measures of popularity only, not acceptance or preference. They are mentioned only if they serve a purpose for comparison.

Reliability

Many of the considerations of reliability are not as applicable to sociometric methods as they are to other psychological measures. Interrater reliability, although calculable for sociometric ratings, rankings, and paired comparisons, is usually not determined for the more commonly used peer nomination methods. Interitem reliability is also less vital in sociometric methods. Many researchers, in fact, use single-item measures to assess behavioral or affective constructs, arguing that the number of respondents and the face validity of questions mitigate the general methodological difficulties of single-item measures (Becker & Luthar, 2007; Parkhurst & Asher, 1992). Popularity, in particular, has been investigated using one or two items (i.e., either a single popularity item or a popularity item and an unpopularity item). This practice is deliberately designed to evoke the participant's definition of the term; adding additional items would be counterproductive to allowing participants to define "popularity" for themselves.

The primary form of reliability to be considered for popularity assessments is test–retest reliability. Cillessen, Bukowski, and Haselager (2000) used a time interval of 3 months, roughly the equivalent of one semester in school, as a practical guideline to distinguish reliability from stability in sociometric research. Test–retest correlations across intervals shorter than 3 months were considered measures of reliability; test–retest correlations across intervals longer than 3 months were considered measures of stability. This guideline is followed here.

Because research on popularity is relatively new, and past studies are more scattered throughout history and substantive fields, less information is available about the reliability of popularity than of acceptance, rejection, and preference. In fact, we know of only one study that determined the test–retest correlations of measures of popularity across intervals shorter than 3 months and that also included measures of acceptance and rejection at the same time for comparison purposes (van den Berg, 2009). In this study, peer nominations of popularity, acceptance, and rejection were collected in grades 7 and 8 across 8-week intervals in the late fall and winter of the school year. High test–retest correlations were found for composite measures of popularity, and they were higher than for concurrent measures of acceptance and rejection. The test–retest reliability of popularity measures in early adolescence appears to be high.

Stability

Stability information is more often reported in sociometric studies. In a meta-analysis, Jiang and Cillessen (2005) reported average stability correlations of about .60 for acceptance, rejection, and preference. The stability correlations for popularity that have been reported in studies tend to be higher than this estimate. Studies that have directly compared the stabilities of popularity with the other sociometric dimensions also consistently find that the stability of popularity is higher than the stabilities of acceptance, preference, and rejection (Cillessen & Borch, 2006; Cillessen & Mayeux, 2004; Rose et al., 2004).

The fact that popularity is more stable than preference makes sense. Popularity is a reputation for which there is, by definition, a certain degree of consensus in the peer group. Preference-based measures reflect individual judgments of liking and disliking that are more heavily influenced by changes in the social behavior of the votee and the level of interaction between the voter and the votee. They do not measure a shared group perception but an individual choice. This argument was confirmed in recent analyses by van den Berg (2009), who conducted a variance componential analysis (Kenny, 1994) on ratings of likeability and popularity within classrooms and showed that ratings of popularity are primarily driven by characteristics of the child being judged (partner variance), whereas ratings of likeability depend more on the combination of rater and the ratee (dyadic variance).

Discriminant Validity: Popularity–Preference Correlations

Researchers have occasionally asked whether measures of popularity are actually all that different from measures of acceptance or preference. Parkhurst and Hopmeyer (1998) initially provided an answer to that question by reporting a correlation of .40 between composite measures of popularity and preference. This correlation was confirmed in later studies that also demonstrated that the distinction between preference and popularity widens across adolescence for both genders, especially for girls (e.g., Cillessen & Mayeux, 2004). The following section reviews the evidence regarding the preference–popularity correlation and also reviews how this association varies by age and gender.

Popularity–Preference Correlations

Quite a few studies have reported correlations between preference and popularity. The majority of these compare preference (acceptance minus rejection) with composite popularity (popularity minus unpopularity). The correlations tend to vary by age and gender. Correlations are moderate to high in middle childhood and early adolescence (Andreou, 2006; Cillessen & Mayeux, 2004; de Bruyn, Cillessen, & Wissink, 2010; de Bruyn & van den Boom, 2005; Košir & Pečjak, 2005; Sandstrom & Cillessen, 2006; Sijtsema, Veenstra, Lindenberg, & Salmivalli, 2009; see Cillessen & Borch, 2006, for an exception) but are lower in middle adolescence (Cillessen & Borch, 2006; Cillessen & Mayeux, 2004; Košir & Pečjak, 2005; LaFontana & Cillessen, 2002; Prinstein & Cillessen, 2003). The gender effect is more consistent; across ages and time points, correlations between social preference and composite popularity are (often significantly) higher for boys than girls (Andreou, 2006; Cillessen & Borch, 2006; Cillessen & Mayeux, 2004; LaFontana & Cillessen, 2002; Prinstein & Cillessen, 2003). Studies reporting correlations between acceptance and popularity scores (i.e., without including aspects of rejection or unpopularity) tend to mirror those that use preference and composite popularity measures; they find that these correlations are moderate to high in middle childhood/early adolescence (Babad, 2001; Lease, Musgrove, et al., 2002) and low to moderate in middle adolescence (Babad, 2001; Košir & Pečjak, 2005; Parkhurst & Hopmeyer, 1998).

Gender Differences

Cillessen and Mayeux (2004) directly addressed the question of why the correlations between social preference and composite popularity tend to be significantly higher for boys than for girls and why, as their results showed, this correlation declines over time for girls more than for boys. They offered two explanations: (1) Boys are able to balance popularity and likeability without the use of aggression, whereas girls increasingly use manipulation and relational aggression (which are related to increased peer rejection; see Crick, Murray-Close, Marks, & Mohajeri-Nelson, 2009, for a review) over time, and (2) boys and girls are both manipulative, but girls are more likely than boys to be rejected when they engage in relationally aggressive actions. Although these explanations are plausible, they are based primarily on the effects of aggression. Further research is needed to explore more fully these and other possible hypotheses for the gender difference in the association between popularity and likeability.

Age Differences

The linear decline in the magnitude of the correlation between popularity and preference may be due to a number of factors. First, social and cognitive faculties are continually developing throughout childhood and adolescence and may provide increasing capacity to understand the complexities of status hierarchies and to make fine distinctions between affective versus consensus-based judgments.

Another explanation for the decreasing popularity–preference correlation may be that, as adolescents develop, the process of remaining popular becomes less conducive to being accepted or vice versa. Whereas some studies have, indeed, shown that popularity is related to increases in antisocial behavior (Mayeux et al., 2008; Sandstrom & Cillessen, 2006), others have shown that popularity in middle school is actually related to small increases in social preference over time (Cillessen & Mayeux, 2004). This pattern of results may make it difficult to explain why the popularity–preference correlation becomes progressively lower during adolescence. However, developmental changes in the prioritizing of status and the factors associated with achieving and maintaining it are likely strong influences in this trend (see Cillessen, Chapter 12, this volume).

Construct Validity: Correlations with Social Behavior

The final issue of importance regards the unique correlates of popularity that confirm its theoretical conceptualization as a measure of impact, visibility, or dominance and that also further distinguish it from social preference. Analogous to earlier research on traditional sociometric status, in particular rejection (see Asher & Coie, 1990), three groups of correlates can be distinguished: social-behavioral, social-cognitive, and emotional. The majority of the recent studies on popularity have focused on the unique behavioral correlates of preference and popularity, and within the behavioral domain a key focus has been on aggression (both overt and relational). This research has consistently shown that whereas preference is typically negatively associated with measures of aggression, the association of aggression (in particular relational aggression) with popularity is positive. These associations with aggression have been a key factor in demonstrating the unique construct validity of preference and popularity.

The unique behavioral, social-cognitive, and emotional correlates of preference and popularity are documented elsewhere in this volume (see Atkins & Litwack, Chapter 7, and Mayeux et al., Chapter 4). It should be noticed, however, that the number of studies that have looked at social-cognitive or emotional variables is small compared with the number of behavioral studies. More research in these other domains is needed. In the final chapter of this volume, Cillessen provides a broader context in which to integrate the unique behavioral, social-cognitive, and emotional correlates of popularity and preference.

ALTERNATIVE MEASURES OF POPULARITY

In addition to sociometric measures of popularity and related constructs (e.g., coolness, admiration) discussed previously, additional measures of popularity have been used in the literature that are not derived from the perspective of peers but rather are based on other sources. These have been used in situations where it is not possible to use peer nominations. We discuss these nonsociometric, non-peer-based alternative measures of popularity next. They are measures of popularity (or related constructs) derived from self-judgments, teacher ratings, or observations conducted by trained coders.

Self-Ratings

A relatively frequently used procedure in peer relations research is to ask children or adolescents to assess their own self-perceived degree of likeability or acceptance in the peer group using single-item ratings or multiple-item scales from existing instruments such as the Harter scales (e.g., Boivin & Bégin, 1989; Cillessen & Bellmore, 1999). Less commonly, as part of a sociometric procedure, children or adolescents are asked to indicate not only who they themselves like most and like least but also who they think likes or dislikes them. Scores for the accuracy of social self-perceptions are then derived from comparisons of the self-perceived nominations with the actual pattern of nominations (see Bellmore & Cillessen, 2003, 2006; Zakriski & Coie, 1996). Another approach is to ask children or adolescents to rate their own popularity in the peer group.

This allows researchers to assess accuracy and evaluate how awareness of one's own place in the peer hierarchy affects behavior or interacts with other factors (such as one's actual popularity level) to affect behavior (see Mayeux & Cillessen, 2008).

Self-perceptions of acceptance and popularity are valuable additions to popularity research. However, they cannot serve as replacements for the perspective from peers. Similar to acceptance, the correlations between self- and peer perceptions of popularity are usually significant and positive but too low to justify that one replaces the other (see, e.g., Mayeux & Cillessen, 2008). Thus, although it is highly recommended to include self-perceptions of popularity in studies that also include peer-based sociometric measures, the self-judgments cannot replace the judgments from peers.

Teacher Ratings

It has often been suggested that teachers may be surveyed instead of peers in order to obtain data about peer status. Teachers have a broad reference group against which they can judge student behavior, making them well able to distinguish students on various behaviors and traits such as aggression and peer sociability (Clarke & Ladd, 2000; Coie & Dodge, 1988). However, teachers are less accurate judges of peer status. They lack the inside perspective on important events in the peer group that often happen in hallways, in bathrooms, or on the way to home or school, outside of their view (Coie, Dodge, & Kupersmidt, 1990). Teacher judgments have the additional disadvantage of reflecting a single viewpoint, whereas peer-report data are based on the composite judgments of multiple informants.

Studies by Cillessen, Terry, Coie, and Lochman (1992) and Pennings (2009) yielded three conclusions regarding teachers' ability to identify peer status. First, teachers are not very accurate judges of traditional sociometric status. Their classification of students into the five status types have low correspondence with the classifications derived from peer nominations. Second, teachers tend to believe that most students are better liked than they actually are. Third, individual teachers vary markedly in their accuracy, although full-time teachers show higher accuracy than part-time teachers, because (presumably) they have more contact with the students.

This latter finding is encouraging because it suggests that teacher ratings are indeed based on the patterns of observations of the peer groups in their classrooms rather than something else (such as their own preferences for students). Yet the relatively low teacher–peer correspondence in general confirms a long-standing consensus that peers tend to have a better idea of each others' social abilities and peer relationships than do teachers (Rubin & Cohen, 1986).

That being said, some influential studies on popularity have appeared that are based on teacher judgments. Rodkin et al. (2000) used teacher judgments to identify high-status peers and then divided them into two subgroups: "toughs" and "models." These subgroups correspond, in terms of their behavioral and other attributes, to students who score high on popularity and acceptance, respectively. This correspondence of results between teacher- and peer-based findings supports the validity of the teacher-report measure of high status. Yet the fact remains that in other studies the correspondence between peer and teacher measures has been less than ideal (e.g., Babad, 2001).

In order to resolve this issue, research is needed on the correspondence between teacher and peer assessments of acceptance and popularity. Because popularity is a reputation for which there is more consensus in the peer group than for likeability, we hypothesize that the teacher–peer correlation will be higher for popularity than for likeability. This hypothesis should be tested to gain further insight into the value of teacher ratings of popularity.

Observations

A third assessment possibility is to observe the indicators of popularity systematically. It is not possible to observe popularity directly because it is an evaluative judgment derived from group members. Yet it is possible to observe the behavioral or other correlates of popularity. For example, observations of interactions between adolescents at a high school dance might suggest who is popular and who is not (see Pellegrini, Roseth, Van Ryzin, & Solberg, Chapter 6, this volume). If observed interaction patterns have previously been validated in studies that also include direct measures of popularity, the observed patterns might become proxies in studies where peer nominations are not possible. Another example of this approach is the early observational work by Vaughn and Waters (1980), who measured visual regard in preschool groups. Children in preschool groups who received the highest amount of visual regard from peers can be considered dominant or socially central. They might be considered popular, but the observations of visual regard were originally intended to observe social dominance (as in ethological research). It is not surprising that observational approaches originated in ethology-inspired research, as in the work of Pellegrini et al. (Chapter 6, this volume) and Vaughn and Waters (1980; see also Hawley, 2003). However, as indicated earlier, observations of social dominance cannot replace peer nominations or ratings of popularity, which remain the gold standard for the assessment of popularity in the peer group.

CONCLUSIONS AND RECOMMENDATIONS

In this chapter we set out to review past and current measures of popularity in the child and adolescent peer group. One primary goal was to review existing terminology and propose a clear set of terms for use in future studies. In past studies, the term *popularity* has been used inconsistently and often used when acceptance, preference, or likeability were actually measured instead. Consistent with previous sociometric studies, the term *acceptance* should be reserved for "liked most" nominations, likeability ratings, and other assessments of likeability. The term *rejection* should be reserved for "liked least" nominations, or the lowest rating points on a likeability scale. *Preference* should be used to refer to the composite score created by using both "liked most" and "liked least" nominations received; it is still very much a measure of likeability in the peer group. *Impact* is the sum of "liked most" and "liked least" nominations received, a less frequently studied construct. Importantly, the term *popularity* should be reserved for measures derived from "most popular" nominations, "most popular" minus "least popular" nominations, or popularity ratings.

As a corollary of this proposal, we suggest that use of the terms *sociometric popularity* and *perceived popularity* should be discontinued. The term *sociometric popularity* is a source of confusion because both forms of high status in the peer group are typically assessed with peer nominations. Sociometric popularity should simply be called "acceptance" or "preference." *Perceived popularity* then simply becomes "popularity."

A challenge of this proposal is how to refer to results from past studies using traditional sociometric status types in which the term *popular* is used for a well-liked, preferred, highly accepted group. In descriptions of results from those studies, instead of using the term "sociometrically popular" for this group, it should instead be referred to by the terms *well-liked, accepted,* or *preferred*. For example, instead of saying that sociometrically popular children are cooperative, whereas perceived popular children are also aggressive, it should be stated that well-liked children are cooperative, whereas popular children (or adolescents) are also aggressive. More consistent use of these status-related terms will yield greater clarity in the popularity literature. A related implication is that measures of network centrality, desired peer affiliation, dominance, admiration, or coolness should not be called popularity, but rather should be transparently described as the psychological constructs that they actually measure.

The terminology in previously published articles obviously cannot and should not be changed, and the reasons for their terminology were valid and logical at the time. However, it seems like an appropriate time to adjust the labels of the traditional sociometric status types *popular, rejected, neglected, controversial*, and *average*. As research on popularity is growing, it seems wise to replace the label "popular" in the traditional sociometric classification system with "accepted." It made sense in the 1980s to call this group "popular," as was done by the researchers who proposed this classification system (Coie et al., 1982; Newcomb & Bukowski, 1983). However, the label "popular" for a group that is defined by acceptance, preference, or likeability has been a source of some confusion in recent research. Therefore, as research on popularity is growing, when summarizing results from past studies using the traditional sociometric types and when conducting new studies with these types, we recommend the use of the label "accepted" instead of "popular" for status types based on "liked most" and "liked least" nominations or other judgments of likeability. "Popular" can then be reserved for sociometric dimensions and groupings based on "most popular" and "least popular" nominations or other popularity judgments.

An important reason for a clear distinction of terms is that empirical studies have shown consistently that preference and popularity are not identical constructs. The correlation between them is low, and, as shown in other chapters in this volume, both correlate uniquely with different concurrent characteristics and later outcomes. What is known about the unique characteristics of preference and popularity is found primarily in the domains of concurrent social behaviors (particularly aggression) and later academic and antisocial behavior outcomes. These characteristics form the beginning of further explorations of the unique features of popularity and how it is different from acceptance or preference. The last chapter of this volume provides a broader theoretical context of these measures and a corresponding research agenda for further popularity research.

REFERENCES

Adler, P. A., & Adler, P. (1998). *Peer power: Preadolescent culture and identity.* New Brunswick, NJ: Rutgers University Press.

Andreou, E. (2006). Social preference, perceived popularity and social intelligence: Relations to overt and relational aggression. *School Psychology International, 27,* 339–351.

Angold, A., Coie, J. D., Burns, B. J., Terry, R., Costello, E. J., Lochman, J., et al. (1990). *Methods for developmental studies of conduct problems: Assessments of service use and peer ratings of social status and behavior.* Unpublished manuscript, Department of Psychology, Duke University, Durham, NC.

Asher, S. R., & Coie, J. D. (Eds.). (1990). *Peer rejection in childhood.* New York: Cambridge University Press.

Asher, S. R., Singleton, L. C., Tinsley, B. R., & Hymel, S. (1979). A reliable sociometric measure for preschool children. *Developmental Psychology, 15,* 443–444.

Babad, E. (2001). On the conception and measurement of popularity: More facts and some straight conclusions. *Social Psychology of Education, 5,* 3–29.

Becker, B., & Luthar, S. S. (2007). Peer-perceived admiration and social preference: Contextual correlates of positive peer regard among suburban and urban adolescents. *Journal of Research on Adolescence, 17,* 117–144.

Bellmore, A. D., & Cillessen, A. H. N. (2003). Children's meta-perceptions and meta-accuracy of acceptance and rejection by same-sex and other-sex peers. *Personal Relationships, 10,* 217–234.

Bellmore, A. D., & Cillessen, A. H. N. (2006). Reciprocal influences of victimization, perceived social preference, and self-concept in adolescence. *Self and Identity, 5,* 209–229.

Bierman, K. L. (2004). *Peer rejection: Developmental processes and intervention strategies.* New York: Guilford Press.

Boivin, M., & Bégin, G. (1989). Peer status and self-perception among early elementary school children: The case of the rejected children. *Child Development, 60,* 591–596.

Bonacich, P. (1987). Power and centrality: A family of measures. *American Journal of Sociology, 92,* 1170–1182.

Boorman, W. R. (1931). *Personality in its teens.* New York: Macmillan.

Buff, S. A. (1970). Greasers, dupers, and hippies: Three responses to the adult world. In L. Howe (Ed.), *The white majority* (pp. 60–77). New York: Random House

Canaan, J. (1987). A comparative analysis of American suburban middle class, middle school, and high school teenage cliques. In G. Spindler & L. Spindler (Eds.), *Interpretive ethnography of education: At home and abroad* (pp. 385–408). Hillsdale, NJ: Erlbaum.

Carlson, W., & Rose, A. J. (2007). The role of reciprocity in romantic relationships in middle childhood and early adolescence. *Merrill-Palmer Quarterly, 53,* 262–290.

Cillessen, A. H. N. (2009). Sociometric methods. In K. H. Rubin, W. M. Bukowski, & B. Laursen (Eds.), *Handbook of peer interactions, relationships, and groups* (pp. 82–99). New York: Guilford Press.

Cillessen, A. H. N., & Bellmore, A. D. (1999). Accuracy of social self-perceptions and peer competence in middle childhood. *Merrill-Palmer Quarterly, 45,* 650–676.

Cillessen, A. H. N., & Borch, C. (2006). Developmental trajectories of adolescent popularity: A growth curve modelling analysis. *Journal of Adolescence, 29,* 935–959.

Cillessen, A. H. N., & Bukowski, W. M. (2000). Conceptualizing and measuring peer acceptance and rejection. In A. H. N. Cillessen & W. M. Bukowski (Eds.), *New directions for child and adolescent development: Vol. 88. Recent advances in the measurement of acceptance and rejection in the peer system.* (pp. 27–53). San Francisco: Jossey-Bass.

Cillessen, A. H. N., Bukowski, W. M., & Haselager, G. J. T. (2000). Stability of sociometric categories. In A. H. N. Cillessen & W. M. Bukowski (Eds.), *New directions for child and adolescent development: Vol. 88. Recent advances in the measurement of acceptance and rejection in the peer system.* (pp. 75–93). San Francisco: Jossey-Bass.

Cillessen, A. H. N., & Mayeux, L. (2004). From censure to reinforcement: Developmental changes in the association between aggression and social status. *Child Development, 75,* 147–163.

Cillessen, A. H. N., & Rose, A. J. (2005). Understanding popularity in the peer system. *Current Directions in Psychological Science, 14,* 102–105.

Cillessen, A. H. N., Terry, R., Coie, J. D., & Lochman, J. E. (1992, April). *Accuracy of teacher-identification of children's sociometric status positions.* Paper presented at the biennial meeting of the Conference on Human Development, Atlanta, GA.

Clarke, K. E., & Ladd, G. W. (2000). Connectedness and autonomy support in parent–child relationships: Links to children's socio-emotional orientation and peer relationships. *Developmental Psychology, 36,* 485–498.

Coie, J. D., & Dodge, K. A. (1988). Multiple sources of data on social behavior and social status in the school: A cross-age comparison. *Child Development, 59,* 815–829.

Coie, J. D., Dodge, K. A., & Coppotelli, H. (1982). Dimensions and types of social status: A cross-age perspective. *Developmental Psychology, 18,* 557–570.

Coie, J. D., Dodge, K. A., & Kupersmidt, J. B. (1990). Peer group behavior and social status. In S. R. Asher & J. D. Coie (Eds.), *Peer rejection in childhood* (pp. 17–59). Cambridge, UK: Cambridge University Press.

Coleman, J. (1961). *The adolescent society.* New York: Free Press.

Crick, N. R., Murray-Close, D., Marks, P. E. L., & Mohajeri-Nelson, N. (2009). Aggression and peer relationships in school-age children: Relational and physical aggression in group and dyadic contexts. In K. H. Rubin, W. M. Bukowski, & B. Laursen (Eds.), *Handbook of peer interactions, relationships, and groups* (pp. 287–302). New York: Guilford Press.

Currie, D. H., Kelly, D. M., & Pomerantz, S. (2007). 'The power to squash people': Understanding girls' relational aggression. *British Journal of Sociology of Education, 28,* 23–37.

de Bruyn, E. H., & Cillessen, A. H. N. (2006a). Heterogeneity of girls' consensual popularity: Academic and interpersonal behavioral profiles. *Journal of Youth and Adolescence, 35,* 435–445.

de Bruyn, E. H., & Cillessen, A. H. N. (2006b). Popularity in early adolescence:

Prosocial and antisocial subtypes. *Journal of Adolescent Research, 21*, 607–627.
de Bruyn, E. H., Cillessen, A. H. N., & Wissink, I. B. (2010). Associations of peer acceptance and perceived popularity with bullying and victimization in early adolescence. *Journal of Early Adolescence, 30*, 543–566.
de Bruyn, E. H., & van den Boom, D. C. (2005). Interpersonal behavior, peer popularity and self-esteem in early adolescence. *Social Development, 14*, 555–573.
Dunnington, M. J. (1957). Investigation of areas of disagreement in sociometric measurement of preschool children. *Child Development, 28*, 93–102.
Eckert, P. (2000). *Linguistic variation as social practice: The linguistic construction of identity in Belten High*. Malden, MA: Blackwell.
Eder, D. (1985). The cycle of popularity: Interpersonal relations among female adolescents. *Sociology of Education, 58*, 154–165.
Eder, D. (1995). *School talk: Gender and adolescent culture*. New Brunswick, NJ: Rutgers University Press.
Folsom, J. K. (1934). *The family: Its sociology and social psychiatry*. New York: Wiley.
Franzoi, S. L., Davis, M. H., & Vasquez-Suson, K. A. (1994). Two social worlds: Social correlates and stability of adolescent status groups. *Journal of Personality and Social Psychology, 67*, 462–473.
Gordon, C. W. (1957). *The social system of the high school*. Glencoe, IL: Free Press.
Gorman, A. H., Kim, J., & Schimmelbusch, A. (2002). The attributes adolescents associate with peer popularity and teacher preference. *Journal of School Psychology, 40*, 143–165.
Gorman, A. H., Schwartz, D., Nakamoto, J., & McKay, T. (2007, March). *She may not be very popular but she is not unpopular.* Paper presented at the biennial meeting of the Society for Research in Child Development, Boston, MA.
Graham, S., & Juvonen, J. (2002). Ethnicity, peer harassment, and adjustment in middle school: An exploratory study. *Journal of Early Adolescence, 22*, 173–199.
Hawley, P. H. (2003). Prosocial and coercive configurations of resource control in early adolescence: A case from the well-adapted Machiavellian. *Merrill-Palmer Quarterly, 49*, 279–309.
Hermans, M. C. (1931). Experiments with gifted pupils. *The English Journal, 20*, 540–547.
Hollingshead, A. (1949). *Elmtown's youth: The impact of social classes on adolescents*. New York: Wiley.
Jennings, H. H. (1937). The structure of leadership. Development and sphere of influence. *Sociometry, 1*(1–2), 99–143.
Jiang, X. L., & Cillessen, A. H. N. (2005). Stability of continuous measures of sociometric status: A meta-analysis. *Developmental Review, 25*, 1–25.
Kenny, D. A. (1994). *Interpersonal perception: A social relations analysis*. New York: Guilford Press.

Kenny, D. A., Kashy, D. A., & Cook, W. L. (2006). *Dyadic data analysis*. New York: Guilford Press.

Koch, H. L. (1933). Popularity in preschool children: Some related factors and a technique for its measurement. *Child Development, 4,* 164–175.

Košir, K., & Pečjak, S. (2005). Sociometry as a method for investigating peer relationships: What does it actually measure? *Educational Research, 47,* 127–144.

LaFontana, K. M., & Cillessen, A. H. N. (1998). The nature of children's stereotypes of popularity. *Social Development, 7,* 301–320.

LaFontana, K. M., & Cillessen, A. H. N. (1999). Children's interpersonal perceptions as a function of sociometric and peer perceived popularity. *Journal of Genetic Psychology, 160,* 225–241.

LaFontana, K. M., & Cillessen, A. H. N. (2002). Children's perceptions of popular and unpopular peers: A multimethod assessment. *Developmental Psychology, 38,* 635–647.

LaFontana, K. M., & Cillessen, A. H. N. (2010). Developmental changes in the priority of perceived status in childhood and adolescence. *Social Development, 19,* 130–147.

Larkin, R. W. (1979). *Suburban youth in cultural crisis*. New York: Oxford University Press.

Lease, A. M., Kennedy, C. A., & Axelrod, J. L. (2002). Children's social constructions of popularity. *Social Development, 11,* 87–109.

Lease, A. M., Musgrove, K. T., & Axelrod, J. L. (2002). Dimensions of social status in preadolescent peer groups: Likability, perceived popularity, and social dominance. *Social Development, 11,* 508–533.

Malloy, T. E., Albright, L., & Scarpati, S. (2007). Awareness of peers' judgments of oneself: Accuracy and process of metaperception. *International Journal of Behavioural Development, 31,* 603–610.

Marks, P. E. L., Cillessen, A. H. N., Andreou, E., Berger, C., Bukowski, W. M., Caravita, S. C., et al. (2010). *International perspectives on popularity: The meanings and constructions of popularity across cultures*. Manuscript submitted for publication.

Mayeux, L., & Cillessen, A. H. N. (2008). It's not just being popular, it's knowing it, too: The role of self-perceptions of status in the associations between peer status and aggression. *Social Development, 17,* 881–888.

Mayeux, L., Sandstrom, M. J., & Cillessen, A. H. N. (2008). Is being popular a risky proposition? *Journal of Research on Adolescence, 18,* 49–74.

Michell, L., & Amos, A. (1997). Girls, pecking order and smoking. *Social Science and Medicine, 44,* 1861–1869.

Milner, M. (2004). *Freaks, geeks, and cool kids*. New York: Routledge.

Moreno, J. L. (1934). *Who shall survive?: A new approach to the problem of human interrelations*. Washington DC: Nervous and Mental Disease Publishing Co.

Moreno, J. L. (1960). *The sociometry reader*. Glencoe, IL: Free Press.

Newcomb, A. F., & Bukowski, W. M. (1983). Social impact and social preference as determinants of children's peer group status. *Developmental Psychology, 19,* 856–867.

Olweus, D. (1996). *The Revised Olweus Bully/Victim Questionnaire*. Bergen, Norway: Research Centre for Health Promotion.

Pakaslahti, L., & Keltikangas-Järvinen, L. (2001). Peer-attributed prosocial behavior among aggressive/preferred, aggressive/non-preferred, non-aggressive/preferred, and non-aggressive/non-preferred adolescents. *Personality and Individual Differences, 30,* 903–916.

Parkhurst, J. T., & Asher, S. R. (1992). Peer rejection in middle school: Subgroup differences in behavior, loneliness, and interpersonal concerns. *Developmental Psychology, 28,* 231–241.

Parkhurst, J. T., & Hopmeyer, A. (1998). Sociometric popularity and peer-perceived popularity: Two distinct dimensions of peer status. *Journal of Early Adolescence, 18,* 135–144.

Pennings, H. J. M. (2009). *The teacher Q-sort sociometric: An alternative for sociometric status identification?* Unpublished master's thesis, Behavioural Science Institute, Radboud University, Nijmegen, The Netherlands.

Polansky, N., Lippitt, R., & Redl, F. (1950). The use of near-sociometric data in research on group treatment process. *Sociometry, 13,* 39–62.

Prinstein, M. J. (2007). Assessment of adolescents' preference- and reputation-based popularity using sociometric experts. *Merrill-Palmer Quarterly, 53,* 243–261

Prinstein, M. J., & Cillessen, A. H. N. (2003). Forms and functions of adolescent peer aggression associated with high levels of peer status. *Merrill-Palmer Quarterly, 49,* 310–342.

Rodkin, P. C., Farmer, T. W., Pearl, R., & Van Acker, R. (2000). Heterogeneity of popular boys: Antisocial and prosocial configurations. *Developmental Psychology, 36,* 14–24.

Rose, A. J., Swenson, L. P., & Waller, E. M. (2004). Overt and relational aggression and perceived popularity: Developmental differences in concurrent and prospective relations. *Developmental Psychology, 40,* 378–387.

Rubin, K. H., & Cohen, J. S. (1986). The Revised Class Play: Correlates of peer assessed social behaviors in middle childhood. *Advances in Behavioral Assessment of Children and Families, 2,* 176–206.

Sandstrom, M. J., & Cillessen, A. H. N. (2006). Likeable versus popular: Distinct implications for adolescent adjustment. *International Journal of Behavioral Development, 30,* 305–314.

Schwartz, D., Gorman, A. H., Nakamoto, J., & McKay, T. (2006). Popularity, social acceptance, and aggression in adolescent peer groups: Links with academic performance and school attendance. *Developmental Psychology, 42,* 1116–1127.

Sebald, H. (1984). *Adolescence: A social-psychological analysis* (3rd ed.). Englewood Cliffs, NJ: Prentice Hall.

Sijtsema, J. J., Veenstra, R., Lindenberg, S., & Salmivalli, C. (2009). Empirical test of bullies' status goals: Assessing direct goals, aggression, and prestige. *Aggressive Behavior, 35,* 57–67.

Thompson, G. G., & Powell, M. (1951). An investigation of the rating-scale approach to the measurement of social status. *Educational and Psychological Measurement, 11,* 440–455.

Tryon, C. M. (1939). Evaluations of adolescent personality by adolescents. *Monographs of the Society for Research in Child Development, 4*.
van den Berg, Y. H. M. (2009). *Interpersonal distance and peer relations: A longitudinal field experiment*. Unpublished master's thesis, Behavioural Science Institute, Radboud University, Nijmegen, The Netherlands.
Vaughn, B. E., & Waters, E. (1980). Social organization among preschoool peers: Dominance, attention, and sociometric correlates. In D. R. Omark, F. F. Strayer, & D. G. Freedman (Eds.), *Dominance relations: Ethological perspectives on human conflict* (pp. 126–141). New York: Garland.
Voigt, C. (1933). *A study of happiness of sixth grade children*. Unpublished doctoral dissertation, Washington University, St. Louis, MO.
Waller, W. (1937). The rating & dating complex. *American Sociological Review, 2*, 727–734.
Watson, G. B. (1927). *Experimentation and measurement in religious education*. New York: Association Press.
Webster, M., Jr., & Driskell, J. E., Jr. (1983). Beauty as status. *American Journal of Sociology, 89*, 140–165.
Xie, H., Li, Y., Boucher, S. M., Hutchins, B. C., & Cairns, B. D. (2006). What makes a girl (or a boy) popular (or unpopular)?: African American children's perceptions and developmental differences. *Developmental Psychology, 42*, 599–612.
Zakriski, A. L., & Coie, J. D. (1996). A comparison of aggressive–rejected and nonaggressive–rejected children's interpretations of self-directed and other-directed rejection. *Child Development, 67*, 1048–1070.

Chapter 3

Being There Awhile

An Ethnographic Perspective on Popularity

Don E. Merten

> Deciding the question is the path to knowledge. ... It is opinion that suppresses questions.
> —Gadamer (1989, p. 366)

There is an impressive corpus of ethnographic studies of children that dates back to the early 20th century (James, 2001), to which many ethnographic studies of adolescents can be added. Although ethnographic research represents a small portion of the literature on children and adolescents, it is still a substantial body of work. An important theme running through descriptions of young peoples' worlds is their concern with status arrangements and popularity. As Adler, Kless, and Adler (1992) noted, "Gaining and maintaining popularity has enormous significance in children's lives, ... influencing their ability to make friends, to be included in fun activities, and to develop a positive sense of self-esteem" (p. 182).

Ethnographers have been especially sensitive to the dynamics of popularity. At first glance, qualitative research, especially ethnography, seems straightforward and relatively simple to undertake. After all, how difficult can it be to observe and talk to youth? Yet there is more to ethnography than may be immediately apparent. This chapter first examines the rationale and practices of ethnography—that is, *why* ethnographers do *what* they do—and then considers the different roles that ethnographers assume as they seek to enter and be part of students' worlds. Finally, I discuss how ethnographic work has contributed to understanding the constructions, meanings, and dynamics of popularity in students' lives.

ETHNOGRAPHY: RATIONALE AND PRACTICES

The essence of ethnography involves determining how people understand and operate in their worlds by observing, listening to, and talking with them. By doing this over an extended time in the places where students live, ethnographic researchers provide a holistic view and interpretation of young people's lives. For example, ethnographers not only examine the meanings secrets have for students but also trace how secrets relate to other important features of peer life, such as the process by which friendships are negotiated. Ethnographers further learn that not all secrets are equally valued insofar as secrets about popular students are especially prized resources and to possess such secrets often increases one's own popularity (Merten, 1999). Thus, although ethnographic research may initially focus on a particular issue of importance to youth, it invariably reveals connections to other features of the sociocultural system and thereby contributes to our overall understanding of young people's worlds.

Rationale

The rationale for ethnography is grounded in a number of conceptual assumptions that are far from widely held among social scientists. For instance, in addition to its other strengths, ethnography is particularly effective in identifying cultural meanings as they are constructed, shared, and vary by context. The importance of recognizing the *constructedness* of social life is not the recognition per se but the thoroughgoing interrogation of the constructedness that such recognition encourages. Although social scientists seldom interrogate that which is natural (e.g., the meaning of breathing), the problem is that researchers often perceive, and therefore treat, cultural constructs as if they were natural. For example, friendship in American society is such a ubiquitous and important social form that it is generally perceived as more natural than constructed. Even when we have problems with friends, we rarely question the social form itself and instead focus on the actions of the individuals involved. Similarly, if we assume it is human nature to aspire to be popular, then we are unlikely to examine what it is about popularity as a cultural construct that makes it so desirable and at times problematic.

Ethnographers also tend to focus on the shared, rather than idiosyncratic, meanings and often privilege *meaning* over descriptions of behavior. Of course, not all meanings are shared by youth, even those living in the same community. What is not shared, however, can be an important marker of group or categorical boundaries and thus signifies important variation among students. For example, young people encounter a number of important transitions as they make their way from childhood to adolescence and from grade school to high school. With each transition, new expectations come into play, but not all individuals immediately accept the new expectations and their associated meanings. In grade school, students who cause trouble in class seldom garner the support of many peers. Creating trouble in a junior high class, however, often elicits support from many students and can enhance an individual's popularity among peers who understand that trouble can now symbolize greater autonomy vis-à-vis adults. Students who do not accept the new meaning of trouble, conversely, are often subjected to their peers' disdain (Merten, 2005).

Ethnographers' interest in the constructed nature of students' worlds and the importance of the shared meanings that students bestow on their actions leads them to participate in those worlds—at least being present in them. This level of participation allows researchers to identify more effectively how *context* shapes the meanings of students' actions. For example, sitting next to someone in a classroom where seating is assigned may have a different meaning than sitting next to someone in the lunchroom where students decide with whom to sit. Likewise, the meanings of popularity may be easier to express in one particular context. Observing a hallway may be more productive than observing a classroom. Banks noted, "Students actively use this space to tout one's identity as superior to another. For example, discourses regarding coolness and popularity are often played out in busy school hallways, with those deemed popular getting the most greetings and laughs" (2005, p. 187). In an even more complex way, contexts in which ethnographers observe and engage youth may also shape the types of insights they gain. If one only engages youth in the classroom context where expressions are restrained, the differences between adult and youth culture are minimized, whereas, as Bloustien (2003) observed, being with young people in unconstrained contexts can produce unexpected insights.

> As an adult woman entering into the teenage world, I repeatedly had to confront the extreme physicality of this world. I had forgotten in my own adult socialization how much I had learned to control and contain bodily action. As I engaged more intimately with the teenage world I realized that I had to "unlearn" my adult body: I had to learn again to be more relaxed, to be "silly." (p. 9)

Being present, however, is not always sufficient to produce quality ethnographic data. One needs an openness that is facilitated by holding in abeyance one's taken-for-granted assumptions about what is likely to happen and what it will mean. Still, the more contexts we share with young people and the greater our immersion in those contexts, the more likely we are to notice and understand the nuances of their lives.

Practices

Regardless of where ethnographers decide to observe and make contact with students, they must enter into their presence without unduly distorting the existing routines. The *entry process* can be daunting. Having to build relationships and gain rapport with students who they seek to understand requires that researchers not allow status differences to stand between themselves as individuals and those they wish to understand. Nor can ethnographers hope to gain trust and rapport by using the authority that adults have over children or even the authority of their research role: Successful entry rests on how they are perceived as individuals. Because students control the social aspects of their worlds that interest ethnographers, their permission is required in order for the researchers to be accepted in their world. However, ethnographers also depend on students' goodwill and patience to help them understand how that world is constituted. Corsaro captured the highly personal nature of entry when he writes about his work with preschool children: "I entered the outside play area of the preschool and walked up to two four-year-old girls, Betty and Jenny, who were sitting in the sandpile" (2003, p. 7). Betty told Corsaro that he could not play with them because he was too big—He was "Big Bill." Corsaro's request to watch, however, was granted and later he was invited to play. Conversely, not all ethnographers are accepted and not all ethnographic research is successful (Schwartz, 1987).

Simply *observing* students may be the least intrusive way to gather ethnographic data, but even observation is somewhat disruptive until students get used to the observer and have some idea why they are being observed. Ethnographic observation does not consist of being a human video camera because, unlike a camera, one cannot record everything within one's field of vision. One is seeking to observe not raw behavior but rather meaningful action that is intended to accomplish a particular goal or convey a particular meaning. Furthermore, one cannot effectively observe without giving prior thought to the forms that particular actions, such as behavioral expressions of popularity, may take in a specific context—one cannot assume to recognize "it" when it occurs. Even though the purpose of observation is to determine the actual patterns of students' actions (Goodwin, 1988), observations also serve as takeoff points for subsequent discussions with students. Not only do the ethnographer and the students share common behavioral referents, but these referents also open the way for the ethnographer to ask why an event occurred the way it did and what the intent behind it was. The process of inscribing the details of what one has seen and heard in field notes (Emerson, Fretz, & Shaw, 2001) does not simply capture the events; it also produces insights, like most writing, that were not fully present before writing. Moreover, field notes record events and provisional interpretations in the present that can be reviewed weeks, or even years, later and thereby provide a record unaltered by memory.

Open-ended interviews (LaFontana & Cillessen, 2002; Merten, 1996; Xie, Boucher, Hutchins, & Cairns, 2006) also create a record of what has occurred over time and stand in contrast to interviews that use fixed questions asked in a fixed order. Like most ethnographic work, open-ended interviews possess the tight–loose quality that characterizes observation and thus are seldom entirely spontaneous. The ethnographer develops an idea of what he or she will ask, the possible responses, and the follow-up questions to those potential responses. Well-planned interviews often seem more conversational than unplanned interviews. By starting with very general questions (e.g., "What is a typical day like for you and your friends?"), a student can offer many possible responses. Such general questions encourage narrative-like responses (Cortazzi, 2001) that are important both for their detail and because students are arranging their experience and ideas in a form that makes sense to them. That is, they move from one topic to the next because they are related to each other according to the cultural logic of their constructed world.

This approach may mean that some planned questions are not asked in a particular interview. However, because ethnographers are present for an extended period, they can take up unaddressed questions or ask for clarifications in subsequent interviews. Furthermore, by interviewing students not as isolated individuals but as friends of other students, ethnographers supplement their knowledge of particular people from what their friends mention about them. Such triangulation, the use of multiple sources of data, helps to determine the nature and extent of variation among youth regarding how they bestow meaning on what they and their peers do.

The longitudinal character of ethnography, which provides the basis for what Geertz (1973) refers to as "thick description," is both obvious and underappreciated. It affords the possibility of reconsidering over time what other data are needed and refining interpretations of that data as additional observations and interviews are conducted. For instance, if one initially assumes that popularity once gained is stable, one is unlikely to ask how it is sustained. Yet if one subsequently is told that popularity is often fragile, then the continuous nature of ethnography allows one to take advantage of this information and ask questions about how students manage to sustain popularity. Likewise, new data allow one to view previous data from the perspective of what one has learned subsequently. For example, one may initially accept a newly popular girl's explanation that she dropped her former best friend because the latter was telling lies about her. However, if the girl provides the same explanation when she drops a new popular friend for an even more popular peer, one has reason to critically reexamine her initial explanation. The longitudinal character of ethnography allows researchers to use the ongoing dialectic between data and interpretation to make adjustments to their research strategy.

RESEARCH ROLES IN ETHNOGRAPHIC WORK

The *ethnographer as researcher* is the traditional role (Corsaro, 2003; Eckert, 1989; Eder, 1985; Fine, 1987; Fordham, 1996) taken by most ethnographers. It reduces the possibility that the researcher role will be confused with other adult roles. Eder (1985), for example, chose not to be introduced to students by school administrators or teachers and instead arrived in the school lunchroom, observed students, and eventually began eating with and talking to them. As she writes, the "goal was to avoid association with adults and adult roles and to enter the adolescents' world as peers rather than as authority figures.... We tried to enter the lunchroom environment much as a new student would" (p. 156). Similarly, Fine (1987), in his study of Little League baseball players, emphasized to players and adults alike that his role as researcher was quite different from the usual adult roles, and he reinforced this stance by not telling players what to do during practices or games. The reasoning behind taking on a research role without a mandate of adult authority is that young people are likely to be more open and candid in telling ethnographers about their lives.

Ethnographers also assume dual roles that provide certain advantages. For example, a *teacher as researcher* may make a systematic record of her observations and conversations with students or ask them to answer a questionnaire to collect data for an educational project, an advanced degree, or just intellectual curiosity (Wiseman, 2002). A reversal of role emphasis occurred in the study by Merten (1996), in which certified teachers were trained to be ethnographers and two *ethnographer-teachers* taught one class per semester, spending the rest of their time conducting research. They identified themselves as researchers to the students who took their class, to students in general, and to school personnel. Their unfettered access to the entire school allowed them to observe a broad range of activities and contexts. In the teachers' lounge, they were privy to discussions about students that contained information that often enabled them to understand better the larger familial and school situation of a student. The open-ended interviews they conducted with students took place at the school in a small room set aside for that purpose. Although students expected the ethnographers to be teachers in classroom matters (evaluating work and maintaining order), they also found that the researchers kept what they were told confidential and did not bring adult/teacher authority to their research.

Perhaps the least common role is that of *parent as researcher*. It has enormous potential for breadth of coverage but, like other dual roles, has potential for ambiguity. No one has described the complexity of this role in greater detail than Patricia and Peter Adler. They identify the benefits as being able to "readily gain entry to the world of children through their own children." They can then capitalize on this "complete membership role" (Adler & Adler, 1998, p. 19). As parents, the Adlers had access to students in school, at athletic venues, during neighborhood gatherings, in other parents' homes, and in their own home. Ethnographers frequently hear students refer to some parents as "cool"—parents who listen to them, can joke with them, and understand about being young. The ethnographer as parent comes close to enacting the persona of the cool parent.[1] Yet because ethnographers know the identity of students, they must take extra precautions to ensure confidentiality. The studies by

---

[1] Cutting across the research roles mentioned are other roles described by Fine and Glassner (1979): friend, observer, supervisor, and leader. These roles vary with regard to the authority they bring to dealing with students. Even when authority is played down as much as possible, however, students rightfully assume that adults can exercise authority. Thus, students invariably test the limits of a nonauthority stance taken by an adult, such as using language they consider inappropriate to use with an adult.

the Adlers and Merten were protected by a certificate of confidentiality that prevented parents or authorities from accessing the data.

THE DYNAMICS OF POPULARITY: AN ETHNOGRAPHIC PERSPECTIVE

The strength of ethnography is its ability to capture the dynamics of sociocultural phenomena like popularity. It is difficult to understand a cultural construct like popularity in isolation, and ethnographers, therefore, trace the conceptual relations and cultural logic that connect popularity to other features of students' worlds. For example, Adler et al. (1992) considered the role of popularity in gender identity. Even when ethnographers have focused on popularity, their interest has been less on defining it and more on identifying the role it played in students' lives, especially the processes by which students acquired, sustained, or lost popularity. This section describes what ethnographic research has reported about popularity and considers how the rationale and practices of ethnography have contributed to understanding popularity.

Attributes of, and Paths to, Popularity

The Adlers' research on grade school students identified the somewhat different attributes and factors found among popular boys and girls. For boys, these attributes were athletic ability, coolness, toughness, savoir faire, cross-gender relations, and academic performance. For girls, the popularity factors were family background, physical appearance, social development, and academic performance (Adler & Adler, 1998). The fewer attributes for girls suggested a narrower construction of popularity and emphasized the Adlers' contention that preadolescent culture was gendered. Eckert found that popular students in junior high, however, shared similar attributes, being "on the whole physically attractive, friendly, strong and well coordinated, perceptive, and bright" (1989, p. 163). Eder (1985) found that being from a family with money also contributed to a girl's chances for popularity. The attributes that ethnographers have found associated with popularity are quite similar despite using somewhat different terms to describe them. Regardless of which factors constituted the bases for popularity (Eder & Kinney, 1995), it is clear that some adolescents, by virtue of possessing the attributes that coincided with local representations of popularity, acquired it almost effortlessly, while the majority of their peers were not so fortunate. Most of the less fortunate students simply focused on their interests and did not drive themselves to achieve popularity in order to feel good about who they were. Other students in the same circumstances, however, did everything they could to become popular and thereby prove their worthiness. However, only some succeeded.

Certain activities, cheerleading being the most notable for girls and football or basketball for boys, were clearly marked paths to popularity. If a boy was an outstanding athlete in a high-profile sport, this immeasurably enhanced his chances of being popular. Games of high-profile sports were well attended and often ballplayers were able to wear their uniform jersey to school on game day. These activities enhanced visibility, at least in junior high, and were an important path to popularity. In fact, simply being known was a key to popularity. The best athletes playing the glamour positions (e.g., quarterback or running back in football) were, of course, the most visible. For girls, cheerleading was the activity that led to the greatest visibility and, therefore, was a well-trod path to popularity. Cheerleaders, like their male athlete counterparts, possessed other attributes associated with popularity (e.g., physical attractiveness and athleticism). Cheerleading was such an important path to popularity that being a friend of a cheerleader was a recognized secondary path (Eder, 1985). Nonetheless, gaining popularity by being a friend of a cheerleader was not as simple as it might seem. First, being friends with a girl before she became a cheerleader did not automatically lead to becoming popular. Such a friend had to be something of a cheerleader facsimile—in other words, have many of the attributes that cheerleaders had—or she was likely to be dropped as a friend. Likewise, girls who became friends of cheerleaders were either already cheerleader-like or had to make changes that would make them so. As Eder (1985; Eder & Kinney, 1995) has shown, the dynamics of popularity and the paths to it are both complex and variable from school to school and grade to grade.

It should be no surprise that being from a privileged stratum in a community or having money enhances students' opportunities to be popular, but the association between economic privilege and popularity is complex. For boys, possessing the economic wherewithal to purchase the "expressive equipment" (Adler & Adler, 1998) to increase one's coolness, to travel and have other experiences that develop one's savoir faire, to attend athletic camps, or to take private lessons are significant advantages for becoming popular. For girls, the visibility that is an important asset for popularity (Eder, 1985) was also linked to being well off. For example, a girl's attractiveness was an important attribute for becoming a cheerleader, and her attractiveness could be enhanced by designer clothes and the other expressive equipment that cost money. Nonetheless, some privileged youth did not choose to do the things that led to popularity. For example, they may have chosen not to participate in the "right" activities, may have chosen to pursue a personal style that was unattractive to most popular students, or may have identified with a status category or crowd that generally eschewed the things that led to popularity. Therefore, the privileges that came with economic affluence did not automatically translate into popularity any more than being less privileged kept some students with desirable attributes (athleticism or physical attractiveness) from becoming popular.

For example, Jackie came from a privileged background and was physically attractive and athletically talented, but her selection as a cheerleader resulted in major turmoil among her junior high peers because Jackie was referred to by the students as a burnout (Merten, 1996). The majority of girls selected for cheerleading at this school were preppies; never had a burnout been selected. Because cheerleaders were icons of popularity, this unexpected event simply could not be dismissed and threatened the link between cheerleading and popularity. At first, students expected Jackie to give up her burnout attitude and behaviors and become a preppie, and then things would return to normal. When this assimilationist scenario did not occur, an unprecedented incongruity existed between the high status of an extracurricular activity and the low status of a participant in it. In addition, Jackie seemed remarkably unimpressed at becoming a cheerleader, judging from the fact that she did not transform herself into a preppy, missed practices, and left practice early when she did attend. The main criticism against her by other cheerleaders, however, was not that she continued to talk openly about her drinking and smoking marijuana (burnout activities), but that she lacked commitment to the hard work of cheerleading. It was not that she failed to execute the cheering routines at games, although she did make mistakes from time to time (as did other girls), but her mistakes were interpreted as resulting from and symbolizing her lack of commitment.

It was not altogether clear what was at issue beyond the unprecedented situation of a burnout being a cheerleader. However, because we were present when this process unfolded, we were able to talk to Jackie, other cheerleaders, and various students, but no one managed to articulate precisely what made this situation so problematic. By having students try to explain to us (and themselves) why a burnout as cheerleader cast doubt on the status of the activity and the popularity of the cheerleaders, we pieced together what this anomalous event meant. The interpretation had a number of different components. Cheering practices were very important, not just for instrumental reasons such as helping girls perfect their routines, but also because the hard work that practice symbolized justified the high status of cheerleading and cheerleaders. In other words, the quasi-ascribed characteristics (Adler et al., 1992) of being pretty, graceful, and perky were not sufficient to warrant cheerleaders' special treatment, visibility, and enhanced popularity. They also needed to demonstrate a level of commitment that justified their special treatment. When Jackie refused to take cheerleading, especially practice, seriously, she undermined the very thing that made other students feel that it was generally acceptable for cheerleaders to be popular. Cheerleaders received both an institutional stage and imprimatur for their specialness, and therefore a seriousness of purpose and commitment was expected.

Before Jackie became a cheerleader, we were unaware of the taken-for-granted meanings that connected cheerleading and popularity, but even if we had had a clue, it probably would not have helped us. It is doubtful that students could have given us more than superficial responses had we asked, "What if a burnout became a cheerleader?" The possibility was largely unthinkable. Nevertheless, we were able to take advantage of this anomalous event not only because we were there but also because we already had established rapport with students. In addition, we took their reactions to this situation seriously, and it raised questions for us about the basis of popularity. It is not simply a matter of being a good athlete or being pretty.

Losing Popularity

Eder's (1995) ethnographic research documented the dynamics of becoming popular but also revealed something unexpected: "Popular girls are not always well liked" (p. 155). By closely observing girls after they became popular, Eder was able to identify the processes by which the initial approval of popular girls was reversed as they dismissed girls who were former friends or excluded girls who wished to be their friend. Rejecting a girl's aspirations to be a cheerleader's friend was tantamount to denying her an opportunity to enhance her popularity by being in the elite group. The exclusion of most girls who sought popularity led cheerleaders and their friends, individually and collectively, to be characterized as snobs and as stuck-up by many nonpopular students. Yet to adults the popularity of children was something desirable because it meant being well thought of and liked by peers. Most parents wanted their children to be at least moderately popular, and many parents worked to increase their children's chances of being popular. Thus, for most adults, the negative aspects of popularity went unnoticed. Eder not only recognized the negative features associated with popularity but, just as important, did not dismiss them because they were contrary to the dominant adult image of popularity. Her willingness to hold in abeyance the positive presuppositions about popularity and to look critically at what was actually happening was the necessary first step in formulating the cyclical nature of popularity. By doing so, Eder's research made a significant contribution to understanding the dynamics by which popularity was gained and lost.

Although popular students may come to be disliked by their nonpopular peers, being a member of a popular clique is usually more than sufficient to maintain a girl's high self-esteem, even in the face of being called "stuck-up." However, the situation is quite different for members of a popular clique who are expelled from it. In this case, no longer being with other popular students can result in a devastating loss of popularity and self-esteem. The Adlers (1998) and Merten (1997) described such precipitous losses of status and popularity, but why popular people should experience such a loss so acutely that they can barely function in school or feel compelled to transfer to another school is not obvious. Part of the answer may be that popularity is not just an individual phenomenon, but it also requires affirmation by other popular students. That is, relatively few students in grade school or junior high have the independence to withstand both the withdrawal of support and the derogatory appraisals by their popular former friends. Moreover, at least for youth who have had to work at being popular, having popular friends discover "flaws" in them can confirm their own doubts regarding the legitimacy of their popularity. To understand better why loss of popularity is experienced so forcefully, therefore, requires research on the psychology of popularity.

The cycle of popularity is somewhat paradoxical in that just as one becomes popular, processes are set in motion that threaten one's popularity; popularity seems as difficult to retain as it is to obtain. For example, shortly after starting our research, we were told by students, teachers, and parents that a clique of very popular girls, mostly cheerleaders, was remarkably mean (Merten, 1997). This led us to ask what, if any, link there was between meanness and popularity. Initially, it seemed to us rather pointless for very popular girls to be mean when they had everything the school and student culture offered. It was also clear that some clique members were disliked by girls outside the clique. A commonsense remedy to being disliked was to be nice and engage other students in a friendly manner. Nonetheless, this response had practical limits. More students wanted the attention and friendship of popular girls than the latter could accommodate, even if they wanted to. These limitations were not, however, the main problem. If popular girls were to accommodate all their peers who wanted to be included, it would debase and dilute their popularity. Thus, popular girls were in a bind. If they did not accept the overtures for affiliation from their less popular peers, they were considered stuck-up snobs, and this reputation diminished their popularity, just as Eder found. If they were nice to all girls by including them, they lost their sense of specialness. By being mean, however, they were able to use the power of their popularity to intimidate girls who characterized them as stuck-up. Thus, meanness, at least for these girls, was used to defend and preserve their popularity by intimidating potential detractors. Their meanness was even more effective by virtue of using it against some girls in the clique, thereby demonstrating to their nonpopular peers what they could expect if they had the audacity to openly criticize them.

The key to understanding how meanness was related to popularity did not come from what students told us about meanness but from what a girl told us about being nice. Sherry identified someone as nice if she was "nice to everybody and treats everybody as equal and stuff like that" (Merten, 1997). This statement, embedded in a narrative about niceness, enabled us to identify the dilemma of popularity and the nexus between popularity and meanness. Students' narratives frequently told ethnographers things about which they did not know to ask. Of course, the subsequent interpretation required recognizing the salience of Sherry's statement about the cultural logic that linked meanness and popularity.

Preserving popularity was not always focused on potential detractors but sometimes on rivals within the group or clique. For example, the Adlers (1998) described the steps the leader of a clique took to ensure his continued popularity. Brad was a leader of a clique of popular boys and Larry was the leader of a subgroup (composed of Mark and Rick) within the larger clique. School administrators previously had avoided placing Brad and Larry in the same homeroom, but in fifth grade this changed. Having Larry in the same homeroom led Brad to remove him from the clique. However, when Mark and Rick, out of loyalty to Larry, left the clique, Brad allowed all three to return. Later Brad found ways to turn Larry and Mark against each other, banished Mark, and became best friends with Larry. The Adlers identified the processes, including adult actions, that resulted in Mark's loss of popularity. This insight was possible because of the relationships they had established with teachers, parents, and young people. They knew about the clique composition and Larry's subgroup; thus, when Brad and Larry's rivalry came to a head in fifth grade, they were already familiar with the plot and characters in this drama. Their interpretation of this extended incident revealed a good deal about clique and friendship dynamics as they were played out in the arena of popularity and power. Moreover, this incident revealed that boys were not averse to using duplicity and manipulation to protect their popularity, actions usually attributed to girls.

Longitudinal research that identifies popular students at several measurement points would have probably picked up that Brad and Larry remained popular within a high-status clique and Mark at some point was no longer a member. The advantage of a continuous ethnographic analysis is that it increases one's chances to identify and understand the processes that sustain or fail to sustain popularity for some students. Making their community their research site allowed the Adlers to pursue their ethnographic work for 8 years. Following students for such a long time enabled them to identify the complex contextual factors that shaped peer dynamics and created change. By being on site over many years, they avoided the predicament of having to speculate as to what processes led to the changes they identified. Instead, they were able to observe and hear about processes of change as they unfolded.

Collective Aspect of Popularity

Research has consistently reported that popular students tend to hang out together (Adler & Adler, 1998; Kinney, 1993). Moreover, when popular students associated with each other, a synergistic effect increased their individual and collective popularity. This networking allowed them, particularly in clique structures, to control popularity as a resource. That is, they were able to leverage their power qua popularity, especially the crucial power to select and reject peers as worthy of joining them. In the popular clique Merten (1997) described, girls who had had to work hard to become popular were especially aggressive in using meanness to sustain the clique's and their own popularity. "Naturally" popular girls also engaged in meanness, but they were more inclined to be friendly toward their nonpopular peers when not in the presence of other clique members. Thus, as suggested previously, the paths to popularity influenced how youth experienced and expressed their status in various contexts.

Members of popular cliques, and especially their leaders, were sensitive to what was needed to maintain popularity, both individually and collectively. An example was Brad's move first to banish Larry and then co-opt him. At other times, clique leaders attacked potential rivals to keep them in their place. As an example, aggressive behavior was targeted toward Melissa, who was very attractive and had become a cheerleader in 7th grade (Merten, 1997). Without even trying, she had become more and more popular with boys. Eventually, her rapid increase in popularity became a threat to at least one clique leader. The clique leaders launched a campaign of meanness against Melissa and enlisted other clique members to participate. By keeping her in the clique but in a submissive state of mind, the leaders avoided the risk of Melissa establishing a competing source of popularity and power. Because Melissa was much nicer than her clique antagonists, she had the potential to become the focal point of a separate clique that could attract other popular classmates. Recurrent conflicts in popular groups occurred as members maneuvered to enhance their status; the members' competing interests were in tension and continuously in play.

Another way in which popular girls in junior high collectively consolidated their popularity was to monopolize going with the popular boys. According to Best (1983), this was possible because "the prettier the girl, the higher her status" (p. 102), and girls learned in grade school that "it was important to win boys because being popular and dating were important" (p. 6). Moreover, girls were more active in initiating relationships than boys and probably in general more sensitive to issues of popularity. They did their utmost to see that they and their friends could go with the most popular boys. Because the duration of relationships was often measured in days or weeks, girls could "go with" a number of popular boys as they recycled them within their group. This practice had the effect of drawing popular boys into the sphere of influence of popular girls. Once drawn in, popular boys were deterred from going with girls outside this circle because doing so tended to separate them from their male friends.

An issue that has received relatively little attention involves the unspecified referent as to the scope or breadth of popularity. For instance, some students were considered popular only within their small circle of several friends, whereas other students' popularity was broader in scope and existed among peers who shared the same status category, such as preps or freaks. Other students claimed schoolwide popularity. In the latter case, as Eckert (1989) points out, when comparing the popularity of burncuts and jocks, to be popular in the scope of the high school required buying into the institutional culture controlled by adults. Even to be allowed to participate on the school stage, a student had to abide by standards of behavior and demeanor (at least publicly) set by the school authorities. Here, socioeconomic class and lifestyle influenced the construction of popularity. Students who were comfortable with impression management, a staple of mainstream American life, found it easier to publicly, if not always privately, enact institutional expectations. Therefore, popularity in its broadest expression was often tied to the prep or jock (or local equivalent) status category; burnouts or freaks often chose not to accept the constraints required to gain popularity on the institutional stage.

The Dark Side: Costs of Popularity

Recently, concern has been raised regarding the costs of popularity (see Schwartz & Gorman, Chapter 11, this volume) because drinking, smoking, and sexual activity are occurring at a high level among popular students (Allen, Porter, McFarland, Marsh, & McElhaney, 2005; Mayeux, Sandstrom & Cillessen, 2008). Yet it is important to consider not just the behaviors, even when problematic, but also their meanings in a particular context. That is, some of the problematic behaviors of popular students and their peers, at least in junior high, were largely symbolic and transient in nature. The behaviors were attempts to negate one's identity as a child while in the transition to adolescence (Merten, 2005). Ironically, the meanness of popular students has garnered more attention than other problematic actions in the media. The film, *Mean Girls*, based on Wiseman's book about queen bees and wannabes (2002), revealed some of the viciousness that popular girls inflict on their peers and each other. Yet the costs of these actions to mean girls themselves are seldom considered (see, however, Sandstrom, Chapter 10, this volume). For example, Darla observes how she and her popular friends treated marginal members of their group: "We would pretty much treat them like shit, but they were our friends. We would treat them like shit, but we would be nice to them, and they would always just come back" (Adler & Adler, 1998, p. 83). An implication of such behavior was that popular students were learning that their high status provided a mandate for gratuitous meanness whenever it fit their mood or needs.

Students not only struggled to be popular but also struggled with the demands for attaining popularity. Often students' critiques of popularity came across as rationalizations, but sometimes they seemed well grounded. For instance, Nicole was on the fringe of a popular clique and was close to attaining popularity both by being friends with a very popular girl and by having achieved some personal visibility. The issue for Nicole was whether she wanted to make the changes her popular friend, Abby, insisted on in order to help Nicole become more popular. Nicole's situation made us wonder whether any student with a legitimate chance to be popular would forego doing so, and, more specifically, was Nicole such a person. We had known Nicole for 2 1/2 years and knew that she was successful in a range of activities that included track and jazz band. Furthermore, she knew how these activities related to her social identity and how she wanted to see herself. Because the criteria for popularity (attractiveness and social adeptness) were expressed in narrow terms, Nicole's choice was more complicated than to be popular or not popular. To pursue popularity was to embark on a number of changes with which she felt uncomfortable. We noted:

> Nicole could have been popular by following Abby's lead, but only at the cost of allowing their friendship to be transformed into a different type of relationship based on different principles. Nicole would have also had to assume a persona that did not correspond to her sense of self. She would have had to concentrate on looking attractive rather than doing what she considered fun, on attracting boys rather than competing with them, and on perfecting her public image based on the narrow standards for popularity. (Merten, 2004, p. 364)

Thus, friendships that facilitated popularity sometimes demanded changes that transformed a student's identity in order to be "eligible" for higher status. The extent of these changes was seldom initially obvious and was appreciated only in retrospect, if at all.

Students who desperately sought to be popular, or wannabes, were not unfamiliar to ethnographers. The Adlers (1998) described them not as individuals but as a loose alliance of convenience for pursing popularity. Based on their conversations with wannabes, other middle school students, and teachers, the Adlers provided a rich description of the wannabes' situation, revealing the costs of popularity for them. Wannabes, located just below the popular clique in the local status hierarchy, based their identity on those above them. Their self-esteem largely depended on the crumbs of acceptance that came with occasionally associating with popular peers. Not only did students outside the wannabe circle notice that the wannabes were manipulated by popular peers, but so did some of the wannabes. As a fourth-grade wannabe, Scott, said, "With the popular group you get to do more stuff, you get to have more play, you get to have more fun at recess.... You play with them [popular peers], but they don't, in football they never pass to you, and in basketball they never really pass to you" (Adler & Adler, 1998, p. 95). Scott recognized that although his popular peers needed someone like him to fill out the team, they had no interest in accepting him as a full member. By describing the wannabes, the Adlers advanced our understanding of how the near-obsessive pursuit of popularity adversely affected students' self-esteem, identity, and relationships.

The costs of popularity are not solely attributable to the actions of students. For instance, Brown (1998) cites an example of a pregnant high school girl, April, from a working-class family who was chosen homecoming queen because, as one student said, "she knows who she is ... she's nice to everyone" (p. 2). Brown described what happens next: "But since April did not fit the ideal of the beauty queen, four school administrators and a teacher 'arranged' for a more likely winner: a cute, bright swimming star" (1998, p. 2). Although it is important to note that other teachers joined April's supporters to protest her removal, examples like this remind us that adults believe they have a stake in how the symbols of popularity are enacted. In this respect, popularity is inextricably embedded in a broader system of meaning that goes beyond its expressions in the cultures of students. Thus, although it is tempting to focus on particular students like Nicole, Scott, or April, it is clear from ethnographic accounts that the construction and dynamics of popularity cannot be understood by simply focusing on students, even collectively.

CONCLUSION

"Being there awhile" positions ethnographers to observe and hear what is happening in the contexts in which students live their lives. The closer researchers are to the events that students give meaning to and derive meaning from, the more likely they are to get the meaning right and make accurate interpretations. It is no coincidence that the Adlers' (1998) lengthy research resulted in a richly comprehensive account of popularity that finds support in the work of Eder, Merten, and other ethnographers.[2] The more one hears students offer similar explanations (e.g., for why popular girls are snobs), the more confident one can be that these are the shared meanings that reveal the power of culture to shape action. Moreover, spending time on site increases the chances that one will encounter the anomalous events that make conscious the tacit assumptions that these anomalies challenge. Immersion over time also works to dissolve the assumptions that distort our understanding of young peoples' lives and that prevent us from asking salient questions. These basic elements

---

[2] This may seem unremarkable, yet the roles and the theoretical frameworks that these ethnographers used were quite different. Thus, even with different researchers in disparate contexts, ethnography produced results that were remarkably consistent.

of ethnography have allowed researchers to reveal important connections between popularity and other aspects of students' lives, to uncover counterintuitive findings about popularity, to elucidate the cultural logic that influenced students' actions to preserve popularity, and to call attention to the often unseen and unappreciated costs of popularity. Ethnography as perspective and process is best understood in its detailed practices and in the conceptual rationale that guides them. What may strike some readers as a low-level description and conceptualization that characterizes the foregoing is intentional. To consider ethnography in more abstract and formulaic terms is to distort its essence: being there awhile.

REFERENCES

Adler, P. A., & Adler, P. (1998). *Peer power: Preadolescent culture and identity.* New Brunswick, NJ: Rutgers University Press.

Adler, P. A., Kless, S. J., & Adler, P. (1992). Socialization to gender roles: Popularity among elementary school boys and girls. *Sociology of Education, 65,* 169–187.

Allen, J. P., Porter, M. R., McFarland, F. C., Marsh, P., & McElhaney, K. B. (2005). The two faces of adolescents' success with peers: Adolescent popularity, social adaptation, and deviant behavior. *Child Development, 76,* 747–760.

Banks, C. A. (2005). Black girls/white spaces: Managing identity through memories of schooling. In P. J. Bettis & N. G. Adams (Eds.), *Geographies of girlhood: Identities in-between* (pp. 177–193). Mahwah, NJ: Erlbaum.

Best, R. (1983). *We've all got scars: What boys and girls learn in elementary school.* Bloomington: Indiana University Press.

Bloustien, G. (2003). *Girl making: A cross-cultural ethnography on the processes of growing up female.* New York: Berghahn Books.

Brown, L. (1998). *Raising their voices: The politics of girls' anger.* Cambridge, MA: Harvard University Press.

Corsaro, W. A. (2003). *We're friends, right? Inside kids' culture.* Washington, DC: Joseph Henry Press.

Cortazzi, M. (2001). Narrative analysis in ethnography. In P. Atkinson, A. Coffey, S. Delamont, J. Lofland, & L. Lofland (Eds.), *Handbook of ethnography* (pp. 384–394). Thousand Oaks, CA: Sage.

Eckert, P. (1989). *Jocks and burnouts: Social categories and identity in high school.* New York: Teachers College, Columbia University.

Eder, D. (1985). The cycle of popularity: Interpersonal relations among female adolescents. *Sociology of Education, 58,* 154–165.

Eder, D., & Kinney, D. A. (1995). The effect of middle school extracurricular activities on adolescents' popularity and peer status. *Youth and Society, 26,* 298–324.

Emerson, R. M., Fretz, R. I., & Shaw, L. L. (2001). Participant observation and fieldnotes. In P. Atkinson, A. Coffey, S. Delamont, J. Lofland, & L. Lofland (Eds.), *Handbook of ethnography* (pp. 352–368). Thousand Oaks, CA: Sage.

Fine, G. A. (1987). *With the boys: Little League baseball and preadolescent culture.* Chicago: University of Chicago Press.

Fine, G. A., & Glassner, B. (1979). Participant observation with children: Promise and problems. *Urban Life, 8,* 153–174.

Fordham, S. (1996). *Blacked out: Dilemmas of race, identity, and success at Capital High.* Chicago: University of Chicago Press.

Gadamer, H. G. (1989). *Truth and method.* New York: Crossroads.

Geertz, C. (1973). *Interpretations of culture.* New York: Basic Books.

Goodwin, M. H. (1988). Cooperation and competition across girls' play activities. In A. D. Todd & S. Fisher (Eds.), *Gender and discourse: The power of talk* (pp. 55–94). Norwood, NJ: Ablex.

James, A. (2001). Ethnography in the study of children and childhood. In P. Atkinson, A. Coffey, S. Delamont, J. Lofland, & L. Lofland (Eds.), *Handbook of ethnography* (pp. 246–257). Thousand Oaks, CA: Sage.

Kinney, D. (1993). From nerds to normals: The recovery of identity among adolescents from middle school to high school. *Sociology of Education, 66,* 21–40.

LaFontana, K. M., & Cillessen, A. H. N. (2002). Children's perceptions of popular and unpopular peers: A multimethod assessment. *Developmental Psychology, 38,* 635–647.

Mayeux, L., Sandstrom, M. J., & Cillessen, A. H. N. (2008). Is being popular a risky proposition? *Journal of Research on Adolescence, 18,* 49–74.

Merten, D. E. (1996). Burnout as cheerleader: The cultural basis for prestige and privilege in junior high school. *Anthropology and Education Quarterly, 27,* 51–70.

Merten, D. E. (1997). The meaning of meanness: Popularity, competition, and conflict among junior high school girls. *Sociology of Education, 70,* 175–191.

Merten, D. E. (1999). Enculturation into secrecy among junior high school girls. *Journal of Contemporary Ethnography, 28,* 107–137.

Merten, D. E. (2004). Securing her experience: Friendship versus popularity. *Feminism and Psychology, 14,* 361–365.

Merten, D. E. (2005). Transitions and "trouble": Rites of passage for suburban girls. *Anthropology and Education Quarterly, 36,* 132–148.

Schwartz, G. (1987). *Beyond conformity and conflict.* Chicago: University of Chicago Press.

Wiseman, R. (2002). *Queen bees and wannabes: Helping your daughter survive cliques, gossip, boyfriends, and other realities of adolescence.* New York: Crown.

Xie, H., Li, Y., Boucher, S., Hutchins, B., & Cairns, B. (2006). What makes a girl (or boy) popular (or unpopular)? African American children's perceptions and developmental differences. *Developmental Psychology, 42,* 599–612.

Part II
DEVELOPMENT OF POPULARITY

Chapter 4

Social Acceptance and Popularity
Two Distinct Forms of Peer Status

Lara Mayeux
John J. Houser
Karmon D. Dyches

It used to be that when a peer relations researcher sat down to describe the results of a study, he or she could use the term *popularity* without any kind of qualification. For many years, popularity referred to one simple thing: being generally well accepted by the peer group and, perhaps indirectly, having all of the positive attributes that went along with that status (e.g., prosocial behavior, low levels of aggression, good social-cognitive and emotion regulation skills). Discussions about having high peer status were straightforward; popularity was a thing to be desired and indicative of positive adjustment and commendable social skills, and there was no mention of a "dark side."

In 1998, two studies published by two separate research teams began to change the way developmental psychologists conceptualized popularity. One study, by Jennifer Parkhurst and Andrea Hopmeyer, was the first to link two distinct research traditions: sociometric popularity, typically conducted by developmental psychologists, and reputational, dominance-based popularity, typically carried out by sociologists. Asking fourth and fifth graders about peers they liked the most and the least and about peers they saw as popular and unpopular, Parkhurst and Hopmeyer found that although reputation-based popularity and sociometric popularity were correlated with each other, they were by no means identical constructs. Sociometric popularity was associated with positive attributes, like kindness and trustworthiness, and with being nonaggressive and not stuck-up. "Peer-perceived popularity" (as they called it) was linked to both positive and negative attributes.

At the same time that Parkhurst and Hopmeyer were puzzling over their results, Kathryn LaFontana and Antonius Cillessen were looking at a similar set of findings. LaFontana and Cillessen had designed a simple vignette study that was meant to replicate the finding that children had universally positive expectations about socially accepted peers. Using hypothetical peers as targets, they asked fourth- and fifth-grade children questions about several different encounters they might have with a popular, unpopular, and neutral peer. The children's responses showed that their stereotypes of popular peers were a combination of positive and negative attributes and expectations, including reports of getting along well with others but also having hostile intent toward peers (LaFontana & Cillessen, 1998). Furthermore, children did not like hypothetical popular peers any more than they liked a hypothetical neutral-status peer, and they made relatively stable attributions for hypothetical popular peers' negative behaviors. These findings were distinctly inconsistent with prior studies of "popular" children, and although they did not surprise everyone—including LaFontana herself, a social psychologist!—they contributed to the small but growing literature suggesting that popularity is not a universally positive thing.

Thus, from two studies using two very different methods, developmental psychologists heard a wake-up call: that the traditional conceptualization of the word *popular* simply wasn't going to cut it anymore. These studies pointed clearly to different types of high status among youth: one that was linked to positive attributes and one that had both positive and negative correlates. This idea made intuitive sense to many researchers who, looking back to their own middle school days, certainly had memories of the "in" crowd. Others studies showing trends similar to those presented by the Parkhurst and the LaFontana studies appeared soon thereafter. Initially, researchers were focused on establishing discriminant validity between the two forms of high status (hereafter referred to as *social acceptance* and *popularity*). Soon, however, they turned to more sophisticated questions of developmental invariance in the correlates of social acceptance and popularity, of developmental precursors and outcomes of status, and of moderation by gender. These lines of research, among others, comprise several of the chapters in this volume.

This chapter addresses that initial research question inspired by Parkhurst and Hopmeyer (1998) and LaFontana and Cillessen (1998): Are social acceptance and popularity really different types of status? If so, how are they different and how are they similar? Even now, some debate exists within the field. We hope to convince you that social acceptance and popularity are, indeed, two distinct constructs.

HOW WE CONDUCTED OUR REVIEW

We base our review primarily on studies relying on a specific method of assessing status: sociometry, in which scores for social acceptance and popularity are computed on the basis of patterns of nominations given by peers (see Cillessen & Marks, Chapter 2, this volume). Several of the studies we discuss use open-ended questions about status, experimental paradigms in which hypothetical peers of varying status are used as targets, and social-cognitive mapping procedures, combined with teacher ratings of status, to identify socially well-connected students. Regardless of the specific research paradigm used, the one criterion that we strictly applied in our review was that in order to be included the study had to contain some assessment of power- or status-based popularity, defined as social visibility, impact, and prestige. In many of the studies we discuss, both social acceptance and popularity were measured and compared directly, although this was not a requirement.

ISSUES OF STABILITY, CHANGE, AND OVERLAP BETWEEN SOCIAL ACCEPTANCE AND POPULARITY

Although we argue that social acceptance and popularity are two distinct constructs in childhood and adolescence, they may not necessarily begin that way, and there is a certain degree of overlap even into the adolescent years. The earliest age at which social acceptance and popularity have been correlated is at 10 years, when the two constructs are correlated at about .40 (LaFontana & Cillessen, 1999). When gender is taken into account, the association between social acceptance and popularity is significantly stronger for boys than for girls (Cillessen & Mayeux, 2004; Litwack, Akins, & Cillessen, 2008). Furthermore, longitudinal data suggest that the two forms of high status remain positively correlated across development for boys, whereas for girls the correlations either disappear or become modestly (but significantly) negative by late high school (Cillessen & Mayeux, 2004). Data that our own research team recently collected from a sample of high school seniors showed a correlation of .40 for boys and .16 for girls (both $ps > .05$). The somewhat inconsistent correlations, particularly in adolescence, likely reflect variability in the peer ecology, including the dynamics of status and the meaning of "coolness," from school to school. The stronger correlations for boys in some studies suggest that boys are better able to balance being liked and being popular than girls are. However, we have a relatively poor understanding of why this is so. As presented next, the correlates of popularity are strikingly similar across genders, suggesting that the issue is not so much one of behavioral differences than of the perceptions and stereotypes of those behaviors held by peers (see Rose, Glick, & Smith, Chapter 5, this volume).

Several research teams have addressed the overlap between social acceptance and popularity by investigating the degree to which popularity is associated with the five sociometric status categories first proposed in 1982 by Coie, Dodge, and Coppotelli: popular, average, rejected, neglected, and controversial. Parkhurst and Hopmeyer's seminal study showed that popularity was most closely aligned with *controversial* status, that is, youth who are liked by many peers but also disliked by many peers and who have a large degree of visibility among the peer group. Other studies have found most popular students to fall into the sociometrically popular or average categories (Kosir & Pecjak, 2005; LaFontana & Cillessen, 1999).

Even fewer studies have addressed the stability of social acceptance and popularity. As with most constructs, short-term stabilities of status are stronger than long-term ones, and popularity has been shown to be significantly more stable than social acceptance. Popularity owes much of its stability to the hardiness of reputations; because social acceptance is based on personal preference, even small changes in behavior or other attributes can quickly lead to a change in that type of status if peers do not like or do not agree with the new behaviors. The 5-year (fifth through ninth grade) stability of social acceptance in one study was .38 for girls and .34 for boys; for popularity, the corresponding coefficients were .55 and .48 (Cillessen & Mayeux, 2004). Using the same dataset, Mayeux and Cillessen (2008) reported 9- to 12th-grade stabilities of .44 and .71 for social acceptance and popularity, respectively. Social acceptance is more stable for boys than for girls during the high school years, whereas popularity is more stable for girls (Mayeux, Sandstrom, & Cillessen,

2008). Cillessen and Borch (2006) have estimated the long-term stability of social acceptance at .40 and popularity at .60.

ASSOCIATIONS BETWEEN STATUS AND AGGRESSION

The bulk of the research establishing discriminant validity between social acceptance and popularity has focused on their associations with various forms of aggression. The earliest sociometric investigations of both forms of status noted that links between overt and relational aggression and social acceptance were generally negative. However, their associations with popularity were positive and in some cases quite strong (LaFontana & Cillessen, 1998, 1999, 2002; Lease, Kennedy, & Axelrod, 2002; Parkhurst & Hopmeyer, 1998; Prinstein & Cillessen, 2003). These studies focused on a relatively wide range of developmental periods, from middle childhood to late adolescence, suggesting that some of the same underlying social and developmental processes were at work at varying ages. Subsequent research, some of it longitudinal, has confirmed these initial studies and provided a more nuanced view of the links between status and aggression (Cillessen & Mayeux, 2004; de Bruyn & Cillessen, 2006; de Bruyn, Cillessen, & Wissink, 2009; Rose, Swensen, & Waller, 2004; Sandstrom & Cillessen, 2006; but see also Hawley, Little, & Card, 2007, which found a nonsignificant link between aggression and both forms of status).

For example, in the first long-term longitudinal study of social acceptance and popularity and their correlates, Cillessen and Mayeux (2004) followed children from fifth grade through ninth grade and assessed social acceptance, popularity, and overt and relational aggression. They found that the negative association between social acceptance and overt aggression became less pronounced over time. On the other hand, the negative association between social acceptance and relational aggression became stronger over time, especially for girls. However, the positive associations between popularity and both forms of aggression became stronger with increasing age. In addition, using structural equation modeling, the authors found support for a model in which gains in popularity predicted subsequent increases in aggressive behavior. In a similar study, Rose and colleagues (2004) found evidence for both causal paths in a cross-sectional investigation of popularity and aggression: Relational aggression predicted increases in popularity for seventh- and ninth-grade girls, and popularity predicted increased relational aggression for both boys and girls. Relational aggression and popularity were found to reciprocally influence each other in a third study of middle schoolers (Puckett, Aikins, & Cillessen, 2008). Thus, the interplay between popularity and aggression is likely bidirectional, with certain forms of aggression being used successfully by some youth to acquire popular status and that popularity then serving as an instigator for increased aggression.

In the most expansive longitudinal study of aggression and status to date, Cillessen and Borch (2006) applied multilevel modeling techniques to data from Cillessen's Manchester Youth Study. Focusing on the longitudinal trajectories of social acceptance and popularity from grades 5 through 12, they found distinct long-term associations between status and both overt and relational aggression. Overt aggression predicted low social acceptance across the 8 years of the study, but increasing popularity, for both boys and girls. Relational aggression predicted low social acceptance across the 8 years of the study, especially for girls, but high popularity across those years.

Although aggression has been shown to be adaptive for some youth, Hawley and her colleagues have presented evidence that aggression is most adaptive if it is paired with more prosocial behaviors. In her research on so-called bistrategic controllers, Hawley (2003) found that children perhaps best described as Machiavellian—those who were best able to balance "getting along and getting ahead"—were among the most popular in school (see also Hawley, Little, & Card, 2008; Pellegrini, Roseth, Van Ryzin, & Solberg, Chapter 6, this volume). In a similar vein, in a sample of middle school students, relationally aggressive adolescents who were also high on leadership, cooperation, peer sociability, and social self-efficacy were more popular than their relationally aggressive peers who did not possess these qualities (Puckett et al., 2008). As the authors contend, "Relational aggression embedded in a larger behavioral repertoire that also includes prosocial behaviors is expected to be the most effective" (p. 565).

In addition to these studies using traditional sociometric assessments of status and behavior, other research teams have found similar results using alternative measures of high status. For example, using measures of *social network centrality*, high socially central and visible members of the peer group have also been shown to be some of the most overtly aggressive (Farmer & Rodkin, 1996). In a study of fourth- through sixth-grade boys, Rodkin, Farmer, Pearl, and Van Acker (2000) used clustering techniques to identify two distinct groups of popular boys. "Tough" boys were overtly aggressive and athletic, whereas "model" boys were athletic, prosocial, and nonaggressive. Both groups were very socially central, suggesting that overt aggression and social connectedness can be quite compatible. Farmer and colleagues followed up with a study of both boys and girls in an investigation of how status and both overt and relational forms of aggression were related. They found evidence for two types of aggressive boys: "Tough" boys were aggressive, popular, and socially skilled; "troubled" boys were aggressive, unpopular, and socially unskilled. Almost identical female groups were identified, except that both "popular" and "troubled" girls were rated by teachers as manipulative instead of overtly aggressive (Farmer, Estell, Bishop, O'Neal, & Cairns, 2003).

One challenge researchers face is the careful study of the longitudinal relationship between aggression and both social acceptance and popularity and what those relationships can tell us about the dynamics of the peer culture. As discussed, the association is likely bidirectional, but how does this translate into a real-world understanding of the schoolyard (or lunchroom or locker room)? It isn't difficult to imagine how aggressive behavior can come to be associated with low social acceptance as children enter middle childhood and begin to learn more appropriate ways of managing conflict. Aggressive peers are upsetting, hurtful, and unpleasant to be around. Most peers recognize this, compare their aggressive peers' aversive behaviors with others' less hurtful (and more acceptable) ones, and develop preferences based on those comparisons. For some aggressive children, this behavior-based rejection kick-starts a self-perpetuating cycle of aggression and rejection (Cillessen & Ferguson, 1989; Cillessen, van IJzendoorn, van Lieshout, & Hartup, 1992), although certainly not all aggressive children face stable, long-term peer relations problems.

It is also relatively easy to imagine how aggression can lead to gains in popularity. Savvy manipulation of the peer group, impressive or intimidating displays of physical force, and, perhaps even more salient to a young person, the demonstration of the willingness to use aggression against someone who may be a threat can all be useful tools in the quest for status. Children and adolescents may ascribe power to peers who express dominance in overt or relational ways because they want to avoid being the target of the next aggressive act. By this rationale, it takes increasingly more powerful displays of force or relational damage, and increasingly savvy levels of manipulation, to climb to the top of the social ladder.

Once attained, however, status may contribute to increases in aggression in a variety of ways. First, popular youth may continue to express their power in aggressive ways as a means of preempting potential threats to their authority. Second, they may use aggression to counteract actual threats to their social position, such as when a lower status peer spreads a rumor to "dethrone" the ringleader. For example, consider an adolescent who wishes to climb the social ladder but feels that her higher status peers are too well respected by others for her ever to take their places in the hierarchy. She may choose to sully the reputation of one of those peers in order to create suspicion and doubt in the minds of others about the peer's integrity or honesty, which might also create enough of a disturbance in the social hierarchy for the instigator of the rumor to position herself for "social climbing." Third, popularity may serve to insulate youth from the typical consequences of behaving badly, resulting in a relatively consequence-free environment in which to aggress. Anecdotal evidence suggests that teachers and parents are often unaware of the aggressive behavior of high-status children and adolescents and are less likely to punish that behavior when it is detected. Whether one of these scenarios is more typical, or all three are common, is a question for future research to address. A more nuanced understanding of the role that aggression plays in popularity is needed, and a variety of research methods, including observations and ethnographies conducted over time, will aid in these efforts.

It remains unclear why hurtful behaviors are so damaging to the peer status of some youth and yet seem to enhance the status of others. The best evidence so far suggests that some children and adolescents simply have what it takes to convince their peers to overlook their misdeeds (see following discussion).

MODERATORS OF THE STATUS–AGGRESSION LINK

Although the just-mentioned studies can give the impression that the associations between status and aggression are relatively straightforward, there is increasing evidence that the links are moderated by a variety of personality, social-cognitive, and demographic factors (including gender; for extensive treatment of the role of gender, see Rose and colleagues, Chapter 5, this volume). One demographic characteristic that has received considerable attention is age. As has been shown numerous times, the associations between aggression and status vary according to the age of the children participating. For example, physical aggression is most strongly associated with peer rejection during the period of middle childhood. However, in both early childhood and adolescence, the link between physical aggression and preference tends to be nonsignificant or modestly positive (Cillessen & Mayeux, 2004; Pope, Bierman, & Mumma, 1989).

When considering popularity, however, the pattern is more consistent. From middle childhood through late adolescence, physical aggression and relational aggression are positively related to popularity (Cillessen & Rose, 2005). Research has also shown that the role of aggression in peer status depends partly on the presence or absence of "peer-valued characteristics" such as having wealth, dressing well, being funny, and being attractive (Vaillancourt & Hymel, 2006). In a study of 6th through 10th graders, boys who were both overtly aggressive and who possessed several of these peer-valued characteristics were more popular and less peer rejected than aggressive boys who did not have these characteristics. Relationally aggressive girls who had peer-valued characteristics were more popular than relationally aggressive girls who did not (although being funny, attractive, and so on did not help their social acceptance at all, unlike for boys). Lease and colleagues (2002) also found a link between popularity and spending power in a sample of early adolescents. Adolescents seem to be quite willing to forgive, and even reward, aversive behaviors if they are enacted by peers who have certain attributes they envy or admire, particularly if those aggressive peers wield some economic power. The Vaillancourt and Hymel study is our best hint yet at the complicated dynamics underlying the aggression–status link. For young people who are lucky enough to have wealthy parents or good looks, the schoolyard is an easy place to get by: Not only do peers want to befriend them and ascribe them significant social power, but they also are willing to overlook and even reward their sometimes nasty behavior. For children who do not have such luck, the road is much more difficult: Peers may not be any less inclined to befriend a lower class peer than an upper class one (no research to date suggests that economic hardship predicts poor peer relations), but being unattractive may make finding friends more difficult for some children (Coie et al., 1982). The addition of aversive behaviors to an already less desirable peer's "total package" is likely to be the proverbial nail in the coffin. Not only will these children have difficulty finding acceptance, but they will be as "out" as their attractive, wealthier, and equally aggressive peers are "in."

External characteristics of the aggressor are not the whole story, however. Adolescents' perceptions of their own status have also been shown to moderate the aggression–status link. Popular high school students who also had high self-perceptions of popularity were the most overtly and relationally aggressive students in ninth grade in a recent study (Mayeux & Cillessen, 2008). Further, being both popular and aware of that popularity predicted increases in overt aggression over the course of high school for both boys and girls. Very different trends were found for social acceptance. Although social acceptance in general was associated with stable low to average levels of aggression, the interactions of peer- and self-perceptions of social acceptance yielded mixed results. In other words, the same combination of peer- and self-perceptions (i.e., being socially accepted and knowing it) was not associated with high initial levels of aggression or with increasing levels of it. Perhaps feeling socially powerful among one's peers inspires the confidence to aggress without fear of censure. Knowing that one is well liked may inspire different feelings, like a wish to maintain those positive relationships and friendships.

Furthermore, factors that tap into so-called social intelligence have also been shown to play a role in the association between aggression and popularity. Peeters, Cillessen, and Scholte (2010), for example, used cluster analysis to identify subtypes of bullies in a sample of eighth graders. They identified clusters of male and female bullies who were particularly high in both popularity and social intelligence. Further, the popular and socially intelligent bullies generally scored higher on measures of aggression than other clusters of bullies. In a recent unpublished study, self-reported Machiavellianism was shown to exacerbate the positive association between popularity and relational aggression for late-adolescent girls (Mayeux, 2009).

ASSOCIATIONS WITH BEHAVIORAL AND ACADEMIC RISK

In addition to addressing relations between peer status and aggressive behaviors, a few recent studies have addressed even more weighty questions of behavioral and academic risk among socially accepted versus popular adolescents (see also Schwartz & Gorman, Chapter 11, this volume). In a study of 10th graders, self-reported sexual behavior was positively associated with peer-reported popularity but negatively associated with peer-reported social acceptance. However, reporting a large number of sexual partners was associated with low, not high, levels of popularity, suggesting a nonlinear relationship between sexual risk behavior and popularity (Prinstein, Meade, & Cohen, 2003). Popularity in 10th grade was found to predict the increased use of alcohol and more risky sexual behavior in 12th grade for both boys and girls in another study of status and risk behaviors (Mayeux et al., 2008). Smoking in 10th grade also predicted increased 12th-grade popularity for boys, suggesting again that the associations between popularity and its correlates are bidirectional. Being socially accepted was not associated with any of the risk behaviors measured, although being disliked was associated with increased sexual behavior over time for girls (Mayeux et al., 2008; however, see Luthar & D'Avanzo, 1999, for evidence that social acceptance is also associated with substance use for boys in certain contexts).

Researchers are also beginning to investigate links between social acceptance and popularity and academic performance. In a short-term longitudinal study, Schwartz, Gorman, Nakamoto, and McKay (2006) collected peer nominations and obtained academic records for a large sample of midadolescents. They found that for aggressive youth short-term increases in popularity predicted concomitant increases in unexplained absences as well as decreases in grade point average. The same trend was not found for changes in social acceptance in either direction (Schwartz et al., 2006; see also Gorman, Kim, & Schimmelbusch, 2002). These findings are also corroborated by a small experimental study in which ninth graders rated the popularity of hypothetical peers based only on information regarding their attractiveness and academic achievement. Attractiveness was strongly associated with popularity; grades were not (Boyatzis, Baloff, & Durieux, 1998; however, see also Xie, Li, Boucher, Hutchins, & Cairns, 2006).

The association with academic risk does not hold for all adolescents, however. In a study of adolescents' perceptions of popular peers, 13- and 14-year-olds identified two subtypes of popularity: *populistic* (popular but not socially accepted) and *popular-prosocial* (popular and well-accepted; de Bruyn & Cillessen, 2006). Whereas populistic peers were described as academically disengaged, popular-prosocial peers were academically oriented. However, populistic peers were seen as more influential, suggesting that teens at the more extreme end of high popularity are more likely to experience academic disengagement.

In summary, popularity is associated with several indices of risk—substance use, sexual behavior, and academic disengagement—whereas social acceptance is not. Mayeux and colleagues (2008) have suggested that popular adolescents are particularly likely to experiment with risky behaviors at the expense of more age-appropriate concerns (e.g., obtaining an education) because of their desire to maintain their dominant status over their peers. Consistent with Moffitt's (1993) theory of adolescence-limited delinquency, popular adolescents may be strongly motivated to bridge the "maturity gap" so that their peers will view them as obvious choices for leadership and influence, and engaging in very adult behaviors (such as sexual activity and alcohol use) is an easy way to bridge that gap. Well-accepted adolescents who are not popular may simply have very different goals, namely, to nurture their friendships and maintain positive relationships with their peers, teachers, and parents. Trying to draw others to them via outward expressions of pseudomaturity is unlikely to serve those functions.

ASSOCIATIONS WITH OTHER SOCIAL BEHAVIORS AND ATTRIBUTES

Although the study of how status relates to aggression and risk taking has been more commonplace in the popularity literature, associations between status and other social behaviors have also been addressed. In a recent study of bullying and defending behaviors, social acceptance was found to be negatively associated with bullying in both childhood and adolescence and positively associated with defending peers from bullies. Interestingly, although popularity was positively linked with bullying at both ages, it was also associated with defending others against bullies in childhood (Caravita, Di Blasio, & Salmivalli, 2008). The authors suggest that it is possible that children who are both popular and well accepted engage in defending behaviors; they have both the prosocial motivation and relational orientation to defend and the social clout to make it effective (and to prevent themselves from being associated with the low-status peers they are defending). These hypotheses are supported by the studies of Hawley and her colleagues in which the most popular children and adolescents used a combination of prosocial and coercive strategies of getting what they want (the bistrategic controllers discussed previously; see Hawley, 2003; Hawley et al., 2008).

These findings are also similar to those of several early studies that found evidence for a bright side to popularity. Most of the earliest studies of high status included measures of both positive (cooperation, leadership) and negative (aggression, being stuck-up) attributes in their protocols. Popularity, like social acceptance, has been linked to cooperation, helpfulness, good leadership, kindness, and trustworthiness (de Bruyn & Cillessen, 2006; Gorman et al., 2002; LaFontana & Cillessen, 1998, 1999, 2002; Parkhurst & Hopmeyer, 1998), particularly if the popular student is also high in social acceptance. Popularity has also been found to be closely associated with athleticism or sports involvement, especially among adolescents (Lease et al., 2002; Rodkin et al., 2000).

Although popularity is associated with some positive attributes, a longer list of beneficial correlates is associated with social acceptance. Take, for example, a sociometric study of midadolescents conducted by de Bruyn and van den Boom (2005). Whereas popular students were described as not boring, as trendy dressers, and as having high social self-esteem, well-accepted peers were described as good at sharing, keeping promises, and cooperating, good at making up after a fight, and as not angry or mean. Socially accepted students, however, were also described as boring. Popular youth have been shown to be better at taking initiative and more creative than their average-status counterparts, although the same study found well-accepted peers to be higher than average on those dimensions as well. The same study also found well-accepted youth to be more persistent and less anxious than average youth. Children who were both accepted and popular tried harder in school, had the best relationships with peers and teachers, were highest on persistence, initiative, and creativity, were the least anxious, and had the highest social self-concept (Košir & Pečjak, 2005). Although research suggests that balancing popularity and social acceptance is difficult, particularly for girls (Cillessen & Mayeux, 2004), the combination of being both socially accepted and popular has undeniable social and intrapersonal benefits (see also de Bruyn & Cillessen, 2006; Parkhurst & Hopemeyer, 1998).

A growing number of studies have investigated the correlates of popularity by simply asking children and adolescents to list attributes they feel are characteristic of popular peers. In a study of fourth to eighth graders, children's perceptions of popular peers were primarily focused on attractiveness and social connectedness (LaFontana & Cillessen, 2002). Xie and colleagues (2006) generally replicated these findings with first-, fourth-, and seventh-grade inner-city African American children. Consistent with the positive association between likeability and popularity at younger ages, first graders associated popularity with prosocial behavior, companionship, and liking. Fourth graders were more likely to describe popular peers as attractive and good at self-presentation and as good students. Seventh graders also noted popular peers' attractiveness and self-presentation skills and added that popularity was determined by involvement in sports and social connectedness. Interestingly, and consistent with LaFontana and Cillessen (2002), aggressive or deviant behaviors were not mentioned at a high frequency by children at any age, although they were most common among seventh graders in the Xie et al. study and were said to be more relevant to boys' versus girls' popularity.

In the de Bruyn and Cillessen (2006) study, which identified populistic and popular-prosocial adolescents, distinct differences were noted by the adolescents asked to describe their popular peers. Populistic peers (who were popular but not well accepted) were seen as aggressive (including bullying) and arrogant and as show-offs. They were also seen as more likely to take advantage of peers and to be insolent and vulgar. Popular–prosocial peers (who were both popular and socially accepted) were described as academically engaged, helpful, and friendly. Both groups were seen as attractive, athletic, and fashionable and as having many friends. Importantly, populistic teens were described as having more leadership power and influence than popular–prosocial teens.

In a more recent study of middle school students, descriptions of popular peers were examined separately by participant gender and level of popularity (Closson, 2008). Boys were more likely than girls to describe popularity in terms of athleticism, sense of humor, and risk-taking behavior; girls were more likely than boys to focus on attractiveness, meanness, snobbishness, and rudeness. Not surprisingly, popular adolescents tended to describe popular youth in positive terms, whereas participants of average or low popularity provided both positive and negative descriptions of popular peers.

STUDIES OF FRIENDSHIPS AND OTHER RELATIONSHIPS

Despite the intuitive implications that popularity has for friendships and romantic relationships, very few studies linking these areas have been published to date. In contrast, the associations between social acceptance and friendship or friendship quality are relatively well understood. Children who enjoy high peer acceptance are more likely to have reciprocated friendships as well as more high-quality friendships (Bukowski & Hoza, 1989; Parker & Asher, 1993) than peer-rejected children.

What we know about the friendships of popular children is limited. Given the associations between popularity and aggressive behavior, it is perhaps not surprising that the first such study of how popularity relates to friendships addressed friendship quality, and in particular friendship conflict, in relation to popularity and social acceptance. Rose and her colleagues found that the association between relational aggression and friendship quality was indeed moderated by status: Relational aggression was associated with increased friendship conflict for disliked children but not for popular ones (Rose et al., 2004). A study of eighth graders' friendships found that social acceptance was associated with high reciprocation among friends and low friendship conflict; popularity was related to high levels of friendship support (Litwack et al., Cillessen, 2008).

Friendship quality has also been shown to vary depending on whether the members of a friendship dyad are of similar levels of perceived popularity (Houser, Mayeux, & Cillessen, 2007). We identified best-friendship dyads that were made up of either two highly popular adolescents, two adolescents of average popularity, or two adolescents who were discordant for popular status (e.g., one member of the dyad was highly popular and the other was only of average popularity). No differences in friendship quality were found among girls, but significant differences were found for boys. When both friends were of average popularity, they reported more companionship, security, and closeness than discordant dyads and had closer friendships than the high-popularity dyads. Discordant dyads perceived less help from their best friends than the high- or average-popularity dyads and were less close than high-popularity dyads. Taken together, these studies suggest that popularity can serve as both a risk factor and a protective factor in the development of friendship quality, and whether the friendships of popular youth are positive may depend partly on how similar the friends are in popularity.

We know even less about how popularity relates to romantic relationships than how it relates to friendships. In the domain of romantic relationships, third through ninth graders who were involved in a reciprocal romantic relationship were more likely to be popular than youth who were not (Carlson & Rose, 2007). This finding is noteworthy because it speaks to the issue of the attractiveness of status itself. A study of young adolescents by Pellegrini and Bartini (2001) found that dominance displays by boys at the beginning of sixth grade predicted their dating status at the end of the year, with more dominant boys engaging in more dating behavior. If dominance and popularity are related (and we argue that they are, given the overlap that both share with aggression and other behaviors), these two studies are highlighting an important function of popularity: the heightening of one's desirability as a romantic partner. This element of popularity has important implications for how adolescents perceive and respond to the negative behaviors of opposite-sex popular peers. For example, in an experimental study using hypothetical vignettes about popular, unpopular, or neutral-status peers, we have found that while adolescents attribute more hostile intent to opposite-sex popular peers than to opposite-sex peers of lower status, they still report liking popular opposite-sex peers more (Samples & Mayeux, 2007). Teens appear to give popular members of the opposite sex the benefit of the doubt when they behave badly, possibly because their romantic interest or desire to be associated with a popular romantic partner clouds their judgment.

Further studies that clarify how popularity relates to both friendships and romantic relationships are sorely needed, in particular, studies of the dynamics within popular friend dyads or popular romantic pairs. For example, Houser and Cillessen (2009) have shown that female friends (and, to a lesser but still significant extent, male friends) are highly similar in their levels of popularity and relational aggression. It will be important to determine whether the friendships of popular youth are characterized by intimate exchange and shared interests or by high levels of aggression and alliances against shared targets and what the implications of these styles of interaction are for friendship quality and stability.

SOCIAL-COGNITIVE FACTORS AND EMOTIONAL ADJUSTMENT

Researchers are also beginning to address questions regarding popular youth's status-related social cognitions as well as their emotional adjustment. In contrast to the very large body of work that exists to explain how peer acceptance or rejection predict social cognitions (see Gifford-Smith & Rabiner, 2004), relatively few published studies have addressed the social cognitions of popular youth. In a recent correlational study, popularity, but not social acceptance, was positively associated with social intelligence (a self-report index composed of social information-processing skills, social skills, and social awareness; Meijs, Cillessen, Scholte, Segers, & Spijkerman, 2010). A similar study of midadolescents found a positive link between self-reported social intelligence and peer-rated popularity among a subset of powerful bullies (Peeters et al., 2010), suggesting that the combination of social intelligence and popularity can be particularly problematic, at least from the perspective of potential peer victims.

In an experimental study using hypothetical vignettes, LaFontana and Cillessen (2010) measured the social goals of individuals in grades 1 to 12. The overarching findings were twofold. First, concerns about popularity and the prioritization of popularity over other goals increased across childhood, peaked in the late middle school and early high school years, and then leveled off and remained stable through college. Second, youth, in particular early adolescents, tended to prioritize status goals over and above other motivations or goals, including friendships, romantic relationships, academic achievement, or compassion toward less fortunate peers. The prioritization of popularity over socially acceptable behavior was most pronounced, with an effect size of .46. Adolescents and young adults were particularly likely to violate norms for acceptable behavior in order to be popular. LaFontana and Cillessen suggest that as youth grow older, they become increasingly aware that being successful sometimes entails being socially self-protective in ways that may harm others or sacrifice other personal goals. This study begs the question of whether the prioritization of popularity is most pronounced among youth who have already achieved popular status or those who wish to be popular. LaFontana and Cillessen did not directly measure peer status in their study; thus, replications of their developmental findings, with the addition of status assessments, will provide a more nuanced view of how status and motivations interact to influence behavior.

A second study investigated adolescents' accuracy in their self-assessments of social acceptance and popularity as well as gender differences in accuracy. Mayeux and Cillessen (2008) assessed both peer and self-perceptions of popularity and social acceptance in their study of high schoolers. The correlations between peer and self-perceptions of social acceptance were generally nonsignificant for girls but significant and moderate for boys; indeed, statistical tests showed that boys in grades 11 and 12 were more accurate in their self-perceptions regarding social acceptance than their female counterparts. Correlations between peer and self-perceptions of popularity were generally moderate and of higher magnitude than those for liking, especially for girls.

Thus, although boys were generally more accurate than girls in their assessments of their social acceptance, girls were more aware of how they fit into the social hierarchy. This is intriguing for two reasons. First, girls have been shown to be more concerned with relationships than boys, so the findings that boys were better able to predict their own acceptance by peers, and that girls were generally inaccurate to begin with, begs the question of what cues the different genders are using in their interpretations of peers' behavior toward them. What important cues are girls missing? Second, these findings suggest that both genders may be more tuned into status-related information than they are to relational cues from peers. Given that status concerns are highest during the adolescent years (see LaFontana & Cillessen, 2010), this does not come as a particular surprise. However, it does bolster the implication that adolescents care more about being popular than about being liked, which has implications for peer-directed behavior like aggression, behaviors that increase personal risk, such as susceptibility to peer influence, and risk-taking behaviors like substance use (see Cohen & Prinstein, 2006).

Studies of the link between popularity and emotional adjustment have yielded mixed results. Eighth-grade popularity was associated with more depressive symptoms in one study (Litwack et al., 2008), but another found a longitudinal link between popularity and lower levels of internalizing symptoms such as depression and social anxiety for adolescent boys (Sandstrom & Cillessen, 2006). This study also found that social acceptance predicted fewer internalizing symptoms over time for girls. Although preliminary, these studies suggest that social acceptance carries with it less risk of depression and other internalized distress than popularity. Further studies are needed to replicate Litwack and colleagues' finding. Although there are intuitive and empirical reasons to expect more internalizing symptoms among popular youth, Sandstrom and Cillessen note that popular children and adolescents receive consistent positive feedback from peers in the form of admiration and social support, which may buffer them against anxiety and depression. Based on the evidence, this may be especially true for boys.

A recent study showed that popularity, but not social acceptance, was associated with higher levels of empathy in childhood (Caravita et al., 2008). This is an important finding that bears replication. If popular youth are particularly socially skilled in this area, it has strong implications for the robust association between popularity and aggression. For example, Sutton, Smith, and Swettenham (1999) have argued that certain forms of bullying, in particular relational aggression and bullying that requires the coordination of multiple peers ("ringleading"), require excellent theory of mind skills and other subtle social perspective-taking abilities. Indeed, Andreou (2006) found relational aggression to be positively correlated with social intelligence in a sample of early adolescents. Although Caravita and her colleagues did not investigate the potential moderating effects of empathy in the association between popularity and bullying in their own data, the intuitive guess would be that empathy does indeed play a role (see also Peeters et al., 2010). The combination of popularity and well-developed socioemotional skills may be a surprisingly dangerous one. Perhaps popular children who are high in empathy are particularly likely to aggress against others or to aggress in especially savvy or hurtful ways because they know how best to hurt a given peer. This is an exciting preliminary finding by Caravita et al. that is sure to influence future research in the field, as investigators continue to examine the complex association between popularity and aggression.

CONCLUSIONS: QUEEN BEES AND DON'T-WANNABES

If you ask your favorite teen about status, you will learn that there are huge differences between being socially accepted and being popular. If you read the developmental literature on the same topic, you walk away with a similar conclusion. Social acceptance and popularity share a number of attributes, such as good leadership, prosocial behavior, and high-quality friendships. However, the two types of status diverge in more ways than they converge. Popularity is associated with elevated levels of both overt/physical and relational/social forms of aggression; social acceptance is not. Popular youth are often strongly disliked by peers; well-accepted youth, by definition, enjoy relatively high levels of peer acceptance by their classmates as a whole. Popular children are both bullies and defenders; well-accepted children defend their peers without coupling it with aggression. Popularity predicts risk taking, including risky sexual behavior and substance use; social acceptance is almost uniformly found to predict low levels of risk taking. Popular youth are more likely to be attractive and well dressed and to have the spending power to afford the trendy clothes or gadgets that their peers covet.

The young queen bee is a paradox. She acts kindly toward some peers, yet knows that being nasty to others will help her climb the social ladder. She acts out in ways that would concern parents and professionals, but yet has strong interpersonal skills, is confident, and is a good leader. We can assume that most children start out the same way (although, admittedly, we have no real data on popular preschoolers, nor do we have a good sense of what popularity would look like at that age, if it does indeed exist in such young children). Parents and teachers stress the importance of compassion, sharing, cooperation, and kindness toward others, and being successful among very young peers reflects the internalization of those values. Yet at some point during development the queen bee learns that being good does not always make one as successful as being bad can and decides that being bad sometimes is worth a shot.

At what point do these children's paths diverge? Does a little boy become popular because of his attributes, such as the combination of being wealthy, funny, and athletic, which then kick-starts a self-perpetuating dynamic of behavioral change and status reinforcement? Or does a child make a conscious decision to be popular and seek out the proper social accoutrements (the "right" friends, the "right" clothes, skillful aggressive acts) to become that way? Researchers have yet to propose a true developmental model of popularity (but see Cillessen, Chapter 12, this volume). Longitudinal studies beginning in early childhood are sorely needed to uncover trajectories of behaviors and other attributes that contribute to the development of popular status in childhood and adolescence. Given that popularity is highly stable, studies that track children into the late childhood or early adolescent years would provide valuable information about the attributes of youth who attain status in the first place. Studies following popular children through adolescence have the potential to contribute to our understanding of how popularity, once attained, changes the developing person. In the grand scheme of things, the study of popularity is a young endeavor, and we have miles to go before we understand the complex dynamics of high status in the peer group. However, researchers would do well to integrate findings from the extant literature into comprehensive longitudinal studies (as difficult as that can be logistically) so that we can begin to figure out how all of these behavioral, emotional, social, and cognitive factors interact with each other to create the queen bees of our children's classrooms.

In any discussion of differences between being well accepted and being popular, it is important to acknowledge that there are also differences in how youth themselves feel about popularity versus social acceptance. The power that popularity holds for any individual child is likely one of the most important predictors of who remains popular from year to year, and how great a role these feelings play in the establishment of popularity is also an important research question that has yet to be explored. As prior studies suggest (e.g., LaFontana & Cillessen, 2010), popularity is not the primary goal of all children or adolescents, but it is for many. We need a better understanding of the variability in children's social goals and how those goals relate to peer-directed behavior and peer status longitudinally. There are clearly reasons to expect to find a subsample of youth who actively seek to improve their status via whatever means prove the most useful, but we should also expect a subsample of youth who eschew social power, in part because they do not wish to engage in hurtful behaviors or associate with hurtful peers. Thus, although we should find wannabes, we should also find "don't-wannabes" in equal or greater numbers.

To end, we come back to our original question: Are social acceptance and popularity really different types of status? A decade of research strongly suggests that they are. Social acceptance and popularity diverge in many more ways than they converge. By middle childhood, children are beginning to solidify their conceptualization of what it means to be popular, and their behaviors reflect it. The true nature of the development of social acceptance versus popularity, including the many factors involved in the divergence, remains to be discovered. As we continue to establish the differences between socially accepted and popular peers, we also challenge researchers to explore developmental antecedents and long-term consequences to popularity. It is by learning the answers to these kinds of questions that developmental scientists will be best able to help parents, educators, and counselors harness the power of the peer group to maximize the potential of each developing child.

REFERENCES

Andreou, E. (2006). Social preference, perceived popularity, and social intelligence: Relations to overt and relational aggression. *School Psychology International, 27*(3), 339–351.

Boyatzis, C. J., Baloff, P., & Durieux, C. (1998). Effects of perceived attractiveness and academic success on early adolescent peer popularity. *Journal of Genetic Psychology, 159*(3), 337–344.

Bukowski, W. M., & Hoza, B. (1989). Popularity and friendship: Issues in theory, measurement, and outcome. In T. J. Berndt & G. W. Lad (Eds.), *Peer relationships in child development* (15–45). Oxford, UK: Wiley.

Caravita, S. C. S., Di Blasio, P., & Salmivalli, C. (2008). Unique and interactive effects of empathy and social status on involvement in bullying. *Social Development, 18*(1), 140–163.

Carlson, W., & Rose, A. J. (2007). The role of reciprocity in romantic relationships in middle childhood and early adolescence. *Merrill-Palmer Quarterly, 53*(2), 262–290.

Cillessen, A. H. N., & Borch, C. (2006). Developmental trajectories of adolescent popularity: A growth curve modeling analysis. *Journal of Adolescence, 29*(6), 935–959.

Cillessen, A. H. N., & Ferguson, T. J. (1989). Self-perpetuation processes in children's peer relationships. In R. P. Weissberg, B. H. Schneider, G. Attili, & J. Nadel (Eds.), *Social competence in developmental perspective* (203–221). New York: Kluwer Academic/Plenum.

Cillessen, A. H. N., & Mayeux, L. (2004). From censure to reinforcement: Developmental changes in the association between aggression and social status. *Child Development, 75*(1), 147–163.

Cillessen, A H. N., & Rose, A. J. (2005). Understanding popularity in the peer system. *Current Directions in Psychological Science, 14*(2), 102–105.

Cillessen, A. H. N., van IJzendoorn, H. W., van Lieshout, C. F., & Hartup, W. W. (1992). Heterogeneity among peer-rejected boys: Subtypes and stabilities. *Child Development, 63*(4), 893–905.

Closson, L. M. (2008). Status and gender differences in adolescents' descriptions of popularity. *Social Development, 18*(2), 412–426.

Cohen, G. L., & Prinstein, M. J. (2006). Peer contagion of aggression and health risk behavior among adolescent males: An experimental investigation of effects on public conduct and private attitudes. *Child Development, 77*(4), 967–983.

Coie, J. D., Dodge, K. A., & Coppotelli, H. (1982). Dimensions and types of status: A cross-age perspective. *Developmental Psychology, 18*, 557–570.

de Bruyn, E. H., & Cillessen, A. H. N. (2006). Popularity in early adolescence: Prosocial and antisocial subtypes. *Journal of Adolescent Research, 21*(6), 1–21.

de Bruyn, E. H., Cillessen, A. H. N., & Wissink, I. B. (2009). Associations of peer acceptance and perceived popularity with bullying and victimization in early adolescence. *Journal of Early Adolescence.*

de Bruyn, E. H., & van den Boom, D. C. (2005). Interpersonal behavior, peer popularity, and self-esteem in early adolescents. *Social Development, 14*(4), 555–573.

Farmer, T. W., Estell, D. B., Bishop, J. L., O'Neal, K. K., & Cairns, B. D. (2003). Rejected bullies or popular leaders? The social relations of aggressive subtypes of rural African-American early adolescents. *Developmental Psychology, 39*(6), 992–1004.

Farmer, T. W., & Rodkin, P. C. (1996). Antisocial and prosocial correlates of classroom social positions: The social network centrality perspective. *Social Development, 5*(2), 174–188.

Gifford-Smith, M. E., & Rabiner, D. L. (2004). Social information processing and children's social adjustment. In J. B. Kupersmidt & K. A. Dodge (Eds.), *Children's peer relations: From development to intervention* (pp. 61–79). Washington, DC: American Psychological Association.

Gorman, A. H., Kim, J., & Schimmelbusch, A. (2002). The attributes adolescents associate with peer popularity and teacher preference. *Journal of School Psychology, 40*(2), 143–165.

Hawley, P. H. (2003). Prosocial and coercive configurations of resource control in early adolescence: A case for the well-adapted Machiavellian. *Merrill-Palmer Quarterly, 49*(3), 279–309.

Hawley, P. H., Little, T. D., & Card, N. A. (2007). The allure of a mean friend: Relationship quality and processes of aggressive adolescents with prosocial skills. *International Journal of Behavioral Development, 31*(2), 170–180.

Hawley, P. H., Little, T. D., & Card, N. A. (2008). The myth of the alpha male: A new look at dominance-related beliefs and behaviors among adolescent males and females. *International Journal of Behavioral Development, 32*(1), 76–88.

Houser, J. J., & Cillessen, A. H. N. (2009, April). *Popularity, relational aggression, and friendship quality in adolescence: A dyadic analysis.* Paper presented at the biennial meeting of the Society for Research in Child Development, Denver, CO.

Houser, J. J., Mayeux, L., & Cillessen, A. H. N. (2007, March). *Popularity and friendship: Associations between status discordance and friendship quality.* Poster presented at the biennial meeting of the Society for Research in Child Development, Boston.

Košir, K., & Pečjak, S. (2005). Sociometry as a method for investigating peer relationships: What does it actually measure? *Educational Research, 47*(1), 127–144.

LaFontana, K. M., & Cillessen, A. H. N. (1998). The nature of children's stereotypes of popularity. *Social Development, 7*(3), 301–320.

LaFontana, K. M., & Cillessen, A. H. N. (1999). Children's interpersonal perceptions as a function of sociometric and peer-perceived popularity. *Journal of Genetic Psychology, 160*(2), 225–242.

LaFontana, K. M., & Cillessen, A. H. N. (2002). Children's perceptions of popular and unpopular peers: A multimethod assessment. *Developmental Psychology, 33*(5), 635–647.

LaFontana, K. M., & Cillessen, A. H. N. (2010). Developmental changes in the priority of perceived status in childhood and adolescence. *Social Development, 19*(1), 130–147.

Lease, A. M., Kennedy, C. A., & Axelrod, J. L. (2002). Children's social constructions of popularity. *Social Development, 11*(1), 87–109.

Litwack, S. D., Aikins, J. W., & Cillessen, A. H. N. (2008). *Considerations of the distinct roles of sociometric and perceived popularity: The interplay with friendship factors for adolescent depression and self esteem*. Manuscript submitted for publication.

Luthar, S. S., & D'Avanzo, K. (1999). Contextual factors in substance use: A study of suburban and inner-city adolescents. *Development and Psychopathology, 11*(4), 845–867.

Mayeux, L. (2009, April). *Machiavelli goes to high school: Machiavellianism moderates the aggression-status link among high school seniors*. Paper presented at the biennial meeting of the Society for Research in Child Development, Denver, CO.

Mayeux, L., & Cillessen, A. H. N. (2008). It's not just being popular, it's knowing it, too: The role of self-perceptions of status in the associations between peer status and aggression. *Social Development, 17*(4), 871–888.

Mayeux, L., Sandstrom, M. J., & Cillessen, A. H. N. (2008). Is being popular a risky proposition? *Journal of Research on Adolescence, 18*(1), 49–74.

Meijs, N., Cillessen, A. H. N., Scholte, R. H. J., Segers, E., & Spijkerman, R. (2010). Social intelligence and academic achievement as predictors of adolescent popularity. *Journal of Youth and Adolescence, 39*, 62–72.

Moffitt, T. E. (1993). Adolescence-limited and life-course-persistent antisocial behavior: A developmental taxonomy. *Psychological Review, 100*(4), 674–701.

Parker, J. G., & Asher, S. R. (1993). Friendship and friendship quality in middle childhood: Links with peer group acceptance and feelings of loneliness and social dissatisfaction. *Developmental Psychology, 29*(4), 611–621.

Parkhurst, J. T., & Hopmeyer, A. (1998). Sociometric popularity and peer-perceived popularity: Two distinct dimensions of peer status. *The Journal of Early Adolescence, 18*(2), 125–144.

Peeters, M., Cillessen, A. H. N., & Scholte, R. H. J. (2010). Clueless or powerful? Identifying subtypes of bullies in adolescence. *Journal of Youth and Adolescence, 39*(9), 1041–1052.

Pellegrini, A. D., & Bartini, M. (2001). Dominance in early adolescent boys: Affiliative and aggressive dimensions and possible functions. *Merrill-Palmer Quarterly, 47*(1), 142–163.

Pope, A. W., Bierman, K. L., & Mumma, G. H. (1989). Relations between hyperactive and aggressive behavior and peer relations at three elementary school grades. *Journal of Abnormal Child Psychology, 17*(3), 253–267.

Prinstein, M. J., & Cillessen, A. H. N. (2003). Forms and functions of adolescent peer aggression associated with high levels of peer status. *Merrill-Palmer Quarterly, 49*(3), 310–342.

Prinstein, M. J., Meade, C. S., & Cohen, G. L. (2003). Adolescent oral sex, peer popularity, and perceptions of best friends' sexual behavior. *Journal of Pediatric Psychology, 28*(4), 243–249.

Puckett, M. B., Aikins, J. W., & Cillessen, A. H. N. (2008). Moderators of the association between perceived popularity and relational aggression. *Aggressive Behavior, 34*(6), 563–576.

Rodkin, P. C., Farmer, T. W., Pearl, R., & Van Acker, R. (2000). Heterogeneity of popular boys: Antisocial and prosocial configurations. *Developmental Psychology, 36*(1), 14–24.

Rose, A. J., Swenson, L. P., & Carlson, W. (2004). Friendships of aggressive youth: Considering the influences of being disliked and of being perceived as popular. *Journal of Experimental Child Psychology, 88*(1), 25–45.

Rose, A. J., Swenson, L. P., & Waller, E. M. (2004). Overt and relational aggression and perceived popularity: Developmental differences in concurrent and prospective relations. *Developmental Psychology, 40*(3), 378–387.

Samples, K. D., & Mayeux, L. (2007, March). *Perceptions of same- and other-sex peers' behaviors: A study of adolescents' stereotypes of perceived popularity*. Poster presented at the biennial meeting of the Society for Research in Child Development, Boston, MA.

Sandstrom, M. J., & Cillessen, A. H. N. (2006). Likeable versus popular: Distinct implications for adolescent adjustment. *International Journal of Behavioral Development, 30*(4), 305–314.

Schwartz, D., Gorman, A. H., Nakamoto, J., & McKay, T. (2006). Popularity, social acceptance, and aggression in adolescent peer groups: Links with academic performance and school attendance. *Developmental Psychology, 42*(6), 1116–1127.

Sutton, J., Smith, P. K., & Swettenham, J. (1999). Social cognition and bullying: Social inadequacy or skilled manipulation? *British Journal of Developmental Psychology, 17*(3), 435–450.

Vaillancourt, T., & Hymel, S. (2006). Aggression and social status: The moderating roles of sex and peer-valued characteristics. *Aggressive Behavior, 32*(4), 396–408.

Xie, H., Li, Y., Boucher, S. M., Hutchins, B. C., & Cairns, B. D. (2006). What makes a girl (or a boy) popular (or unpopular)? African American children's perceptions and developmental differences. *Developmental Psychology, 42*(4), 599–612.

Chapter 5

Popularity and Gender
The Two Cultures of Boys and Girls

AMANDA J. ROSE
GARY C. GLICK
RHIANNON L. SMITH

Children and adolescents spend much of their days in the company of their peers. Not surprisingly, their lives are strongly affected by their status in the peer group, including the degree to which they are seen by peers as being popular. Perhaps for this reason there is a rich history of ethnographic research that seeks to describe the social worlds of popular youth through systematic observation and qualitative analysis (e.g., Eder, 1985; Merten, 1997; Adler, Kless, & Adler, 1992). More recently, quantitative methods that emphasize measurement and statistical associations have been applied to the study of popularity (see Cillessen & Rose, 2005). A goal of these later studies has been to use correlational designs to confirm and extend the earlier ethnographic work.

The emerging pattern of findings from these different approaches does suggest notable differences in the peer relationships of girls and boys. Research on popularity and other aspects of children's social adjustment with peers has continually highlighted the need to consider the role of gender (for a review, see Rose & Rudolph, 2006). Although there has been some disagreement regarding the strength and consistency of the relevant effects (Thorne, 1993; Underwood, 2004), the full pattern is striking enough that some investigators have referred to the "two cultures" of boys and girls (Maccoby, 1990; Maltz & Borker, 1982; Thorne, 1986). As very basic examples, compared with girls, boys play in larger groups (e.g., Ladd, 1983), are more focused on competitive sports and games (e.g., Mathur & Berndt, 2006), and engage in higher rates of overt aggression (Card, Stucky, Sawalani, & Little, 2008). Conversely, girls are characterized by greater self-disclosure in friendships (e.g., Rose, 2002) and higher rates of prosocial behavior (e.g., Crick & Grotpeter, 1995) than boys. Girls are also likely to perceive indirect and socially manipulative forms of aggression (e.g., relational aggression, social aggression) as more hurtful (e.g., Paquette & Underwood, 1999) than boys.

An implication of this "two-cultures" conceptualization is that girls and boys should value and reinforce different behaviors. This process could then lead to socialization of gender-specific behaviors. Consistent with this suggestion, children are somewhat more accepting of gender-typed behavior than behavior that is gender atypical (Fagot, 1985; Smith & Leaper, 2005). Likewise, behaviors that are particularly common or especially salient within gender (e.g., sports participation for boys, relational aggression for girls) might have a particularly strong association with popularity. Thus, a two-culture model also would be consistent with the expectation that the behavioral correlates of popularity will be different for girls and boys.

Interestingly, ethnographic studies describe popular girls and boys in ways that fit with the gendered theoretical framework that we describe. As we summarize in the following sections, the ethnographic work highlights important differences in the behaviors of popular girls and boys as well as divergence in the consequences of popularity. The results from quantitative research lead to somewhat different conclusions but still shed light on potential gender differences in the determinants of popularity.

The goal of this chapter is to examine popularity in the context of the two cultures. We will highlight gender similarities and differences in the determinants, concurrent correlates, and outcomes associated with popularity. Our objective is to develop predictive models that have validity for both boys and girls. To this end, we review both ethnographic and quantitive studies, and we summarize findings across disciplines.

CONCURRENT CORRELATES AND PREDICTORS OF POPULARITY

Ethnographic Perspectives

Ethnographers, including Adler and Adler (1998; Adler et al., 1992), Eder (1985; Eder, Evans, & Parker, 1995), and Merten (1997; Chapter

3, this volume, have conducted qualitative analyses examining the social interactions of high-status youths. A clear message from this work is that an understanding of gender differences is critical for research on popularity. Some of the relevant studies have been narrowly focused on one gender, most often including only girls (i.e., Eder, 1985; Merten, 1997). The implicit assumption of these projects seems to be that correlates of popularity are so different for boys and girls that one should not include both genders in the same study. Other investigations included both genders for the purpose of directly examining differences (Adler et al., 1992).

Ethnographic descriptions of popular girls indicate that they are likely to be attractive, affluent, and involved in prestigious school activities (particularly cheerleading). The issue of physical attractiveness had been an especially persistent theme in this work. For example, Adler and colleagues (1992, p. 179) noted that "girls who were deemed pretty by society's socially constructed standards were attractive to boys and had a much greater probability of being popular." These researchers also reported that popular youth had a heightened focus on their appearance, adhering to strict norms with respect to fashion, makeup, hairstyles, and accessories (e.g., Adler et al., 1992).

Not surprisingly, a degree of affluence is necessary to stay in touch with the latest fashions. For this reason, economic resources can be central to the determination of status for girls. Adler and colleagues (Adler & Adler, 1998; Adler et al., 1992) and Eder (Eder, 1985; Eder & Kinney, 1995) documented the tendency for popular girls to come from high socioeconomic status families. In these studies, girls who came from advantaged family environments had access to coveted designer clothes and other desirable material goods. They were also able to participate in central extracurricular activities (because parents could afford costs associated with the activities and could take them to practices).

High-profile school activities, such as cheerleading (with the associated connotations of attractiveness, leadership, and athletic ability), may also represent an efficient path to popularity. Several ethnographies have stressed the importance of cheerleading and related pursuits for girls' popularity (Eder, 1985; Eder et al., 1995; Merten, 1997). Eder (1985, p. 158) wrote, "There were two main avenues for mobility into the elite group—being a cheerleader or being a friend of a cheerleader." One caveat is that other girls felt some ambivalence toward the legitimacy of particular girls being cheerleaders. These envious peers may have perceived that cheerleaders were chosen primarily for their attractiveness instead of skill (see Eder et al., 1995).

Another factor that can elicit ambivalence from their peers is the mixed behavioral patterns displayed by popular girls. Ethnographers described popular girls as alternating fluidly between friendly behaviors and snobby, exclusive, or manipulative behaviors. According to Eder (1985), "The popular girls in the school were considered snobbish" (p. 160). Adler et al. (1992, p. 181) found that popular girls "form elite social groups using such negative tactics as gossiping, the proliferation of rumors, bossiness, and meanness." Merten (1997, p. 175) further argued that popular girls "used meanness instrumentally to gain a competitive advantage in pursuit or protection of popularity." Merten (1997) also noted that the popular girls he studied would sometimes threaten to physically harm peers but generally did not follow through on these threats. Collectively, the ethnographic studies suggest that popular girls may possess superior social skills, yet wield them in self-serving and manipulative ways.

The emerging picture with regard to boys differs somewhat from the corresponding pattern for girls, emphasizing athletic competences, aggressiveness, and social skills as primary themes. For boys, ethnographic researchers have consistently found athletic ability to be the critical determinant. As Adler et al. (1992, p. 172) argued, "The major factor that affected the boys' popularity was athletic ability" "In both schools we observed, the best athlete was also the most popular boy in the grade." Likewise, Eder (1985, p. 155) wrote, "Athletic activities provide males with a clear avenue for status."

Although there does not seem to be an emphasis on physical attractiveness per se for boys, their self-presentation skills also were found to be important for popularity. Concretely, popular boys must wear the right clothes and hairstyles (Adler et al., 1992). Adler et al. (1992, p. 173) noted, "There was a shared agreement among the boys as to what type of expressive equipment, such as clothing, was socially defined as cool. Although this apparel was worn mostly by the popular boys, boys in other groups also tried to emulate this style."

In terms of social behavior, popular boys were especially socially skilled and sophisticated. Adler and colleagues (1992, p. 174) commented that popular boys' "behaviors included such interpersonal communication skills as being able to initiate sequences of play and other joint lines of action, affirmation of friendships, role-taking and role-playing abilities, social knowledge and cognition, providing constructive criticism and support to one's peers, and expressive feelings in a positive manner." Popular boys also were found to have a good sense of humor (Eder et al., 1995) and often were viewed as "class clowns" (Adler et al., 1992).

Aggressive attributes, such as "toughness," may also be an important correlate of popularity for boys. Eder and colleagues (1995, p. 37) highlighted that "physical and verbal fighting skills ... and (a) willingness to be daring and defy politeness norms further enhanced the likelihood of being in the top group." Adler and colleagues (1992, p. 172) noted that "fighting, whether formal fights or informal pushing, shoving, or roughhousing, was a means of establishing social order. The more popular boys often dispensed these physical actions."

This general inclination toward antisocial attributes also seems to carry over for attitudes toward school. Adler et al. (1992) reported that although boys who had serious academic problems were excluded from the high-status peer group, being seen as highly engaged in academics also detracted from boys' popularity. These researchers also noted that popular boys often were overtly defiant toward teachers. In fact, doing well in school carried a "potentially degrading stigma" (p. 176) so that popular boys often downplayed achievement or failed to work to their full potential. In contrast, they observed that "although not all popular girls were smart or academic achievers, they did not suffer any stigma from performing well scholastically" (p. 182).

In summary, the ethnographic work suggests notable differences in the determinants of popularity for boys and girls. Popular girls and boys were both portrayed as socially skilled and sophisticated and having strong self-presentation skills in terms of looking stylish or "cool." However, factors such as attractiveness, intelligence, and economic resources appear to be more central for girls than boys. Conversely, popular boys were more likely than girls to be characterized as being athletic, "tough" (and physically aggressive), and disengaged from school. For boys, the most prestigious social activities seemed to involve sports team membership, whereas girls achieved status from cheerleading.

As a general rule, peer perceptions of popular youth seemed more negative for girls than boys. In fact, popular girls were often perceived as being manipulative and snobby. Perhaps because popular boys were not seen as being exclusive, they were viewed as being more good-natured and likeable than popular girls. This pattern fits with the findings that popular boys were likely to be "class clowns" and have a good sense of humor.

Ethnographers have also suggested that popularity carries more aversive consequences for girls than boys. Girls were found to covet the social standing of popular peers, creating a breeding ground for feelings of jealousy and resentment (Merten, 1997). Eder (1985) described a "cycle of popularity." When a girl became popular, other girls desired her friendship to increase their own popularity. If their bids for friendship were refused (because the popular girls were being exclusive or simply because they had more bids for friendship than they could accept), the other girls came to dislike them despite their high social status. In this way, popularity was more of a "double-edged sword" for girls than it was for boys.

Quantitative Perspectives

Developmental psychologists have sought to build on prior work with quantitive approaches to the study of popularity. The full picture from this research is not completely consistent with conclusions that might be drawn on the basis of earlier ethnographic studies. Overall, the pattern of results suggests considerable overlap in the correlates of popularity across gender albeit with some notable differences. We next summarize the available findings, with studies organized according to specific sets of correlates.

Social Skills

Prosociability is often conceptualized as an important indicator of social competence (see Aikins & Litwack, chapter 7, this volume). Accordingly, a number of popularity researchers have assessed this dimension of social behavior. The findings of the relevant studies suggest that prosocial tendencies have a moderately strong association with popularity in middle childhood and adolescence (Gorman, Kim, & Schimmelbusch, 2002; Lease, Kennedy, & Axelrod, 2002; Parkhust & Hopmeyer, 1998). For example, Gorman et al. (2002) found that popular adolescents tend to be identified as cooperative and friendly by their peers. Conversely, when investigators have asked children or adolescents to describe the factors that make peers popular, the results have generally not suggested a central role for prosociability (LaFontana & Cillessen, 2002; Xie, Li, Boucher, Hutchins, & Cairns, 2006). In any case, none of these studies found a gender difference in the relation between prosocial behavior and popularity. Like ethnographic researchers, quantitive researchers have viewed social skills as an important determinant of popularity for boys and girls.

Physical Appearance

Recall that ethnographers have frequently emphasized the idea that being up to date with the latest fashions in clothing and hair is related to popularity for both genders (Adler et al., 1992). Quantitative researchers have reached similar conclusions. For example, Vaillancourt and Hymel (2006) reported that peer nomination scores for dressing well and being in style were related to popularity, with no differences in the effects by gender.

There is greater divergence between the ethnographic and quantitive research traditions with regard to the role of physical attractiveness. Ethnographers have suggested that attractiveness is likely to be most relevant for girls, whereas quantitive researchers have concluded that physical attractiveness is a significant issue for both genders. Boyatzis, Baloff, and Durieux (1998) asked ninth graders to rate the popularity of hypothetical attractive and unattractive peers. Ratings did not differ as a function of the gender of the peer depicted in the vignette but were highest when the hypothetical peer was described as attractive. Likewise, Vaillancourt and Hymel (2006) found that peer nomination scores for attractiveness were correlated with popularity in a similar manner for both boys and girls.

As we consider these findings, it is important to keep in mind differences in what is considered attractive for each gender. For example, Wang, Houshyar, and Prinstein (2006) found a linear relation between body size and popularity for adolescent girls, with the thinnest girls being most popular. In contrast, these researchers found a curvilinear relationship for boys, suggesting that being too skinny or too heavy was detrimental to boys' popularity.

Affluence

Ethnographic work also suggests that having an affluent family is especially important for girls' popularity. Conversely, the few relevant quantitative studies that have been conducted suggest that economic advantage is a central factor for both boys and girls. Vaillancourt and Hymel (2006) found that, during early adolescence, affluence (assessed via peer nominations) was related to popularity for both genders. Similarly, Lease et al. (2002) found that spending power (assessed via teacher rating) was associated with popularity for both boys and girls. Xie et al. (2006) reported consistent findings.

Academic Competence

Associations between popularity and academic functioning have been examined by a number of researchers. Generally, the findings suggest a modest positive association between academic competence and popularity before middle adolescence (LaFontana & Cillessen, 2002). There may be important developmental shifts in this pattern, however. In some high school samples, popularity is related to a low grade point average and unexplained absences (Gorman et al., 2002), with the effects being particularly marked for those youth who are also aggressive (Schwartz, Gorman, Nakamoto, & McKay, 2006). Still, regardless of the age group considered, there is little evidence that associations between academic competence and popularity differ as a function of gender. Indeed, we identified only one study that reported a gender difference (LaFontana & Cillessen, 2002). These findings seem particularly notable given that the early ethnographic work suggested that being smart and doing well in school was more closely tied to popularity for girls, and that disengagement from school may be a marker of the "antisocial swagger" that is characteristic of some popular boys.

One explanation for the disparities in results might be that the ethnographic and quantitative studies evaluated different aspects of academic engagement. The quantitative studies assessed peers' perceptions of being smart and doing well in school (LaFontana & Cillessen, 2002; Xie et al., 2006) or actual academic performance and attendance (Gorman et al., 2002; Schwartz et al., 2006). In contrast, the ethnographic work focused largely on popular boys' overtly expressed attitudes toward school. Popular boys' academic disengagement may manifest itself primarily with regard to their outwardly contrarian behavior toward teachers and less with regard to their actual academic performance (especially if their performance does not differ noticeably from their classmates).

School Activities

As might be expected, quantitive researchers have concluded that athletic ability is an especially important factor in the social status of boys. Two studies found that peer nominations for "who is good at sports" were associated with popularity for both girls and boys, but the relations were significantly stronger for boys (LaFontana & Cillessen, 2002; Vaillancourt & Hymel, 2006). A similar pattern emerged in research involving fourth through eighth graders' descriptions of what makes peers popular or unpopular (LaFontana & Cillessen, 2002). We are not aware of quantitative research addressing high-profile school activities that may be more relevant for girls (i.e., cheerleading).

Manipulative Behavior, Relational Aggression, and Exclusiveness

The centrality of relationally aggressive behavior in the social lives of popular youth has been well documented (e.g., Cillessen & Mayeux, 2004). Other researchers have described associations between popularity and snobby or "stuck-up" behaviors (Gorman et al., 2002; Lease et al., 2002; Parkhurst & Hopmeyer, 1998). Nonetheless, in most of the relevant projects, the effects are similar across genders (LaFontana & Cillessen, 2002; Rose, Swenson, & Waller, 2004; Vaillancourt & Hymel, 2006). Despite this pattern of null findings, it may be too early to draw strong conclusions. In contrast to the findings we have just described, Cillessen and Mayeux (2004) found that relational aggression was related to popularity more strongly for girls than for boys during the early to middle adolescent years. Importantly, these researchers conceptualized social preference as a "control variable" in their analyses. One implication of the Cillessen and Mayeux study might be that researchers need to consider "pure" indices of popularity that are not confounded with liking by peers.

It may also be important to consider the *function* of relational aggression. Prinstein and Cillessen (2003) asked youth to identify the circumstances under which their peers used relational aggression. Reactive forms of relational aggression (i.e., relational aggression used in retaliation to provocation) were associated with popularity for both girls and boys. Conversely, instrumental goal-oriented subtypes of relational aggression were associated with popularity only for girls. Thus, popular girls and boys may both rely on relational aggression, but it is the girls who are most likely to use these behaviors as a purposeful strategy for reaching external goals.

In terms of longitudinal associations, the ethnographies imply that girls may be especially likely to strategically use relational aggression to establish or increase their popularity (Merten, 1997). The few longitudinal studies that have been conducted provide only limited support for this suggestion. Rose et al. (2004) found that relationally aggressive behavior predicted increases in popularity for girls only. Nonetheless, other investigators have failed to detect similar patterns of gender effects (Cillessen & Mayeux, 2004; Prinstein & Cillessen, 2003).

Taken together, the findings are mixed regarding whether manipulative/exclusive behaviors, such as relational aggression, are more characteristic of popular girls than boys. Quantitative studies that specifically assess *strategic* relational aggression, as opposed to relational aggression more generally, may be the most likely to find gender differences in relations with popularity. This hypothesis fits with Prinstein and Cillessen's (2003) finding that instrumental (but not reactive) relational aggression was related to popularity more strongly for girls than boys. Moreover, if the gender difference does lie primarily in strategic or instrumental relational aggression, then considering the targets of relational aggression may be particularly important. That is, popular girls may be more likely than popular boys to specifically target viable social status competitors for their relational aggression.

Toughness and Physical Aggression

Whether being tough or aggressive is linked to popularity more closely for boys than girls depends on how the construct is assessed. One study (Vaillancourt & Hymel, 2006) addressed the question directly by asking 6th through 10th graders to nominate peers who were "tough." Toughness was positively related to popularity for both boys and girls. Consistent with predictions, the association was stronger for boys.

Rodkin, Farmer, Pearl, and Van Acker's (2000) research on the different behavioral constellations of popular youth also offers some insights into the role of the toughness construct. These researchers identified a subgroup of "tough," popular boys who scored high on teacher and self-reports of getting in fights, getting in trouble, and arguing and high on peer reports of starting fights, getting in trouble, and being disruptive. Interestingly, a similar study that included only girls (Estell, Farmer, Pearl, Van Acker, & Rodkin, 2008) did not identify a corresponding subgroup of antisocial popular girls. In fact, Estell et al. found that the subgroup of girls with a "tough" profile were only average in popularity. Taken together, these results may suggest that toughness is more central to popularity for boys. An important caveat, however, is that these studies differed with regard to age group identified; the girls in the Estell et al. (2008) study were younger than the boys in Rodkin et al.'s (2000) investigation. Thus, different findings may have emerged because antisocial dispositions become more closely associated with popularity over the course of development.

Other relevant research focuses on overt aggression (i.e., direct verbal and/or physical aggression). There are positive bivariate correlations between overt aggression and popularity during childhood and adolescence (LaFontana & Cillessen, 2002; Parkhurst & Hopmeyer, 1998; Vaillancourt & Hymel, 2006). Nonetheless, investigators have generally not reported gender differences in these associations (LaFontana & Cillessen, 2002; Vaillancourt & Hymel, 2006; Xie et al., 2006). In addition, none of the relevant longitudinal studies indicate gender differences in predictive relations between overt aggression and popularity (Cillessen & Mayeux, 2004; Prinstein & Cillessen, 2003; Rose et al., 2004).

Attempts to detect gender effects may be complicated by statistical overlap between overt and relational aggression. Earlier, we described evidence that relational aggression is linked with popularity, and investigators have also argued that relatively subtle relationally aggressive behaviors may be especially effective for manipulating the social world in ways that increase one's own social standing (Cillessen & Rose, 2005). Therefore, it seems important to consider the possibility that overt aggression may be linked to popularity primarily because overtly aggressive youth also tend to be characterized by more relational forms of aggression. In the Rose et al. (2004) study, significant positive correlations that emerged between overt aggression and popularity for seventh and ninth graders became nonsignificant when relational aggression was controlled. Moreover, three separate longitudinal studies, each of which controlled for relational aggression, found that overt aggression did not predict increases in popularity over time (ranging from 6 months to 17 months; Cillessen & Mayeux, 2004; Prinstein & Cillessen, 2003; Rose at al., 2004).

Research on dominance, another construct potentially related to toughness, has also yielded inconsistent findings. Most studies find that popularity is related to greater dominance and lower submissiveness (Lease et al., 2002; Gorman et al., 2002; Parkhurst & Hopmeyer, 1998). With regard to gender differences, Vaillancourt and Hymel (2006) found that power was associated with popularity for both adolescent girls and boys, but the effect was stronger for boys. These researchers generated a composite power score based on peer nominations of who has power over others, who is a leader, and who kids will listen to and follow (Vaillancourt & Hymel, 2006). Conversely, Xie and colleagues (2006) found that children and adolescents describe both popular girls and boys as dominant.

Together, the quantitative studies do not provide compelling support for the idea that popular boys are characterized by toughness more than popular girls. Nonetheless, in working toward a better understanding of the role of gender in the relation between toughness and popularity, it may useful to replicate the previous results that did indicate gender differences. We might consider assessments that are oriented toward social power (e.g., Vaillancourt & Hymel, 2006) as well as person-centered analyses (e.g., Estell et al., 2008; Rodkin et al., 2000).

To gain a better understanding of gender differences in the association between popularity and overt aggression, more specific behavioral assessments may be important. Almost all of the studies combined assessments of physical aggression, verbal aggression, and threats or other attempts at intimidation (e.g., Cillessen & Mayeux, 2004; LaFontana & Cillessen, 2002; Xie et al., 2006). We suspect that a more targeted assessment of physical aggression would facilitate identification of gender differences in associations with popularity. Given that engaging in actual acts of physical aggression is especially inconsistent with gender norms for girls, this specific behavior may be linked with popularity more for boys than girls. In fact, one study that did include a unidimensional assessment of physical aggression ("starts fights"; Parkhurst & Hopmeyer, 1998) found that the relation with popularity was strongest for boys. This possibility also fits with Merten's (1997) suggestion that both popular girls and boys may make physical threats but only popular boys actually carry these threats out. Accordingly, if additional quantitative research finds that physical aggression (but not verbal aggression or threats) is tied more closely with popularity for boys than for girls, this would help reconcile the differences in the literature regarding toughness and boys' popularity.

Good-Natured/Funny

As noted, there is an implication in the ethnographies that popular boys are more good-natured and likeable than popular girls. There is some limited quantitve support for this conclusion. Vaillancourt and Hymel (2006) found that 6th through 10th graders' nominations of having a good sense of humor and making people laugh predicted popularity more strongly for boys.

Reconciling Conclusions from the Ethnographic and Quantitative Literature

In summary, the quantitative research suggests more similarities across genders than would be expected based on the ethnographic studies. The specific factors underlying the differences in conclusions that can be drawn based on the two research traditions are not yet clear. For now, we suggest that researchers will need to move forward with caution and that closer examination of gender differences in the social worlds of popular youth will be required.

GENDER DIFFERENCES IN THE PSYCHOSOCIAL OUTCOMES ASSOCIATED WITH POPULARITY

To this point, our focus has been primarily on the concurrent correlates and predictors of popularity. Our hope has been to shed light on the determinants of social status within the framework of the two cultures model. From a developmental perspective, it is also to vital to consider the implications of popularity for longer term functioning. Potential links between popularity and negative outcomes are considered in greater detail elsewhere in this volume (Schwartz & Gorman, Chapter 11). Nonetheless, before we move on to our concluding comments, we pause to examine evidence regarding the differential impact of popularity on the adjustment of boys and girls.

Aggression and Other Forms of Antisocial Behavior

Ethnographic researchers have described back-and-forth exchanges of relational aggression in high-status peer groups (i.e., Eder, 1985; Merten, 1997). In these social contexts, popular youth will have ample exposure to relationally aggressive role models. Therefore, popularity could provide an opportunity for youth to expand their repertoire of social forms of aggression. Consistent with this suggestion, longitudinal researchers have shown associations between popularity and increases in relational aggression over time. These findings have been replicated across different time frames and age groups (Cillessen & Mayeux, 2004; Prinstein & Cillessen, 2003; Rose et al., 2004; Sandstrom & Cillessen, 2006).

The ethnographies have particularly emphasized the importance of manipulative behavior in the interactions of high-status girls (Merten, 1997). Furthermore, the significance of relational aggression in girls' peer groups has been well documented (Crick & Grotpeter, 1995). Despite this pattern, there is little empirical evidence that the association between popularity and increases in relational aggression differs for boys and girls (Prinstein & Cillessen, 2003; Rose et al., 2004; Sandstrom & Cillessen, 2006). One notable exception is an important longitudinal investigation conducted by Cillessen and Mayeux (2004). These researchers reported that popularity resulted in stronger increases in relational aggression for girls than boys from grades 6 to 7 and from grades 8 to 9.

The pattern of gender effects for overt aggression is even less convincing. Rose et al. (2004) found that popularity in the fall did not predict changes in overt aggression by spring. Cillessen and Mayeux (2004) also did not find changes from grades 6 to 7 or grades 7 to 8. However, popularity predicted increased overt aggression across grades 5 to 6 and grades 8 to 9. The effects in these studies were not moderated by gender. In two other studies, gender effects emerged but were inconsistent. Sandstrom and Cillessen (2006) found that popularity in grade 5 predicted overt aggression in grade 8 more strongly for boys than girls. In contrast, Prinstein and Cillessen (2003) found that popularity predicted increased overt aggression over 17 months for girls only. In sum, there is not strong or consistent evidence that the impact of popularity on either relational or overt aggression differs by gender.

With regard to other forms of externalizing and nonaggressive antisocial behavior, popularity research is at an early stage of development, and the limited data that are available do not suggest a compelling pattern of gender differences. Sandstrom and Cillessen (2006) found that popularity in grade 5 predicted increased disruptive behaviors in grade 8 similarly for girls and boys. Mayeux, Sandstrom, and Cillessen (2008) found that popularity in grade 10 predicted increased alcohol use and sexual activity in grade 12 and that the effects were consistent across genders.

Academic Adjustment

Theorists have long expressed concern that popular students may encounter social pressures to disengage from school (Steinberg, Dornbusch, & Brown, 1992). Adler et al. (1992) hypothesized that these pressures would be marked for boys in particular. Moreover, cluster analytic studies have identified subgroups of popular youth who are aggressive and characterized by negative attitudes toward school (Rodkin et al., 2000). Based on this work, we might expect popularity to predict academic disengagement in a particularly strong fashion for boys. Unfortunately, we are not yet in a secure position to evaluate this hypothesis because relevant longitudinal data are currently limited. Insofar as we are aware, there is only one published investigation that examines longitudinal relations between popularity and academic difficulties. Schwartz et al. (2006) followed students across the 9th and 10th grades and found that higher popularity predicted declines in GPA and increases in unexplained absences from school (especially for those youth who were concurrently aggression). These investigators did not find any evidence of potential gender differences in the described trajectories.

Internalizing

The ethnographic studies that we described earlier seem to portray the social worlds of popular youth as filled with pressure, competition, and stress. Under these conditions, we might expect some link between high status and internalizing disorders. Still, the limited data that are available seem to suggest that popular youth are relatively unlikely to experience internalized distress. In fact, Sandstom and Cillessen (2006) reported some evidence that popularity serves to reduce risk for internalizing (especially for boys). These researchers reported that boys' popularity in fifth grade was negatively associated with internalizing problems in the eighth grade, with the corresponding effect failing to reach significance for girls.

Liking by Peers

Considerably more research has addressed the relation between popularity and social acceptance, or being well liked by peers. Studies examining concurrent relations indicate that popularity is associated with social acceptance more strongly for boys than for girls (Cillessen & Mayeux, 2004; LaFontana & Cillessen, 2002; Prinstein & Cillessen, 2003). Moreover, this gender difference becomes stronger with age. Cillessen and Mayeux (2004) found that popularity and social acceptance were strongly positively correlated for both boys and girls in the 5th grade. By the 9th grade, the association was still positive for boys but near zero for girls. Mayeux and colleagues (2008) found that, by later adolescence, the associations were smaller but still positive for boys ($rs = .44$ in 10th grade and $.24$ in 12th grade). For girls, these associations had become negative.

Longitudinal research further supports this gender difference. Cillessen and Mayeux (2004) found that across each 1-year period as youth moved from 5th grade to 9th grade, popularity predicted increases in social acceptance for boys. The associations for girls were significantly weaker across three of the four time periods. Although the effects for girls were still significant and positive from 5th to 6th grade and from 7th to 8th, the effects were not significant from 6th to 7th grade and from 8th to 9th grade. Moreover, in later adolescence, popularity seems to actively damage girls' likeability. Mayeux and colleagues (2008) found that popularity in 10th grade predicted decreases in social acceptance for girls by 12th grade. This effect was not significant for boys.

Given that being well liked by peers is a strong predictor of positive adjustment throughout childhood and adolescence, it is important to consider why being popular has positive or neutral implications for boys (depending on their age) but is increasingly damaging to girls' social acceptance. On the basis of ethnographic work, we might suspect that this gender difference emerges because popular boys are more likeable than popular girls. As discussed, the quantitative research suggests that the role of gender in popularity is not as strong as suggested by the ethnographic research. Nevertheless, the quantitative studies provide at least partial support for the idea that popular boys may be especially likeable (e.g., in terms of having a good sense of humor and displaying less relational aggression), and perhaps these effects are strong enough to drive the gender difference in social acceptance. Moreover, as also discussed, more nuanced behavioral assessments might reveal stronger gender differences in quantitative studies that more closely parallel the ethnographies.

Another possibility is that gender differences in social acceptance are not due to differences in popular girls and boys themselves but rather to the reaction of their peers. The ethnographies suggest that girls have more aspirations of becoming popular (e.g., Eder, 1985), which could lay the groundwork for girls who achieve "popularity" to become disliked by other girls as a result of jealousy. This possibility is consistent with the "cycle of popularity" described by Eder (1985). As noted, Eder proposed that when girls become popular, other girls want to be their friends to increase their own popularity. However, when popular girls refuse friendship bids (which is inevitable given all the bids they receive), they are increasingly seen as stuck-up and, as a result, become increasingly disliked. It is feasible that this cycle of popularity does not occur with boys if they are less desperate to be popular. A direction for future research is to examine these predictions quantitatively. This research could track changes in popularity, social acceptance, and friendship nominations over short intervals (e.g., once a week) for a semester or school year to test whether there is a "cycle of popularity" for girls but not boys. Moreover, by assessing internalizing adjustment, such research could test whether popularity is more protective for boys than girls (e.g., Sandstrom & Cillessen, 2006), because popular boys reap the benefits of high social acceptance.

CONCLUSIONS AND FUTURE DIRECTIONS

A conceptualization of the social worlds of boys and girls as constituting two separate cultures may lead us to predict strong gender differences in the behavioral attributes that are associated with popularity. We might also wonder about the developmental implications of popularity with a focus on the distinct trajectories for boys and girls. Certainly, the prevailing sentiment from early qualitative studies would support such a focus. Nonetheless, a careful review of the quantitative studies on popularity reveals more similarities between genders than differences.

Despite the somewhat mixed pattern of findings in the developmental literature, we still contend that it is premature to remove consideration of gender effect from future research on popularity. We suspect that more nuanced assessments of behavior in quantitative studies (e.g., examining expressed attitudes toward school in addition to academic achievement, examining motivations for relational aggression) would shed new light on the role of gender. Research of this nature could potentially bring the quantitative work more in line with the qualitative research. In addition, much of the qualitative work was conducted between the 1970s and the early 1990s, whereas much of the quantitative work was conducted more recently. It also is possible that results from more contemporary qualitative work would be more in line with the quantitative findings.

A larger issue concerns the interpretation of nonsignificant effects. Of course, we must always guard against the temptation to accept the null hypothesis. There are a host of methodological issues that can result in ambiguous findings and lead researchers to underestimate meaningful group differences. We may overlook differences between boys and girls because of issues related to measurement and design. For now, we can only conclude that the available data are not sufficient to allow for strong conclusions regarding gender and popularity.

We further point out that research on popularity has not considered many of the behaviors for which gender differences are found with peers, which may be crucial for better understanding the role of gender. In doing so, simultaneously considering the constellation of behaviors that make up sex-linked interpersonal styles may be important. For example, a boy with a sex-typed interpersonal style may have a relatively large and interconnected social network, spend time in competitive sports and games, and engage in direct verbal and physical behaviors when he does aggress. He would not engage in long interactions with friends that are characterized by disclosure. A girl with a sex-typed style would display the reverse behavioral profile. It may be that individual behaviors in this constellation (e.g., self-disclosure) are not related to popularity. Nevertheless, the degree to which youth fit an overall sex-typed profile may predict popularity. Likewise, youth with gender atypical styles may be especially likely to be unpopular. Such findings would clearly fit within a "two-cultures" conceptualization of peer interactions.

Having a sex-typed interpersonal style that is predictive of popularity could facilitate gender socialization. According to social learning theories (e.g., Bussey & Bandura, 1999), individuals who observe others rewarded for behaving in particular ways are motivated to engage in those behaviors. Thus, if youth who see peers with sex-typed styles rewarded with high status could encourage them to adopt these styles in order to reap the same benefits.

Finally, with regard to outcomes, we must consider the possibility that outcomes of popularity for girls and boys that are seemingly similar may nevertheless have different implications for adjustment. For example, popularity predicted increased sexual activity similarly for girls and boys (Mayeux et al., 2008). Insofar as these behaviors are riskier for girls (i.e., the risk of pregnancy) and perceived more negatively by peers when enacted by girls (as a result of a double standard), then the true consequences of popularity would actually be worse for girls. It has been acknowledged previously that predicting the developmental trajectories of popular youth is challenging given that they display characteristics typical of both well-adjusted youth and at-risk youth (Cillessen & Rose, 2005). Predicting outcomes may be further complicated by the possibility that they are different for girls and boys. Considering these outcomes is a concern and a critical direction for future research given that many youth, of both genders, aspire to be popular.

ACKNOWLEDGMENT

During the preparation of this chapter, Amanda J. Rose was partially supported by National Institute of Mental Health Grant No. R01 MH 073590.

REFERENCES

Adler, P. A., & Adler, P. (1998). *Peer power: Preadolescent culture and identity.* New Brunswick, NJ: Rutgers University Press.

Adler, P. A., Kless, S. J., & Adler, P. (1992). Socialization to gender roles: Popularity among elementary school boys and girls. *Sociology of Education, 65,* 169–187.

Boyatzis, C. J., Baloff, P., & Durieux, C. (1998). Effects of perceived attractiveness and academic success on early adolescent peer popularity. *Journal of Genetic Psychology, 159,* 337–344.

Bussey, K., & Bandura, A. (1999). Social cognitive theory of gender development and differentiation. *Psychological Review, 106,* 676–713.

Card, N. A., Stucky, B. D., Sawalani, G. M., & Little, T. D. (2008). Direct and indirect aggression during childhood and adolescence: A meta-analytic review of gender differences, intercorrelations, and relations to maladjustment. *Child Development, 79,* 1185–1229.

Cillessen, A. H., & Mayeux, L. (2004). From censure to reinforcement: Developmental changes in the association between aggression and social status. *Child Development, 75,* 147–163.

Cillessen, A. H., & Rose, A. J. (2005). Understanding popularity in the peer system. *Current Directions in Psychological Science, 14,* 102–105.

Crick, N. R., & Grotpeter, J. K. (1995). Relational aggression, gender, and social-psychological adjustment. *Child Development, 66,* 710–722.

Eder, D. (1985). The cycle of popularity: Interpersonal relations among female adolescents. *Sociology of Education, 58,* 154–165.

Eder, D., Evans, C. C., & Parker, S. (1995). *School talk: Gender and adolescent culture.* New Brunswick, NJ: Rutgers University Press.

Eder, D., & Kinney, D. A. (1995). The effect of middle school extracurricular activities on adolescents' popularity and peer status. *Youth and Society, 26,* 298–324.

Estell, D. B., Farmer, T. W., Pearl, R., Van Acker, R., & Rodkin, P. C. (2008). Social status and aggressive and disruptive behavior in girls: Individual, group, and classroom influences. *Journal of School Psychology, 46,* 193–212.

Fagot, B. (1985). Beyond the reinforcement principle: Another step toward understanding sex role development. *Developmental Psychology, 21,* 1097–1104.

Gorman, A. H., Kim, J., & Schimmelbusch, A. (2002). The attributes adolescents associate with peer popularity and teacher preference. *Journal of School Psychology, 40,* 143–165.

Ladd, G. W. (1983). Social networks of popular, average, and rejected children in school settings. *Merrill-Palmer Quarterly, 29,* 283–307.

LaFontana, K. M., & Cillessen, A. H. N. (2002). Children's stereotypes of popular and unpopular peers: A multi-method assessment. *Developmental Psychology, 38,* 635–647.

Lease, A. M., Kennedy, C. A., & Axelrod, J. L. (2002). Children's social constructions of popularity. *Social Development, 11,* 87–109.

Maccoby, E. E. (1990). Gender and relationships: A developmental account. *American Psychologist, 45,* 513–520.

Maltz, D. N., & Borker, R. A. (1982). A cultural approach to male-female miscommunication. In J. J. Gumperz (Ed.), *Language and social identity* (pp. 195–216). New York: Cambridge University Press.

Mathur, R., & Berndt, T. J. (2006). Relations of friends' activities to friendship quality. *Journal of Early Adolescence, 26,* 365–388.

Mayeux, L., Sandstrom, M. J., & Cillessen, A. H. N. (2008). Is being popular a risky proposition? *Journal of Research on Adolescence, 18,* 49–74.

Merten, D. (1997). The meaning of meanness: Popularity, competition, and conflict among junior high school girls. *Sociology of Education, 70,* 175–191.

Paquette, J. A., & Underwood, M. K. (1999). Gender differences in young adolescents' experiences of peer victimization: Social and physical aggression. *Merrill-Palmer Quarterly, 45,* 242–266.

Parkhurst, J. T., & Hopmeyer, A. (1998). Sociometric popularity and peer-popularity: Two distinct dimensions of peer status. *Journal of Early Adolescence, 18,* 125–144.

Prinstein, M. J., & Cillessen, A. H. N. (2003). Forms and functions of adolescent peer aggression associated with high levels of peer status. *Merrill-Palmer Quarterly, 49,* 310–342.

Rodkin, P. C., Farmer, T. W., Pearl, R., & Van Acker, R. (2000). Heterogeneity of popular boys: Antisocial and prosocial configurations. *Developmental Psychology, 36,* 14–24.

Rose, A. J. (2002). Co-rumination in the friendships of girls and boys. *Child Development, 73,* 1830–1843.

Rose, A. J., & Rudolph, K. D. (2006). A review of sex differences in peer relationship processes: Potential trade-offs for the emotional and behavioral development of girls and boys. *Psychological Bulletin, 132,* 98–131.

Rose, A. J., Swenson, L. P., & Waller, E. M. (2004). Overt and relational aggression and popularity: Developmental differences in concurrent and prospective relations. *Developmental Psychology, 40,* 378–387.

Sandstrom, M. J., & Cillessen, A. H. N. (2006). Likeable versus popular: Distinct implications for adolescent adjustment. *International Journal of Behavioral Development, 30,* 305–314.

Schwartz, D., Gorman, A. H., Nakamoto, J., & McKay, T. (2006). Popularity, social acceptance, and aggression in adolescent peer groups: Links with academic performance and school attendance. *Developmental Psychology, 42,* 1116–1127.

Smith, T. E., & Leaper, C. (2005). Self-perceived gender typicality and the peer context during adolescence. *Journal of Research on Adolescence, 15,* 91–103.

Steinberg, L., Dornbusch, S. M., & Brown, B. B. (1992). Ethnic differences in adolescent achievement: An ecological perspective. *American Psychologist, 47,* 723–729.

Thorne, B. (1986). Girls and boys together ... but mostly apart: Gender arrangements in elementary schools. In W. W. Hartup & Z. Rubin (Eds.), *Relationships and development* (pp. 167–184). Hillsdale, NJ: Erlbaum.

Thorne, B. (1993). *Gender play: Girls and boys in school.* New Brunswick, NJ: Rutgers University Press.

Underwood, M. K. (2004). Gender and peer relations: Are the two gender cultures really all that different? In J. B. Kupersmidt & K. A. Dodge (Eds.), *Children's peer relations: From development to intervention* (pp. 21–36). Washington, DC: American Psychological Association.

Vaillancourt, T., & Hymel, S. (2006). Aggression and social status: The moderating roles of sex and peer-valued characteristics. *Aggressive Behavior, 32,* 396–408.

Wang, S. S., Houshyar, S., & Prinstein, M. J. (2006). Adolescent girls' and boys' weight-related health behaviors and cognitions: Associations with reputation- and preference-based peer status. *Health Psychology, 25,* 658–663.

Xie, H., Li, Y., Boucher, S. M., Hutchins, B. C., & Cairns, B. D. (2006). What makes a girl (or a boy) popular (or unpopular)? African American children's perceptions and developmental differences. *Developmental Psychology, 42,* 599–612.

Chapter 6

Popularity as a Form of Social Dominance

An Evolutionary Perspective

ANTHONY D. PELLEGRINI
CARY J. ROSETH
MARK J. VAN RYZIN
DAVID W. SOLBERG

In this chapter, we examine overlap between popularity and social dominance in school peer groups. As is discussed throughout this volume, popularity is a dimension of social standing that is characterized by visibility, prestige, and status with peers. Social dominance is a related process that is the product of naturally occurring differences in resource-control status among members of a group (de Waal, 1986; Hawley, 1999; Pellegrini, 2008). Informed by an evolutionary perspective, we contend that these aspects of social experience are linked through a common foundation in the strategic use of aggression.

The role of aggression in children's and adolescents' lives has often been conceptualized by developmental psychologists in terms of social-cognitive deficits. More specifically, aggression is viewed as a maladaptive behavior that is the product of faulty social information processing (e.g., the tendency to perceive benign stimuli as provocative). The infusion of evolutionary-oriented theory into the discussion has challenged such assumptions. The ubiquity of aggression among invertebrate and vertebrate species suggests that these behaviors are a product of natural selection and can be viewed as functional instead of indicative of a deficit (Archer, 1988). Thus, the proposition that aggression may have positive implications for some children or adolescents should not be rejected.

Research that is influenced by an evolutionary orientation has explained the functional dimensions of aggression in terms of social dominance. According to this work, a combination of aggressive and affiliative strategies predicts peer group centrality and control of social resources. We suggest that popularity involves similar processes, reflecting a behavioral style that simultaneously incorporates prosocial skills and effective use of aggression.

In both developmental psychology (e.g., Dodge, Coie, & Lynam, 2006) and ethology (McGrew, 1972), dimensions of peer affiliation, such as cooperative behavior, peer group centrality, and popularity, have traditionally been contrasted with aggression. Aggression is typically considered to have "dispersive" effects on social groupings, whereas affiliation keeps individuals together (e.g., McGrew, 1972). Correspondingly, the use of aggression in peer interactions, especially in middle childhood, has traditionally been linked to peer rejection (see Coie & Dodge, 1998). Aggression also negatively forecasts typical measures of peer affiliation, such as acceptance and peer group centrality (Coie & Dodge, 1998).

More recently, peer relations researchers (e.g., Cillessen & Mayeux, 2004; Hawley, Little, & Rodkin, 2007; Rodkin, Farmer, Pearl, & Van Acker, 2000; Schwartz, Gorman, Nakamoto, & McKay, 2006) and evolutionary-oriented psychologists (e.g., Cairns, Cairns, Neckerman, Gest, & Gariepy, 1988; Hawley, 1999; Pellegrini, 2008; Vaughn & Santos, 2007) have begun to reconsider associations between aggression and popularity. Accumulating evidence from this research indicates that aggression is *positively* related to dimensions of peer status indicative of social prominence and visibility. The role of aggression in social status, it has become clear, depends on what dimension of status is considered.

An organizing theme in this chapter is the role of aggression in social dominance and popularity. Our focus is primarily on studies that link aggression with popularity, conceptualized as a form of social dominance. We also review evidence that the role of aggression in enhancing or diminishing peer status depends on several other factors, including the form of the aggression (proactive vs. reactive), the co-occurrence of affiliative behaviors such as cooperation and reconciliation with the aggression, the type of social situation involved (contest vs. scramble competition), school transitions, and the history of the peer group in which the aggression takes place.

Distinctions between popularity and other forms of social status crystallize during the transition from middle childhood to adolescence (Cillessen & Mayeux, 2004). Reflecting this developmental pattern, popularity researchers have focused primarily on the later stages of childhood and adolescence. In contrast, ethological perspectives on social dominance have often emphasized preschool samples (perhaps because observational research methods are particularly viable with this age group). Our strategy is to extrapolate cautiously from earlier developmental stages to adolescence. Insofar as is appropriate, we use lessons from research conducted with preschoolers to generate hypotheses that are relevant for later stages of development.

POPULARITY AS SOCIAL DOMINANCE

Peer relations researchers have emphasized distinctions between the concepts of "being liked" (i.e., social acceptance) and "being highly visible" (i.e., popularity; e.g., Cillessen & Mayeux, 2004; Parkhurst & Hopmeyer, 1998). In contrast to being liked, popularity emphasizes social prominence, visibility, and peer reputational salience. Popular youth are viewed as cool, athletic, and influential in their grade. Importantly, popularity is also associated with physical and relational aggression (Adler & Adler, 1998; Cillessen & Mayeux, 2004; Farmer, Estell, Bishop, O'Neal, & Cairns, 2003; LaFontana & Cillessen, 2002; Parkhurst & Hopmeyer, 1998; Rodkin et al., 2000; Rose, Swenson, & Lockerd, 2003). This latter finding gives aggression a key role in differentiating between popularity as "being liked" and "being highly visible." Presumably, the effective use of aggression in the service of a larger goal, such as accessing heterosexual contacts in adolescence (e.g., Bukowski, Sippola, & Newcomb, 2000; Pellegrini & Long, 2007) or challenging adult norms (Moffitt, 1993), enhances one's peer group reputation and visibility, at the cost of diminished likeability (Schwartz & Gorman, Chapter 11, this volume).

More generally, relations among aggression, group salience, and popularity can be integrated if considered in terms of social dominance. Social dominance involves individuals competing for resources (Dunbar, 1988; Pellegrini, 2008). These competitions are realized at two levels of social abstraction: the dyad and the group (Hinde, 1978). In the dyadic case, aggression, in a variety of forms, is typically used in competitions for limited resources between same-sex children (Pellegrini et al., 2007) or adolescents (Pellegrini & Long, 2002, 2007). The results of these contests are defined in terms of winners (those accessing the resources) and losers (those who do not). From the outcomes of dyadic contests, group-level dominance hierarchies can be constructed (Savin-Williams, 1987; Strayer, 1980; Vaughn & Waters, 1981). For example, two children may be observed in the school playground, each trying to gain access to a swing. Child A pushes child B and A gains access to the swing. In this instance, child A is the winner and child B the loser. Such dyadic encounters determine *dominance relationships*. The number of dyadic contest wins in the group determines each group member's *dominance rank* or status in relation to the group. If child A defeats child B and B defeats C, the hierarchy is child A over B over C and is assumed to be transitive.

One of the assumed functions of these social dominance relationships is to minimize within-group aggression and the costs of within-group competition (de Waal, 1986; Hawley, 1999; McGrew, 1972; Pellegrini et al., 2007; Vaughn & Santos, 2007). Presumably, dominant and subordinate group members alike benefit from avoiding within-group aggression (Hawley & Little, 1999; Pellegrini, 2008). Use of aggression by dominant individuals is costly. If their status is already established, they have little to gain relative to what they may lose (e.g., injury, social sanction). Similarly, subordinate individuals' use of aggression has high costs, because they may be defeated and win nothing. It follows that, in the context of social dominance relationships, the goal of aggression is to maximize an individual's status, reputational salience, and "visibility" within the social group, with the function of reducing the chance of more serious aggression that will critically destabilize the group.

Scholars have noted the similarity between this social dominance process and the phenomenon of peer group popularity (see Schwartz & Gorman, Chapter 11, this volume). Consistently, they have measured dominance in terms of visibility in the group, or attention structure. In research with preschool children, dominance status has been operationally defined in terms of the number of peers looking at one child at various points in time (e.g., Chance, 1967; Pellegrini et al., 2007; Vaughn & Waters, 1981). In these studies, attention structure is indeed significantly correlated with winning dyadic disputes ($r = .34$ in Pellegrini et al., 2007), social dominance rank ($rs = .60–.68$ in LaFreniere & Charlesworth, 1983; $r = .40$ in Vaughn & Waters, 1981), observed cooperation ($r = .67$ in Pellegrini et al., 2007), and peer affiliation ($rs = .49–.60$ in LaFreniere & Charlesworth, 1983). To our knowledge, attention structure has not yet been used in studies of older children or adolescents. However, a related metric—the number of peers observed in the presence of a focal child—is positively and significantly correlated with primary school children's peer nominations for being athletic ($r = .29$) and teachers' rating of children for being good at games ($r = .24$; Pellegrini, Kato, Blatchford, & Baines, 2002). Correlations in adolescent samples (e.g., popularity's association with athleticism and leadership) further support the link between popularity and social dominance (e.g., Cillessen & Mayeux, 2004, 2007; Mayeux, Sandstrom, & Cillessen, 2008; Rodkin et al., 2000).

Although aggression is associated with social dominance (Hawley, 1999; Pellegrini, 2008) and popularity (Cillessen & Mayeux, 2004), there may be important differences in the implications of specific subtypes of aggressive behavior. The association between aggression and popularity–dominance also is influenced by the larger social and behavioral contexts. In the next sections, we examine how different forms of aggression (i.e., proactive and reactive) relate to social dominance and perceived popularity and then review these important contextual factors.

DO DIFFERENT FORMS OF AGGRESSION RELATE DIFFERENTLY TO POPULARITY?

Bullying in school can be viewed as a form of instrumental, or *proactive*, aggression used to attain dominance as students enter a new social group (Pellegrini & Bartini, 2001; Pellegrini, Bartini & Brooks, 1999; Rodkin et al., 2000). In contrast, *reactive* aggression involves angry, aggressive responses to peer provocation. Reactive aggression is typically seen in "aggressive victims" (also bully victims, provocative victims; Schwartz, 2000). These youth emerge as frequent victims of bullying but respond aggressively when provoked. Aggressive victims often have troubled backgrounds, including hostile or abusive treatment by caregivers. They also lack social competence and are at high risk for behavior problems at school (Schwartz, Proctor, & Chen, 2001).

The literature is somewhat unclear on the relationship between bullying and social dominance. Although reactive aggression is clearly related to rebuff by peers, the link between bullying or other forms of proactive aggression and peer status is more complex. Proactively aggressive children have been found to be popular in some studies (Rodkin et al., 2000). Other research suggests that proactively aggressive bullies may be popular only within a highly aggressive peer group and less popular with other students (Pellegrini et al., 1999). In a recent study with adolescents, de Bruyn and Cillessen (2009) found very clear positive associations between bullying and popularity, while controlling for social preference.

As part of a further effort to clarify these issues, we used person-centered analyses (e.g., von Eye & Bogat, 2006) to examine the associations among bullying, social dominance, popularity, and prosocial behavior in early adolescence. Our results (Van Ryzin & Pellegrini, in press) revealed different clusters of bullies and socially dominant youth. Specifically, some bullies were also high in social dominance while others were low. The high-bullying/low-dominance group appeared to be similar to the aggressive victims found in other research (Schwartz, 2000), given that they were frequently victimized, low in proactive aggression, and relatively high in reactive aggression. Moreover, these adolescents lacked social competence, which is consistent with extant theory (Pellegrini et al., 1999). Perhaps as a result of their tendencies toward reactively aggressive behavior, the high-bullying/low-dominance group was also highly disliked and had few peer-nominated friends (e.g., Dodge, 1991).

In contrast, a low-bullying/high-dominance group represented the opposite end of the spectrum. These youth were characterized by prosocial behavior, sophisticated peer communication skills, and low levels of aggression. They received frequent friendship nominations and were the most well-accepted group in school. Social acceptance, in this case, may be attributed in part to low bullying. In fact, the low-bullying/high-dominance group was significantly more well liked than the high-bullying/high-dominance group despite similar levels of social dominance. More likely, however, acceptance by peers was multiply determined by the combination of high social dominance, low bullying, and high prosocial behavior. The relatively high levels of peer communication of the low-bullying/high-dominance group may be indicative of their ability to verbally attenuate any damage done in dominance encounters. These findings suggest that youth who use proactive aggression effectively, in combination with prosocial behaviors to repair damage done in aggressive confrontations, tend to be well liked by peers as well as socially dominant (see also Cillessen & Mayeux, 2004). Thus, understanding the role of aggression in peer status most likely involves more than differentiating between different forms of aggression. The place of aggression in the larger behavioral stream must also be considered.

AFFILIATION AS A MODERATOR OF THE RELATION BETWEEN AGGRESSION AND PEER STATUS

The proposition that social dominance and popularity are not the result of aggression alone is widely accepted (e.g., Francis, 1988; Hawley & Little, 1999; Strayer, 1980). Indeed, the co-occurrence of aggressive and affiliative behaviors in social dominance and resource-control encounters has been clearly recognized by scholars of children's social development, at least since the publication of Blurton Jones's (1967) influential observational studies. Over the years, numerous scholars have concluded that social dominance is not simply a matter of "toughness"; rather, children use a combination of aggressive and affiliative behaviors (such as cooperation and reconciliations) to control resources, such as toys, treats, and peer attention (Hawley, 1999; La Freniere & Charlesworth, 1983; Pellegrini, 2008; Rowe, Maughan, Worthman, Costello, & Angold, 2004; Savin-Williams, 1987; Vaughn, Vollenweider, Bost, Azria-Evans, & Snider, 2003). Children using both of these strategies—so-called bistrategic resource controllers (e.g., Hawley, 2002)—are particularly adept in this regard and, as a consequence, enjoy increased levels of peer status, attention, and affiliation (Hawley, 2003; LaFreniere & Charlesworth, 1983; Pellegrini et al., 2007; Roseth et al., 2007).

The linking of aggression to positive social attributes in the service of resource control challenges traditional views of social competence. Still, the behavioral processes underlying this relation remain unclear. For example, does "bistrategic" merely imply that some youth use both strategies some of the time? Game theory leads us to expect that individuals' choices of behaviors during conflict are dynamic (Pusey & Packer, 1997; Stephens & Krebs, 1986). According to this view, individuals' initiations and responses are affected by information gained from preceding behaviors and anticipating future behaviors. From this perspective, it is important to examine sequences of behavior surrounding resource contests to determine not only how individuals access resources initially but also how they maintain their dominance after they win initially. In the next section, we present results from our work with preschoolers, where we took a closer look at behavioral sequences when aggressive and affiliative behaviors were used in establishing and maintaining social dominance. We emphasize those results concerned with children's use of reconciliatory strategies after aggression.

Moving to the context in which aggression is embedded, we have shown that aggression is related to dominance and popularity when it is used in concert with affiliative strategies, such as cooperative behavior. Yet it is not enough to merely say that they co-occur when there are recognizable and systematic contextual variations in their use, as we discuss. Even trait theorists recognize that this level of generality is not sufficient to invoke a trait or a combination of traits to explain the co-occurrence of aggressive and affiliative behaviors in social dominance and group leadership (Parten, 1933; Zaccaro, 2007).

One place to start is with postaggressive affiliations and reconciliations in competitive encounters. Postaggression reconciliation, although widely studied in nonhuman primates (Aureli, Cords, & van Schaik, 2002), has been understudied in children. The data that do exist suggest that after dominant children use aggression to control resources in contests, they follow up with an affiliative strategy (Pellegrini et al., 2007). It is not enough, however, to show that affiliation occurs after aggressive encounters. If postconflict affiliation is to be linked convincingly to the preceding aggressive bout, it must also be shown that affiliation occurs more often after competitive conflict than during free play and that it occurs selectively between former opponents (de Waal, 2000).

To test for reconciliation while controlling for these contingencies, de Waal and Yoshihara (1983) developed the post-conflict-matched control method, otherwise known as the *attracted-pairs* method. Using this method, Roseth (2006; Roseth et al., in press) showed evidence of preschoolers' reconciliation, with postconflict affiliation occurring selectively between former opponents, even after controlling for baseline rates of affiliation during free play. Results also showed that reconciliation was positively correlated with preschoolers' social dominance, supporting the view that dominant preschoolers reconcile strategically, using postconflict affiliation after winning contests as a way of keeping defeated peers as affiliates or simply so the latter will not defame them to peers or adults.

At the group level, these results support the view that combining coercive resource control with reconciliation increases group-level cohesion by bringing former opponents together more often than occurs in the absence of competitive bouts (de Waal, 1986, 2000). In other words, reconciliation allows interpersonal competition, even coercive, aggressive forms, to enhance peer affiliation by allowing peers to negotiate interpersonal conflict while avoiding alienation (de Waal, 2000; Pellegrini, 2008; Pellegrini et al., 2007; Roseth, 2006).

In a second study of preschoolers' social dominance and reconciliation (Pellegrini et al., in press), we sought to clarify these processes further by focusing on who, in the course of conflict resolution, initiated and who responded to reconciliatory attempts. We assessed children's dominance status by both the observed ratio of wins and teacher ratings of children's number of wins across all dyads in their classroom. Both dominance measures were significantly and positively correlated with initiating postcontest reconciliations (r's = .44 and .56, respectively) and with responding to others' reconciliations (r's = .35 and .40, respectively). The different magnitudes of these correlations favored the relation between dominance and initiating reconciliations over dominance and responding to reconciliations. Dominant children appear to be likely to initiate reconciliations, perhaps reflecting their strategic use of prosocial behaviors for resolution of conflicts. This strategy, or what Whiten and Byrne (1988) labeled "Machiavellian," is consistent with research by Sutton, Smith, and Swettenham (1999). Adding to the full picture, the tendency to initiate reconciliations correlated significantly with teacher ratings of children being deceptive ($r = .28$) but not accepting others' reconciliations.

The results also showed that initiating reconciliation after dominance bouts paid dividends in terms of liking by peers. Initiating reconciliations was significantly correlated with social acceptance ($r = .30$), but responding to reconciliations was not. Correspondingly, responding to reconciliations was significantly correlated with peer rejection ($r = .40$), but initiating reconciliations was not. These findings support the claim that high-status children tend to combine aggressive resource-control behaviors with initiating reconciliations with defeated peers to attenuate damage done to their peer status associated with using aggression. We cautiously predict that similar processes hold during the adolescent years, although relevant observational data are not yet available.

COMPETITIVE CONTEXTS: CONTEST VERSUS SCRAMBLE COMPETITION

Different forms of competition provide another dimension that influences which strategies children or adolescents use to access and maintain resources. There are two forms of competition that predict variations in aggressive and affiliative behaviors to access resources: *scramble* and *contest*. In scramble competition, resources are abundantly present to the extent that all group members get a share (Parker, 2000). Consequently, group members use "low-cost" affiliative strategies, such as cooperation, to access resources (Pellegrini, 2008; Pellegrini et al., 2007). When resources are abundant or "cheap," the use of "costly" strategies such as aggression is not efficient because its risks of injury and social sanction outweigh its benefits. In contest competitions, there are winners and losers, and the winners can "take all." In this case, aggression is more likely than cooperation because it is more likely to "pay off." Such a costly strategy is balanced by the relatively high value of the resources being contested, because they can be monopolized (Parker, 2000; Pellegrini, 2008; Pellegrini et al., 2007).

To our knowledge, only one study has examined the behavioral predictors of social dominance in scramble and contest competitions (Pellegrini et al., 2007). Contest wins were defined in terms of the ratio of dyadic wins: total dyadic resource contests observed across a school year as well as teacher ratings of children in hypothetical contest situations. The scramble measure was an experimental task, developed by Gunnar and colleagues to assess social dominance (e.g., Tarullo, Mliner, Gustafson, & Gunnar, 2003). This task is considered a scramble because all children get access to the resource.

Consistent with the predictions, children's observed cooperative behavior predicted access to resources in scramble competitions but not in contest competitions. Teacher ratings of social dominance (a measure of contest wins) were significantly related to observed wins but not to observed cooperation. These results support the view that scramble competitions elicit more affiliation than aggression, whereas the reverse might be true for contest competitions. They also support the idea that peers' positive regard for successful resource control may be attributed to the *strategic* combination of prosocial and coercive strategies in different competitive contexts.

In adolescence, a common, visible, and valued form of contest competition involves youth competing for access to opposite-sex relationships (Charlesworth, 1988; Low, 2000). Research from two studies of early adolescents making the transition from primary to middle school supports the hypothesis that boys' use of aggression relates to contact with the opposite sex, a dimension of perceived popularity that is especially salient during adolescent-related transitions (Schwartz & Gorman, Chapter 11, this volume). First, using diary-reported rates of aggression and peer nominations of invitations of opposite-sex peers to a hypothetical party, Pellegrini and Bartini (2001) found that boys' aggression predicted their being nominated by girls to a hypothetical party. Correspondingly, a significant relation was reported between peer nominations of aggression and opposite-sex friendship in a Canadian sample of adolescents (Bukowski et al., 2000). In both studies, the formation of new groups may have made aggression an especially appropriate male strategy to access heterosexual contact. In these studies, youth were either making the transition from primary to secondary school (Pellegrini & Bartini, 2001) or recently enrolled in secondary school (Bukowski et al., 2000). This may work not only for boys but also for girls. Cillessen and Mayeux (2004) found that girls' use of relational aggression before the transition from middle to high school predicted their higher popularity status in the first year of high school, controlling for earlier measures of peer status.

Another study of early adolescents' use of aggression to access heterosexual contact was conducted by Pellegrini and Long (2007), who directly observed middle school students (ages 12–14 years) at monthly dances across a school year, a prime but underutilized venue for studying heterosexual interaction (Low, 2000). Following sexual selection theory, Pellegrini and Long (2007) predicted that boys' use of aggression and girls' attractiveness would predict cross-sex contact at school dances. Interestingly, they found that aggression and attractiveness predicted cross-sex contact for adolescent girls and boys alike.

SCHOOL TRANSITIONS

School transitions (from primary to middle school and from middle to high school) and the corresponding history of group formation also illustrate how aggressive and affiliative behaviors relate differently to status with peers. Research in this tradition (e.g., Cillessen & Mayeux, 2007; Pellegrini & Long, 2002) has found that aggression increases with the transition to a new school and then decreases. Savin-Williams's (1987) studies of 12- to 17-year-olds at summer camp also found that rates of agonism (i.e., contests) were initially high but decreased with time, as youth came to know each other. These findings are consistent with the argument that adolescents' use of aggression during such transitions is an important predictor of social reputation. From this perspective, it is probably the case that aggression is strategically used to establish dominance in new social groupings, and once dominance is established, rates of aggression decrease (Pellegrini, 2008).

Similar patterns have been observed among preschoolers. Rates of efficacious aggression (i.e., the number of aggressive bouts that are effective in securing resources divided by the total number of aggressive bouts) increase across the first few months of school, when dominance is being established, and then decline after dominance is stable (Pellegrini et al., 2007; Roseth et al., 2007; Roseth et al., in press). As with early adolescents, these change trajectories in preschoolers' aggression also depend on social dominance, even when controlling for age, presumably reflecting the strategic use of aggression in establishing dominance and the strategic decline in aggression in order to maintain it.

In an effort to take a closer look at changing rates of aggression and affiliation during the primary to middle school transition, we examined predictors of social dominance during group stabilization (Pellegrini & Bartini, 2001). Aggression (self- and diary recorded) but *not* affiliation (peer nominations and self-reports) predicted a contest-oriented teacher measure of social dominance in the fall of 6th grade, the first term in a new school. In the spring of the 6th grade, both measures of affiliation and only one measure of aggression (diary report) predicted social dominance.

We have also documented time-related changes in the way preschoolers' social dominance and reconciliation correlated with social acceptance. During the fall term, reconciliation correlated positively with indicators of disliking by peers and social impact. Thus, high visibility in the fall seemed to come at the cost of social rejection. By the spring term, however, a positive correlation between reconciliation and friend nominations emerged. We hypothesized that decreasing coercion, ongoing high rates of affiliative behavior, and a history of reconciliation combined dynamically to buffer the effects of aggression and enhance peer liking. Supporting this view, being liked in the spring did not come at the cost of preschoolers' dominance. In fact, social dominance was positively associated with acceptance by peers across both fall and spring terms.

These findings point to the importance of the role of dynamic social ecologies in moderating the effects of aggression on peer status. Specifically, peers' liking of dominant peers may be attributed to the strategic combination of affiliative and aggressive behaviors in the service of controlling resources (de Waal, 1986; Hawley, 1999; Pellegrini, 2008; Roseth, 2006; Roseth et al., in press). The idea of resource control, however, is probably much too general to the extent that one set of strategies, such as aggression, may be used to access resources in contests, but another set of more affiliative strategies may be more successful in maintaining control of resources.

CONCLUSIONS

Researchers studying peer status and aggression are increasingly making analogies between popularity and social dominance. We have extended this discussion by stressing the importance of examining specific forms of aggression in the context of social dominance. Specifically, we have presented evidence that some forms of aggression are used strategically in contest competitions, especially in initial encounters as a group is being formed and dominance status is being negotiated. After resources are secured and children recognize their relative status in the group, aggression decreases and affiliation increases. In adolescence, Pellegrini and Bartini (2001) found these patterns across a school year. At a microanalytical level, Roseth's (2006; Roseth et al., in press) work with preschoolers, following de Waal's (1986) theorizing, demonstrates that dominant children, relatively soon after winning contest competitions with peers, engage in reconciliations. It may be that dominant children reconcile peers to keep them as allies, to form coalitions, or to achieve and maintain peer status. Future research should not only document the ways in which different strategies are used to control resources, including peer group visibility and popularity, but should make a distinction between accessing and maintaining control of resources. Both theory and data suggest that different strategies are invoked.

There are important methodological and theoretical implications of this discussion. First, following game theory, researchers wishing to understand the meaning and function of a behavior must begin to examine sequences of behavior within the dynamic social and behavioral contexts in which they occur, and not simply as summary variables aggregated across time. As demonstrated with observations of preschoolers, aggression may be used initially to access resources in contests, but within a few minutes the winners of these contests affiliate with their peers, often initiating reconciliations with them. Thus, it seems too simple to treat social behaviors as isolated variables impacting an outcome. Although this type of thinking fits neatly into regression models, it does not accurately model social interactive processes. The natural ecology of social interaction does not unfold in these terms; children's or adolescents' behaviors are contingent on the preceding behaviors of their peers as well as the anticipation of future behaviors. Although some theories, such as game theory, and indeed common sense point in this direction, our research methods and analytic strategies have yet to follow. Utilization of dynamic models with longitudinal data (e.g., Long & Pellegrini, 2003) provide important tools to examine the moderating roles of cooperation and reconciliation in trajectories of contest-related aggression. When aggression is examined in the dynamic contexts in which it is used, it is not only an unequivocal risk factor but also a predictor of popularity and social dominance.

REFERENCES

Archer, J. (1988). *The behavioural biology of aggression.* Cambridge, UK: Cambridge University Press.

Aureli, F., Cords, M., & van Schaik, C. P. (2002). Conflict resolution following aggression in gregarious animals: A predictive framework. *Animal Behaviour, 64,* 325–343.

Blurton Jones, N. G. (1967). An ethological study of some aspects of social behaviour of children in nursery school. In D. Morris (Ed.), *Primate ethology* (pp. 347–368). London: Weidenfeld & Nicolson.

Bukowski, W. M., Sippola, L. A., & Newcomb, A. F. (2000). Variations in patterns of attraction to same- and other-sex peers during early adolescence. *Developmental Psychology, 36*, 147–154.

Cairns, R. B., Cairns, B. D., Neckerman, H. J., Gest, S. D., & Gariepy, J.-L. (1988). Social networks and aggressive behavior. *Developmental Psychology, 24*, 815–823.

Chance, M. R. A. (1967). Attention structure as a basis for primate rank order. *Man, 2*, 503–518.

Charlesworth, W. R. (1988). Resources and resource acquisition during ontogeny. In K. MacDonald (Ed.), *Sociobiological perspectives on human development* (pp. 24–77). New York: Springer.

Cillessen, A. H. N., & Mayeux, L. (2004). From censure to reinforcement: Developmental changes in the association between aggression and social status. *Child Development, 75*, 147–163.

Cillessen, A. H. N., & Mayeux, L. (2007). Expectations and perceptions at school transitions: The role of peer status and aggression. *Journal of School Psychology, 45*, 567–586.

Coie, J. D., & Dodge, K. A. (1998). Aggression and antisocial behavior. In N. Eisenberg (Ed.), *Manual of child psychology, Vol. 3, Social, emotional, and personality development* (pp. 779–862). New York: Wiley.

de Waal, F. B. M. (1986). The integration of dominance and social bonding in primates. *Quarterly Review of Biology, 61*, 459–479.

de Waal, F. B. M. (2000). The first kiss. In F. Aureli & F. B. M. de Waal (Eds.), *Natural conflict resolution* (pp. 13–33). Berkeley: University of California Press.

de Waal, F. B. M., & Yoshihara, D. (1983). Reconciliation and redirected affection in rhesus monkeys. *Behaviour, 85*, 224–241.

Dodge, K. A., Coie, J. D., & Lynam, D. (2006). Aggression and antisocial behavior in youth. In W. Damon (Series Ed.) & N. Eisenberg (Vol. Ed.), *Handbook of child psychology, Vol. 3: Social, emotional, and personality development* (6th ed.). New York: Wiley.

Dunbar, R. I. M. (1988). *Primate social systems.* Ithaca, NY: Cornell University Press.

Francis, R. C. (1988). On the relationship between aggression and dominance. *Ethology, 78*, 223–237.

Hawley, P. H. (1999). The ontogenesis of social dominance: A strategy-based evolutionary perspective. *Developmental Review, 19*, 97–132.

Hawley, P. H. (2003). Prosocial and coercive configurations of resource control in early adolescence. *Merrill-Palmer Quarterly, 49*, 279–309.

Hawley, P. H., & Little, T. D. (1999). On winning some and losing some: A social relations approach to social dominance in toddlers. *Merrill-Palmer Quarterly, 45*, 185–214.

Hawley, P. H., Little, T. D., & Rodkin, P. C. (Eds.). (2007). *Aggression and adaptation: The bright side of bad behavior.* Mahwah, NJ: Erlbaum.

Hinde, R. A. (1978). Dominance and role. Two concepts with two meanings. *Journal of Social Biology Structure, 1,* 27–38.

LaFreniere, P. J., & Charlesworth, W. R. (1983). Dominance, attention, and affiliation in a preschool group: A nine-month longitudinal study. *Ethology and Sociobiology, 4,* 55–67.

Long, J. D., & Pellegrini, A. D. (2003). Studying change in dominance and bullying with linear mixed models. *School Psychology Review, 32,* 401–417.

Low, B. S. (2000). *Why sex matters: A Darwinian look at human behavior.* Princeton, NJ: Princeton University Press.

Mayeux, L., Sandstrom, M. J., & Cillessen, A. H. N. (2008). Is being popular a risky proposition? *Journal of Research on Adolescence, 18,* 49–74.

McGrew, W. C. (1972). *An ethological study of children's behaviour.* London: Methuen.

Moffitt, T. E. (1993). Adolescent-limited and life-course-persistent anti-social behavior: A developmental taxonomy. *Psychological Review, 100,* 674–701.

Parker, G. A. (2000). Scramble in behaviour and ecology. *Philosophical Transactions of the Royal Society of London, 355,* 1637–1645.

Parten, M. (1933). Leadership among preschool children. *Journal of Abnormal and Social Psychology, 27,* 430–440.

Pellegrini, A. D., Van Ryzin, M., Bohn-Gettler, C., Dupuis, D., Hickey, D., Roseth, C., & Solberg, D. (in press). Behavioral and Social Cognitive Processes in Preschool Children's Social Dominance. *Aggressive Behavior.*

Pellegrini, A. D. (2008). The roles of aggressive and affiliative behaviors in resource control: A behavioral ecological perspective. *Developmental Review, 28,* 461–487.

Pellegrini, A. D., & Bartini, M. (2001). Dominance in early adolescent boys: Affiliative and aggressive dimensions and possible functions. *Merrill-Palmer Quarterly, 47,* 142–163.

Pellegrini, A. D., Bartini, M., & Brooks, F. (1999). School bullies, victims, and aggressive victims: Factors relating to group affiliation and victimization in early adolescence. *Journal of Educational Psychology, 91,* 216–224.

Pellegrini, A. D., Kato, K., Blatchford, P., & Baines, E. (2002). A short-term longitudinal study of children's playground games across the first year of school: Implications for social competence and adjustment to school. *American Educational Research Journal, 39,* 991–1015.

Pellegrini, A. D., & Long, J. D. (2002). A longitudinal study of bullying, dominance, and victimization during the transition from primary to secondary school. *British Journal of Developmental Psychology, 20,* 259–280.

Pellegrini, A. D., & Long, J. D. (2007). An observational study of early heterosexual interaction at middle school dances. *Journal of Research in Adolescence, 17,* 613–638.

Pellegrini, A. D., Roseth, C. J., Mliner, S., Bohn, C. M., Van Ryzin, M., Vance, N., et al. (2007). Social dominance in preschool classrooms. *Journal of Comparative Psychology, 121,* 54–64.

Pusey, A. E., & Packer, C. (1997). The ecology of relationships. In J. Krebs & N.

B. Davies (Eds.), *Behavioural ecology: An evolutionary approach* (4th ed., pp. 254–283). Oxford, UK: Blackwell.

Rodkin, P. C., Farmer, T. W., Pearl, R., & Van Acker, R. (2000). Heterogeneity of popular boys: Antisocial and prosocial configurations. *Developmental Psychology, 36,* 14–24.

Roseth, C. J. (2006). *Effects of peacekeeping and peacemaking on preschoolers' conflict: A multi-method longitudinal study.* Unpublished doctoral thesis, University of Minnesota, Twin Cities.

Roseth, C. J., Pellegrini, A. D., Dupuis, D. N., Bohn, C. M., Hickey, M. C., Hilk, C. L., & Peshkam, A. (In press). Preschoolers' bistrategic resources control, reconciliation, and peer regard. *Social Development.*

Rowe, R., Maughan, B., Worthman, C. M., Costello, E. J., & Angold, A. (2004). Testosterone, antisocial behavior, and social dominance in boys: Pubertal development and biosocial interaction. *Biological Psychiatry, 55,* 546–552.

Savin-Williams, R. C. (1987). *Adolescence: An ethological perspective.* New York: Springer.

Schwartz, D. (2000). Subtypes of aggressors and victims in children's peer groups. *Journal of Abnormal Child Psychology, 28,* 181–192.

Schwartz, D., Gorman, A. H., Nakamoto, J., & McKay, T. (2006). Popularity, social acceptance, and aggression in adolescent peer groups: Links with academic performance and school attendance. *Developmental Psychology, 42,* 1116–1127.

Stephens, D. W., & Krebs, J. R. (1986). *Foraging theory.* Princeton, NJ: Princeton University Press.

Strayer, F. F. (1980). Social ecology of the preschool peer group. In W. A. Collins (Ed.), *Minnesota symposium on child development* (Vol. 13, pp. 165–196). Hillsdale, NJ: Erlbaum.

Sutton, J., Smith, P. K., & Swettenham, J. (1999). Social cognition and bullying: Social inadequacy or skilled manipulation. *British Journal of Developmental Psychology, 17,* 435–450.

Van Ryzin, M., & Pellegrini, A. D. (in press). Socially competent and incompetent aggressors in middle school: The non-linear relation between bullying and dominance in middle school. *Aggressive Behavior.*

Vaughn, B. E., & Santos, A. J. (2007). An evolutionary-ecological account of aggressive behavior and trait aggression in human children and adolescents. In P. H. Hawley, T. D. Little, & P. C. Rodkin (Eds.), *Aggression and adaptation: The bright side of bad behavior* (pp. 31–64). Mahwah, NJ: Erlbaum.

Vaughn, B. E., Vollenweider, M., Bost, K. K., Azria-Evans, M. R., & Snider, J. B. (2003). Negative interactions and social competence for preschool children in two samples: Reconsidering the interpretation of aggressive behavior for young children. *Merrill-Palmer Quarterly, 49,* 245–278.

Vaughn, B. E., & Waters, E. (1981). Attention structure, sociometric status, and dominance: Interrelations, behavioral correlates, and relationships to social competence. *Developmental Psychology, 17,* 275–288.

von Eye, A., & Bogat, G. A. (2006). Person-oriented and variable-oriented research: Concepts, results, and development. *Merrill-Palmer Quarterly, 52,* 390–420.

Whiten, A., & Byrne, R. W. (1988). The manipulation of attention in primate tactical deception. In R. W. Byrne & A. Whiten (Eds.), *Machiavellian intelligence: Social expertise and the evolution of intellect in monkeys, apes, and humans* (pp. 207–233). Oxford, UK: Clarendon.

Zaccaro, S. J. (2007). Trait-based perspectives of leadership. *American Psychologist, 62,* 6–16.

Chapter 7
Prosocial Skills, Social Competence, and Popularity

JULIE WARGO AIKINS
SCOTT D. LITWACK

The peer group is a critical context for social and emotional development in childhood and adolescence. Researchers have focused extensively on the implications of peer relationships for adjustment and their developmental significance in general. Much of this attention has been concerned with peer rejection, demonstrating a link between a lack of adequate peer relationships and later maladaptive outcomes (e.g., delinquency, school dropout, externalizing disorders; see, for a review, Bierman, 2004). Considerable effort has also been directed toward exploring the implications and significance of positive relationships with peers, expressed in peer acceptance and popularity as defined by Cillessen and Marks (Chapter 2, this volume).

An important conclusion from early work on positive peer relations is that children and adolescents who are well accepted by their peers score high on prosocial tendencies and other dimensions of social competence. Research on the behavioral, cognitive, and emotional correlates of peer acceptance has highlighted the role of social skills. Generally, the most highly liked youth are cooperative, socially skilled, and unaggressive.

As investigators expanded their focus on positive peer relationships or high status in the peer group to include popularity in addition to acceptance, a more complex picture began to emerge. This research has shown that, unlike acceptance, popularity is not associated exclusively with positive features but rather has a mixed set of correlates (see Cillessen & Rose, 2005). Not surprisingly, there are associations between popularity and various dimensions of social competence. However, more unexpectedly, antisocial attributes, and especially some forms of aggression, also emerged as correlates of popularity. The realization that aggression can sometimes be associated with high peer group status motivated new research. A central theme in the resulting body of literature has been the role of aggression and other forms of disruptive behavior in the social lives of popular youth (see Mayeux, Houser, & Dyches, Chapter 4, this volume).

Because popularity researchers have subsequently emphasized aggression as a pathway to high status in the peer group, the role of social competence and prosociability that initially motivated research on positive peer relationships has been underestimated or underemphasized in recent research on popularity. The goal of the current chapter is to correct this view and bring back into focus the idea that popularity is a balance that also includes prosocial skills. As part of this effort, we present a theoretical model that summarizes the link between prosocial skills and popularity. A broad definition of social competence is needed to fully understand the processes underlying popularity. In this conceptualization, the *effectiveness of social interaction* is the defining feature.

In the absence of an extensive body of findings on the role of social competence in popularity, the literature on the social competence determinants of peer acceptance is used for our initial hypotheses. A central theme of this volume is that acceptance and popularity are not equivalent dimensions of the peer group (Cillessen & Marks, Chapter 2, and Mayeux et al., Chapter 4, this volume). Nonetheless, research on well-accepted children and adolescents does offer important insights into the nature of social competence that can be used to understand popularity.

BEHAVIORAL COMPONENTS OF SOCIAL COMPETENCE

We begin by identifying the behavioral components of social competence. What do we mean when we describe a child or adolescent as "socially skilled" or "socially competent?" Rubin, Bukowski, and Parker (1998) defined social skills as "discrete behaviors that lead children to solve social tasks or achieve social success" (p. 644). Behavioral attributes that may be part of this conceptualization are prosociability, assertiveness, self-control, and successful peer group entry. These specific skills are supported by a child's social knowledge and emotional functioning, two areas that we believe are also important for popularity.

Prosociability is a critical aspect of social competence with peers. Social psychologists conceptualize prosocial behavior as being characterized by empathy, concern for others, and interest in enhancing personal relationships (e.g., Twenge, Baumeister, DeWall, Ciarocco, & Bartels, 2007). These characteristics lay the groundwork for achieving interpersonal goals and maintaining relationships (Newcomb, Bukowski, & Patee, 1993). Indeed, children or adolescents who are cooperative, helpful, and willing to share are typically positively evaluated by their peers (Coie & Dodge, 1988; Coie & Kupersmidt, 1983; Hartup, Glazer, & Charlesworth, 1967; Walker, 2004; Wentzel, 2003).

Of course, social competence involves more than just taking the perspective of others. Socially skilled children or adolescents must also be able to attend assertively to their own needs. Social competence involves a range of assertive and sociable attributes that enhance functioning in peer group interactions. Some relevant behaviors might include asking others for information, introducing oneself, and initiating contact. These assertive strategies can foster individuals' own social objectives while maintaining an awareness of the rights of others.

Self-control refers to the capacities of children and adolescents to cope with changing circumstances and respond flexibly to provocative stimuli. Capacities to focus on longer term objectives (e.g., getting along with others) and ignore prepotent responses (i.e., behaviors that shaped by short-term reinforcers) are also central to self-control. An example is responding appropriately to teasing or bullying (Maag, Vasa, Reid, & Torrey, 1995; Stuart, Gresham, & Elliot, 1991). In fact, well-accepted children tend to cope adaptively with provocations such as a peer breaking a personal possession (Matson, Esveldt-Dawson, & Kazdin, 1983).

Self-control, assertiveness, and sociability all contribute to success in peer group entry bids (Putallaz & Wasserman, 1990). Socially skilled youth can patiently read the goals and activities of a group before attempting to join it and are accordingly effective in smooth entry attempts (Dodge, Schlundt, Schocken, & Delugach, 1983; Putallaz, 1983; Putallaz & Gottman, 1981; Putallaz & Wasserman, 1989). Such youth also imitate the group's actions and contribute only relevant conversation. The outcome of their general approach is blending into the group rather than disrupting the existing interaction (Dodge et al., 1983; Putallaz & Gottman, 1981).

It should be recognized that the meaning of some of these specific skills might differ by gender. Sebanc, Pierce, Cheatham, and Gunnar

(2003) showed that boys and girls develop unique "cultures." As a result, the outcomes of specific behaviors depend on the gender composition of a peer group. In a task in which four peers had to negotiate preferred and unpreferred roles, assertiveness (indicated by commands and demands) was a positive predictor of acceptance for boys but a negative predictor for girls (Sebanc et al., 2003). Others have found that girls are more skilled than boys on general measures of social skill (e.g., responding appropriately to various situations; Achenbach & Edelbrock, 1983; Gresham & Elliott, 1990; Matson et al., 1983).

A larger question concerns the components of social competence that are specifically relevant for popularity. As indicated, existing conceptualizations of social competence have focused on peer acceptance and emphasized prosocial tendencies. Popularity may require a different constellation of skills. For example, social acceptance is associated with a patient and deferential peer entry style (Putallaz & Wassserman, 1990). In contrast, the status that popular youth have established may afford them the ability to be more forceful in disrupting the stream of ongoing interaction. As a result, they may be less attentive to group dynamics and enter in a manner that calls attention to themselves, their thoughts, and their interests. Such behavior may be effective to maintain one's position in the peer hierarchy. Youth who are both well accepted and popular may exhibit more considerate and accommodating initiation behaviors.

There is also evidence that prosocial behaviors are more closely associated with acceptance than popularity. Popular children and adolescents do engage in high rates of cooperative and sociable behavior (LaFontana & Cillessen, 2002; Xie, Li, Boucher, Hutchins, & Cairns, 2006). However, Sandstrom and Cillessen (2006) found that, when controlling for peer acceptance, popularity was not uniquely associated with these prosocial behaviors.

Another factor in the effects of particular behaviors on acceptance and popularity is group context. Peer group norms and expectations influence how behavior is perceived. Prosocial behaviors that lead to peer acceptance may not be the valued behaviors that lead to popularity in the same peer group. For instance, attempting to be liked by *all* classmates may not fit with the value of exclusivity in the popular group. In her ethnography of middle school girls, Eder (1985) described how popular girls ignored the social overtures of less popular peers. By encouraging social aggression and discouraging friendliness and interpersonal sensitivity, popular girls created and sustained power. The controlled use of prosocial behavior (e.g., deciding when to use it and toward whom) may be key in creating popularity.

UNDERLYING PROCESSES

Social-Cognitive Competencies

To elaborate the theoretical perspectives on the nature of social competence, the underlying mechanisms are critical to consider. One relevant area of inquiry is the literature on social-cognitive processes (e.g., Ladd & Mize, 1983; Rubin & Krasnor, 1986). Crick and Dodge (1994) posited a multistep processing sequence to explain individual differences in socially competent behavior. According to this model, children and adolescents enter social situations with predispositions based on previous experiences and biological capabilities. As they receive social cues from the environment, they generate and evaluate behavioral responses and strategies based on their interpretation of the situation and their social goals. The outcome of this process determines whether or not youth's predominant behavioral response styles are prosocial in orientation (e.g., Ladd & Oden, 1979; Renshaw & Asher, 1983; Richard & Dodge, 1982).

Although much of the social information-processing literature has focused on rejected and aggressive youth (e.g., Bierman, 1986; Renshaw & Asher, 1983), it has also examined the youth who are well liked by their peers (e.g., Asher & Renshaw, 1981; Gottman, Gonso, & Rasmussen, 1975; Ladd & Oden, 1979). Across each processing step, differences have been found between accepted children and their peers, supporting the hypothesis that skillful social information processing contributes to positive peer outcomes.

The initial mental representations of children's social selves and their social worlds determine how they attend to, encode, and interpret social cues (Crick & Dodge, 1994). Accepted children have higher social self-concept and perceived competence (Chambliss, Muller, Hulnick, & Wood, 1978; Kurdek & Krile, 1982; Patterson, Kupersmidt, & Griesler, 1990) and a broader interpersonal understanding (Kurdek & Krile, 1982) than less accepted children. Social schemas of competence bolster accepted children's feelings of efficacy and enable them to attend to and encode social cues. Keane and Parrish (1992) found that accepted children made better use of affective cues to explain hypothetical peers' intentions than rejected children, whose interpretations were based on their own biases rather than on actual information (e.g., a peer's affect). The ability to use social cues allows well-accepted children to respond to their peers in appropriate ways and adjust their behavior if needed.

With higher interpersonal understanding, well-accepted children may have a broader context in which to place their social experiences and, therefore, may be able to interpret them more accurately. Rejected children use biased processing in their interpretation of social information. For example, they attribute hostile intentions to peers' behaviors in ambiguous situations (e.g., Dodge & Frame, 1982; Dodge & Somberg, 1987), whereas well-accepted children attribute benign intentions (Dodge, Murphy, & Buchsbaum, 1984). By appraising these situations in a nonhostile way, and feeling confident that prosocial behaviors can lead to positive outcomes (Pettit, Harrist, Bates, & Dodge, 1991), well-liked children are primed to construct prosocial goals and generate positive strategies to reach them.

Among accepted youth, social knowledge and understanding contribute to the generation of solutions and goals and the subsequent enactment of effective strategies to implement the solutions (Renshaw & Asher, 1983; Wentzel & Erdley, 1993). Social goals motivate and direct social behavior. If children choose inappropriate goals, their behaviors to achieve them will be maladaptive as well (Crick & Dodge, 1994; Jarvinen & Nicholls, 1996; Renshaw & Asher, 1983; Wentzel & Erdley, 1993). Accepted children's social goals are characterized by the desire to maintain or enhance existing relationships and form new ones (Rubin et al., 1998). Well-accepted children also generate more and higher quality solutions that are prosocial, assertive, relevant, and adaptive (Asarnow & Callan, 1985; Ladd & Oden, 1979, Richard & Dodge, 1982). For instance, well-accepted children identify friendly-assertive strategies as leading to relationship enhancement and conflict resolution (Hart, Ladd, & Burleson, 1990).

Crick and Ladd (1990) found that both rejected and accepted children engaged in assertive and controlling strategies. Coie and Kupersmidt (1983) found that the prosocial nature of accepted children's strategies and their emphasis on setting norms for social behavior contributed to their acceptance. Importantly, the impact of strategy knowledge on peer acceptance may be mediated by social behavior. Understanding and selecting competent strategies may contribute to adaptive social behaviors, which then promote higher levels of peer acceptance. In contrast, strategy knowledge deficits are associated with aggressive and antisocial behaviors that undercut peer acceptance and contribute to rejection (Wentzel & Erdley, 1993).

To date, limited research has examined social-cognitive differences among popular youth. Only one study demonstrated a positive association between peer-rated social intelligence (social awareness, social skills, and social information processing) and popularity (Andreou, 2006). Therefore, it is unclear whether popular youth process and interpret social cues differently than their nonpopular peers and whether this results in different attributions or outcome expectations for peer behavior. However, it has been theorized (LaFontana & Cillessen, 1998) that popular youth may demonstrate *particularly well developed and sophisticated* social-cognitive skills that allow them to simultaneously use aggression (to manipulate the peer group and attain high status) and prosocial behaviors (to mitigate the negative ramifications of the aggression). Thus, popular youth may demonstrate quantifiably different approaches than their peers in terms of goal selection, strategy generation, and strategy evaluation.

Akin to this idea of advanced social-cognitive skills potentiating "social success," Sutton, Smith, and Swettenham (1999) suggested that bullies may achieve power (potentially a form of social success) in the peer group through advanced social-cognitive skills that allow them to accurately assess and respond to situational demands. This notion challenges the idea that bullies have impoverished social information processing and theory of mind. Sutton and colleagues (1999) proposed that relational bullying requires an understanding of the social context and strategic choices of allies and targets.

Research on bistrategic resource controllers and Machiavellianism also provides insight into the parallel role of social goals and strategies for popular children. Hawley and colleagues (Hawley, 2002; Hawley, Little, & Card, 2007; Hawley, Little, & Pasupathi, 2002) have suggested that children's competition for resources and group dominance contributes to the adoption of prosocial, coercive, or bistrategic (a combination of prosocial and coercive) approaches. Through the use of both prosocial and coercive strategies, bistrategists attain their instrumental goals in a manner that is "prosocial enough" to mitigate the potentially negative repercussions of their coercive behaviors. Although socially accepted individuals who use primarily prosocial behaviors are believed to be driven by intrinsic motivations of achieving pleasure and feeling self-fulfillment, bistrategists are believed to be inspired by both these intrinsic goals and the extrinsic goal of attaining power and popularity.

Sutton et al.'s (1999) and Hawley's (2002) theories lead to the hypothesis that although accepted and popular children may engage in the same prosocial behaviors, these behaviors may serve different goals and may be mediated by different cognitions. The prosocial behaviors of well-accepted children may be motivated by the desire to solve interpersonal problems and facilitate positive interactions. The prosocial behaviors of popular youth may be meant to ease the negative impact of their coercive behaviors and promote the achievement of even higher status.

The differential use of prosocial and aggressive behavior may also characterize different subtypes of popularity.

Emotional Functioning

Key processes of social competence also include emotional functioning. Youth's capacities to read others' emotional states, to recognize and effectively communicate their own emotions, and to modulate negative affect are central for interactions with peers. Whereas socially competent behavior is supported by adaptive functioning in this domain, difficulties in emotional understanding and regulation set the stage for less desirable interactions with peers.

Children's ability to identify other's emotions through nonverbal facial expressions (Edwards, Manstead, & MacDonald, 1984; Mostow, Izard, Fine, & Tretacosta, 2002), vocal tone (Leppänen & Hietanen, 2001; Nowicki & Duke, 1992), and situational cues (Denham, McKinley, Couchoud, & Holt, 1990; Goldman, Corsini, & deUrioste, 1980; Rubin & Maioni, 1975) has been linked to positive social outcomes across development. Accurate identification of others' emotions is a core component of a prosocial disposition (Eisenberg et al., 1997; Mostow et al., 2002; Rubin, Coplan, Fox, & Calkins, 1995) and facilitates positive interactions (Campos, Mumme, Kermonian, & Campos, 1994; Miller et al., 2005). Correct decoding of emotions potentiates interpersonal responsivity, guides appropriate reactions to peers, and allows youth to adjust their behavior to the situation. Misperceptions result in behaviors that "miss their mark" (Edwards et al., 1984; Mostow et al., 2002).

A related set of capacities involves recognizing and communicating one's own emotional state. The ability to accurately express underlying emotional states can enhance functioning with peers and contribute to the communication of needs (e.g., for support in case of sadness) rather than leaving a peer guessing about the emotional undertone of the interaction (Miller et al., 2005). In contrast, children who have difficulties expressing their feelings verbally sometimes use aggression as an outlet for their emotional state (Casey, 1996; Olson, 1992).

Not only must children and adolescents be able to gauge their behaviors in response to their peers' emotions, but they must also regulate their internal experience and external display of emotions to support socially competent behavior (Hubbard & Dearing, 2004). Indeed, successful emotion regulation consistently predicts positive social outcomes with peers (Cole, Zahn-Waxler, Fox, Usher, & Welsh, 1996; Denham et al., 1990; Eisenberg et al., 1993; Hubbard, 2001). By modulating behavioral expressions of feelings and impulses, shifting attention toward or away from provocative stimuli, and activating or inhibiting behavior in the service of emotion regulation, children are better able to engage in adaptive social behaviors.

Not surprisingly, researchers have found that efficient emotion regulation is linked to peer acceptance. Denham et al. (1990) found that peer acceptance was positively related to well-modulated displays of happiness and negatively related to anger in young children. Likewise, the ability to regulate anger in response to provocations using less aggressive and more verbally mediated coping is associated with acceptance (Eisenberg, Fabes, Nyman, Bernzweig, & Pinuelas, 1994; Fabes & Eisenberg, 1992).

Although the association between emotional functioning and socially competent behavior has been explored extensively in research on social acceptance, less is known with specific regard to the determinants of popularity. Nonetheless, we expect that emotional knowledge, understanding, and regulation would be important correlates of popularity. These capacities can contribute to the savviness that characterizes popular youth and facilitate socially competent behavioral strategies that mitigate the negative impact of their deliberate use of aggression. Of course, popular youth will likely use their skills in this domain to reach a very specific set of social goals. Their abilities to regulate and express emotion could foster control of the social environment and help promote their status in the peer group.

We speculate that popularity will require children and adolescents to use their regulatory capacities in very purposeful ways. Display rules for the optimal expression of affect (Cole, Zahn-Waxler, & Smith, 1994; Underwood, Coie, & Herbsman, 1992) can play an important role in the pursuit and maintenance of popularity. Popular youth may be particularly good at keeping their own emotions in check while exhibiting the emotion that is most beneficial in a given context. Consider, for example, a popular early adolescent who feels disappointment after losing a game but exhibits indifference as a way of showing that he is "too cool" for the situation.

The strategic and instrumental use of aggression by popular youth could be another example of successful affect regulation. In this case, aggression would not be driven by impulsive anger, but rather would reflect a modulated and goal-driven strategy to reach goals (i.e., achieve dominance in the peer group). Likewise, popular children and adolescents may use their emotional understanding to optimize the outcomes associated with aggression. For example, they may understand when a peer is particularly vulnerable and use it to aggress or manipulate this person to their own advantage.

Although much remains to be learned, we contend that the aspects of emotional functioning discussed in this section play a critical role in the socially competent behavior of popular youth. Further research exploring the implication of emotion regulation and expression seems warranted. In the meantime, the absence of theorizing and empirical work examining the link of these processes to popularity represents a significant gap in the extant literature.

DEVELOPMENTAL TRAJECTORIES

Changing Relations between Prosocial Skills and Popularity

So far, our discussion of the association between social competence and popularity has not emphasized development. We have described the behavioral components of social skills and generated hypotheses regarding the underlying mechanisms. For the most part, we have generalized across childhood and adolescence and have not emphasized developmental changes On the one hand, there may be some constancy of the skills of high-status youth across development. On the other hand, the association between social skills and popularity may not be entirely invariant across development either. Indeed, evidence suggests that there are significant shifts in the nature and implications of social competence beginning in adolescence.

Changing associations between acceptance and popularity might provide important clues regarding developmental transitions. Researchers have consistently reported associations between acceptance and popularity and their overlapping correlates (e.g., Cillessen & Mayeux, 2004; Parkhurst & Hopmeyer, 1998; Sandstrom & Cillessen, 2006), but the concordance between acceptance and popularity appears to attenuate across development. In their 5-year longitudinal study, Cillessen and Mayeux (2004) found that the correlation between acceptance and popularity decreased dramatically from .52 in middle childhood to .15 in early adolescence. We suggest that social, cognitive, and contextual changes underlie this shifting association.

Throughout development, prosocial behavior is a critical determinant of acceptance by peers. During early childhood, prosocial behavior is also a primary predictor of popularity. By early adolescence, however, aggression, deviance, and dominant behaviors emerge as more powerful markers of popularity (Allen, Weissberg, & Hawkins, 1998; Bukowski,

Sippola, & Newcomb, 2000). At the same time, prosociability is increasingly less predictive of popularity. Thus, adolescence appears to bring divergence in the predictors of popularity and acceptance.

Findings by Xie, Li, Boucher, Hutchins, and Cairns (2006) are consistent with the developmental pattern we are hypothesizing. Using the methodology of LaFontana and Cillessen (2002), they asked first, fourth, and seventh graders to describe the attributes of popular children. First graders defined popularity in terms of prosocial behavior, peer acceptance, and companionship. By fourth grade, children had a clear conception of popularity and its association with attractiveness, self-presentation, being a good student, and prosociability. In seventh grade, aggression, attractiveness, self-presentation, extracurricular activity involvement, social connectedness, and the popularity of one's friends played additional roles. These findings suggest that popularity is not well defined in early childhood because group inclusion is an overriding mandate from adult caregivers (e.g., "We don't say 'You can't play'"), and notions of power and visibility are not salient. However, as children get older and play a more directive role in their own peer interactions without the high level of management by adults, other social factors move to center stage. Because of this shift, prosocial tendencies become a less significant aspect of the social landscape, at least in terms of determining the social hierarchy.

At the same time, children's growing cognitive abilities allow them a more nuanced understanding of popularity. Adolescents begin to understand that acceptance and popularity can be distinct, and that pursuing acceptance or popularity represents two separate social goals (e.g., LaFontana & Cillessen, 2010). The transition to middle school also contributes to the increasing disjuncture between acceptance and popularity (LaFontana & Cillessen, 1999). Middle school brings distinct friendship groups, cliques, and crowds. Stereotypes regarding these groups limit contact across them, which contributes to the maintenance of biases and stereotypes. It is plausible that in their own peer groups, popular youth demonstrate prosocial behavior that promotes liking. However, the aggressive behaviors that they use to maintain their visibility and status in the larger peer group undermines their likeability in the peer group at large and contributes to the increasing divide between overall peer acceptance and popularity.

Although acceptance and popularity reflect similar constructs in early childhood that are built on the same social competencies, the changing social, contextual, and cognitive world of adolescence causes an increasing differentiation. Growth curve models have examined the longitudinal contribution of aggression to acceptance and popularity (e.g., Cillessen & Mayeux, 2004), but similar analyses have yet to be completed with prosocial characteristics. Studies that use longitudinal methods might establish a more definitive picture of the changing influence of social competence on acceptance versus popularity.

Reciprocal Relations and Causal Models

As part of our efforts to elaborate a longitudinal perspective on social skills and popularity, we consider the direction of causality. The assumption underlying much of the research on popularity is that social standing is the result of youth's skills and abilities. Thus, from the perspective of our focus on social competence, we might view popularity as a by-product of prosocial skills, peer entry strategies, capacities for self-control, and assertive sociability. We predict that efficient social information processing and emotion regulation lead to socially competent behavior, which, in turn, predicts popularity.

An alternative pathway is one in which peer experiences drive the development of specific social skills. Popular youth have many positive experiences in the peer group that allow them to build and practice their behavioral competencies, adaptive social cognitions, and emotional regulation skills. These youth are likely to interact with other skilled peers, who further model and reinforce efficient social functioning. Consequently, their skills and abilities further contribute to the maintenance or amplification of their status in the peer group.

We might also posit a transactional model in which socially competent behavior and popularity are mutually dependent and linked through reciprocal feedback loops. Socially competent behavior determines status, and status simultaneously influences the acquisition of new adaptive behavioral tendencies. This perspective suggests that social skills and popularity are simultaneously linked and are jointly causal.

There is some precedent for the reciprocal models that we are proposing. Research on popularity and aggression (e.g., Cillessen & Mayeux, 2004) has hypothesized that aggression is both a predictor and a product of status. Adolescents, in particular, may use aggression to dominate peers and establish their preeminent position in the peer group. In turn, popularity provides an opportunity for youth to intensify their aggressive behaviors, as modeled by the other high-status peers with whom they associate (Schwartz & Gorman, Chapter 11, this volume).

Earlier theoretical discussions of the link between peer rejection and maladjustment have touched on related issues. Most notably, Parker and

Asher (1987) described causal and incidental models of peer relationships. In the incidental model, rejection is a by-product of an underlying dysfunction that predicts both pathology and peer difficulties. In the causal model, peer rejection is a stressor that leads to negative outcomes. Framed in terms of the specific issues of this chapter, we wonder whether popularity is an outcome of social competence or whether social competence and popularity are incidentally linked through third-variable processes.

Complex transactional models may be needed to explain the co-evolution of popularity and social skills across development. Longitudinal studies on the emergence and maintenance of popularity and social skills over time can illuminate the reciprocal processes that we are proposing and test causal and incidental models. In the mean time, caution is warranted when considering the validity of simple unidirectional models.

HETEROGENEITY IN THE BEHAVIORAL PRESENTATION OF POPULAR YOUTH

As noted in the beginning of this chapter, much of the research on popularity has focused on the role of antisocial behaviors, particularly aggression. To provide a more complete picture, we have attempted to review evidence regarding links between popularity and positive behavioral features. Despite the limited consideration of social competence in the extant popularity literature, the predominant view seems to be that many high-status youth demonstrate a mixed pattern of aggressive and prosocial behaviors (Cillessen & Mayeux, 2004; Cillessen & Rose, 2005). One explanation for this pattern might be that the strategic use of prosocial behaviors mitigates the negative effects of aggression (e.g., Cillessen & Rose, 2005). An alternate explanation is that popularity is associated with both aggression and prosociability as a reflection of behavioral heterogeneity among high-status youth.

Cluster analytic studies have shown that popular children and adolescents are distinguishable by varying levels of aggression, prosociability, and academic orientation (de Bruyn & Cillessen, 2006; Luthar & McMahon, 1996; Rodkin, Farmer, Pearl, & Van Acker, 2000). Different classification systems have been proposed based on the specific features examined by researchers: popular–studious (prosocial) versus popular–disengaged (antisocial; de Bruyn & Cillessen, 2006); popular–prosocial (model) versus popular–antisocial (tough; Rodkin et al., 2000); and prosocial–popular versus aggressive–popular (Luthar & McMahon,

1996). A common theme across these topographies is the distinction between popular youth who are well liked and prosocial and those who are highly disliked and aggressive.

Given these subtypes of popularity, it seems reasonable that the associations of popularity with varying antecedents, correlates, and outcomes are obscured when popular youth are seen as a homogenous group. Inconsistent findings among previous studies may also be the result of this oversight. For example, ethnographic studies and some quantitative studies have regularly found an association of popularity with academic disengagement and negative feelings toward achievement (e.g., Adler, Kless, & Adler, 1992; Merten, 1997), whereas other studies have shown academic success to be an indicator of popularity (e.g., LaFontana & Cillessen, 2002; Lease, Kennedy, & Axelrod, 2002).

Although it is sensible that socially skilled youth may attain popular status, the fact that aggressive youth become popular is less intuitive. Perhaps popular youth, regardless of their placement on the prosocial–aggressive continuum, all demonstrate one or more personal attributes (i.e., attractiveness, wealth, athleticism, academic success) or group memberships that are valued by peers (e.g., Vaillancourt & Hymel, 2006). Eder (1985) vividly depicted the role of extracurricular activities (i.e., cheerleading), attractiveness, and friendship with high-status peers in the establishment of popularity among middle school girls. Adler and colleagues (1992) found that athletic ability was the most important predictor of popularity among elementary school boys. Empirical work has linked popularity and attractiveness for both genders (Boyatzis, Baloff, & Durieux, 1998; LaFontana & Cillessen, 2002; Lease et al., 2002; Weisfeld, Bloch, & Ivers, 1984) as well as athletic involvement (LaFontana & Cillessen, 2002; Kennedy, 1995; Meisinger, Blake, Lease, Palardy, & Olejnik, 2007; Weisfeld et al., 1984).

These findings suggest that prosociability may not be the only route to popularity, and we speculate that these status-conferring attributes may be effective in diminishing the impact of aggression within the peer group and help to maintain visibility, power, and status. In fact, such attributes may allow the individual to gain status in the context of aggressive behaviors (e.g., the cool football player who teases others may be particularly powerful in the peer context and as such may solidify his position at the top of the peer hierarchy).

Rodkin and colleagues (2000) found that "tough" boys were aggressive and antisocial, but were also seen as cool and athletic and were rated as highly popular. Troubled boys demonstrated similar levels of aggression but were rarely identified as cool or athletic and, therefore, were not afforded the same peer regard (Rodkin et al., 2000). Similarly, the antisocial popular–disengaged group identified by de Bruyn and Cillessen (2006) was also seen as highly fashionable. The behaviors of some aggressive children may lead to popularity simply because they create some kind of special visibility, perhaps challenging group or contextual norms (e.g., exhibiting disruptive behaviors at school; Merten, 1996) or seeming elite or admirable. Taken together, these findings suggest that socially desirable physical attributes, visibility gained by extracurricular activities, and the importance and selectivity of youth's group memberships may be potent predictors and perhaps even more so in the context of aggression.

RECONCEPTUALIZATION OF SOCIAL COMPETENCE

Although empirical data are limited, the research summarized suggests that advanced social skills, social cognitions, and emotional functioning promote prominent standing in the peer group. However, we have yet to emphasize the capacities that allow popular youth to read and manipulate the social context to their advantage. In this final section, we contend that an understanding of popularity necessitates a broader perspective on social competence that moves beyond molecular skills. Consistent with Rose-Krasnor's (1997) conceptualization of social competence, popular youth's capabilities may be best defined in terms of their ability to be effective in peer group interactions and to achieve dominance.

The conceptualization we are proposing reflects a functional view of social competence in which goals and contexts are considered to determine an individual's social success. Ford (1982; Ford & Ford, 1987) proposed that socially competent youth must organize their behavior and direct it to the desired goal, monitor progress toward the goal, and monitor success to alter their behavior if it fails to achieve the desired end. Notably absent from this model is the description of a set of behaviors that are judged to be competent. Instead, the focus is on evaluating the competence of the behaviors in light of their success in achieving the initial goal.

Popularity can take on greater importance than achievement, romantic relationships, and friendships for some adolescents (LaFontana & Cillessen, 2010). Adolescents may be willing to pursue and achieve this valued status through a number of different strategies, including coercive behaviors that can lead to disliking. In these circumstances, social success will depend on youth's social skills, adaptive social cognitions, and emotional functioning, but may also reflect the wider context. In striving for popularity, socially skilled behavior could involve the capacity to strategically coordinate prosocial and antisocial behaviors. Youth who have a complex understanding of their social context and engage in social behaviors that promote popularity, even if they have antisocial "side effects," may also be considered socially competent.

Rose-Krasnor (1997) also suggested that social competence reflects the quality of youth's interactions and relationships. To date, limited research has examined the friendships of popular youth; however, preliminary evidence suggests that although popular youth have supportive friendships (Rose, Swenson, & Carlson, 2004), they may also be contentious and unstable. In this regard, Litwack and Wargo Aikins (2008) hypothesized that popular youth's need to constantly jockey for position undermines the formation of high-quality stable friendships. If social competence is more broadly construed as social success, it is necessary to know what the end goals are. If achieving popularity is regarded as the pinnacle of social success regardless of the impact on intimate friendships, then perhaps popularity by "any means necessary" should be defined as social competence in the peer group. However, it must be noted that this form of popularity harms other relationships, which are also indicators of social success.

Who judges this success may also be an important component of this reconceptualization of social competence. The observation that youth's antisocial behaviors contribute to success may be unsettling for parents, educators, and interventionists. If we accept the definition of social competence as social effectiveness, in this case the achievement of popularity, we cannot judge individual behaviors outside the context of their success. From this perspective, black-and-white perceptions of antisocial behavior as maladaptive and prosocial behaviors as adaptive may reflect adult conceptions of competence rather than the reality of child and adolescent peer relationships. Although perhaps controversial, the broader conception of social competence suggests that the coordinated use of both sets of behavior or the use of antisocial behavior in concert with other valued attributes may best define social competency in the peer context.

CONCLUSION

Despite the recent empirical focus on popularity among social developmentalists, we have only a preliminary understanding of the positive correlates and prosocial skills of popular youth. Because the study of peer acceptance has a longer history, the social competencies and positive correlates of socially accepted children are more clearly understood. Although this chapter provides a summary of the literature thus far, it is a "call to arms," pointing out gaps in the literature that are ready for investigation. Research that further examines the behavioral, social-cognitive, and emotional correlates of popularity, as well as developmental changes in these associations, is warranted to clarify further the nature of popularity in the peer group. It is our hope that this chapter also raises discussion about how to best define social competence given the challenge that popularity poses to previous conceptualizations.

REFERENCES

Achenbach, T., & Edelbrock, C. (1983). *Child Behavior Checklist and Revised Behavior Profile*. Burlington: University of Vermont.

Adler, P. A., Kless, S. J., & Adler, P. (1992). Socialization to gender roles: Popularity among elementary school boys and girls. *Sociology of Education, 65*, 169–187.

Allen, J. P., Weissberg, R. P., & Hawkins, J. A. (1989). The relation between values and social competence in early adolescence. *Developmental Psychology, 25*, 458–464.

Andreou, E. (2006). Social preference, perceived popularity, and social intelligence: Relations to overt and relational aggression. *School Psychology International, 27*, 339–351.

Asarnow, J. R., & Callan, J. W. (1985). Boys with peer adjustment problems: Social cognitive processes. *Journal of Consulting and Clinical Psychology, 53*, 80–87.

Asher, S. R., & Renshaw, P. D. (1981). Children without friends: Social knowledge and social-skill training. In S. R. Asher & J. M. Gottman (Eds.), *The development of children's friendships* (pp. 273–296). New York: Cambridge University Press.

Bierman, K. L. (1986). The relationship between social aggression and peer rejection in middle childhood. In R. J. Prinz (Ed.), *Advances in behavioral assessment of children and families* (pp. 151–178). Greenwich, CT: JAI Press.

Bierman, K. L. (2004). *Peer rejection: Developmental processes and intervention strategies*. New York: Guilford Press.

Boyatzis, C. J., Baloff, P., & Durieux, C. (1998). Effects of perceived attractiveness and academic success on early adolescent popularity. *Journal of Genetic Psychology, 159*, 337–344.

Bukowski, W. M., Sippola, L. K., & Newcomb, A. F. (2000). Variations in patterns of attraction of same- and other-sex peers during early adolescence. *Developmental Psychology, 36*, 147–154.

Campos, J. J., Mumme, D. L., Kermonian, R., & Campos, R. G. (1994). A functionalist perspective on the nature of emotion. In N. A. Fox (Ed.), The development of emotion regulation: Biological and behavioral considerations. *Monographs of the Society for Research in Child Development, 59,* 284–303.

Casey, R. J. (1996). Emotional competence in children with externalizing and internalizing disorders. In M. Lewis & M. W. Sullivan (Eds.), *Emotional development in atypical children* (pp. 161–183). Mahwah, NJ: Erlbaum.

Chambliss, J., Muller, D., Hulnik, R., & Wood, M. (1978). Relationships between self-concept, self-esteem, popularity, and social judgments of junior high school students. *Journal of Psychology, 98,* 91–98.

Cillessen, A. H. N., & Mayeux, L. (2004). From censure to reinforcement: Developmental changes in the associations between aggression and social status. *Child Development, 75,* 147–163.

Cillessen, A. H. N., & Rose, A. J. (2005). Understanding popularity in the peer system. *Current Directions in Psychological Science, 14,* 102–105.

Coie, J. D., & Dodge, K. A. (1988). Multiple sources of data on social behavior and social status in school: A cross-age comparison. *Child Development, 59,* 815–829.

Coie, J. D., & Kupersmidt, J. B. (1983). A behavioral analysis of emerging social status in boys' groups. *Child Development, 54,* 1400–1416.

Cole, P. M., Zahn-Waxler, C., Fox, N. A., Usher, B. A., & Welsh, J. D. (1996). Individual differences in emotion regulation and behavior problems in preschool children. *Journal of Abnormal Psychology, 105,* 518–529.

Cole, P. M., Zahn-Waxler, C., & Smith, K. D. (1994). Expressive control during disappointment: Variations related to preschoolers' behavior problems. *Developmental Psychology, 30,* 835–846.

Crick, N. R., & Dodge, K. A. (1994). A review and reformulation of social information-processing mechanisms in children's social adjustment. *Psychological Bulletin, 115,* 74–101.

Crick, N. R., & Ladd, G. W. (1990). Children's perceptions of the outcomes of social strategies: Do the ends justify being mean? *Developmental Psychology, 26,* 612–620.

de Bruyn, E. H., & Cillessen, A. H. N. (2006). Popularity in early adolescence. Prosocial and antisocial subtypes. *Journal of Adolescent Research, 21,* 607–627.

Denham, S. A., McKinley, M., Couchoud, E. A., & Holt, R. (1990). Emotional and behavioral predictors of preschool peer ratings. *Child Development, 61,* 1145–1152.

Dodge, K. A., & Frame, C. L. (1982). Social cognitive biases and deficits in aggressive boys. *Child Development, 53,* 620–635.

Dodge, K. A., Murphy, R. R., & Buchsbaum, K. (1984). The assessment of intention-cue detection skills in children: Implications for developmental psychopathology. *Child Development, 55,* 163–173.

Dodge, K. A., Schlundt, D. C., Schocken, I., & Delugach, J. D. (1983). Social competence and children's sociometric status: The role of peer group entry strategies. *Merrill-Palmer Quarterly, 29,* 309–336.

Dodge, K. A., & Somberg, D. R. (1987). Hostile attributional biases among aggressive boys are exacerbated under conditions of threat to self. *Child Development, 58,* 213–224.

Eder, D. (1985). The cycle of popularity: Interpersonal relations among female adolescents. *Sociology of Education, 58,* 154–165.

Edwards, R., Manstead, A. S. R., & MacDonald, C. J. (1984). The relationship between children's sociometric status and ability to recognize facial expression of emotion. *European Journal of Social Psychology, 14,* 235–238.

Eisenberg, N., Fabes, R. A., Nyman, M., Bernzweig, J., & Pinuelas, A. (1994). The relations of emotionality and regulation of children's anger-related reactions. *Child Development, 65,* 109–128.

Eisenberg, N., Fabes, R. A., Shepard, S. A., Murphy, B. C., Guthrie, I. K., Jones, S., et al. (1997). Contemporaneous and longitudinal prediction of children's social functioning form regulation and emotionality. *Child Development, 68,* 642–664.

Eisenberg, N., Vailente, C., Fabes, R. A., Smith, C. L., Reiser, M. Shepard, S. A., et al. (2003). The relations of effortful control and ego control to children's resiliency and social functioning. *Developmental Psychology, 39,* 761–776.

Fabes, R. A., & Eisenberg, N. (1992). Young children's coping with interpersonal anger. *Child Development, 69,* 642–664.

Ford, D., & Ford, M. (1987). Humans as self-constructing living systems: An overview. In M. Ford & D. Ford (Eds.), *Humans as self-constructive livings systems: Putting the framework to work* (pp. 1–46). Hillsdale, NJ: Erlbaum.

Ford, M. (1982). Social cognition and social competence in adolescence. *Developmental Psychology, 18,* 323–340.

French, D. C. (1988). Heterogeneity of peer-rejected boys: Aggressive and nonaggressive subtypes. *Child Development, 59,* 976–985.

Goldman, J. A., Corsini, D. A., & deUrioste, R. (1980). Implications of positive and negative sociometric status for assessing the social competence of young children. *Journal of Applied Developmental Psychology, 1,* 209–220.

Gottman, J. M., Gonso, J., & Rasmussen, B. (1975). Social interaction, social competence, and friendship in children. *Child Development, 46,* 709–718.

Gresham, F. M., & Elliott, S. N. (1990). *Social Skills Rating System: Manual.* Circle Pines, MN: American Guidance Service.

Hart, C. H., Ladd, G. W., & Burleson, B. R. (1990). Children's expectations of the outcomes of social strategies: Relations with sociometric status and maternal disciplinary styles. *Child Development, 61,* 127–137.

Hartup, W. W., Glazer, J. A., & Charlesworth, R. (1967). Peer reinforcement and sociometric status. *Child Development, 38,* 1017–1024.

Hawley, P. H. (2002). Social dominance and prosocial and coercive strategies of resource control in preschoolers. *International Journal of Behavioral Development, 26,* 167–176.

Hawley, P. H., Little, T. D., & Card, N. A. (2007). The allure of a mean friend: Relationship quality and processes of aggressive adolescents with prosocial skills. *International Journal of Behavioral Development, 31,* 170–180.

Hawley, P. H., Little, T. D., & Pasupathi, M. (2002). Winning friends and influencing peers: Strategies of peer influence in late childhood. *International Journal of Behavioral Development, 26,* 466–474.

Hubbard, J. A. (2001). Emotion expression processes in children's peer interaction: The role of peer rejection, aggression, and gender. *Child Development, 72,* 1426–1438.

Hubbard, J. A., & Dearing, K. F. (2004). Children's understanding and regulation of emotion in the context of their peer relations. In J. B. Kupersmidt & K. A. Dodge (Eds.), *Children's peer relations: From development to intervention* (pp. 243–267). Washington, DC: American Psychological Association.

Jarvinen, D. W., & Nicholls, J. G. (1996). Adolescents' social goals, beliefs about the causes of social success, and satisfaction in peer relations. *Developmental Psychology, 32,* 435–441.

Keane, S. P., & Parrish, A. E. (1992). The role of affective information in the determinants of intent. *Developmental Psychology, 28,* 159–162.

Kennedy, E. (1995). Correlates of perceived popularity among peers: A study of race and gender differences among middle school students. *Journal of Negro Education, 64,* 186–195.

Kurdek, L. A., & Krile, D. (1982). A developmental analysis of the relation between peer acceptance and both interpersonal understanding and perceived social self-competence. *Child Development, 53,* 1485–1491.

Ladd, G. W., & Mize, J. (1983). A cognitive-social learning model of social skills training. *Psychological Review, 90,* 127–157.

Ladd, G. W., & Oden, S. L. (1979). The relationship between peer acceptance and children's ideas about helpfulness. *Child Development, 50,* 402–408.

LaFontana, K. M., & Cillessen, A. H. N. (1998). The nature of children's stereotypes of popularity. *Social Development, 7,* 301–320.

LaFontana, K. M., & Cillessen, A. H. N. (1999). Children's interpersonal perceptions as a function of sociometric and peer-perceived popularity. *Journal of Genetic Psychology, 160,* 225–242.

LaFontana, K. M., & Cillessen, A. H. N. (2002). Children's perceptions of popular and unpopular peers: A multimethod assessment. *Developmental Psychology, 38,* 635–647.

LaFontana, K. M., & Cillessen, A. H. N. (2010). Developmental changes in the priority of perceived status in childhood and adolescence. *Social Development, 19,* 130–147.

Lease, A. M., Kennedy, C. A., & Axelrod, J. L. (2002). Children's social constructions of popularity. *Social Development, 11,* 87–109.

Leppanen, J. M., & Hietanen, J. K. (2001). Emotion recognition and social adjustment in school-aged girls and boys. *Scandinavian Journal of Psychology, 42,* 429–435.

Litwack, S. D., & Wargo Aikins, J. (2008, March). *The influence of friendship factors in the adaptation of sociometrically and perceived popular adolescents.* Paper presented at the biennial meeting of the Society for Research in Adolescence, Chicago.

Luthar, S. S., & McMahon, T. J. (1996). Peer reputation among inner-city ado-

lescents: Structure and correlates. *Journal of Research on Adolescence, 6,* 581–603.
Maag, J. W., Vasa, S. F., Reid, R., & Torrey, G. K. (1995). Social and behavioral predictors of popular, rejected, and average children. *Educational and Psychological Measurement, 55,* 196–205.
Matson, J. L., Esveldt-Dawson, K., & Kazdin, A. E. (1983). Validation of methods for assessing social skills in children. *Journal of Clinical Child Psychology, 12,* 174–180.
Meisinger, E. B., Blake, J. J., Lease, A. M., Palardy, G. J., & Olejnik, S. F. (2007). Variant and invariant predictors of perceived popularity across majority-black and majority-white classrooms. *Journal of School Psychology, 45,* 21–44.
Merten, D. E. (1996). Visibility and vulnerability: Responses to rejection by nonaggressive junior high school boys. *Journal of Early Adolescence, 6,* 581–603.
Merten, D. E. (1997). The meaning of meanness: Popularity, competition, and conflict among junior high school girls. *Sociology of Education, 70,* 175–191.
Miller, A. L., Kiely, K., Seifer, R. E. P., Zakriski, A., Eguia, M., & Vergnani, M. (2005). Emotion knowledge skills in low-income elementary school children: Associations with social status and peer experiences. *Social Development, 14,* 637–651.
Mostow, A. J., Izard, C. E., Fine, S., & Trentacosta, C. J. (2002). Modeling emotional, cognitive, and behavioral predictors of peer acceptance. *Child Development, 73,* 1775–1787.
Newcomb, A. F., Bukowski, W. M., & Patee, L. (1993). Children's peer relations: A meta- analytic review of popular, rejected, neglected, controversial, and average sociometric status. *Psychological Bulletin, 113,* 99–128.
Nowicki, S., & Duke, M. P. (1992). The association of children's nonverbal decoding abilities with their popularity, locus of control, and academic achievement. *Journal of Genetic Psychology, 153,* 385–393.
Olson, S. L. (1992). Development of conduct problems and peer rejection in preschool children: A social systems analysis. *Journal of Abnormal Child Psychology, 20,* 327–350.
Parker, J. G., & Asher, S. R. (1987). Peer acceptance and later personal adjustment: Are low-accepted children "at risk"? *Psychological Bulletin, 102,* 357–389.
Parkhurst, J. T., & Hopmeyer, A. (1998). Sociometric popularity and peer-perceived popularity: Two distinct dimensions of peer status. *Journal of Early Adolescence, 18,* 125–144.
Patterson, C. J., Kupersmidt, J. B., & Griesler, P. C. (1990). Children's perceptions of self and of relationships with others as a function of sociometric status. *Child Development, 61,* 1335–1349.
Pettit, G. S., Harrist, A. W., Bates, J. E., & Dodge, K. A. (1991). Family interaction, social cognition and children's subsequent relations with peers at kindergarten. *Journal of Social and Personal Relationships, 8,* 383–402.

Putallaz, M. (1983). Predicting children's sociometric status from their behavior. *Child Development, 54,* 1417–1426.
Putallaz, M., & Gottman, J. M. (1981). An interactional model of children's entry into peer groups. *Child Development, 52,* 986–994.
Putallaz, M., & Wasserman, A. (1989). Children's naturalistic entry behavior and sociometric status: A developmental perspective. *Developmental Psychology, 25,* 297–305.
Putallaz, M., & Wasserman, A. (1990). Children's entry behavior. In S. R. Asher & J. D. Coie (Eds.), *Peer rejection in childhood* (pp. 60–89). New York: Cambridge University Press.
Renshaw, P. D., & Asher, S. R. (1983). Children's goals and strategies for social interaction. *Merrill-Palmer Quarterly, 29,* 353–374.
Richard, B. A., & Dodge, K. A. (1982). Social maladjustment and problem solving in school-aged children. *Journal of Consulting and Clinical Psychology, 50,* 226–233.
Rodkin, P. C., Farmer, T. W., Pearl, R., & Van Acker, R. (2000). Heterogeneity of popular boys: Antisocial and prosocial configurations. *Developmental Psychology, 36,* 14–24.
Rose, A. J., Swenson, L. P., & Carlson, W. (2004). Friendships of aggressive youth: Considering the influences of being disliked and of being perceived as popular. *Journal of Experimental Child Psychology, 88,* 25–45.
Rose-Krasnor, L. (1997). The nature of social competence: A theoretical review. *Social Development, 6,* 111–135.
Rubin, K. H., Bukowski, W. M., & Parker, J. G. (1998). Peer interactions, relationships, and groups. In W. Damon & N. Eisenberg (Eds.), *Handbook of child psychology: Vol. 3. Social, emotional, and personality development* (5th ed., pp. 619–700). New York: Wiley.
Rubin, K. H., Coplan, R. J., Fox, N. A., & Calkins, S. D. (1995). Emotionality, emotion regulation, and preschoolers' social adaptation. *Development and Psychopathology, 7,* 49–62.
Rubin, K. H., & Krasnor, L. R. (1986). Social-cognitive and social behavioral perspectives on problem solving. In M. Perlmutter (Ed.), *Minnesota Symposium on Child Psychology* (Vol. 18, pp. 1–68). Hillsdale, NJ: Erlbaum.
Rubin, K. H., & Maioni, T. L. (1975). Play preference and its relationship to egocentrism, popularity, and classification skills in preschoolers. *Merrill-Palmer Quarterly, 21,* 171–179.
Sandstrom, M. J., & Cillessen, A. H. N. (2006). Likeable versus popular: Distinct implications for adolescent adjustment. *International Journal of Behavioral Development, 30,* 305–314.
Sebanc, A. M., Pierce, S. L., Cheatham, C. L., & Gunnar, M. R. (2003). Gendered social worlds in preschool: Dominance, peer acceptance and assertive social skills in boys' and girls' peer groups. *Social Development, 12,* 91–106.
Stuart, D. L., Gresham, F. M., & Elliot, S. N. (1991). Teacher ratings of social skills in popular and rejected males and females. *School Psychology Quarterly, 6,* 16–26.
Sutton, J., Smith, P. K., & Swettenham, J. (1999). Social cognition and bullying:

Social inadequacy or skilled manipulation? *British Journal of Developmental Psychology, 17,* 435–450.

Twenge, J. M., Baumeister, R. F., DeWall, N. C., Ciarocco, N. J., & Bartels, M. J. (2007). Social exclusion decreases prosocial behavior. *Journal of Personality and Social Psychology, 92,* 56–66.

Underwood, M. K., Coie, J. D., & Herbsman, C. R. (1992). Display rules for anger and aggression in school-aged children. *Child Development, 63,* 366–380.

Vaillancourt, T., & Hymel, S. (2006). Aggression, social status and the moderating role of sex and peer-valued characteristics. *Aggressive Behavior, 32,* 396–408.

Walker, S. (2004). Teacher reports of social behavior and peer acceptance in early childhood: Sex and social status differences. *Child Study Journal, 34,* 1328.

Weisfeld, G. E., Bloch, S. A., & Ivers, J. W. (1984). Possible determinants of social dominance among adolescent girls. *Journal of Genetic Psychology, 144,* 115–129.

Wentzel, K. R. (2003). Sociometric status and adjustment in middle school: A longitudinal study. *Journal of Early Adolescence, 23,* 5–28.

Wentzel, K. R., & Erdley, C. A. (1993). Strategies for making friends: Relations to social behavior and peer acceptance in early adolescence. *Developmental Psychology, 29,* 819–826.

Xie, H., Li, Y., Boucher, S. M., Hutchins, C., & Cairns, B. (2006). What makes a girl (or boy) popular (or unpopular)? African American children's perceptions and developmental differences. *Developmental Psychology, 42,* 599–612.

Part III
POPULARITY IN CONTEXT

Chapter 8

Popularity in Peer Group Perspective

The Role of Status in Adolescent Peer Systems

B. BRADFORD BROWN

Few facets of child and adolescent social interactions have been the subject of as much research and controversy over the past decade as the concept of popularity. Through extensive study of childhood populations in the latter portion of the 20th century, sociometric researchers derived a categorization scheme that designated popular youth as individuals routinely nominated by peers as well liked (or close friend or desirable activity companion) and rarely nominated as disliked (or not a friend or unwelcome activity companion). As they began studying older youth, these scholars were surprised to discover that adolescents have their own definition of the term *popular*, and it fails to correspond to standard sociometric terminology. Although often admired and emulated, the "populars" are not necessarily well liked and harbor behaviors and characteristics inconsistent with the common portrait of sociometrically popular children. To resolve this definitional dilemma, sociometric scholars now routinely designate two forms of popularity among adolescents: one referring to an individual's likeability or acceptance among peers and the other to the person's social status (Cillessen & Rose, 2005).

Although expedient, this solution obviates an understanding of popularity from the perspective of the adolescent social system. Why is popularity so important in this social system? Why do young people seek popularity and yet deride those who have it? Why do popular youth manifest a mix of prosocial and antisocial behaviors? To address these questions, I review another body of research—much of it ethnographic and typically emanating from more sociological or social-psychological perspectives—that elucidates the meaning and purpose of popularity within the adolescent peer system (Merten, Chapter 3, this volume). I then offer suggestions for future research that may help to bridge these two research traditions and their respective theoretical perspectives on popularity.

THE SOCIAL IMPETUS FOR POPULARITY

Adolescence is routinely perceived as a period of intensified peer interest and interaction (Brown & Larson, 2009). The reason for the increased salience of peers at this life stage lies in the consequences of a combination of biological, psychological, and social developments that are fundamental to adolescence in contemporary U.S. society. The three most important changes concern puberty, autonomy, and social expansion. Pubertal development is routinely regarded as the initiator of adolescence. One of its primary consequences is heightened interest in sexual and romantic relationships. Such interest directs most young people to interactions and relationships with peers of the other sex. Because such peers have been largely ignored or avoided in middle and late childhood (Maccoby, 1988), there is a fair amount of social learning required to become adept at other-sex relationships.

Although young people might be able to turn to adults for instruction in how to interact with the other sex or how to be effective in mixed-sex social situations, a second fundamental change discourages this option. The transition to adolescence is accompanied by increased expectations for autonomy, expectations that are manifest in the minds of both young people and their elders. Early adolescents display an increasing interest in taking responsibility for their own decisions (Soenens & Vansteenkiste, 2005). They begin to question the legitimacy of parents' rule making or oversight of their behavior, especially in matters that they regard as more personal than moral or prudential (Smetana & Asquith, 1994). Parents are less eager to relinquish their authority, but still acknowledge that in some cases their children should be granted more of a voice in decisions about their activities (Smetana & Asquith, 1994). Teacher–student relationships also become less personal with the transition to secondary school in early adolescence (Eccles et al., 1983). This is partly because of the structural arrangement of secondary schools (teachers see more students for less time each day than in elementary school), but also because of a sense that their students do not desire as close a relationship with school adults as in younger grades (Finders, 1997). The drive toward autonomy prompts young people to rely more extensively on peers to guide them into the heterosocial world of adolescence.

Turning to peers becomes more challenging because of a third development common in adolescence, namely the transition to a much larger and more diverse nexus of age-mates. With the move to secondary school, young people typically encounter a greater number of classmates, often from more demographically diverse backgrounds and almost certainly extending beyond the geographical boundaries of the immediate or nearby neighborhoods served by their elementary school. A daily routine of shifting classes exposes students to a much larger share of age-mates than they encountered in elementary school. Extracurricular activities (after-school programs or community sports teams) often draw from this larger pool of peers as well. Not only are these changes likely to disrupt existing friendship networks, but they also heighten the need to get to know—and to be known by—the new, larger network of peers. Given the difficulty of establishing personal relationships with everyone in this greatly expanded peer setting, establishing one's identity or reputation and discerning the identity of everyone else become critical tasks at the outset of adolescence.

Collectively, these developmental changes plunge early adolescents into a new and challenging social environment. Reluctant to rely on adults as much as they have earlier in their lives, young people naturally look to peers for assistance in developing the skills necessary to thrive in this new environment. A peer system evolves to meet adolescents' developmental needs. That system is charged with developing norms for social interaction, especially as they pertain to mixed-gender systems of relationships, establishing mechanisms that allow expression of autonomy and identity, and deriving a means of maintaining the boundaries of acceptable attitudes and activities. As I indicate in the sections that follow, popularity is a central feature of the peer system. It endows certain individuals with the authority to set and enforce norms, anchors a process of peer socialization regarding system norms, and helps to organize the specification of acceptable social identities.

The magnitude of this task should not be underestimated. Popularity is a central feature of a system charged not merely with establishing and maintaining the norms of one peer group but with facilitating the formation and operation of a larger system that spawns numerous peer groups and regulates their interactions. The peer system arises in part to foster key social relationships (romantic affiliations and more intimate friendship bonds), but it also addresses other major developmental tasks. Preoccupations with autonomy and identity that are so central to adolescence in individualistic societies also become woven into the peer group structure in such cultures (Brown, Mory, & Kinney, 1994; Newman & Newman, 2001). To understand popularity's role in this venture, one must first appreciate the basic organizational and operational features of the emerging peer system.

ORGANIZATIONAL AND OPERATIONAL PRINCIPLES OF THE ADOLESCENT PEER SYSTEM

"When you're in junior high, everything's different." Finders (1997) uses this statement from one of her study participants as the heading for her book's first chapter to underscore how dramatic young people regard the transition between elementary and middle school social systems. Although some elements are retained across the transition—early adolescents still form friendships and cluster together in friendship or activity groups—new types of relationships and new levels of interaction emerge to create a more complex social structure (Brown & Larson, 2009). More important, one's actions and affiliations are held up to public scrutiny in a way that is disquieting to many early adolescents. As one of Merten's (1996a, p. 56) middle school respondents noted about her peers, "They're judging you this year, and that's what I don't like. Because they never used to judge you last year. They wouldn't judge [you] on what you looked like; they would judge you on your personality. This year they're judging you on what you look like, what clothes you wear, what kind of friends you hang out with. Like, if your friend is a burnout then you're a burnout." Some young people even argue that peer social dynamics trump the school's intended mission of academic learning and advancement. Duncan's (2004, p. 143) sample of British girls confessed that they would advise a new student to establish her position within the peer system before attending to classes and academic requirements. "It was highly important to understand the peer hierarchy and to find a comfortable position within it."

What is the nature of the changes that young people regard as so radical and disturbing?

Organizational Changes

Sociometric studies often use the entire grade level as the nomination pool for ratings of adolescent popularity or related behaviors, under the assumption that this unit forms a coherent, unified system comparable to self-contained classrooms in elementary school settings. Such an assumption is questionable in light of the restructuring that occurs in early adolescence. Except in small and very homogeneous contexts, the peer system is composed of an array of groups. Adolescents typically conceive of groups in two different ways. One involves sets of peers who commonly hang out and do things together. Social scientists typically refer to these interaction-based groupings as *cliques*. On average, cliques tend to have between five and eight members, which investigators point out is an optimum size for maintaining reasonably close relationships among all dyads in the group (Dunphy, 1969; Kindermann, 2007; Larkin, 1979).

The other conception of groups clusters individuals who are perceived as sharing a common image, lifestyle, or pattern of behaviors, even if they don't all routinely hang out together. Typically, these reputation-based clusters are called *crowds*. The central defining feature of crowds is that each proffers a unique provisional identity—a set of values, music and grooming styles, activity preferences, orientations toward school, and so on that, collectively, set it apart from any other group (Brown & Larson, 2009). Thus, any peer system that includes multiple crowds automatically features multiple identity or lifestyle choices. In other words, both across and within adolescent peer systems, there is more heterogeneity than is often apparent in depictions of the youth culture, including many sociometric studies of popularity.

Heuristically, cliques and crowds seem to be noticeably distinct, and social scientists work diligently to emphasize their differences. Merten (1996a, p. 57), for example, cautions that "it is important to keep in mind that in junior high school the terms like *preppie* refer to status *categories*—not groups with identifiable boundaries and specific criteria for membership. The designation of specific individuals as representatives of these categories makes the categories seem more substantial than they actually are."

Other scholars affirm Merten's distinction between crowd categories and clique groups (Cross & Fletcher, 2009), but adolescents are not so facile at differentiating the two terms. Kindermann (2007) used the social-cognitive mapping technique, in which adolescents name all the different groups of peers they can think of who hang out together, to map the clique structure in one middle school sample. When he then asked respondents to give each group a name signifying "what the group was about," participants offered up common crowd labels, including jocks, brains, nerds, the cool crowd, and in-betweeners. Ethnographers also note the tendency for adolescents to think of cliques in terms of crowd labels, even if they recognize that the crowd may extend beyond one particular clique (Eder, 1985; Milner, 2004; Wiseman, 2002).

An additional organizational change, slower to develop, is the transformation of peer groups from largely gender-homogeneous to mixed-gender units. This transformation seems to occur at different rates among various peer groups, sometimes not becoming apparent until middle adolescence (high school). Dunphy (1969) observed that the transition to mixed-gender groups typically occurred when a clique of girls commingled with an all-boys clique, spurred by the development of a dating relationship between each clique's leader. Scholars have not determined whether this mode of merger is common among current-day U.S. youth, but the commingling of genders within cliques is obvious (Connolly, Furman, & Konarski, 2000) and underscores the capacity of adolescent peer groups to adjust to developmental needs driven by puberty.

Beyond these structural transformations is another change that is particularly important for the study of popularity, namely the strong tendency for cliques and crowds to be arranged into a status hierarchy (Garner, Bootcheck, Lorr, & Rauch, 2006). Scholars have debated the basis for the hierarchy. Some studies provide evidence that peer group divisions simply replicate socioeconomic strata apparent in adult society (Eckert, 1989; Hollingshead, 1949) or reflect the surrounding society's emphasis on consumerism (Milner, 2004). Others suggest that group position reflects success at stage-specific attributes such as athletic prowess, social skills, or physical attractiveness (Coleman, 1961). In most cases, status systems seem to strike a careful balance between mimicking and rejecting adult standards. For example, it is common for peer systems to value academic success but not academic effort (Friedenberg, 1963; Gordon, 1957) or to admire the skill in getting along well with adults but not subjugation to adult rules or authority (Garner et al., 2006). In this way, peer groups can nurture healthy autonomy development without encouraging alienation from adults.

Garner et al. (2006) reported substantial variation in the nature of status hierarchies that could be observed in the high schools of various communities. Organization ranged from a traditional pyramid structure, in which one or two groups enjoyed the highest status position and increasing numbers of cliques occupied positions further down the hierarchy, to pluralistic systems, in which no one group dominated and there was a climate of egalitarianism and tolerance, to oppositional structures featuring hostile relationships between the popular crowd and at least one other peer group. These distinctions, however, portray peer structures in middle adolescence and point to developmental changes in peer groups that I describe later in this chapter. In early adolescence, the more hegemonic pyramid structure is a consistent theme in research studies. Such a structure may better serve the developmental needs of young people as they try to navigate the new peer social system.

Operational Principles

In the United States, these structural changes in the peer system are most likely to occur as young people transition into middle or junior high school, typically at age 11 or 12. Spurred by the presence of older youth in more advanced grade levels, the peer system quickly infiltrates new arrivals to the school. There is a scramble to consolidate friendship networks into viable cliques and to identify high-status cliques and clique leaders. Criteria for popularity or high status typically replicate those for older students. In fact, popular cliques in older grades have a vested interest in promulgating their status criteria among new students—and even selecting the "popular group" leaders—as a means of maintaining their favored position in the peer system (Bishop, Bishop, & Bishop, 2003). Once high-status cliques are identified and the criteria for judging status established, other cliques can find their place along the hierarchy, according to their adeptness at conforming to status norms and forging friendly relations with high-status groups or their members (Milner, 2004). "Once status systems become well established," Milner (2004) reports, "they are relatively stable. Adolescents repeatedly report the difficulty of changing their status once their peers have categorized them" (p. 83). Individuals who defy the popular group's norms too dramatically may have difficulty finding or forming a clique. Payne (2007) indicated that the sexual minority youth whom they observed were not successful in forming a friendship group until the later years of high school.

Combined with all of the academic adjustments that young people confront in the school transition (Eccles et al., 1983), the intense negotiations over group affiliations and group status positions can seem overwhelming, especially when the criteria for judgments shift substantially, from personality to grooming styles or friendship affiliations, as one of Merten's (1996b) respondents noted. The salience of group affiliations over personality in the quest for popularity or acceptance is particularly important. Other contributions to this volume detail personal characteristics that are associated with sociometrically derived popularity scores (Aikins & Litwack, Chapter 7, and Mayeux, Houser, & Dyches, Chapter 4, this volume). Certainly, such characteristics contribute to an individual's ability to become part of the popular crowd, but in the final analysis popularity is designated by membership in a high-status peer group. One can attain popular status simply by being friends or romantic partners of popular clique leaders and thereby gaining admission to their clique. There is a certain "guilt by association" (if your friend is a burnout, then you're a burnout). And although particular characteristics—athletic prowess, physical attractiveness, material wealth—are generally advantageous, the specific traits valued by the peer system are context specific and can vary considerably among communities (Coleman, 1961). In this regard, popularity is more a characteristic of the peer group or peer system than the individual.

Given the amount of energy that early adolescents invest in establishing their place in the peer group system, it is surprising how reluctant they are to articulate their position. Several investigators have noted the inclination of early adolescents to disavow membership in a given crowd, to claim membership in multiple groups, or to characterize their own clique as just a group of friends, even as they readily supply crowd labels—often derogatory—for other clusters of peers (Brown, Von Bank, & Steinberg, 2008; Cross & Fletcher, 2009; Dunphy, 1969; Eckert, 1989; Finders, 1997). The derogation of out-groups is a common feature of intergroup relations when groups are competing for a limited resource (such as status), according to social identity theory (Tajfel, 1982). For lower status crowd members, denying their group affiliation may be a face-saving strategy because group status is associated with self-esteem. In fact, Brown et al. (2008) demonstrated that adolescents who were rated by peers as members of low-status crowds did not suffer as much loss of self-esteem if they disavowed their crowd affiliation or claimed membership in no crowd than if they affirmed peers' assessment of their group membership. Such findings serve as a caution about the validity of self-ratings of crowd affiliation.

The challenges that young people face as they enter a secondary school environment are quite foreboding. They must become aware of the prevailing peer norms, discern the various crowds within the peer context, decide how they want peers to perceive them, perhaps compete with others for affiliation in popular groups, and assemble or work their way into a group of friends who will help them achieve their social goals. They need to accomplish all of this quickly, mindful of the potential social cost of missteps (gaining a reputation that is difficult to alter).

The peer system appears to be well organized to assist in this mission. Building on the work of Corsaro and Eder (1990), Youniss, McLellan, and Strouse (1994) discerned four fundamental principles underlying the social adjustment process. First, young people behave in a rule-like fashion. Second, they operate as if they share meanings for actions and norms for procedures that they establish through mutual understanding. Third, group activities focus on repeatable themes that all group members recognize. Finally, young people believe that the activities in which they participate are orderly and necessary. These principles, according to Youniss and his colleagues, arise from interactions in the situation, among participants, rather than from some code of rules or laws that exist outside the setting. In this way, on a broader level, the peer system reflects the budding sense of autonomy that is so salient to individuals' developmental agenda at this stage of life.

Summary

In adolescence, popularity is a key component of the fundamental organization of adolescent peer systems. Peer groups emerge and are arranged into a status hierarchy, which allows a particular group of peers (those who are leaders and members of the popular crowd or highest status groups) to take leadership in defining the dominant norms governing individual behavior and intergroup interactions within the social system. The widespread desire to gain membership in the popular crowd (Coleman, 1961; Eder, 1985) legitimizes the authority of high-status youth and their efforts to establish and maintain norms, thereby assuring a well-functioning peer system. The shared meanings for which early adolescents strive and their belief in the legitimacy of operational procedures provide stability to what otherwise could be a chaotic social system through this time of transition. Popularity is defined by the peer system and embodied in its organization as high-status group membership. However, these general principles do not reveal much about the specific practices that keep the system running—and in some cases undermine its efficiency. It is to these practices that I now turn attention.

POPULARITY AND PEER GROUP DYNAMICS

The social system that emerges from the restructuring in early adolescence is likely to include a variety of groups or crowds. These groups can be categorized in numerous ways (see, e.g., Sussman, Pokhrel, Ashmore, & Brown, 2007), but in terms of popularity or status, four types of groups can be discerned. First among these are the populars, who enjoy high status and are charged with the task of demarcating and enforcing the dominant group norms within the peer setting. Second are the unpopulars, who manifest a general lack of social maturity and ineptitude in adjusting to the normative demands of the new peer system (Merten, 1996b; Canaan, 1987). In some settings, these are the only two groups to become apparent in middle school (Eder, 1985; Kinney, 1993), but in most cases at least one other category is visible, which could be labeled mid-rangers. Groups in this category are neither particularly high nor low in status but may be arranged in various intermediary points along the status hierarchy. Finally, there may be iconoclasts. Likely to emerge later than the other groups, often not until high school, these groups display norms that are oppositional to the popular crowd and often antagonistic toward adult standards or expectations as well; they tend to have hostile relationships with high-status groups in the peer system.

In patterns of social interaction, particularly intergroup relations, each type of group harbors different motivations. Popular crowds strive to maintain their dominance over the social system and enforce their own norms. They tend to be particularly derisive of the unpopulars, who, as a result, are motivated to avoid the derogation or abusive treatment that they receive from peers, particularly the populars. In some respects, their objective is to become invisible (Merten, 1996b) or too strange or intimidating to contend with (Bešić & Kerr, 2009). Mid-rangers have a split objective. On the one hand, they strive to become candidates for membership in higher status crowds, thus trying to befriend the populars and mimic their attributes, attitudes, interests, and activities. On the other hand, especially if their group lies toward the bottom of the status hierarchy, they are motivated to avoid association with unpopulars (Milner, 2004), making them eager to join in the derision levied upon unpopular group members. They can become avid cheerleaders or bystanders of populars' relational aggression and bullying of low-status peers. The iconoclasts, on the other hand, are more assertive or aggressive in challenging populars' authority. They are motivated to be everything that populars are not, to disrupt the populars' hegemony of the peer system, and to visibly articulate their differences with the prevailing norms of the social system (Eckert, 1989). The more rigid the hierarchy within a peer setting, the more distinctive the motives and actions are among these different types of peer groups (Garner et al., 2006). These group-dependent motives form the backdrop for intra- and intergroup interactions.

Conformity and Visibility

Conformity to clique norms is an especially salient issue for high-status group members because it is usually a prerequisite to moving up the dominance hierarchy within a clique. The stronger one's allegiance to group norms, the more likely group leaders are to recognize and trust a member, possibly elevating the person's status over less conforming members (Wiseman, 2002). However, adolescents throughout the peer system acknowledge strong peer pressure to conform to clique norms. They understand that nonconformity can lead to expulsion from the group, leaving them without any friends (Larkin, 1979). This is true even among oppositional groups (freaks, Goths) who rail against the tight conformity of high-status cliques (Larkin, 1979; Milner, 2004).

To obtain a high rank in this system, one has to anticipate the criteria by which status will be judged and then pursue those criteria or, better yet, control the process of stipulating criteria. This is why leaders of high-status cliques tend to complicate or elaborate group norms in ways that will give them a competitive advantage (Milner, 2004). Leaders then endeavor to maintain strict allegiance to group norms among all members. This effort sometimes can be taken to extremes, as Finders (1997) observed in one popular middle school clique:

> Because group identity was privileged over individual identity, allegiance to peer group remained central. ... Physical appearance, dress, social behavior, academic achievement, and reading and writing preferences were carefully monitored by the girls to present a united front. Not only did the girls arrange their hair and dress similarly, but on weekends they exchanged grocery bags full of clothing so that the next week each girl could come to school dressed in the same outfits as those of her tight circle of friends" (pp. 48–49).

To maintain their ranking in the system, high-status groups strive for maximum visibility, often by controlling activities within the context that offer such visibility (Canaan, 1987). Visibility brings attention from others, which serves as its own reward beyond its effect on enhancing social status (Eder, 1985). In schools in the United States, cheerleading, glory sports such as football or basketball, leadership positions (e.g., student council or class officers), social distinctions (prom queen or king), and pictures in the yearbook are frequent sources of high visibility. Accordingly, members of popular crowds strive to control the election or selection process into these positions (Eder & Kinney, 1995; Finders, 1997).

Peer Socialization

Popular clique leaders have a variety of methods at their disposal to inspire or induce conformity to group norms. Some appear to be more prosocial, others more aggressive or punitive (Brown, Bakken, Ameringer, & Mahon, 2008). Dunphy (1969), for example, detailed clique leaders' efforts to inculcate heterosocial skills and interests among group members. Leaders first set an example by pursuing a romantic relationship with a member of an other-sex clique, then offered encouragement for fellow group members to follow their lead with other members of the other-sex clique. They structured opportunities for the cliques to interact so that members could locate potential romantic partners and hone their skills at pursuing romantic relationships. This combination of behavioral display, encouragement, and structuring opportunities proved very effective in helping cliques integrate into heterosocial units. An essential factor in the leader's success was his or her own skill in the behavior that defined the clique. When Dunphy examined nonelite crowds, such as the more aggressive and delinquent "wharfie" cliques, he found that the same principle applied, except that the crucial skill shifted from interacting with the other sex to more deviant behavior. Likewise, in Macleod's (1987) study of the deviantly oriented "hallway hangers," the leader tactfully ceded authority temporarily to a more athletically oriented group member when the clique competed in basketball because his relatively inept leadership on the basketball court could threaten his control of the clique in other situations.

Most studies of group dynamics focus on more antagonistic socialization techniques. These range from gentle teasing of group members who fall short of the normative ideal (Eder, 1993) to ignoring members who display undesirable or unapproved behavior to more aggressive efforts to demean individuals or demote their group status (Merten, 1997). Wiseman (2002), whose ethnography was the basis for a full-length feature film, *Mean Girls*, provides a catalog of all of the socialization and control strategies in a popular group leader's arsenal. She describes how leaders may use selective attention to reward certain followers and punish others, create gossip to undermine someone threatening their authority, displace someone's role in the group and thereby the person's status, verbally berate someone in front of other group members, arrange for the individual to be temporarily shunned by other group members, or in extreme cases expel the individual from the clique.

Fearing the leader's power and angling for any opportunity to move up the status hierarchy, other group members generally endorse the leader's actions, but the leader must be careful not to venture too far in these aggressive socialization strategies. If she appears to break the rules for interpersonal interactions or violate shared meanings of the group (recall Youniss's principles), the clique can turn out the leader and lift someone else into power. Milner (2004, p. 89) noted that "in the competition for status, people (especially leaders) often vacillate between being nice and being mean, depending on whether they see the other person as a supporter or as a threat. Conversely, followers are usually nice to those above them in the hope of being accepted as an intimate, and hence raising their status. At the same time they often resent the deference they have to show. Frequently, those with high status are talked about and envied, but disliked."

The need for this arsenal of supportive and combative social skills explains why sociometric studies have found that high-status individuals are associated by peers with both prosocial and antagonistic interpersonal behaviors. What seems most impressive about popular youth's interpersonal behaviors is not that they vacillate between positive and negative interactions but that they do so strategically, in a way that serves to maintain their dominance both within their own clique and across the peer system as a whole.

Intergroup Interactions

Turning attention from intragroup to intergroup relations, investigators' reports tend to emphasize more negative strategies of socialization and control. Although popular group members can treat out-group peers kindly, they are better known for antagonistic interactions. Initially, this may simply serve as an indicator of their qualifications to be popular. One prerequisite to entry into a high-status group is renouncing allegiance to adult conventions and authority. Aggressive behaviors accomplish this, signaling to peers one's budding maturity and openness to the new (adolescent) social system (Merten, 2005). Such behaviors enhance visibility, a key element in admission to popular cliques. Among his sample of British schoolgirls, Duncan (2004, p. 147) noted that "one could be popular within one's own clique, but to be known as one of *the* popular girls implied that you would be brash, aggressive, and involved in rumors and fights amongst the girls."

Adler and Adler (1998) argue that high-status group members are verbally aggressive to outsiders simply because they can get away with it. "Clique members join together in disparaging outsiders; they learn that those in the in-group can freely demean out-group members, and that their targets will return for renewed attempts at acceptance" (p. 158). However, they also acknowledge that such tactics build cohesion among group members. Once the jockeying for position among peer groups is completed in early adolescence and the new popular crowds are established, they will work diligently to defend their position. One way of doing so is to demean groups who are lower in the status hierarchy or who refuse to conform to popular group norms (Bishop et al., 2003). Disparaging peers who are not part of the high-status groups serves to lower outsiders' status and discourage group members from befriending them or following the outsiders' norms (Milner, 2004).

Canaan (1987) found a pattern of relational aggression among high-status middle school girls and more physical aggression toward outsiders by high-status boys. Top-group boys were said to gang up on a low-group member in places unmonitored by adults and then shove the boy around until he was reduced to tears. "This is not a playful thing," one respondent confided, "This is serious. They usually don't stop until the low group member throws a fit. Then the top group gang says 'Calm down, you faggot'" (Canaan, 1987, p. 393). Girls' relational aggression can be equally pointed. Finders (1997) described how a clique of popular middle school girls openly characterized many of their classmates either as "dogs" (unattractive to boys) or "babies" (still conforming to adult rules and expectations). In the presence of the former they would bark loudly and then giggle as they walked away.

The popular group's behavior can have a domino effect, in which individuals outside of the high-status groups pick up the pattern of verbally or physically harassing low-status peers as a sign of allegiance to the popular group norms. Merten (1996b), for example, described how middle school students would pick on members of the low-status "mels" simply to conform to expectations or urgings of other peers, with little regard for the impact of their actions on their victims. Picking on the mels also diminished chances that they would be associated with the mels and thereby become a target of victimization by others (the agenda of mid-rangers that I have already mentioned).

Adults may regard the bullying that Merten (1996b) observed as shameful, but to adolescents it is understandable, and consistent with unspoken rules about who aggresses against whom and for what reasons. When Horn (2003) provided a sample of white, middle-class high school students with scenarios in which a low-status group member was excluded by a high-status peer from a prototypically high-status activity, she found that most ninth graders found the scenario believable and acceptable, often invoking stereotypes about high- and low-status groups to justify the popular peer's actions.

Only in peer settings containing iconoclast crowds are the popular groups likely to be challenged directly. Eckert (1989) conducted an ethnographic study among high school youth in a largely white, working- to middle-class midwestern community, finding the peer system anchored by two major crowds. The high-status jocks were counterpoised against the iconoclastic burnouts, who prided themselves on being the antithesis of the jock crowd: largely working class, following more of a vocational than college-bound academic curriculum, disengaged from athletics and school activities, cool if not hostile toward school adults, and more openly deviant. Each group claimed a different portion of the school property for social interactions; jocks generally preferred to take the long way around between classes rather than risk running the burnout gauntlet by cutting across the courtyard where burnouts congregated. Because the jocks retained friendly relations with school adults, the burnouts' intimidation and opposition did little to undermine the jocks' status, but it certainly dampened the aggression that jocks could mete out against other groups.

The portrait of antagonistic intergroup interactions must be tempered by two factors. First, it underrepresents reports of more measured approaches that popular group members may take to maintain their group boundaries or their control of high-status activities. Dunphy (1969), for example, discovered that when adolescents tried to "crash" a given crowd's social function, group leaders tended to simply ignore the uninvited guests rather than drive them away in a more hostile fashion. Likewise, Merten (1996a) recounted that when a burnout infiltrated the ranks of the cheerleading squad, which heretofore had been staffed exclusively by popular girls, the popular crowd fumed and grumbled to each other but took few steps besides ignoring the interloper to remove her. Second, most accounts of intergroup relations are taken from a narrow and fairly homogeneous range of peer settings: middle schools with the traditional pyramid status system. Without further study of more diverse settings, it is not clear how common the popular group's aggressive and antagonistic behaviors are across secondary schools.

Dyadic Relationships

Patterns of intergroup and intragroup interactions affect the quality and character of dyadic relationships that adolescents form with peers. Some of the impact seems to be related to status striving, but status position is also a factor.

Status Striving

Youth who are striving to attain or retain high status among peers must be mindful of some basic principles about patterns of association. Affiliating with higher status peers enhances opportunities to raise one's status, whereas affiliating with lower status peers threatens to diminish one's own position. This applies to within- as well as across-clique relationships. The implication of affiliating with adults depends on the nature of the association: Dependent relationships drive one's status down sharply (Merten, 1996b; Milner, 2004); relationships that are more egalitarian or manipulative (in which the young person is able to gain certain privileges from adults without being subservient to them) harbor the prospect of raising peer status (Eckert, 1989). Although scholars sometimes fault secondary school teachers for maintaining more distant relationships with students than is common in elementary school settings (Eccles et al., 1983), early adolescents themselves—or rather the demands of their peer system—may bear major responsibility for the estrangement.

Status striving can affect the selection of friends, especially in early adolescence. Part of the "cycle of popularity" that Eder (1985) describes among middle school girls reflects concerns about popularity. Eder observed that a girl who was reasonably well liked just before being accepted into the popular clique became even more sought after for friendship after her move into the clique, only to have her reputation fall when she failed to respond to peers' overtures of friendship. Peers were put off when their offer of friendship was rejected, thereby diminishing their own prospects for admission to the popular clique. The newly popular girl, on the other hand, felt overwhelmed by so much attention from would-be friends and worried that responding to the overtures would jeopardize her newfound position in the popular clique.

Status can play a role in romantic attachments as well. Brown (1999) theorized that, after learning how to relate to potential romantic partners (typically, other-sex peers), adolescents become sensitive to how peers might respond if they become romantically involved with a specific peer, especially whether the relationship will enhance or demean their status among peers. This is particularly true among members of high-status groups because romantic alliances can elevate the romantic partner into the popular crowd, and there is the threat of censure or expulsion if fellow group members do not approve of the individual's romantic choice.

Status Position

Because objectives for peer interactions vary across different types of groups, norms governing dyadic relationships, especially friendships, also vary. The status vigilance of popular crowds carries over into their friendship patterns. Even though these groups sit atop the status hierarchy, they still promulgate a hierarchy within the clique, so that members enjoy different levels of authority (Finders, 1997; Wiseman, 2002). Ever mindful of threats to their position and aware that clique mates represent the most likely individuals to supplant them in the hierarchy, popular group members remain guarded in their friendship patterns. Although they profess true loyalty and affection for each other, they remain open to opportunities to break off relationships or form new alliances if it will improve their position. As a result, their friendships appear to be shallow and opportunistic (Eckert, 1989; Finders, 1997).

Unpopulars are in a challenging situation. They need close friendships for support, especially in early adolescence when they are so often the target of bullying and ridicule, but their low status makes them unattractive candidates for relationships except among fellow members of the unpopular crowd. Because of the "guilt by association" principle, forging friendships with fellow unpopulars increases the risk of physical or verbal attacks from peers. So friendships are both a valuable and risky proposition. Merten (1996b) reported that the unpopular youth whom he observed maintained tenuous bonds. They offered support and advice to each other in private, but often would publicly disavow any affiliation or shy away if their friend was threatened or attacked by peers so as to avoid becoming a secondary target.

Information on mid-rangers and iconoclasts is more limited, but existing evidence suggests that their friendship bonds are much more intimate and enduring than in either of the other types of groups. Finders's "tough cookies" clique evidenced stable friendship ties and a consistent group structure (in terms of the centrality of group members) in contrast to the high-status "social queens," whose within-group status was more tenuous and vacillating. Unable to exert much influence over the peer system as a whole, the "middle group" that Canaan (1987) observed turned much of their attention inward, on relationships within the clique. Eckert's (1989) iconoclastic group of burnouts formed especially tight and enduring friendships. Like the tough cookies, the burnouts emphasized group and individual loyalty and support.

Although provocative, these depictions of differences in dyadic relationships stemming from status striving or status position should be regarded with some skepticism. The information base from which they are drawn is quite limited. In most cases, they arise from ethnographic observations of small and sometimes unusual samples. Few investigators follow their respondents for more than a few months, and most studies focus on early adolescent populations. Closer, more systematic study of the issue, in which a broader array of research strategies is applied to a more diverse set of samples, is needed to reach definitive conclusions about the conditions under which popularity and status affect relationship dynamics. Nevertheless, existing findings do converge consistently on a theme, suggesting that membership in remarkably high- or low-status groups tends to promote less advanced and reliable dyadic affiliations.

DEVELOPMENTAL CHANGES IN STATUS STRUCTURES

So much attention has been devoted to the nature of popularity and the organization and operation of cliques and crowds in early adolescence that investigators can easily forget an essential component of the adolescent peer system: It is a dynamic system that continues to evolve across adolescence. The rich ethnographic database on the organization and operation of early adolescent cliques has no counterpart in middle or later adolescence. The close scrutiny of status strivings among middle school peer groups stands in stark contrast to limited evidence about status in high school crowds. With rare exceptions (e.g., Kinney, 1993), investigators do not follow their study participants across the middle school years, let alone across the transition from middle or junior high school to high school. Thus, much of what can be said about developmental changes in the adolescent peer system remains speculative. Like the associations between group affiliations and relationship dynamics, developmental trajectories—and their implications for popularity—are supported by a limited body of evidence.

The early adolescent/middle school years might best be construed as a period of initiation and consolidation of the peer system. Young people can be expected to spend much of the first year in secondary school simply trying to decipher the new peer system and negotiate their position within the system. This helps to explain the crude features of peer relationships in ethnographic reports of this age group: sharp distinctions between popular groups and nonpopular groups (Canaan, 1987; Eder, 1985); rigid conformity to group norms, even to the point of sharing wardrobes (Finders, 1997); and aggressive tactics to enforce group norms and punish or deride those who refuse to disengage from adult-dependent relationships and enter the more heterosocially oriented world of peer interactions (Finders, 1997; Merten, 1996b; Wiseman, 2002).

Through the remainder of the middle school years, young people presumably grow more comfortable with the new peer system and more resigned to their position within it. A continued press toward heterosociality (Connolly et al., 2000) may precipitate further rearrangements of status and group affiliations as bolder or more skillful players pursue relationships more aggressively and successfully. The popular crowd, segmented by gender in the beginning of middle school, tends to meld into a single, mixed-sex group by the end of middle school. Generally, however, there is little reason to expect major alterations in the basic elements or operation of the system during this time period.

The transition to high school generally marks a shift from early to middle adolescence. In many cases, high schools encompass a larger student population than middle or junior high schools, thus signaling a second major expansion in the size of the peer system. Obviously, they cater to an older set of adolescents who are encountering ever-expanding domains of autonomy: obtaining a driver's license, earning the right to vote, making independent health care decisions, and so on. A broader array of extracurricular activities provides more opportunities to demonstrate exceptional talents or abilities. All of these factors carry the potential for major changes in the peer system.

Kinney (1993) found that the increase in the size of the school and scope of activities prompted an expansion in the number of peer crowds available to students. Crowds also began to unite individuals across grade levels, so that freshmen cliques dominated by a particular crowd type would closely affiliate with, if not encompass, members from older grade levels who had the same reputation among peers. Contact with older students provided greater credibility to crowds, even if they occupied the midrange of the status hierarchy. This seemed to diminish students' preoccupation with popularity and status. If they gained the attention of upperclass students, the need to be recognized or directed by popular peers in their own grade level diminished.

Other investigators point to additional transformations in the peer system in middle adolescence that undermine the stature of the popular peer group. The sheer size of the school, coupled with diversification of lifestyles through various extracurricular activities, makes it more difficult for the popular crowd to attain and maintain the high visibility that is critical to establishing and enforcing a dominant set of norms. In some instances, high-status individuals become partitioned into disparate crowds (Canaan, 1987), often creating confusion about the criteria by which status is achieved. Accompanying the increase in school size may be greater diversity in the ethnic and socioeconomic composition of the student body. Tendencies toward racial segregation within the student body can set the stage for a pluralistic status system, in which separate status structures emerge within various racial groups, or the basic social division of students along racial and ethnic lines undermines the importance of previous social divisions based on clique or crowd identities (Garner et al., 2006; Foley, 1990; Larkin, 1979; Milner, 2004). The growth of autonomy and diversification of activities or lifestyles provides fertile grounds for iconoclastic crowds that openly challenge the norms of high-status groups (Milner, 2004). Finally, because of all the privileges that age itself bestows upon young people, age becomes an alternative source of status. Bishop et al. (2003) found that upperclassmen enjoyed more prestige than underclassmen, often without regard to their crowd affiliation.

All of these factors suggest that the social environment of high school is not likely to be as consistent across schools, as in the case of middle or junior high schools. This may explain why Garner et al. (2006) found such an array of status structures across the high schools that they studied. In the face of such diversity in social systems, it seems unlikely that investigators will find as consistent a set of correlates of popularity among middle adolescents as they have found among early adolescents. However, the key to the meaning of popularity still seems to lie in the organization of the peer system in which it is measured. Schools that manifest the traditional pyramid status structure should harbor popular-crowd dynamics similar to what seems to be common among middle school youth. In social settings with pluralistic or fragmented status structures, popularity may not prove to be a very distinctive or meaningful factor in students' lives.

As middle adolescence unfolds, the very forces that brought status strivings and peer groups to the fore in early adolescence seem to progress beyond the need for these structures. As young people grow more comfortable with their emerging sense of identity, they may find a crowd's provisional identity, once a source of comfort and support, constraining to their identity development. Group identity gives way to individual identity. Many high school students, for example, claim membership in multiple crowds (Cross & Fletcher, 2009). Likewise, in the face of continued autonomy development, they may chafe at the conformity demands of cliques and crowds. Interests shift away from group relationships to deeper, individual ties in romantic dyads; cliques and crowds no longer serve much of a function in such relationships (Brown, 1999; Connolly & Goldberg, 1999). Cliques draw members from multiple crowds, further obscuring the reputation and status of clique members (Brown et al., 1994; Urberg, Değirmencioğlu, Tolson, & Halliday-Scher, 2000).

As status striving and peer group conformity fade as organizing principles of the peer system, it makes sense that the correlation between status and likeability will weaken as well. Indeed, by the beginning of late adolescence, the connection between popularity and status has diminished to statistical and practical nonsignificance, so that, just as in childhood, popular youth are simply those who are well liked by peers (e.g., Cillessen & Mayeux, 2004).

CULTURAL PERSPECTIVES

Studies cited in this chapter support the assertion that the meaning and significance of popularity in adolescence stem from the organization and operation of a new social system that emerges in early adolescence and then continues to evolve over the course of the middle and high school years. Status structures that help to identify popular youth and endow them with certain privileges and responsibilities assist young people in adjusting to a new social system that itself is designed to facilitate the major developmental mandates of the adolescent period.

Although this standard script has been observed in a number of communities across the United States, it is important not to overgeneralize study findings. Most investigators have concentrated on a narrow demographic: predominantly (if not exclusively) white, middle-class populations of youth in the United States. There is some evidence that peer crowds share a similar organization in North America and Europe (Bešić & Kerr, 2009; Delsing, ter Bogt, Engels, & Meeus, 2007; Thurlow, 2001), but the evidence is still quite circumscribed. Investigations of adolescent peer social dynamics in more collectivist cultures are rare and sorely needed, especially because the developmental demands of autonomy and identity may be organized quite differently in those contexts (Kagitçibasi, 2005).

There are several levels of analysis that scholars can pursue in exploring cultural influences on popularity and peer group dynamics. One is to examine the impact of family culture. Finders (1997), for example, discovered that members of the tough cookies clique were essentially sidelined from pursuing popularity by family values and resources. Their mothers commented that they did not have the money to buy the styles of clothing, pay for the extracurricular activities, or even pay the cost of a yearbook, all of which were de rigueur for acceptance into the popular crowd. Likewise, in Eckert's (1989) study of jocks and burnouts, the tradition of close reliance on peers among working-class youth and their unfamiliarity with the "corporate" style of relationships with peers and adults left them ill equipped to negotiate the status struggles that characterized cliques among the high-status jock crowd.

A somewhat broader level of cultural assessment involves community culture: the prevailing norms within the community in which adolescents reside. Even though Coleman (1961) railed against adolescents for eschewing adult values, he acknowledged the potential of communities to influence value systems in the "leading crowd." For example, the importance that high-status peers accorded to academic achievement seemed to vary directly with the rate of college completion among community adults.

The level of cultural analysis most familiar among scholars in the United States involves ethnic comparisons. Studies of multiethnic high schools suggest that ethnicity may overshadow popularity or status as a means of differentiating peer groups (Foley, 1990; Larkin, 1979). Milner (2004) argues that the proliferation of multiethnic communities has increased the tendency of U.S. schools to feature pluralistic peer social systems rather than systems that feature a singular social hierarchy. Such contexts could encompass two or three distinct groups of popular youth or could manifest so little consensus among students that it is unclear who, if anyone, enjoys high status among peers.

At all of these levels, as well as the level of national comparisons already mentioned, scholarship is very limited. It may seem ironic to call for more careful investigation of these cultural components when I have argued that the adolescent peer system operates relatively independent of adults. The fact that adults no longer control peer relations with the advent of adolescence does not mean that they have no significant influence over these relationships; clearly, they do. Moreover, the degree to which adults absent themselves from adolescents' peer interactions, or even permit relatively autonomous peer interactions, is culturally variable. As with so many aspects of adolescent development and behavior, it is not possible to understand popularity and peer group dynamics without including cultural components.

STUDYING POPULARITY IN PEER CONTEXTS: IMPLICATIONS FOR RESEARCH

From the broader, sociological perspective of adolescent peer systems, popularity emerges as a key factor in the definition of status and operation of peer socialization within and among peer groups. As these peer systems emerge and evolve, and as they differ in form and function across cultures or communities, so do the nature and significance of popularity. In treating popularity as an individual-difference variable based primarily on internal characteristics of a person, investigators misconstrue its meaning and significance among adolescents.

A better approach is to regard popularity as an interaction between individual interests or abilities and peer system structures and demands. Both the individual and peer system characteristics on which popularity is based are likely to evolve over the course of adolescence, so popularity ought to be studied as a dynamic trait, shifting over time in response to individual and system developments.

The peer system is not uniform across adolescence or within any period of this life stage. It emerges in different forms in different school or community contexts. Variations in the nature or degree of status differentiation should affect the salience of popularity as well as the individual characteristics that are most important to it. Generalizations about popularity ought to be situated within a social context. That is, investigators should refer to the nature of popularity within highly stratified peer systems, or within pluralistic peer contexts, rather than in more general terms.

Another important question to explore is whether or not popularity is perceived similarly across various segments of the adolescent peer system. Do young people in moderate- or low-status groups regard the same peers as popular as those in high-status groups? Gorman, Kim, and Schimmelbusch (2002) reported that the preponderance of nominations of high-status peers came from adolescents who themselves had fairly high status ratings. Considering evidence that depictions of particular peer groups vary systematically by a rater's own crowd affiliation (Stone & Brown, 1998), it is possible that adolescents may not enjoy as broad a base of popularity as sociometric studies suggest, or that beyond identification of extreme cases (those who are markedly high in popularity or unpopularity) sociometric ratings of popularity are volatile and contingent on the nominators' group affiliations.

It may also be useful to differentiate "local" from "regional" popularity. Some adolescents may enjoy considerable popularity or status within their own clique or crowd, even if they are not recognized as popular within the broader peer system. Given the normative developmental trajectory of peer systems, it seems likely that the distinction between local and regional popularity will grow more important as young people move from early to middle and late adolescence. With age, status within a friendship group or peer crowd may have more significance for individual adjustment and peer group functioning than status across the peer system as a whole.

Finally, it is important to acknowledge that I have overstated the clarity of adolescent peer systems and their evolution. Clique membership is unstable, especially in early adolescence (Kindermann, 2007; Rubin, Bukowski, & Parker, 2006). The stability of crowd affiliations has not been carefully considered because there are hardly any longitudinal investigations of the issue (Cross & Fletcher, 2009). The use of social network programs to define peer groups produces somewhat arbitrary arrangements of individuals, often prohibiting young people from being assigned to more than one group, even though observations indicate that many youth have multiple clique affiliations (Kindermann, 2007). When given an opportunity, a significant share of adolescents will claim membership in more than one peer crowd (Youniss et al., 1994) or disavow affiliation with any crowd. In other words, the adolescent peer group system is inherently fuzzy and dynamic, greatly complicating the study of important constructs such as popularity.

Sociometric studies have identified some general patterns, in which likeability and social status become distinct in adolescence, moderately related early in this period but not so much later on, with prosocial characteristics linked to both facets of popularity but aggressive behavior more common among high-status youth. Seen through the lens of sociological and ethnographic studies, these features of popularity appear to be part of group dynamics that facilitate identity and autonomy development in adolescence through the organization of peer group allegiances and status relationships. However, the peer group system allows for multiple group affiliations, fuzzy group boundaries, and considerable variation on the general theme of a hierarchical status system—variations that are sensitive to cultural or contextual characteristics as well as the course of development across adolescence. Young people's understanding of popularity is embedded within a complex and dynamic peer system, which in turn is embedded within cultural frameworks that, despite adolescents' efforts at autonomy, still influence their behavior. As researchers continue to explore the intriguing issues concerning popularity in adolescence, they should work from more of a multilevel conceptual perspective, seeking to understand the varying forms that popularity takes in different populations of adolescents.

REFERENCES

Adler, P. A., & Adler, P. (1998). *Peer power: Preadolescent culture and identity.* New Brunswick, NJ: Rutgers University Press.

Běsić, N., & Kerr, M. (2009). Punks, goths, and other eye-catching peer crowds: Do they fulfill a function for shy youths? *Journal of Research on Adolescence, 19,* 113–121.

Bishop, J. H., Bishop, M., & Bishop, M. M. (2003). *Peer harassment: A weapon in the struggle for popularity and normative hegemony in American secondary schools* (CAHRS working paper no. 03–19). Ithaca, NY: Cornell University, School of Industrial and Labor Relations, Center for Advanced Human Resource Studies.

Brown, B. B. (1999). "You're going with *who?!*": Peer group influences on adolescent romantic relationships. In W. Furman, B. B. Brown, & C. Feiring (Eds.), *The development of romantic relationships in adolescence* (pp. 291–329). London: Cambridge University Press.

Brown, B. B., Bakken, J. P., Ameringer, S. W., & Mahon, S. D. (2008). A comprehensive conceptualization of the peer influence process in adolescence. In M. J. Prinstein & K. Dodge (Eds.), *Understanding peer influence in children and adolescents* (pp. 17–44). New York: Guilford Press.

Brown, B. B., & Larson, J. (2009). Peer relationships in adolescence. In R. M. Lerner & L. Steinberg (Eds.), *Handbook of adolescent psychology* (3rd ed., pp. 74–103). New York: Wiley.

Brown, B. B., Mory, M., & Kinney, D. A. (1994). Casting adolescent crowds in relational perspective: Caricature, channel, and context. In R. Montemayor, G. R. Adams, & T. P. Gullotta (Eds.), *Advances in adolescent development: Vol. 6. Personal relationships during adolescence* (pp. 123–167). Thousand Oaks, CA: Sage.

Brown, B. B., Von Bank, H., & Steinberg, L. (2008). Smoke in the looking glass: Effects of discordance between self- and peer rated crowd affiliation on adolescent anxiety, depression and self-feeling. *Journal of Youth and Adolescence, 37,* 1163–1177.

Canaan, J. (1987). A comparative analysis of American suburban middle class, middle school and high school teenage cliques. In G. Spindler & L. Spindler (Eds.), *Interpretive ethnography of education: At home and abroad* (pp. 385–406). Hillsdale, NJ: Erlbaum.

Cillessen, A. H. N., & Mayeux, L. (2004). Sociometric status and peer group behavior: Previous findings and current directions. In J. B. Kupersmidt & K. A. Dodge (Eds.), *Children's peer relations: From development to intervention* (pp. 3–20). Washington, DC: American Psychological Association.

Cillessen, A. H. N., & Rose, A. J. (2005). Understanding popularity in the peer system. *Current Directions in Psychological Science, 14,* 102–105.

Coleman, J. S. (1961). *The adolescent society.* Glencoe, IL: Free Press.
Connolly, J., Furman, W., & Konarski, R. (2000). The role of peers in the emergence of heterosexual romantic relationships in adolescence. *Child Development, 7,* 1395–1408.
Connolly, J., & Goldberg, W. (1999). Romantic relationships in adolescence: The role of friends and peers in their emergence and development. In W. Furman, B. B. Brown, & C. Feiring (Eds.), *The development of romantic relationships in adolescence* (pp. 266–290). London: Cambridge University Press.
Corsaro, W. A., & Eder, D. (1990). Children's peer cultures. *Annual Review of Sociology, 16,* 197–220.
Cross, J. R., & Fletcher, K. L. (2009). The challenge of adolescent crowd research: Defining the crowd. *Journal of Youth and Adolescence, 38,* 747–764.
Delsing, M. J. M. H., ter Bogt, T. F. M., Engels, R. C. M. E., & Meeus, W. H. J. (2007). Adolescents' peer crowd identification in The Netherlands: Structure and associations with problem behaviors. *Journal of Research on Adolescence, 17*(2), 467–480.
Duncan, N. (2004). It's important to be nice, but it's nicer to be important: Girls, popularity, and sexual competition. *Sex Education, 4,* 137–152.
Dunphy, D. C. (1969). *Cliques, crowds, and gangs.* Melbourne, Victoria, Australia: Cheshire.
Eccles, J. S., Midgley, C., Wigfield, A., Buchanan, C. M., Reuman, D., Flanagan, C., et al. (1983). Development during adolescence: The impact of stage-environment fit on young adolescents' experiences in schools and in families. *American Psychologist, 48,* 90–101.
Eckert, P. (1989). *Jocks and burnouts: Social categories and identity in the high school.* New York: Teachers College Press.
Eder, D. (1985). The cycle of popularity: Interpersonal relations among female adolescents. *Sociology of Education, 58,* 154–165.
Eder, D. (1993). "Go get ya a French!": Romantic and sexual teasing among adolescent girls. In D. Tannen (Ed.), *Gender and conversational interaction* (pp. 17–31). New York: Oxford University Press.
Eder, D., & Kinney, D. A. (1995). The effect of middle school extracurricular activities on adolescents' popularity and peer status. *Youth and Society, 26,* 298–324.
Finders, M. J. (1997). *Just girls: Hidden literacies and life in junior high.* New York: Teachers College Press.
Foley, D. E. (1990). *Learning capitalist culture: Deep in the heart of Tejas.* Philadelphia: University of Pennsylvania Press.
Friedenberg, E. (1963). *Coming of age in America: Growth and acquiescence.* New York: Vintage Press.
Garner, R., Bootcheck, J., Lorr, M., & Rauch, K. (2006). The adolescent society revisited: Cultures, crowds, climates, and status structures in seven secondary schools. *Journal of Youth and Adolescence, 35,* 1023–1035.
Gordon, C. W. (1957). *The social system of the high school.* Glencoe, IL: Free Press.
Gorman, A. H., Kim, J., & Schimmelbusch, A. (2002). The attributes adolescents

associate with peer popularity and teacher preference. *Journal of School Psychology, 40,* 143–165.

Hollingshead, A. B. (1949). *Elmtown's youth: The impact of social classes on adolescents.* New York: Wiley.

Horn, S. S. (2003). Adolescents' reasoning about exclusion from social groups. *Developmental Psychology, 39,* 71–84.

Kagitçibasi, Ç. (2005). Autonomy and relatedness in cultural context: Implications for self and family. *Journal of Cross-Cultural Psychology, 36,* 403–422.

Kindermann, T. A. (2007). Effects of naturally existing peer groups on changes in academic engagement in a cohort of sixth graders. *Child Development, 78,* 1186–1203.

Kinney, D. (1993). From "nerds" to "normals": Adolescent identity recovery within a changing social system. *Sociology of Education, 66,* 21–40.

Larkin, R. (1979). *Suburban youth in cultural crisis.* New York: Oxford University Press.

Maccoby, E. (1988). Gender as a social category. *Developmental Psychology, 24,* 755–765.

Macleod, J. (1987). *Ain't no makin' it. Leveled aspirations in low-income neighborhoods.* Boulder, CO: Westview Press.

Merten, D. E. (1996a). Burnout as cheerleader: The cultural basis for prestige and privilege in junior high school. *Anthropology and Education Quarterly, 27,* 51–70.

Merten, D. E. (1996b). Visibility and vulnerability: Responses to rejection by nonaggressive junior high school boys. *Journal of Early Adolescence, 16,* 5–26.

Merten, D. E. (1997). The meaning of meanness: Popularity, competition, and conflict among junior high school girls. *Sociology of Education, 70,* 175–191.

Merten, D. E. (2005). Transitions and "trouble": Rites of passage for suburban girls. *Anthropology and Education Quarterly, 36,* 132–148.

Milner, M. (2004). *Freaks, geeks, and cool kids: American teenagers, schools, and the culture of consumption.* New York: Routledge.

Newman, B. M., & Newman, P. R. (2001). Group identity and alienation: Giving the we its due. *Journal of Youth and Adolescence, 30,* 515–538.

Payne, E. C. (2007). Heterosexism, perfection, and popularity: Young lesbians' experiences of the high school social scene. *Educational Studies, 41,* 60–79.

Rubin, K. H., Bukowski, W. M., & Parker, J. G. (2006). Peer interactions, relationships, and groups. In N. Eisenberg, W. Damon, & R. M. Lerner (Eds.), *Handbook of child psychology: Vol. 3. Social, emotional, and personality development* (6th ed., pp. 571–645). Hoboken, NJ: Wiley.

Smetana, J. G., & Asquith, P. (1994). Adolescents' and parents' conceptions of parental authority and personal autonomy. *Child Development, 65,* 1147–1162.

Soenens, B., & Vansteenkiste, M. (2005). Antecedents and outcomes of self-determination in 3 life domains: The role of parents' and teachers' autonomy support. *Journal of Youth and Adolescence, 34,* 589–604.

Stone, M., & Brown, B. B. (1998). In the eye of the beholder: Adolescents' perceptions of peer crowd stereotypes. In R. E. Muuss & H. D. Porton (Eds.), *Adolescent behavior and society: A book of readings* (5th ed., pp. 158–169). New York: McGraw-Hill.

Sussman, S., Pokhrel, P., Ashmore, R. D., & Brown, B. B. (2007). Adolescent peer group identification and characteristics: A review of the literature. *Addictive Behaviors, 32,* 1602–1627.

Tajfel, H. (1982). Social psychology of intergroup relations. *Annual Review of Psychology, 33,* 1–39.

Thurlow, C. (2001). The usual suspects? A comparative investigation of crowds and social-type labelling among young British teenagers. *Journal of Youth Studies, 4,* 319–334.

Urberg, K. A., Değirmencioğlu, S. M., Tolson, J. M., & Halliday-Scher, K. (2000). Adolescent social crowds: Measurement and relationship to friendships. *Journal of Adolescent Research, 15,* 427–445.

Wiseman, R. (2002). *Queen bees and wannabes: Helping your daughter survive cliques, gossip, boyfriends, and other realities of adolescence.* New York: Crown.

Youniss, J., McLellan, J. A., & Strouse, D. (1994). "We're popular but we're not snobs": Adolescents describe their crowds. In R. Montemayor, G. R. Adams, & T. P. Gullotta (Eds.), *Advances in adolescent development: Vol. 6. Personal relationships during adolescence* (pp. 101–122). Thousand Oaks, CA: Sage.

Chapter 9

Peer Popularity in the Context of Ethnicity

AMY BELLMORE
ADRIENNE NISHINA
SANDRA GRAHAM

Consider the peer experiences of a Latina student attending a large public school that is 90% African American and 10% Latino. Are you surprised to learn that she is the most popular student in her grade? Given this information, what expectations do you have about her or her peers? Alternatively, what conclusions might you draw if she was the least popular student in her grade? In many ways, the latter case is easier to reconcile because there is congruence between her low social status among her peers and the numerical minority status of her ethnic group within the school. Popularity may be a reflection of visibility or power within a peer group. Thus, any behaviors or characteristics that enhance prominence should also promote popularity, whereas those that limit prominence and power should weaken popularity.

Students who are in the numerical majority in their school may have power and prominence based on their representation in the peer group. Thus, it might be easier for the Latina just described to achieve status and prominence in a different setting (e.g., a Latino-majority school). However, an adolescent like our Latina may also be able to transcend the limitations placed on her because of the relatively low numerical representation of her ethnic group. She may possess other characteristics that increase her status at school. In this case, the low numerical representation of her ethnic group at school may serve to enhance her standing, because it makes her stand out more from the crowd. In ethnically diverse settings, our student's popularity may be more dependent on her personal and individual attributes than her ethnic group membership. In this chapter, we elaborate on these speculations as we argue that ethnicity can either promote or limit popularity depending on the ethnic composition of the peer group.

The notion that both individual characteristics (e.g., Latino group membership) and peer group composition (e.g., a predominantly African American school population) influence popularity draws directly from conceptualizations of popularity as both an individual- and group-oriented phenomenon (Rubin, Bukowski, & Parker, 2006) that depends on interactions between individuals and their social contexts (Boyce et al., 1998; Bronfenbrenner, 1979; Coie & Cillessen, 1993; Moreno, 1934).

There are also key reasons why we should consider both ethnicity and the ethnic composition of the peer group. First, the ethnicity of individuals triggers racial stereotype-based expectations from peers. These expectations can cut both ways in influencing popularity: If they match behaviors associated with popularity, status will benefit; but if they match behaviors associated with low status, status will suffer. Second, there are unique challenges associated with being a numerical ethnic minority. Ethnic minority youth may face adopting behaviors that lead to acceptance or prominence by the ethnic majority even when their own ethnic group does not endorse them. These youth must negotiate both costs and benefits when they stick to their own norms and disregard those of the larger peer group. For example, this may gain them status in their own ethnic group but reduce their status in the peer group at large. In contrast, minority youth who conform to the majority norms may attain broader status but lose respect and status in their own ethnic group.

Understanding how ethnicity influences popularity is especially important as Western societies, both North American and European, become increasingly ethnically diverse. In the United States, ethnic diversity increased in all states in the decade between the 1990 and 2000 census (Brewer & Suchan, 2001). In both North American and European schools, students are now navigating settings with increased levels of ethnic diversity.

In this chapter, the term *ethnicity* includes race but is also determined by other factors, including culture, nationality, language, and identity. We begin by reviewing the small but emerging literature on ethnic group differences in the correlates of popularity and peer acceptance in the United States. The significance of popularity to the lives of children and adolescents has been examined across nations and cultures, including China (Schwartz et al., in press), Greece (Andreou, 2006), Slovakia (Košir & Pečjak, 2005), and the Netherlands (de Bruyn & Cillessen, 2006) to name just a few. Marks et al. (2010) provide a comprehensive overview of current international research on popularity. In this chapter, we focus on the experiences of U.S. students because this allows us to consider the unique ethnic makeup of the country, historical and current policies related to race and ethnicity, and the distinctive immigration experiences of children from different ethnic groups. After reviewing this literature, we discuss several issues central to understanding the relevance of ethnicity to popularity that have yet to be addressed in research.

ETHNIC GROUP DIFFERENCES OR SIMILARITIES?

Researchers who have studied peer status in multiethnic settings have generally recognized the significance of the ethnic composition of the peer group when making conclusions about ethnic differences. For example, although a number of investigators have attributed differences in acceptance to specific ethnic group membership (e.g., being African American) rather than numerical representation within the setting, all of them have been careful either to control for ethnic composition in some way or to interpret the results in light of the ethnic composition of the peer group. In our review, we use the same ethnic labels reported in each study and highlight the assumptions of the researchers.

It is important to point out that, even though researchers have recognized the significance of ethnicity to peer status, few studies of popularity have examined ethnicity explicitly (see Graham, Taylor, & Ho, 2008). This deficit in the literature may be partially due to the fact that many study samples do not allow for rich explorations of ethnicity. In early sociometric studies of peer acceptance, samples were either predominantly white (e.g., Coie, Dodge, & Coppotelli, 1982) or predominantly black (Coie & Kupersmidt, 1983). Moreover, most samples that included more than one ethnic group were composed primarily of white and black participants (e.g., Parkhurst & Hopmeyer, 1998). Thus, while little is known about popularity for ethnic minority groups in general, even less is known about groups such as Latinos and Asians. Finally, in cases where samples did allow ethnic group comparisons, they were often not reported. As a result, this review marks only the beginning of understanding how ethnicity affects popularity.

Using Ethnicity and Peer Acceptance as a Starting Point

One of the first studies to use a classification system to examine social status based on "like most" and "like least" nominations used a 68% white and 32% black sample of third-, fifth-, and eighth-grade students (Coie et al., 1982). In this study, proportionally fewer black students (12.5%) were classified as "popular" compared with white students (25.4%). The authors noted this difference but were careful to point out potential difficulties in examining ethnic group differences when the ethnic representation is not equal. It should also be noted that Coie et al. used the term popular for a sociometric classification category and were not assessing popularity as conceptualized in this volume (see Cillessen & Marks, Chapter 2).

When ethnic group representation is not balanced in a setting, popularity and acceptance may be influenced by two distinct processes: in-group preferences and majority-group preferences. Reflecting the tendency of children, adolescents, and adults to view members of their own group more favorably than members of another group (Tajfel, 1982), acceptance among one's own ethnic group members has been found to be overwhelmingly stronger than acceptance by out-group members. Sociometric research with children and adolescents in ethnically balanced (i.e., 50% African American and 50% Caucasian) academic settings has consistently indicated that both African American and Caucasian students like same-ethnicity peers more than other-ethnicity peers (Graham & Cohen, 1997; Sagar, Schofield, & Snyder, 1983; Schofield & Whitley, 1983; Singleton & Asher, 1979; Shrum, Cheek, & Hunter, 1988).

Concurrent with these in-group preferences, average acceptance tends to be relatively high for children who belong to the ethnic group that is in the numerical majority in a particular setting. In unbalanced settings with white–black samples, several studies have shown that students in the numerical ethnic majority within their classrooms were more accepted among both same- and other-ethnicity peers than were students in the numerical ethnic minority (Hallinan & Smith, 1985; Kistner, Metzler, Gatlin, & Risi, 1993; Shaw, 1973; St. John & Lewis, 1975). Thus, rather than one ethnic group being more accepted regardless of context, in black-majority classrooms black students were the most accepted, and in white-majority classrooms white students were the most accepted. This pattern has been attributed to the greater availability of students in the numerical ethnic majority for both same- and other-ethnicity students to interact with them and create positive perceptions. It may also reflect the higher perceived status of the group that holds the majority in a school (Nesdale, 1999).

There is little evidence of one group being more accepted than other groups after these two factors are taken into consideration. One exception is a study by Jackson, Barth, Powell, and Lochman (2006) with a sample of fifth graders that was 41% white and 53% black. They found that the peer acceptance of black children increased as their proportion in the classroom increased. White children were generally rated as more accepted than black children except when black children were the strong majority within the classroom (defined as > 66%). Even in that case, the ratings of white students were not much lower than when they held the strong majority. These findings suggest that in some cases both black and white children may be favorably biased toward white peers. Unfortunately, these results are somewhat reflective of earlier concerns about how minority status, or the status with low perceived power, may affect the social experiences of ethnic minorities in white-majority schools (Khmelkov & Hallinan, 1999; Nesdale, 1999). However, note that acceptance for both ethnic groups continued to be influenced by the relative representation of each ethnic group in the context.

For the few studies including more than African American and Caucasian groups, the main conclusion is that peer acceptance does not differ across ethnic groups and that the ethnic composition of a peer group influences all students similarly. No difference in acceptance was found with a kindergarten and third-grade sample of European American, Spanish American, African American, and Asian American students (Howes & Wu, 1990) or a 60% European American, 30% African American, 10% Asian American, and multiethnic sample of kindergartners attending multiethnic schools (Phillipsen, Bridges, McLemore, & Saponaro, 1999). When the effect of classroom ethnic composition was examined in a sixth-grade sample of African Americans, Asian Americans, Latinos, and European Americans, students from ethnic groups that represented a larger proportion of the classroom were more accepted. This trend existed for all ethnic groups (Bellmore, Nishina, Witkow, Graham, & Juvonen, 2007).

This research on ethnic group differences in peer acceptance reveals consistent effects of peer group ethnic composition that appear to hold for all groups. Yet to be determined is whether these effects also hold for popularity. Because of the greater emphasis on visibility and power for popularity over acceptance, a similar pattern may emerge, but the magnitude of the influence of ethnic majority or minority status could be stronger. That is, students who are part of the ethnic group in the numerical minority in a peer group may be especially unlikely to achieve popular status. It is also possible that ethnic group membership will override the effects of peer group ethnic composition in predicting popularity. Stereotypes about behaviors and values that are tied to certain ethnic groups may be more or less correlated with popularity.

Peer Discrimination as an Index of Low Peer Status

As for popularity, ethnic group differences in unpopularity and the associated influences of peer contexts have yet to be examined. However, at least with regard to peer rejection, there do not appear to be consistent group differences that can be attributed to ethnicity. When interethnic peer preferences are examined, more in-group liking than out-group derogation emerges (Cameron, Alvarez, Ruble, & Fuligni, 2001; Nesdale, 1999; Pfeifer, Brown, & Juvonen, 2007). That is, in-group preferences are stronger than out-group rejections. If we extend this model, we would expect unpopularity to be less impacted by ethnic group membership than popularity. An alternative model that focuses on peer discrimination as an index of low status may also be useful to understand how ethnic group membership may influence unpopularity.

Ethnic discrimination by peers is defined as being ridiculed, called bad names, or being hit because of one's ethnicity (Brown & Bigler, 2005). In multiethnic samples of adolescents, Asian American students have reported more instances of discrimination by their peers than other students (Greene, Way, & Pahl, 2006; Fisher, Wallace, & Fenton, 2000; Rosenbloom & Way, 2004). One reason may be that in these studies Asian American students were always the group with the smallest numerical representation within their schools.

We can look to this work on peer discrimination to inform us about how popularity may be influenced by ethnicity. This work also calls attention to the significance of generational status. Previous popularity studies tend to lack sufficient ethnic diversity to examine basic ethnic group differences (focusing mainly on black and white youth). Studies with samples that also consider the generational status of different ethnic groups are even rarer. The few studies that do exist find that students report intraethnic peer discrimination from same-ethnicity peers who are of different generational status. In a New York high school sample, recent Chinese immigrants suffered at the hands of students who had emigrated from China when they were very young and considered themselves more "Americanized" (Rosenbloom & Way, 2004). In Dutch samples, racial victimization similarly appears to be ordered hierarchically, corresponding with historical societal differences between ethnic groups (Verkuyten & Thijs, 2002). Thus, ethnicity and immigration status may both prohibit the attainment of popular status, of course depending on the composition of the peer group and even when the individual is a member of the numerical majority. Ethnicity and immigration status may also increase the likelihood of being on the receiving end of discriminating or victimizing behaviors, which are linked to low acceptance.

Correlates of Popularity

Popularity is associated with many domains of child and adolescent functioning. Factors correlated with popularity include externalizing behaviors, internalizing behaviors, social functioning, and academic adjustment (see Schwartz & Gorman, Chapter 11, this volume). A second way to understand the significance of ethnicity in the lives of high-status youth is to consider whether these correlates of popularity are similar or different across ethnic groups.

Existing work on the behavioral, psychological, and academic profiles of popular youth is derived from diverse theoretical and methodological traditions. We have learned much from ethnographic studies by anthropologists and sociologists interested in understanding microsocieties present within peer settings (see Merten, Chapter 3, this volume). Normative and atypical experiences of social development have also been studied quantitatively. Much of the work in both traditions has recognized the significance of the values and norms of a peer group to identify the behaviors associated with popularity (e.g., Adler & Adler, 1995; Boivin, Dodge, & Coie, 1995). To the extent that members of an ethnic group might value certain attributes over others or set the behavioral norms in their peer group, we might expect different behaviors to be associated with popularity across ethnic groups. Indeed, Meisinger, Blake, Lease, Palardy, and Olejnik (2007) found that the behavioral correlates of popularity differed across classrooms depending on which ethnic group was in the numerical majority. Next, we review how popularity is associated with two specific dimensions of adjustment: aggression and academic achievement. We contend that peer group norms play a large role in these associations.

Aggression

Aggression is a characteristic that illustrates differences both between popular youth and their peers and between youth who are well liked versus popular. In studies of white youth in predominantly white suburban schools, aggressive behavior detracts from likeability. However, even in these settings, aggression can be used skillfully to gain or maintain popularity (Cillessen & Mayeux, 2004; Parkhurst & Hopmeyer, 1998; Rose, Swenson, & Waller, 2004). Both boys and girls, particularly in adolescence, may strategically use overt and relational aggression to manipulate the social dynamics of the peer group to enhance their own popularity (Adler & Adler, 1995, 1998; Eder, 1985; Evans & Eder, 1993; Kinney, 1993; Merten, 1997). Similar conclusions have emerged with black samples in rural schools that were predominantly black (Farmer, Estell, Bishop, O'Neal, & Cairns, 2003; Lease, Kennedy, & Axelrod, 2007).

When researchers have classified students based on combinations of peer reputational characteristics, they have found that these classifications are influenced by ethnicity. For example, Luthar and McMahon (1996) found that African American students were overrepresented in the aggressive–popular group of a multiethnic urban high school. Rodkin, Farmer, Pearl, and Van Acker (2000) reported similar findings that may be attributed to the ethnic makeup of their classrooms. In their study, proportionally more black than white boys were assigned to the popular–antisocial group, particularly when the ethnic makeup of the classrooms was mostly white. These findings could indicate that popularity and aggression are more strongly linked for black youth than for white youth. However, because these constructs are typically assessed via peer nominations, aggression stereotypes held about black youth by other students need to be considered. It is important to examine whether these links are maintained when aggression scores are derived from other sources that may be more objective. Finally, as indicated, little is known about the popularity–aggression link in other groups, such as Asian and Latino youth.

In summary, aggression seems to have similar implications for acceptance and popularity in ethnically homogenous settings. Still, some differences may emerge in multiethnic settings. In more diverse contexts, factors at play might include the particular ethnic groups present, their relative representation in school, the behaviors that each group may value, and the stereotypes that their peers may have about them. Any one of these factors may account for ethnic differences in multiethnic settings.

Academic Achievement

In order to understand ethnic group differences in adolescent academic achievement, researchers have looked at peers as socializing agents that may either facilitate or inhibit academic success (Steinberg, Dornbusch, & Brown, 1992). Fordham and Ogbu (1986) generated one of the most well-known hypotheses implicating peers. On the basis of their ethnographic work with adolescents, they argued that ethnic groups in the United States that are "involuntary" minorities, such as African Americans, have peer values that discourage the adoption of values and behaviors of the ethnic majority. In contrast, "voluntary minorities," including some Asian and Latino groups who came to the United States to achieve safety and economic security, adopt majority values in the belief that they promote success. As a result, youth from these groups are believed to be more likely to strive for academic success because they have the support of their group members to do so.

Based on these ideas, a negative association might be expected between popularity and academic achievement for African Americans, whereas a positive association would be expected for white, Asian, and Latino students. However, these expectations have not been confirmed in empirical research. Gorman, Kim, and Schimmelbusch (2002) found that lower grade point averages (GPAs) and higher absenteeism were associated with popularity for both white and Latino high school students. Using a nationwide sample of eighth graders from the National Educational Longitudinal Study, Kennedy (1995) found an identical positive association between popularity and achievement for Asian, black, Latino, and white youth. Also in contrast to the expectations derived from Fordham and Ogbu's theory, academic success was the strongest predictor of popularity for black females. However, there does seem to be an important distinction between correlates of the attainment of popularity and striving toward popularity. Kiefer and Ryan (2008) reported that sixth-grade African American girls who desired to be popular regardless of their actual standing were less engaged in school than white girls or boys of either ethnicity.

The fact that most of these findings do not support Fordham and Ogbu's (1986) theory may be attributed, in part, to the peer reference group. Fordham and Ogbu's account implies that same-ethnicity peers are the reference group. The expected differences between ethnic groups may emerge when only same-ethnicity peers are the reference group for popularity in a multiethnic context. It is also possible that peer group values are shaped by other forces. Conchas and Noguera (2004) described how the creation of a small school community designed to promote academic achievement within a larger urban high school resulted in a strong pro-academic ideology in which African American boys promoted academic success among their peers.

Overall, regardless of the approach to studying ethnic group differences in the association of academic achievement and popularity, consistent differences unique to one ethnic group have not emerged. This suggests that other processes may interact with ethnicity to explain when peers are significant for achievement. Relevant factors include socialization by parents, school climate, tracking practices within schools, and disparities between schools. Peers can also socialize achievement values through peer networks or friendship dyads rather than popularity.

KEY FACTORS FOR UNDERSTANDING POPULARITY AND ETHNICITY

As indicated, investigating how ethnic group membership influences popularity is complex. Important factors to consider are the ethnic groups to be studied, the other ethnic groups that are present and their number of members, and the method of assessing whether the social dynamics of the immediate peer group ever trump larger societal dynamics. These issues are now examined further, because they are vital to understand the mechanisms at play.

Can Ethnicity Be Distinguished from Majority or Minority Status?

Researchers are inconsistent in specifying whether their conclusions about popularity should be attributed to ethnic group differences or majority–minority status differences. This distinction is critical and further complicated by the fact that majority–minority status must be conceptualized both at the level of the immediate peer group setting (classroom or school) and at the societal level. At the level of the peer group, students who are in the numerical majority are not required to interact with those in the minority, but this is not the case for those in the minority. Moreover, the norms, values, and stereotypes determining behaviors and peers' responses to them are subject to numerous cultural influences (Garcia Coll, 1996). Children of color, in particular, may experience strong expectations about their ethnic group based on their position as minorities in society. We expect such processes to be especially relevant to understanding how ethnicity may influence popularity. Ethnic minority youth need to overcome status hierarchies not only in a peer group but also at the broader societal context.

An example of these larger societal influences comes from a study of ethnic group differences in the long-term adjustment outcomes of sociometric status in a sample of adolescents that was 69% white and 31% black (Kupersmidt & Coie, 1990). In this study, negative outcomes (school dropout, police contact, school suspension, grade retention, and truancy) were associated with earlier sociometric status for white students only. The authors proposed that one reason why sociometric status was a better predictor for white students may be that black students face other more significant stressors than being rejected by their peers.

Alternative explanations for these findings illustrate the importance of disentangling ethnicity from majority–minority status. Because black students were in the numerical minority, their status depended on nominations from white students (out-group members). However, negative peer outcomes might be more dependent on black students' status among in-group members. Alternatively, the unbalanced representation of white and black students in the peer group may have enabled self-preserving attributions among minority black students who were not well accepted by out-group peers. Indeed, Graham, Bellmore, Nishina, and Juvonen (2009) found that peer victimization did not necessarily elicit self-blaming attributions (e.g., "It's something about me") for Latino and African American sixth graders when they were in the numerical minority within their schools. Thus, numerical-minority youth may explain their lack of popularity as a function of their minority group membership as opposed to personal flaws. Given that self-blame is linked to negative outcomes (Graham & Juvonen, 1998; Graham et al., 2009), this group-based attribution may serve as a protective factor for numerical-minority youth.

Unpacking ethnic group differences from relative representation effects at the local and macro levels may not be possible. It is clear that popularity is simultaneously influenced by group membership, majority–minority status in the peer group, and majority–minority status in society at large. Therefore, investigators should be cautious in their conclusions about the association between popularity and ethnicity.

Measuring Ethnicity and the Effects of Ethnicity

Whether the goal is to understand differences between ethnic groups or within a single ethnic group, it is critical to establish how ethnicity will be defined. Given the fluidity of the meaning of ethnicity, there is no single agreed-upon standard about the measurement of ethnicity. At younger ages, parents may assign an ethnic label to their child while older children and adolescents may be asked to define their own ethnicities. In some school-based studies, teachers have provided these data or researchers have relied on school district data (often provided by parents). In addition to variation of the informant, the measurement approaches can be as varied as providing a checklist containing a small group of predetermined categories to using open-ended questions with no prompts. The effects of such variability in the measurement of ethnicity on popularity can only be assessed when researchers are explicit about how ethnicity is measured.

What Are the Relevant Groupings?

In most research on popularity to date, investigators have relied on panethnic labels, labels that group individuals based on a shared characteristic such as geographic region of origin, skin color, or language. Phinney (1996) has argued against such simple classifications because ethnicity consists of several different aspects such as cultural attitudes and behaviors, a sense of ethnic identity, and experiences associated with minority status that are themselves multidimensional. These various aspects are ignored when people are classified in predetermined categories. Rosenbloom and Way (2004) categorized students according to both a panethnic label and an ethnic label tied to nationality. These two measures lead to different results. Latino students reported less between-group peer discrimination than Asian American youth, who reported physical and verbal discrimination by other groups. However, within the Latino group, students from the Dominican Republic often reported that Puerto Rican students discriminated against them. A challenge for researchers is to balance the use of existing categories with the need to distinguish the most relevant groups in a study population, and with sample size concerns that may preclude fine distinctions.

Researchers may be particularly guilty of oversimplification when considering youth from multiple ethnic backgrounds. Multiethnic youth are frequently classified into a single category with labels such as "other" or "multiethnic" (Herman, 2004). Children are sometimes asked to designate one ethnic group that they identify with most strongly. Because of the difficulty in categorizing multiethnic youth, they are also frequently excluded from analyses. These trends in the literature are unfortunate because there is much to learn about the role of ethnicity in influencing popularity through the experiences of youth who have complex backgrounds. Multiethnic youth may face significant challenges in peer interactions (e.g., discrimination from peers based on one or more of their ethnic backgrounds). They may also be able to capitalize on unique benefits that come with multiple-group membership such as strategically identifying with the ethnic group who has the higher perceived status within their peer group (Nishina, Bellmore, Witkow, & Nylund-Gibson, in press).

According to studies of adolescent friendships, it appears that multiethnic youth are able to profit from their multiple backgrounds in forming relationships with peers. When exploring how multiethnic adolescents choose their friends, Doyle and Kao (2007) reported that multiracial youth demonstrate "amalgamation," a greater preference for friends of one ethnic background over another (e.g., a white–black adolescent choosing more black than white friends). Interestingly, Doyle and Kao did not find "homophily" among these youth (choosing friends of only one ethnicity). Moreover, certain multiracial youth demonstrated "blending," which is a pattern of friendships that bridges more than one ethnic group (i.e., the pattern of choices for a white–black adolescent would be similar to those of both white and black monoracial youth). Thus, multiethnic students may be better able to cross ethnic lines within their peer settings. This, in turn, might affect their popularity positively.

Once having defined ethnic categories, the next step is to determine the peer reference group in which to measure popularity. Most studies have relied on all peers within the classroom or school. This approach is most relevant to determining who is most visible or most well liked in a broad social context. However, if the focus is on the behaviors and outcomes associated with popularity, perhaps the reference group should be same-ethnicity peers. If ethnic groups form different subcultures in a large grade or school, students' popularity in the broader context could be less meaningful and reflective of their daily social experiences than their social standing in their subculture. The importance of social standing in subcultural groups may be particularly important in large schools.

The use of an ethnic subgroup as the reference group may be especially relevant for African American youth. African American students are more likely to nominate same-ethnicity peers across the board for acceptance and popularity, whereas students with white, Asian, and Latino backgrounds tend to only demonstrate within-group preferences for acceptance but not popularity (Bellmore et al., 2007). The strength of this preference may be further magnified when students identify strongly with their ethnic group (Wade & Okesola, 2002).

Ethnic Identity

Ethnic identity is a person's sense of belonging to their ethnic group and the feelings associated with that group membership (Phinney, 1989). A vast and growing literature has documented the association between a strong ethnic identity and positive outcomes (see, for a review, Quintana, 2007). Students who feel good about their ethnic group membership report higher self-esteem, higher academic achievement, and less engagement in risky behavior. Less is known, however, about how a strong ethnic identity is related to popularity. There is evidence that a strong ethnic identity can buffer some of the negative consequences of unpopularity, defined as discrimination by peers (Sellers, Copeland-Linder, Martin, & Lewis, 2006). Ethnic identity is hypothesized to provide an important source of in-group social support, which enables an individual to better cope with and recover from peer discrimination. Nonetheless, we know almost nothing about whether popularity is enhanced by positive feelings about one's ethnicity (strong ethnic identity → popularity linkage) or whether heightened ethnic pride is a positive outcome of popularity among peers (popularity → strong ethnic identity linkage). We suspect that these associations depend in part on the ethnic composition of the context and whether a target student is a member of the numerical minority or majority. Recall the Latina student from the beginning of this chapter: a popular girl attending a school that was 90% African American and 10% Latino. On the one hand, her minority status might make her ethnic identity especially salient and distinctive (McGuire, McGuire, Child, & Fujioka, 1978). On the other hand, she may struggle with her distinctiveness among her African American peers who embrace her as popular. We believe that the association among popularity, ethnic identity, and majority–minority group status is a particularly ripe topic for future research.

Ethnic Identification

Further complicating the study of ethnicity and social status, social motivations of being well liked or popular might also drive students' ethnic identification (i.e., the ethnic group within which they share membership). Nishina et al. (in press) found that middle school students switched their ethnic identification as a function of the ethnic context of the school. Students who identified as multiethnic at the beginning of sixth grade were likely to switch to African American if they attended an African American-majority school or to Mexican or Latino if they attended a Mexican/Latino-majority school but to continue to identify as multiethnic if they attended a diverse school. Although Nishina and her colleagues did not assess the social functioning of youth who switched ethnic identification to be concordant with their school, students may have benefited from aligning themselves with their school's majority group.

Acculturation

The motivation to be popular may also drive the acculturation process of youth. Because there are cultural differences in the behaviors that are acceptable in peer interactions (for a review, see Chen & French, 2008), the behaviors that promote popularity will also vary. Youth who desire to be popular and whose cultural backgrounds emphasize behaviors that do not promote popularity in the larger peer culture face unique challenges. They may adopt certain acculturation strategies that promote popularity but compromise their adjustment in other ways.

There are generally two dimensions of acculturation strategies: preference for maintaining one's own culture and preference for participating in the larger society through interactions with all cultural groups (Berry, 2007). Research with immigrant youth in the United States often portrays the acculturation process as a source of tension between intracultural family expectations and extracultural peer expectations (usually from the dominant European American culture). Lee (2004) described the unique choices of three Hmong American high school boys and their unique consequences for relationships with peers and family, academic achievement, and psychosocial adjustment. Although her account does not focus on strivings toward popularity per se, it illustrates the compromises made by these Asian American boys depending on whether their goal was to maintain their status at home or at school among their peers. The descriptions also suggest that when home and peer culture clash, adoption of the peer values that promote popularity will likely come at some cost to family relations. In any peer context, there are individuals who adopt the behaviors associated with popularity in the peer culture at the expense of their cultural background. Others reject peer-valued behaviors in favor of their own culture. Still others can create a balance between both to reap the benefits of popularity while also staying close to their family background. Thus, the popularity of immigrant youth can be influenced not only by the ethnic composition of their peer group but also by the acculturation strategies they adopt.

Ethnically Diverse School Contexts

As described, most approaches to defining the ethnic composition of the peer group have focused on the specific groups present in the setting (e.g., the proportion of white students in the school). Another way of defining ethnic context is to measure the amount of ethnic diversity present in a given context. One formula for ethnic diversity, used by researchers as different as biologists studying ecological diversity

(Simpson, 1949) and sociologists (Blau, 1977) studying diversity within human groupings, is

$$D_C = 1 - \sum_{i=1}^{g} p_i^2$$

In this formula, p is the proportion of students in ethnic category i across g ethnic groups in peer context C. D_C can range from 0 to approximately 1 and takes into account the number of ethnicities present and their relative representation. Substantively, D_C indexes the likelihood that two randomly drawn individuals from the peer context are from different ethnic groups. The category proportions are usually derived from students' self-reported ethnicity, but D_C can be computed from any of the just-discussed measures of diversity.

Research with this measure has shown that in ethnically diverse schools adolescents have many cross-ethnic friendships (Moody, 2001) and are rarely victimized by peers (Juvonen, Nishina, & Graham, 2006). Students attending these schools also report relatively low levels of loneliness and social anxiety (Bellmore, Witkow, Graham, & Juvonen, 2004).

As far as is known, the impact of ethnic diversity on popularity has not yet been examined. Yet a number of interesting effects are possible. First, given that ethnic diversity reflects balance in ethnic composition and the lack of a clear numerical majority, students from any ethnic background in a diverse setting should have equal opportunities to achieve the highest levels of popularity. Second, the usual hierarchical peer structure of middle and early high school (Brown & Klute, 2006) can be reduced in an ethnically diverse setting. Balance among ethnic groups could extend to the peer structure so that there will not be marked differences between students at the top and bottom of the popularity spectrum. Third, ethnically diverse contexts could foster tolerance of deviance from expected behaviors. Acceptance of divergence from local norms means that there will not be strong expectations placed on individuals' behavior based on their ethnic background. It is also possible that diversity will influence associations between certain behaviors or traits and popularity in general. Behavioral norms would have less power to constrain behavior. Direct tests of these hypotheses have yet to be conducted but are needed given the significance of school ethnic contexts for social development.

Barriers to Cross-Ethnic Interaction

One factor that could negate the effects of ethnic diversity is the occurrence of segregation. Segregation may occur in contexts in which socioeconomic or immigration status are confounded with ethnic background. Several organizational features of schools make such an eventuality possible. Many schools rely on ability groupings or tracking that effectively divides the school population into racially segregated units (Khmelkov & Hallinan, 1999). This will limit opportunities for relationships with peers of all ethnicities and for visibility among all peers. At the same time, such segregation maintains or exacerbates existing stereotypes and discrimination. Stereotypes between ability groups may also play a role in determining popularity. In schools in which tracking is confounded with ethnicity, it is important to determine the proper reference group. It could be, as for ethnic groups described previously, that students sort themselves by track. Thus, a student's track may be the most important reference group as opposed to his or her grade or school.

A second factor that may limit opportunities to achieve popularity, even in ethnically diverse schools, are limitations regarding the availability of extracurricular activities. On a per capita basis, student involvement in extracurricular activities drops as school size increases (Crosnoe, Kirkpatrick, & Elder, 2004). This may be due to competition for access to activities by a relatively large number of students. As a result, only certain students are able to participate in the most sought-after activities. Across studies, specific types of activity involvement, in particular athletics, are more strongly associated with popularity than others (e.g., Eder & Kinney, 1995; Farmer et al., 2003; Kennedy, 1995). Eder and Kinney attributed this effect to the high visibility of sports like basketball and football, which are attended by many members of the school community. To the extent that members of certain ethnic groups are inclined to participate in such athletics, their popularity will be positively impacted. In this way, participation in extracurricular activities that facilitate visibility can boost the peer status of minority students. A small literature on racial/ethnic differences in extracurricular activity rates indicates that black students are disproportionately more likely to participate in basketball and track than white students (e.g., Clotfelter, 2002). It is not known whether such participation boosts these students' popularity or further segregates them from the mainstream (e.g., McNeal, 1998).

The broader local context may also influence the way in which school ethnic diversity impacts student popularity. Geographically bound racial relations and discrimination within the broader community may spill over to the school context. On the basis of historical interactions between groups, economic factors (e.g., competition for jobs), and ethnic minority migration patterns, diverse schools in communities with interethnic tensions may look very different socially than diverse schools in communities where interethnic relationships are less strained. Ethnographic studies of school desegregation provide moving portrayals of how ethnic minority students' social positions in school are shaped by the historical and cultural forces driving school integration initiatives (e.g., Patchen, 1982; Schofield, 1989).

CONCLUSIONS

Whether it is a marker, precursor, or consequence of social competence or power and visibility, popularity plays an important role in the social lives of children and adolescents. This chapter highlighted the ways in which ethnicity may influence popularity, particularly in ethnically diverse peer contexts in the United States. However, the basic principles identified here may apply to other countries and cultures across the world that are also increasingly diverse, even when the specific ethnic groups and their unique representations are different.

As researchers study popularity in ethnically diverse populations, they are charged with considering several contextual layers that influence popularity. These include proximal peer factors such as behavioral norms and social skillfulness that apply across all ethnic groups. They also include distal factors, such as culture, history, and geography, that define ethnic groups and their relationships with other ethnic groups within the same larger setting. Only through exploration of all layers will the full significance of ethnicity to popularity be established.

REFERENCES

Adler, P. A., & Adler, P. (1995). Dynamics of inclusion and exclusion in preadolescent cliques. *Social Psychology Quarterly, 58,* 145–162.

Adler, P. A., & Adler, P. (1998). *Peer power: Preadolescent culture and identity.* New Brunswick, NJ: Rutgers University Press.

Andreou, E. (2006). Social preference, perceived popularity, and social intelligence. *School Psychology International, 27,* 339–351.

Bellmore, A. D., Nishina, A., Witkow, M. R., Graham, S., & Juvonen, J. (2007). The influence of classroom ethnic composition on same- and other-ethnicity peer nominations in middle school. *Social Development, 16,* 720–740.

Bellmore, A. D., Witkow, M. R., Graham, S., & Juvonen, J. (2004). Beyond the individual: The impact of ethnic context and classroom behavioral norms on victims' adjustment. *Developmental Psychology, 40,* 1159–1172.

Berry, J. (2007). Acculturation strategies and adaptation. In J. E. Lansford, K. Deater-Deckard, & M. H. Bornstein (Eds.), *Immigrant families in contemporary society* (pp. 69–82). New York: Guilford Press.

Blau, P. M. (1977). *Inequality and heterogeneity.* New York: Free Press.

Boivin, M., Dodge, K. A., & Coie, J. D. (1995). Individual-group behavioral similarity and peer status in experimental play groups of boys: The social misfit revisited. *Journal of Personality and Social Psychology, 69,* 269–279.

Boyce, W. T., Frank, E., Jensen, P. S., Kessler, R. C., Nelson, C. A., & Steinberg, L. (1998) Social context in developmental psychopathology: Recommendations for future research from the MacArthur Network on Psychopathology and Development. *Development and Psychopathology, 10,* 143–164.

Brewer, C. A., & Suchan, T. A. (2001). *Mapping Census 2000: The geography of U.S. diversity* (U.S. Census Bureau, Census Special Reports, Series CENSR/01-1) [Electronic version]. Washington, DC: U.S. Government Printing Office.

Bronfenbrenner, U. (1979). Contexts of child rearing: Problems and prospects. *American Psychologist, 34,* 844–850.

Brown, B. B., & Klute, C., (2006). Friendships, cliques, and crowds. In G. R. Adams & M. D. Berzonsky (Eds.), *Blackwell handbook of adolescence* (pp. 330–348). Malden, MA: Blackwell.

Brown, C. S., & Bigler, R. S. (2005). Children's perceptions of discrimination: A developmental model. *Child Development, 76,* 533–553.

Cameron, J. A., Alvarez, J. M., Ruble, D. N., & Fuligni, A. J. (2001). Children's lay theories about ingroups and outgroups: Reconceptualizing research on prejudice. *Personality and Social Psychology Review, 5,* 118–128.

Chen, X., & French, D. C. (2008). Children's social competence in cultural context. *Annual Reviews of Psychology, 59,* 591–616.

Cillessen, A. H. N., & Mayeux, L. (2004). From censure to reinforcement: Developmental changes in the association between aggression and social status. *Child Development, 75,* 147–163.

Clotfelter, C. (2002). Interracial contact in high school extracurricular activities. *Urban Review, 34,* 25–46.

Coie, J. D., & Cillessen, A. H. N. (1993). Peer rejection: Origins and effects on children's development. *Current Directions in Psychological Science, 2,* 89–92.

Coie, J. D., Dodge, K. A., & Coppotelli, H. (1982). Dimensions and types of social status: A cross-age perspective. *Developmental Psychology, 18,* 557–570.

Coie, J. D., & Kupersmidt, J. B. (1983). A behavioral analysis of emerging social status in boys' groups. *Child Development, 54,* 1400–1416.

Conchas, G. Q., & Noguera, P. A. (2004). Understanding the exceptions: How small schools support the achievement of academically successful black boys. In N. Way & J. Y. Chu (Eds.), *Adolescent boys: Exploring diverse cultures of boyhood* (pp. 317–337). New York: New York University Press.

Crosnoe, R., Kirkpatrick, M., & Elder, G. (2004). School size and the interpersonal side of education: An examination of race/ethnicity and organizational context. *Social Science Quarterly, 85,* 1259–1274.

de Bruyn, E. H., & Cillessen, A. H. N. (2006). Popularity in early adolescence: Prosocial and antisocial subtypes. *Journal of Adolescent Research, 21,* 607–627.

Doyle, J. M., & Kao, G. (2007). Friendship choices of multiracial adolescents: Racial homophily, blending, or amalgamation? *Social Science Research, 36,* 633–653.

Eder, D. (1985). The cycle of popularity: Interpersonal relations among female adolescents. *Sociology of Education, 58,* 154–165.

Eder, D., & Kinney, D. A. (1995). The effect of middle school extracurricular activities on adolescents' popularity and peer status. *Youth and Society, 26,* 298–324.

Evans, C., & Eder, D. (1993). "No exit": Processes of social isolation in the middle school. *Journal of Contemporary Ethnography, 22,* 139–170.

Farmer, T. W., Estell, D. B., Bishop, J. L., O'Neal, K. K., & Cairns, B. D. (2003). Rejected bullies or popular leaders? The social relations of aggressive subtypes of rural African American early adolescents. *Developmental Psychology, 39,* 992–1004.

Fisher, C. B., Wallace, S. A., & Fenton, R. E. (2000). Discrimination distress during adolescence. *Journal of Youth and Adolescence, 29,* 679–695.

Fordham, S., & Ogbu, J. U. (1986). Black students' school success: Coping with the "burden of acting white." *Urban Review, 18,* 176–206.

Garcia Coll, C., Crnic, K., Lamberty, G., & Wasik, B. H. (1996). An integrative model for the study of developmental competencies in minority children. *Child Development, 67,* 1891–1914.

Gorman, A. H., Kim, J., & Schimmelbusch, A. (2002). The attributes adolescents associate with peer popularity and teacher preference. *Journal of School Psychology, 40,* 143–165.

Graham, J. A., & Cohen, R. (1997). Race and sex as factors in children's sociometric rating and friendship choices. *Social Development, 6,* 355–372.

Graham, S., Bellmore, A., Nishina, A., & Juvonen, J. (2009). "It must be me": Ethnic diversity and attributions for peer victimization in middle school. *Journal of Youth and Adolescence, 38,* 487–499.

Graham, S., & Juvonen, J. (1998). Self-blame and peer victimization in middle school: An attributional analysis. *Developmental Psychology, 34,* 587–599.

Graham, S., Taylor, A. Z., & Ho, A. Y. (2008). Race and ethnicity in peer relations research. In K. H. Rubin, W. M. Bukowski, & B. Laursen (Eds.), *Handbook of peer interactions, relationships, and groups* (pp. 394–413). New York: Guilford Press.

Greene, M. L., Way, N., & Pahl, K. (2006). Trajectories of perceived adult and peer discrimination among black, Latino, and Asian American adolescents: Patterns and psychological correlates. *Developmental Psychology, 42,* 218–238.

Hallinan, M. T., & Smith, S. S. (1985). The effects of classroom racial composition on students' interracial friendliness. *Social Psychology Quarterly, 48,* 3–16.

Herman, M. (2004). Forced to choose: Some determinants of racial identification in multiracial adolescents. *Child Development, 75,* 730–748.

Howes, C., & Wu, F. (1990). Peer interactions and friendships in an ethnically diverse school setting. *Child Development, 61,* 537–541.

Jackson, M. F., Barth, J. M., Powell, N., & Lochman, J. E. (2006). Classroom contextual effects of race on children's peer nominations. *Child Development, 77,* 1325–1337.

Juvonen, J., Nishina, A., & Graham, S. (2006). Ethnic diversity and perceptions of safety in urban middle schools. *Psychological Science, 17,* 393–400.

Kennedy, E. (1995). Correlates of perceived popularity among peers: A study of race and gender differences among middle school students. *Journal of Negro Education, 64,* 186–195.

Khmelkov, V. T., & Hallinan, M. T. (1999). Organizational effects on race relations in schools. *Journal of Social Issues, 55,* 627–645.

Kiefer, S. M., & Ryan, A. M. (2008). Striving for social dominance over peers: The implications for academic adjustment during early adolescence. *Journal of Educational Psychology, 100,* 417–428.

Kinney, D. A. (1993). From nerds to normals: The recovery of identity among adolescents from middle school to high school. *Sociology of Education, 66,* 21–40.

Kistner, J., Metzler, A., Gatlin, D., & Risi, S. (1993). Classroom racial proportions and children's peer relations: Race and gender effects. *Journal of Educational Psychology, 85,* 446–452.

Košir, K., & Pečjak, S. (2005). Sociometry as a method for investigating peer relationships: What does it actually measure? *Educational Research, 47,* 127–144.

Kupersmidt, J. B., & Coie, J. D. (1990). Preadolescent peer status, aggression, and school adjustment as predictors of externalizing problems in adolescence. *Child Development, 61,* 1350–1362.

Lease, A. M., Kennedy, C. A., & Axelrod, J. L. (2002). Children's social constructions of popularity. *Social Development, 11,* 87–109.

Lee, S. J. (2004). Hmong American masculinities: Creating new identities in the United States. In N. Way & J. Y. Chu (Eds.), *Adolescent boys: Exploring diverse cultures of boyhood* (pp. 13–30). New York: New York University Press.

Luthar, S. S., & McMahon, T. J. (1996). Peer reputation among inner-city adolescents: Structure and correlates. *Journal of Research on Adolescence, 6,* 581–603.

Marks, P. E. L., Cillessen, A. H. N., Andreou, E., Berger, C., Bukowski, W. M., Caravita, S. C. S., et al. (2010). *International perspectives on popularity: The meanings and constructions of popularity across cultures.* Manuscript submitted for publication.

McGuire, W., McGuire, C., Child, P., & Fujioka, T. (1978). Salience of ethnicity in the spontaneous self-concept as a function of one's ethnic distinctiveness in the social environment. *Journal of Personality and Social Psychology, 36,* 511–520.

McNeal, R. (1998). High school extracurricular activities: Closed structures and stratifying patterns of participation. *Journal of Educational Research, 91,* 183–191.

Meisinger, E. B., Blake, J. J., Lease, A. M., Palardy, G. J., & Olejnik, S. F. (2007). Variant and invariant predictors of perceived popularity across majority-black and majority-white classrooms. *Journal of School Psychology, 45,* 21–44.

Merten, D. E. (1997). The meaning of meanness: Popularity, competition, and conflict among junior high school girls. *Sociology of Education, 70,* 175–191.

Moody, J. (2001). Race, school integration, and friendship segregation in America. *American Journal of Sociology, 107,* 679–716.

Moreno, J. L. (1934). *Who shall survive? A new approach to the problem of human interrelations.* Washington, DC: Nervous and Mental Disease Publishing Co.

Nesdale, D. (1999). Developmental changes in children's ethnic preferences and social cognitions. *Journal of Applied Developmental Psychology, 20,* 501–519.

Nishina, A., Bellmore, A., Witkow, M. R., & Nylund-Gibson, K. (in press). Longitudinal consistency of adolescent ethnic identification across varying school contexts. *Developmental Psychology.*

Parkhurst, J. T., & Hopmeyer, A. (1998). Sociometric popularity and peer-perceived popularity: Two distinct dimensions of peer status. *Journal of Early Adolescence, 18,* 125–144.

Patchen, M. (1982). *Black-white contact in schools: Its social and academic effects.* West Lafayette, IN: Purdue University Press.

Pfeifer, J. H., Brown, C. S., & Juvonen, J. (2007). Teaching tolerance in schools: Lessons learned since Brown v. Board of Education about the development of reduction of children's prejudice. *Social Policy Report, 21,* 3–23.

Phillipsen, L. C., Bridges, S. K., McLemore, T. G., & Saponaro, L. A. (1999). Perceptions of social behavior and peer acceptance in kindergarten. *Journal of Research in Childhood Education, 14,* 68–77.

Phinney, J. S. (1989). Stages of ethnic identity development in minority group adolescents. *Journal of Early Adolescence, 9,* 34–49.

Phinney, J. S. (1996). When we talk about American ethnic groups, what do we mean? *American Psychologist, 51,* 918–927.

Quintana, S. M. (2007). Racial and ethnic identity: Developmental perspectives and research. *Journal of Counseling Psychology, 54,* 259–270.

Rodkin, P. C., Farmer, T. W., Pearl, R., & Van Acker, R. (2000). Heterogeneity of popular boys: Antisocial and prosocial configurations. *Developmental Psychology, 36,* 14–24.

Rose, A. J., Swenson, L. P., & Waller, E. M. (2004). Overt and relational aggression and perceived popularity: Developmental differences in concurrent and prospective relations. *Developmental Psychology, 40,* 378–387.

Rosenbloom, S. R., & Way, N. (2004). Experiences of discrimination among African American, Asian American, and Latino adolescents in an urban high school. *Youth and Society, 35,* 420–451.

Rubin, K. H., Bukowski, W. M., & Parker, J. G. (2006). Peer interactions, relationships, and groups. In W. Damon & N. Eisenberger (Eds.), *Handbook of child psychology* (6th ed.): *Vol 3. Social, emotional, and personality development* (pp. 571–645). New York: Wiley.

Sagar, H. A., Schofield, J. W., & Snyder, H. N. (1983). Race and gender barriers: Preadolescent peer behavior in academic classrooms. *Child Development, 54,* 1032–1040.

Schofield, J. W. (1989). *Black and white in school: Trust, tensions, or tolerance.* New York: Teachers College Press.

Schofield, J. W., & Whitley, B. E. (1983). Peer nomination vs. rating scale measurement of children's peer preferences. *Social Psychology Quarterly, 46,* 242–251.

Schwartz, D., Tom, S., Chang, L., Xu, Y., Duong, M. T., & Kelly, B. M. (2010). Popularity and acceptance as distinct dimensions of social standing for Chinese children in Hong Kong. *Social Development, 19,* 681–697.

Sellers, R. M., Copeland-Linder, N., Martin, P.P., & Lewis, R. L. (2006). Rational identity matters: The relationship between racial discrimination and psychological functioning in African American adolescents. *Journal of Research on Adolescence, 16,* 187–216.

Shaw, M. E. (1973). Changes in sociometric choices following forced integration of an elementary school. *Journal of Social Issues, 29,* 143–157.

Shrum, W., Cheek, N. H., & Hunter, S. M. (1988). Friendship in school: Gender and racial homophily. *Sociology of Education, 61,* 227–239.

Simpson, E. H. (1949). Measurement of diversity. *Nature, 163,* 688.

Singleton, L. C., & Asher, S. R. (1979). Racial integration and children's peer preferences: An investigation of developmental and cohort differences. *Child Development, 50,* 936–941.

St. John, N. H., & Lewis, R. G. (1975). Race and the social structure of the elementary classroom. *Sociology of Education, 48,* 346–368.

Steinberg, L., Dornbusch, S. M., & Brown, B. B. (1992). Ethnic differences in adolescent achievement. *American Psychologist, 47,* 723–729.

Tajfel, H. (1982). Social psychology of intergroup relations. *Annual Review of Psychology, 33,* 1–39.

Verkuyten, M., & Thijs, J. (2002). Racist victimization among children in The Netherlands: The effect of ethnic group and school. *Ethnic and Racial Studies, 25,* 310–331.

Wade, J. C., & Okesola, O. (2002). Racial peer group selection in African American high school students. *Journal of Multicultural Counseling and Development, 30,* 96–109.

Part IV
POPULARITY AND ADJUSTMENT

Chapter 10

The Power of Popularity
Influence Processes in Childhood and Adolescence

MARLENE J. SANDSTROM

    Imbedded in our conceptualization of social competence (see Aikins & Litwack, Chapter 7, this volume) is the assumption that popular children exert *power*. We assume that a key element of popularity is the ability to influence, in both obvious and subtle ways, the behaviors and attitudes of peers. Colloquially, we apply the description of "popular" to those children who appear to define the social agenda for their peers, to shape the contours of what is valued in the group, and to draw other children into their gravitational pull through the strength of their personal charisma. Although the past decade has witnessed a sharp increase in research on the correlates and consequences of popularity in childhood, surprisingly little is known about the nature of influence processes. It is not clear *how* popular children hold sway or what the extent of their persuasive powers might be.

    The current chapter takes a closer look at the interplay between popularity and social influence processes. Before focusing on the role of popularity specifically, I begin with a brief overview of the literature on peer influence more generally. Research on topics such as conformity, peer pressure, and contagion effects converge to suggest that children exert significant influence on each other during the school-age years and shape the trajectory of each others' attitudes and behavior in important ways. In the second section of this chapter, I take a closer look at research examining the role of popularity in social influence more specifically. Readers will see that existing literature on this topic is quite scarce, and that the bulk of the work is naturalistic and descriptive (showing associations between indices of social status and various aspects of dominance, centrality, or influence). Only a handful of studies use laboratory paradigms or experimental designs to examine the interplay between popularity and influence processes. I review these studies and consider what they can and cannot tell us about influence processes. In the third section, I highlight the limitations and gaps in our current body of literature and identify three key theoretical issues to guide future research: (1) mechanistic processes (i.e., *how* popular children influence their peers), (2) moderating effects (i.e., *why* some children are more susceptible to the influence of popular peers than others), and (3) developmental issues (i.e., *when* particular forms of peer influence exert their strongest effect). I conclude with specific suggestions for the design of future studies.

THE POWER OF PEERS: INFLUENCE TAKES MANY FORMS

After experiencing a heyday in the 1960s and 1970s, interest in peer influence processes languished for many decades as researchers turned their attention to other topics, such as causes, correlates, and consequences of rejection and aggression in childhood (Hartup, 1999, 2005). However, as is so often the case with academic trends, what goes around comes around. Interest in peer influence processes has been renewed in recent years, as theorists have begun to highlight socialization processes as primary forces in the emergence, maintenance, and desistance of many forms of dysfunction in childhood and adolescence (e.g., Prinstein & Dodge, 2008).

Conformity

Early studies on peer influence focused on conformity, or the extent to which children make choices on the basis of group norms rather than personal judgments. Following Asch's (1956) classic illustration of adult conformity, developmental researchers began to examine children's tendency to conform to group consensus at various ages. In these scenarios, children were presented with a perceptual task (e.g., judging the length of lines, distance between lights, or number of clicks) and were asked to draw their own conclusions after being exposed to an erroneous (but unanimous) response from peers. Although some studies suggested that children become increasingly less susceptible to conformity effects over time (e.g., Allen & Newston, 1972; Berenda, 1950; Cohen, Bornstein, & Sherman, 1973; Walker & Andrade, 1996), others found the opposite (e.g., Hamm & Hoving, 1969). Still other researchers reported a curvilinear association, indicating that conformity increases throughout childhood, peaks in late childhood, and then decreases in adolescence (Costanzo & Shaw, 1966; Iscoe, Williams, & Harvey, 1963). To some extent, inconsistency across studies may be due to differences in the ambiguity of the experimental task. When tasks are clearly unambiguous, conformity appears to decrease with age (Walker & Andrade, 1996). As revealed later, the extent to which conformity may be moderated by social status variables (e.g., the popularity of the source or target of influence) has received relatively little attention in the literature.

Peer Pressure

Along with conformity tasks, which tend to focus on affectively and morally neutral judgments, researchers have also examined the extent to which children can be swayed by peers to endorse behaviors or values with ethical connotations. In a typical study of this genre, participants are presented with a hypothetical dilemma in which peers actively encourage either a prosocial or an antisocial choice (e.g., skipping school or helping a peer in trouble). The bulk of studies using this approach suggest that susceptibility to peer pressure rises slowly until midadolescence and then begins to decline (Berndt, 1979; Brown, Clasen, & Eicher, 1986; Steinberg & Monahan, 2007; Steinberg & Silverberg, 1986). Moreover, it appears that the increased susceptibility to peer pressure in adolescence may be particularly salient among boys and in the context of antisocial, rather than prosocial, behavior (Berndt, 1979; Erickson, Crosnoe, & Dornbusch, 2000).

As the influence of peers increases during adolescence, there is also ample evidence to suggest that the influence of parents simultaneously declines (e.g., Allen & Newston, 1972; Berenda, 1950; Utech & Hoving, 1969). Further, it appears that children are differentially susceptible to peer influence as a function of the social context. In one study, for example, children who expected parents to review their responses were more resistant to peer pressure than those who believed their responses were anonymous. In contrast, children who expected peers to review their responses were significantly more conforming than those in the anonymous condition (Bixenstine, DeCorte, & Bixenstine, 1976).

A common thread woven through most of the peer pressure literature is its heavy reliance on hypothetical vignettes. Very few studies have used experimental designs or in vivo peer influence sessions to examine the influence process directly. In one exception, Gardner and Steinberg (2005) randomly assigned participants from three age groups (children, college students, and adults) to complete risk-taking measures either alone or in the company of two same-age peers. Clear age differences in response to peer exposure emerged; working alongside peers doubled the amount of risky behavior endorsed by children, increased it by 50% among college undergraduates, and had no impact on the responses of adult participants.

In another experimental study, Berndt, Laychak, and Park (1990) asked eighth graders to respond to school achievement dilemmas individually (e.g., "Should I study for tomorrow's exam, or attend an elite social event?"), and then randomly assigned them to talk to a friend about the dilemma or an unrelated issue. After the discussion, participants responded to the dilemmas independently once again. The discrepancy in friends' ratings was smaller on the posttest than on the pretest for participants in the experimental condition but not for those in the control condition, suggesting that a targeted discussion between friends successfully influenced teens' attitudes about academic achievement (Berndt et al., 1990). Together, these results show that children are highly sensitive to the presence of peers, who can influence their behavioral choices in both direct and indirect ways. The extent to which popularity (of influencers and targets) moderates the outcome of these peer pressure tactics is discussed shortly.

Peer Contagion

In contrast to the literature on conformity (children's passive adoption of a unanimous majority's behavior) and peer pressure (children's susceptibility to the active suggestions and prompts of peers), the literature on peer contagion emphasizes a more subtle "spread" of particular behaviors throughout a peer network. As the public health connotation implies, the term *contagion* is typically used to describe the transmission of "unhealthy" behaviors from "infected" to previously "healthy" youth. Interest in contagion effects has grown over the past decade, stemming in large part from the realization that group interventions for deviant youth can result in inadvertent increases, rather than decreases, in problematic behavior (e.g., Dishion, McCord, & Poulin, 1999). Presumably, group placements provide peers with an opportunity to transmit new forms of deviant behavior to each other (e.g., sharing cigarettes, exchanging information about where to procure fake ID cards). Indeed, research has documented contagion effects for a wide variety of deviant behaviors, including substance use (Dishion & Medici Skaggs, 2000), lying and stealing (Keenan, Loeber, Zhang, Stouthamer-Loeber, & van Kammen, 1995), violent offenses (Elliot & Menard, 1996), and high-risk sexual behavior (Dishion, 2000).

Interestingly, contagion effects appear to be quite specific, varying as a function of the particular group–target combination. For example, Boxer, Guerra, Huesmann, and Morales (2005) found that individual changes in children's level of aggression over the course of a small-group prevention program were related to the average level of aggression of the other children in the pull-out group. Highly aggressive children who were placed in less aggressive groups reduced their aggression over time, whereas less aggressive children placed in highly aggressive groups showed increases in aggression. Notably, the degree to which children were "infected" by the group appeared to be directly proportional to their initial discrepancy from the group average. Children who began the prevention program with more extreme levels of aggression showed the greatest contagion effects over time. Thus, results demonstrate that an identical group placement can influence two children in completely different ways as a function of their preexisting behavioral tendencies (Boxer et al., 2005).

Taken together, the combined literature on conformity, peer pressure, and contagion effects suggests that children *do* look to each other as primary guides and arbiters of appropriate behavior. Complex social interactions present a nearly infinite number of behavioral choices; the peer group plays an important role in constraining and shaping the options. But do all members of the peer group possess the same degree of influence potential? Anecdotally, most of us would argue otherwise. Some children, as a function of their personal attributes, group status, or personal relationships, seem to wield more influence than others. What does the empirical literature tell us about the role of popularity in social influence? Are popular children particularly persuasive? Do their opinions and behaviors hold more sway?

It turns out that the bulk of research on social influence paints with a rather broad brush and fails to examine how the status of particular peers affects their potency as agents of behavioral change. Only a small number of studies have directly explored the interconnections between popularity and social influence. This research is examined next, beginning with a set of descriptive studies showing differences in the perceived social power of highly likeable versus highly popular children and then moving on to a small number of experimental studies in which the status of potential sources of influence is manipulated.

ARE POPULAR AND ACCEPTED CHILDREN EQUALLY POWERFUL?

As described in previous chapters, the operational definition of high standing with peers varies as a function of researchers' disciplinary roots. Developmental and clinical psychologists have focused on "well-accepted" children (those who are liked by the majority of their peers), while sociologists and educational psychologists have highlighted "popular" children (those who are at the center of attention and who hold sway over the prevailing attitudes and behaviors of their peers). It is the latter conceptualization that has been most consistently and robustly associated with indices of social influence. For instance, ethnographic studies routinely describe popular children as commanding attention from their peers, setting trends, using highly developed interpersonal skills to control others, and defining the boundary between in-groups and out-groups by choosing which peers to include or exclude (e.g., Adler & Adler, 1998; Eder, Evans, & Parker, 1995). Further, elementary and middle school children spontaneously include dimensions of dominance and power when asked to provide open-ended descriptions of popular, but not well-accepted, children (LaFontana & Cillessen, 2002).

In addition to qualitative studies (which typically rely on a combination of interviews, surveys, and naturalistic observations), a number of researchers have used peer nomination methods to examine the unique and joint relations among acceptance, popularity, and aspects of social influence. Once again, results suggest that it is popularity rather than acceptance that is most strongly associated with social dominance (defined as the ability to wield more social influence and power relative to peers across a variety of social contexts). In fact, the association between acceptance and indices of social influence, such as admiration, leadership, or social control, typically diminishes when the effect of popularity is statistically controlled (e.g., Lease, Kennedy, & Axelrod, 2002; Parkhurst & Hopmeyer, 1998; Vaillancourt & Hymel, 2006). Popular children appear to be more powerful than well-accepted children in direct comparisons as well. For example, Lease, Musgrove, and Axelrod (2002) used cluster analysis to identify two distinct groups of dominant children: one that was high in popularity and another that was high in acceptance. Results revealed that children in the popular, more dominant, group were perceived as more cool and admired and as wielding social control than their accepted–dominant counterparts.

MOVING BEYOND DESCRIPTION: LAB PARADIGMS AND EXPERIMENTAL DESIGNS

A significant limitation of descriptive research is its inability to identify causal mechanisms or directions of influence. Studies revealing statistical associations between popularity and social influence are consistent with the notion that popularity, as a commodity, affords children the power to influence others. Such data do not, however, rule out competing alternatives. Perhaps the possession of power leads to popularity rather than the other way around. That is, children who repeatedly get their way or set trends in the peer group may subsequently come to be seen as the most central, visible, and dominant members of the group. Alternatively, some other characteristic, such as propensity toward risk taking, emotional intelligence, or rebellious behavior, might simultaneously engender high levels of popularity and social influence. Testing the causal impact of popularity on children's ability to influence others requires the use of experimental design.

In an early attempt to explore this issue, Harvey and Rutherford (1960) examined the impact of status on social influence at different age levels. A questionnaire was used to obtain self-reported measures of social status among a sample of 3rd-, 6th-, 9th-, and 11th-grade students. In addition, all participants viewed a series of pairs of artwork and were asked to choose a preference from each pair. After making their selections, participants were exposed to information about how two peers (a high-status classmate and a low-status classmate) had purportedly responded to one of the stimulus pairs. Participants were randomly assigned to one of two possible feedback conditions. In one condition, participants were told that a high-status peer had disagreed with their stated preference while the low-status peer had agreed; in the second condition, participants were told that the low-status peer had disagreed with their earlier choice while the high-status peer had agreed. After the influence session, participants once again reported their preferences.

Results revealed a significant effect of condition on children's tendency to change their opinions after receiving peer feedback. Among 6th and 11th graders, more children changed their preference in the condition in which the high-status peer, as opposed to the low-status peer, disagreed. There were also significant gender differences. The tendency toward greater influence on the part of the high-status source was more pronounced for girls than boys from the third through ninth grades; however, this pattern was reversed in the 11th-grade. Finally, results demonstrated that the status of the participants played a role in their susceptibility to influence: Children who rated themselves as low in popularity were significantly more likely to change their responses in reaction to peer influence. Participants' self-ratings of acceptance by peers, however, were not related to their susceptibility to influence. Although this study provides initial support for the notion that popular sources of influence are more effective than their lower status counterparts, confidence in the results is limited by the reliance on self-ratings (as opposed to peer ratings) of social status as well as the curious inconsistencies in status effects as a function of age (e.g., no effects for 3rd and 9th graders).

In a modern version of this study, Cohen and Prinstein (2006) used a chat room paradigm to examine the impact of status on susceptibility to peer influence. During the first phase of the study, 11th graders nominated their "most liked" and "most popular" classmates and responded to hypothetical scenarios assessing their likelihood of engaging in a variety of aggressive/health risk behaviors (e.g., deciding whether to use vs. refuse an illegal drug or to help vs. tease a vulnerable peer). Next, a subgroup of boys was selected to participate in the experimental phase of the study. These boys were led to believe that they were interacting with three classmates via Internet chat technology. In the chat room, they responded to the same set of hypothetical scenarios presented earlier. This time, however, the boys were exposed to their chat partners' responses before making their own choices. Unbeknownst to the participating boys, the identity and responses of the chat partners ("e-confederates") were experimentally manipulated by the researchers. Some of these boys were led to believe that they were interacting with high-status peers (those who had been identified as high in both acceptance and popularity by their classmates), while others were led to believe that they were interacting with low-status peers. Consistent with Harvey and Rutherford's (1960) earlier work, the participants displayed greater conformity to their chat partners' responses when they believed the e-confederates were high in peer status. Interestingly, the boys who were randomly assigned to interact with high-status peers showed not only higher levels of public conformity but also higher levels of private conformity as well as greater willingness to aggress against a group member when other members did so first.

The use of e-confederates highlighted the impact of status on participants' tendency to be swayed by peers. Indeed, the results provided evidence that not all peers are created equal: Popular peers *do* hold more sway. One limitation of Cohen and Prinstein's (2006) design, however, is their conflation of popularity and acceptance. Because high-status peers were identified as those classmates who scored more than 1 *SD* above the mean on peer nominations for either dimension, it is impossible to know whether the effect was driven by acceptance, popularity, or a combination. In an attempt to parse these constructs, Sandstrom and Romano (2007) revived the chat room paradigm and randomly assigned participants to interact with an e-confederate who was described as (1) high in acceptance and popularity, (2) high in acceptance but low in popularity, (3) low in acceptance but high in popularity, or (4) low in both. Similar to the previous study, participants responded to hypothetical vignettes independently (using paper and pencil), and subsequently to the same vignettes using chat technology, after first being exposed to the e-confederate's responses. On target items, the e-confederate always chose a response that was more antisocial than participants' initial judgments.

Results indicated that, overall, participants showed greater shifts in an antisocial direction after being exposed to a partner who was depicted as high in acceptance. The effect of popularity, in contrast, was minimal. Notably, the only case in which the popularity of the e-confederate mattered was one in which the scenario involved a public decision (deciding whether to defend a peer who was being teased on the bus). For this scenario, the highest level of conformity to antisocial behavior occurred when participants believed they were interacting with an e-confederate who was both well accepted and popular. These preliminary results suggest that although popular peers may be particularly influential in group settings, the behaviors and attitudes of well-accepted peers may play a stronger role in shaping children's choices in dyadic or private settings. Future research is necessary to explore the specificity of these effects.

In addition to asking whether characteristics such as popularity and acceptance enable children to induce higher levels of conformity from their peers, a related question might be whether the ability to persuade peers (or to be persuaded by them) predicts adjustment outcomes. Allen, Porter, and McFarland (2006) argued that the ability to assert autonomy with peers represents an important developmental milestone in adolescence. They hypothesized that children who are unduly influenced by their peers (as opposed to being able to assert themselves effectively) would experience higher levels of social and emotional difficulties over time. In this study, participants were presented with a hypothetical dilemma ("Which subset of fictional characters should be saved from an intergalactic disaster?") and asked to come to an independent solution. Next, participants and their close friends were brought together to discuss the dilemma and come to a mutual agreement. Susceptibility to peer influence was defined as the percentage of times that participants changed their initial answer to match that of their friend.

Results demonstrated that high levels of susceptibility to peer influence within the lab task were associated with high levels of concurrent deviant behavior and substance use outside the lab (at home and school). Further, susceptibility to peer influence in the lab showed strong predictive effects; children who acquiesced more frequently within the lab paradigm showed significant declines in popularity and increases in depressive symptoms when assessed 1 year later (Allen et al., 2006). These results are among the first to suggest that the establishment of autonomy (and a healthy degree of influence) with one's peers may be an important marker of psychological adjustment.

THREE ELEPHANTS IN THE ROOM: WHAT WE STILL DON'T KNOW ABOUT POPULARITY AND INFLUENCE

Perhaps the best way to describe the current state of our knowledge is "limited." We know that indices of popularity and influence are related, that popular children tend to be more persuasive sources of influence than their less popular counterparts, and that the ability to exert social dominance can be adaptive. Still, a large number of unanswered questions await empirical investigation. This section highlights the three aspects of popularity and social influence that pose the most pressing (and still relatively unexplored) questions:

1. *How* do popular children influence their peers (mechanistic processes)?
2. *Why* are some children more powerful/more susceptible than others (moderating effects)?
3. *When* do particular forms of peer influence exert their strongest effects (developmental models)?

Mechanisms of Influence

Although it is clear that popular peers can shape the behaviors and attitudes of their classmates, very little research has focused on mechanisms of action. That is, what are the *processes* (both overt and covert) that induce children and adolescents to shape their behaviors in accordance with popular peers? What are the key components of social power? Several constructs have been nominated as important factors in the influence process, including overt reinforcement (deviance training), strategic use of aggression, and embodiment of antiestablishment values.

What all three of these mechanisms share is their reliance on the display of deviant behavior as a form of social leverage. In the case of peer contagion, for example, researchers have discovered that antisocial peers selectively engage in and reinforce "rule-breaking talk" as a means of encouraging their friends to engage in problematic behaviors. In landmark research, Dishion, Spracklen, Andrews, and Patterson (1996) videotaped conversations of adolescent boys and their friends in a laboratory setting. Results indicated clear differences between delinquent and nondelinquent dyads in both the types of topics they introduced as well as their responses to particular topics. Nondelinquent dyads reacted more positively to normative talk and were less likely to laugh in response to rule-breaking talk while delinquent dyads displayed the opposite pattern. Results suggested that delinquent boys used laughter as a way to reinforce (and subsequently increase) their partner's choice of deviant topics. Even more striking, however, was the discovery that this reinforcement pattern, dubbed "deviancy training," emerged as a significant predictor of increased delinquent behavior over a 2-year period, even after controlling for boys' initial levels of delinquency (Dishion et al., 1996). Thus, it appears that selective reinforcement of particular topics of conversation plays an important role in the spread of deviant behavior from one peer to another.

There is also evidence to suggest that the tactical and calculated use of aggressive strategies may help some children maintain control and dominance over their peers. For instance, Hawley's (2002) exploration of resource-control strategies among an elementary school-age sample found that children who combined the use of prosocial and coercive tactics (bistrategic controllers) were seen by their classmates as the most dominant and socially attractive members of the peer group. Further, teachers rated bistrategic children higher on popularity and leadership dimensions compared with those who relied more exclusively on prosocial strategies (Hawley, Johnson, Mize, & McNamara, 2007). Self-report data have yielded similar findings; bistrategic controllers report higher mean levels of social control than other children, including prosocial controllers (Hawley, Little, & Pasupathi, 2002). These studies raise the possibility that it is not popularity per se that bestows social control but rather the combination of popularity and calculated use of force.

In further support of this notion, peer nomination data from middle and high school students demonstrate that children who are viewed as highly popular by their peers are also rated as engaging in high levels of aggressive behavior (Cillessen & Mayeux, 2004; Sandstrom & Cillessen, 2006). As a complement to the existing correlational data, longitudinal evidence suggests that the strategic use of aggression leads to increases in popularity over time. For example, one study of middle and high school students demonstrated that relationally aggressive girls (those who were viewed by peers as engaging in high levels of exclusion, gossip, and rumor spreading) showed increases in peer-rated popularity over 6 months (Rose, Swenson, & Waller, 2004). These results lend support to the notion that the strategic use of aggressive behavior aids in the attainment and maintenance of high status, and that persuasive leaders must be, as Machiavelli advised, both "severe and gracious."

Rather than focusing on the use of aggressive or coercive behavior per se, some theorists posit that it is the display of antiestablishment values and behavior more generally that makes some children particularly influential among their peers. Moffitt (1993) argued that teens who personify the rebel role become intensely appealing models to their peers in adolescence, because their behavior highlights the two most salient goals of that developmental period: personal autonomy and independence. For adolescents who are looking to exert personal power and to separate from their families of origin, legitimate pathways to independence (e.g., employment, marriage, and procreation) are not viable options. In this atmosphere of thwarted self-determination, rebels (peers who "do *what* they want *when* they want") emerge as potent sources of influence.

Indeed, converging findings demonstrate that there *is* an important connection between popularity and antiestablishment behaviors. It is clear that a subgroup of popular children are characterized by their display of "tough" or antisocial characteristics (e.g., Estell, Farmer, Pearl, Van Acker, & Rodkin, 2008; Luthar & McMahon, 1996; Rodkin, Farmer, Pearl, & Van Acker, 2000). Further, emerging evidence suggests that adolescents who engage in antiestablishment behaviors such as cigarette smoking and early sexual activity are perceived by their peers as kids who "other kids listen to" and who "set the trends for other kids" (Miller-Johnson, Costanzo, Coie, Rose, Browne, & Johnson, 2003) and are nominated by their classmates as highly popular (Mayeux, Sandstrom, & Cillessen, 2008). Teens who are seen as popular by members of the opposite sex tend to endorse greater acceptance of "mature" behaviors such as openness to smoking, drinking, and/or dating (Harton & Latané, 1997). Further, popular children demonstrate higher levels of academic misconduct, including lower teacher preference, lower grade point average, and higher rates of absenteeism (Gorman, Kim, & Schimmelbusch, 2002).

The bulk of research linking popularity with rebellion relies on correlational designs, making it difficult to draw causal conclusions about the role deviant behavior actually plays in promoting popularity and influence over time. Does popularity trigger engagement in rule-breaking behavior, or does experimentation with risky behaviors lead to increases in status and power over time? Longitudinal data suggest that adolescents who are viewed as highly popular by their peers engage in higher levels of peer-supported misconduct, such as minor levels of drug use and delinquency, 1 year later (Allen, Porter, McFarland, Marsh, & McElhaney, 2005). Thus, to some extent, popularity may afford greater opportunities to engage in risky behaviors. Other researchers have found that engagement in risky behaviors, such as alcohol use and sexual activity, leads to increases in popularity over time (Mayeux et al., 2008).

In another longitudinal study, Killeya-Jones, Nakajima, and Costanzo (2007) tracked the status and risk behaviors of high school students over the course of a school year and compared the social status of students who engaged in early (fall semester) versus late (spring semester) risk-taking behaviors. Teens who reported using alcohol or cigarettes in the fall were more socially central and well connected than their nonusing counterparts and tended to maintain their status in the spring (even when they reported no further substance use at that time). In contrast, there was no difference in social centrality between students who engaged in risky behaviors for the first time in the spring versus spring abstainers. These results support the premise that the timing of rebellious behavior matters: Teens who push the envelope and are among the first to experiment with adult roles appear to reap the greatest social benefits (Killeya-Jones et al., 2007). Together, these studies suggest that popular children who are willing to break adult rules in prescribed ways may emerge as especially compelling leaders in the peer group.

Although all of the mechanistic processes proposed thus far revolve around rebellious or aggressive behavior, there are many other attributes that may serve to amplify popular children's social influence over peers. For instance, what role does physical attractiveness play in the social influence process? A broad body of research demonstrates that the "beauty is good" stereotype emerges in childhood; attractive youth are perceived as more well accepted, intelligent, and prosocial than their less attractive counterparts (e.g., Vaughn & Langlois, 1983). Given this finding, we might posit that physical attraction is a key mechanism driving the social power of popular children, and that physically attractive children are particularly successful at influencing their peers, acquiring resources, and controlling the social norms in their classrooms. Nonetheless, empirical evidence for such links is surprisingly scarce. In one of the few studies to examine correlations among power, dominance, popularity, and physical attractiveness, Hawley and colleagues (2007) demonstrated that evidence in support of the "attractive–influential" link is mixed. Although indices of social prominence were predicted by teacher ratings of physical attractiveness for boys, no such relationship emerged for girls. Further, there were no significant associations between indices of social influence or prominence and physical attractiveness when ratings of attractiveness were made by unfamiliar observers. Thus, it appears that the association between prominence and attractiveness for boys is due, at least in part, to the teachers' familiarity with the children in question. Indeed, it may be the case that prominence and popularity lead certain boys to be perceived as attractive rather than the other way around. At any rate, such findings suggest that the associations between beauty and power may be more complex than initially believed.

The mechanistic processes described here represent just a few examples of how popularity may translate into power, but the range of possibilities is large. Future researchers need to cast a broad net to identify more of the key mechanisms involved in the social influence process. It is only through a better understanding of *how* children exert control over one another and encourage engagement in particular behaviors that we can build better models of developmental psychopathology and prevention.

Moderators of Peer Influence

In addition to considering the mechanisms through which influence operates, it is also important to identify factors that act to exacerbate or dampen the influence process. Moderators can be broken down into three categories: (1) individual-differences moderators (characteristics of sources and/or targets), (2) relational moderators (characteristics of the association between source and target), and (3) contextual moderators (situational characteristics surrounding sources and targets).

Individual-Differences Moderators

Children vary in the extent to which they are susceptible to peer influence. A number of characteristics appear to contribute to this variability, including gender, family functioning, personal identification with the peer group, and psychological factors (e.g., self-regulation, social anxiety).

Converging results across a number of studies suggest that boys may be more susceptible to peer influence than girls. For instance, girls are more likely than boys to stand up for their personal beliefs and resist conformity (e.g., Berndt, 1979; Steinberg & Monahan, 2007; Steinberg & Silverberg, 1986), and girls report greater feelings of self-reliance than boys (Greenberger, 1982; Steinberg & Silverberg, 1986). In some ways, these findings run counter to the widely held view that girls are less agentic than boys or that girls prioritize communal/relational goals over personal strivings (Maccoby, 1990). If this is the case, shouldn't girls engage in *higher* levels of conformity in an attempt to please their partners, avoid conflict, or establish greater intimacy?

One way to unravel this paradox is to reconsider the function of conformity. It is possible, for example, that conformity serves an agentic purpose rather than a relational one during particular phases of childhood. Perhaps boys rely on behavioral conformity as a means of establishing and illustrating a clear dominance hierarchy in the peer group. If acquiescing to the behavioral choices of higher status boys is a tangible marker of a boy's current status that can be easily broadcast to the larger group, then conformity might serve a key developmental function for boys. Girls, in contrast, may place more emphasis on dyadic exchanges and relationship building than dominance hierarchies. If so, then behavioral conformity may not be as relevant or useful as a social tool. Further research is required to test this premise empirically.

In addition to gender, exposure to particular parenting styles also appears to determine children's susceptibility to peer influence. For instance, evidence suggests that although changes in teens' grade point average and drug use are predicted by their friends' grades and drug use, this effect is moderated by teens' reports of authoritative parenting. The positive impact of a high-achieving friend is stronger among teens whose parents are more authoritative, whereas the negative impact of a drug-using friend is stronger among teens whose parents are less authoritative (Mounts & Steinberg, 1995). Additional research will help us determine whether the impact of authoritative parenting spans across all forms of influence or is circumscribed to particular behaviors.

Another important moderator of social influence is the extent to which children feel personally connected to the peer group; greater identification and investment in a group should lead to increased conformity to its norms. Indeed, empirical evidence suggests that group identification *does* moderate the association between a group's initial level of problem behavior and individual group members' problem behavior 1 year later (Kiesner, Cadinu, Poulin, & Bucci, 2002). These results suggest that social influence is jointly determined by peers' behavior *and* individual group members' identification with the group. It is possible, then, that decreasing children's identification with problematic groups may be one way to reduce the likelihood of socialization effects, especially in those cases in which total exposure cannot be decreased.

Finally, it is likely that certain psychological features determine susceptibility to group influence. For example, children who are generally more adept at regulating their behaviors and emotions (e.g., setting goals, planning, and persisting in tasks) might be better able to resist negative peer influence than those with self-regulatory difficulties. Indeed, there is some support for this notion in the context of antisocial behavior; Gardner, Dishion, and Connell (2008) found that children's self-regulatory ability moderated the association between peer deviance and later self-reported antisocial behavior, even after accounting for initial levels of delinquency. This suggests that it is easier for children to resist the short-term temptations associated with conformity (e.g., entertainment, temporary peer favor) when they are able to keep track of more valuable long-term goals.

Another psychological variable that may be particularly relevant to peer influence is children's subjective fear of negative evaluation. Theoretically, children who experience heightened levels of social anxiety may engage in higher levels of conformity in an attempt to fit in, make a good impression, and reduce their insecurities. Preliminary evidence supports the role of social anxiety as a moderator of peer influence. Prinstein (2007) found that socially anxious girls are particularly likely to report depressive symptoms that corresponded with those of their close friends. Moreover, socially anxious boys are especially prone to conform to aggressive and health risk behaviors when prompted by a high-status peer (Cohen & Prinstein, 2006).

Relational Moderators

In addition to individual factors, it is reasonable to expect that relational factors determine, in part, children's susceptibility to particular sources of influence. Surprisingly, however, remarkably little is known about the extent to which children are more strongly influenced by individual peers (such as close friends) versus larger groups (such as a popular clique or crowd). To make matters more complicated, various sources of influence are not entirely independent, because children's social interactions play out across multiple levels at once (Bronfenbrenner, 1979). That is, friendships exist within the context of cliques, cliques exist within the context of larger crowds, and so on. As children get older, their exchanges gradually shift from predominantly dyadic exchanges to those that occur in the context of larger groups (Crockett, Losoff, & Petersen, 1984). What do these changes in proximal context mean for peer influence?

In one attempt to unravel the impact of friends versus groups, Urberg (1992) found that best friends, rather than social crowd, were the major source of influence on high school students' smoking behavior. Although the absolute frequency of smoking varied by social crowd, *change* in smoking over a year was predicted only by best friend and not social crowd influence. Subsequent research has demonstrated that the relative influence of friends versus larger groups varies as a function of the behavior in question. Although influence from closest friends emerged as the best predictor of *initiation* of cigarette use, only friendship group significantly predicted transition into current cigarette use. In contrast, only close friend use predicted transition into current alcohol use, while both the group and the close friend jointly contributed to the prediction of drinking to intoxication (Urberg, Değirmencioğlu, & Pilgrim, 1997).

Interestingly, research on influence within dyadic relationships has produced mixed findings on the importance of reciprocity. Some studies suggest that mutual or high-quality friends exert considerably more influence on one another than do unilateral or poor-quality friends (Epstein, 1983; Stevens & Prinstein, 2005; Urberg, Luo, Pilgrim, & Değirmencioğlu, 2003), whereas others have found that teens whose friendship choices are not reciprocated or are of lower quality are more influenced by their friend's values than teens in mutual/high-quality relationships (Juvonen & Ho, 2008; Prinstein, 2007). Both findings make some intuitive sense. On the one hand, mutual friends likely spend more time with each other, providing greater exposure to each other's behaviors and values. On the other hand, children with unrequited friendships may feel greater pressure to adapt their behavior in an attempt to "woo" a disinterested peer or to gain additional emotional intimacy. Future research will need to consider the impact of reciprocal and nonreciprocal friends on a wide range of behaviors to determine whether certain types of relationships hold more sway in the context of particular behavioral domains.

Contextual Moderators

While individual and relational moderators of social influence focus on characteristics of the source and target, contextual factors encompass broader situational characteristics, such as the composition and structure of the wider peer group, presence of an ally, or cultural values and norms about the acceptability of particular behaviors. It is this category of moderator effects that has received the least empirical attention. For example, even though it has been well documented that the presence of a single ally can dramatically increase an adult's resistance to group pressure, this phenomenon remains relatively unexplored among children.

One contextual factor that has received some empirical attention recently is the extent to which the status of particular groups influences the degree to which those groups influence their members. For instance, Ellis and Zarbatany (2007) investigated whether groups that are perceived as "well liked" or "high status" (i.e., highly central and visible) by the larger peer group exert greater socializing pressure on their members than do less admired groups. In general, results suggested that high-status groups were more successful in socializing a range of behaviors, including school misconduct, relational aggression, deviant behavior, and prosocial behavior than low-status groups. Perceived likeability of the group, in contrast, had a less striking effect.

Another important contextual factor that has received scant research attention in the social influence literature involves ethnic/cultural norms. Deeply held cultural or ethnic traditions that serve to encourage or discourage particular behaviors may shape the extent to which children are susceptible to peer influence in those domains. For example, Becker and Luthar (2007) found that substance use showed stronger links with peer admiration among Latino inner-city teens than African American teens. Does this imply that that Latino youth are more vulnerable to peer suggestion in this domain? To test such hypotheses, we need to know more about culturally based differences in the value placed on particular behaviors (e.g., academic achievement, substance use, early sexual activity) as well as the extent to which peer pressure succeeds in shaping the behavior of individuals in those cultural contexts.

Influence across Development

The third major question facing peer researchers interested in social influence processes has to do with developmental effects. Existing literature suggests that children's ability to influence and be influenced by each other begins as soon as they are able to have meaningful interactions with their peers. Imitation, which emerges as early as infancy, may be the earliest and most primitive manifestation of peer influence. When infants are presented with an imitation task, for instance, those who are exposed to a peer regularly outperform those who are exposed to an adult (Ryalls, Gul, & Ryalls, 2000). Thus, children seem predisposed to influence each other. What is not clear, however, is how peer influence processes might vary over the course of development. To date, we lack a clear model indicating whether particular *sources* of influence (e.g., friends, cliques, or crowds) are more potent at particular time points, whether particular *behaviors* (e.g., deviant, prosocial) are more amenable to influence at particular times, and whether particular *mechanisms* of influence (e.g., reinforcement, coercion) are prominent during particular developmental periods.

It seems likely that there are developmental differences on all three fronts. For example, it may be the case that although friends and other dyadic partners play a dominant role in shaping children's behavior during early childhood, the major source of influence shifts to the larger peer group in middle childhood and then to reputation-based crowds (e.g., jocks, brains) during adolescence. Although such a model fits with existing knowledge about how children's affiliations and social interactions shift over time, the specifics await empirical investigation. Similarly, future research will need to consider whether particular methods of social influence are age specific or general. Research on deviancy training processes provides a good example. Although the bulk of this research has been conducted with adolescent samples, emerging evidence suggests that differential patterns of reinforcement for rule-breaking talk emerge as early as kindergarten (Snyder, Schrepferman, & McEachern, 2008). Thus, deviancy training may be a general mechanism of peer influence that operates across multiple ages.

In contrast, there is some evidence to suggest that other mechanisms, such as the strategic use of aggressive strategies, may not become an important source of influence among popular children until middle childhood. In support of this distinction, Estell (2007) noted that although cluster analysis of high-status children typically reveals a popular–aggressive subtype among older children and adolescents, no such cluster emerges in kindergarten samples. Estell (2007) used this finding as evidence for the developmental argument that children need to accrue a certain level of developmental skill and social savvy before they are able to strategically use aggression in ways that promote their interests without hurting their social standing.

PRACTICAL IMPLICATIONS

As a field, what can we hope to accomplish with a better understanding of social influence processes? The answer is twofold. First, a more clearly delineated understanding of the processes through which peers shape each other's behavior will help us build better models of developmental psychopathology. If we want to be able to make accurate predictions about which children will become depressed, anxious, delinquent, or academically accomplished over time, it will serve us to know more about the company they keep. Second, a better grasp on the ways in which peers naturally influence each other in positive and negative ways may ultimately allow interventionists to harness that power and guide it in productive directions.

Already, there is some evidence to suggest that popular opinion leaders—highly central and dominant peers in the classroom—can serve as effective change agents, and use their personal charisma to encourage adaptive choices among their peers. For instance, opinion leaders have been used successfully in school-based programs geared toward the prevention of HIV (e.g., Kelly, St. Lawrence, & Diaz, 1991; Stevens, Leybas-Amedia, Bourdeau, McMichael, & Nyitray, 2006), smoking (Clarke, MacPherson, Holmes, & Jones, 1986; Elder, Wildey, de Moor, & Sallis, 1993; Klepp, Halper, & Perry, 1986), and other forms of substance use (Miller-Johnson & Costanzo, 2004). Although the possibility of using peer opinion leaders is fascinating, the limitations of this strategy are unknown. Issues requiring further study include leadership stability (do opinion leaders retain their power after being co-opted by school officials?), iatrogenic effects (do opinion leaders inadvertently spread unwanted behaviors to their peers in the context of these programs?), and feasibility (are school officials comfortable allowing unconventional yet popular leaders to assume these positions of authority?). Answers to such questions are needed to determine how interventions can use peers as agents of change in targeted and effective ways.

MOVING FORWARD

Despite a burgeoning interest in peer influence processes over the past decade, the field remains full of questions and opportunities for inquisitive researchers. At this point, peer researchers have accrued a great deal of descriptive data documenting the existence of conformity, peer pressure, and contagion effects. With this knowledge at our disposal, it is now time to turn to a new phase of research that can extend existing theoretical models and applied interventions. To that end, researchers should focus their investigations on the mechanisms, moderators, and developmental processes of peer influence rather than description alone.

Second, researchers should be mindful of the methodological limitations that have hindered previous work. One pervasive flaw has to do with an overreliance on self-report measures. For example, researchers have frequently used children's reports of their friends' behavior as stand-ins for an actual assessment. To the extent that children exaggerate their similarities with their friends, this method of assessing peer influence produces questionable conclusions. Future research should broaden its assessment armamentarium. This includes gathering behavioral data from multiple sources (including peers and unbiased observers) as well as developing new and innovative assessment strategies. One clever example involves the use of handheld computers to track influence effects. By having children "beam" opinions to each other's handheld electronic devices before and after a series of dyadic discussions in the classroom, for instance, Guryan, Jacob, Kopfer, and Groff (2008) were able track how individual student's opinions evolved over the course of their interactions with specific partners. This type of technology opens up many exciting possibilities for the study of influence processes.

Finally, a parting suggestion for future researchers is to broaden the scope of inquiry about influence processes. The lion's share of existing research focuses on the spread of maladaptive behavior (e.g., deviancy, drug use, academic disengagement, iatrogenic effects of group treatment). Given the costs of such problems to individuals, families, and society, it is clear that this line of inquiry must continue. Nevertheless, more attention needs to be paid to the impact of peer influence on the positive end of the adjustment continuum. In what ways do peers influence each other to engage in competent, adaptive, and prosocial behaviors? The more we know about *all* forms of peer power (both positive and negative), the better prepared we will be to harness that power in adaptive and successful ways.

REFERENCES

Adler, P. A., & Adler, P. (1998). *Peer power: Preadolescent culture and identity*. New Brunswick, NJ: Rutgers University Press.

Allen, J. P., Porter, M. R., & McFarland, C. F. (2006). Leaders and followers in adolescent close friendships: Susceptibility to peer influence as a predictor of risky behavior, friendship instability, and depression. *Development and Psychopathology, 18,* 155–172.

Allen, J. P., Porter, M. R., McFarland, C. F., Marsh, P. A., & McElhaney, K. B. (2005). The two faces of adolescents' success with peers: Adolescent popularity, social adaptation, and deviant behavior. *Child Development, 7,* 747–760.

Allen, V. L., & Newston, D. (1972). Development of conformity and independence. *Journal of Personality and Social Psychology, 22,* 18–30.

Asch, S. E. (1956). Studies of independence and conformity: A minority of one against a unanimous majority. *Psychological Monographs, 70,* 1–71.

Becker, B. E., & Luthar, S. S. (2007). Peer-perceived admiration and social preference: Contextual correlates of positive peer regard among suburban and urban adolescents. *Journal of Research on Adolescence, 17,* 117–144.

Berenda, R. (1950). *The influence of the group on the judgments of children.* New York: Kings Crown Press.

Berndt, T. J. (1979). Developmental changes in conformity to peers and parents. *Developmental Psychology, 15,* 606–616.

Berndt, T. J., Laychak, A. E., & Park, K. (1990). Friends influence on adolescents' academic achievement motivation: An experimental study. *Journal of Educational Psychology, 82,* 664–670.

Bixenstine, V. E., DeCorte, M. S., & Bixenstine, B. A. (1976). Conformity to peer-sponsored misconduct at four grade levels. *Developmental Psychology, 12,* 226–236.

Boxer, P., Guerra, N. G., Huesmann, L. R., & Morales, J. (2005). Proximal peer-level effects of a small-group selected prevention on aggression in elementary school children: An investigation of the peer contagion hypothesis. *Journal of Abnormal Child Psychology, 33,* 325–338.

Bronfenbrenner, U. (1979). *The ecology of human development: Experiments by nature and design.* Cambridge, MA: Harvard University Press.

Brown, B. B., Clasen, D. R., & Eicher, S. A. (1986). Perceptions of peer pressure, peer conformity dispositions, and self-reported behavior among adolescents. *Developmental Psychology, 22,* 521–530.

Cillessen, A. H. N., & Mayeux, L. (2004). From censure to reinforcement: Developmental changes in the association between aggression and social status. *Child Development, 75,* 147–163.

Clarke, J., MacPherson, B., Holmes, D., & Jones, R. (1986). Reducing adolescent smoking: A comparison of peer-led, teacher-led, and expert interventions. *Journal of School Health, 56,* 102–106.

Cohen, G. L., & Prinstein, M. J. (2006). Peer contagion of aggression and health risk behavior among adolescent males: An experimental investigation of effects of public conduct and private attitudes. *Child Development, 77,* 967–983.

Cohen, R., Bornstein, R., & Sherman, R. C. (1973). Conformity behavior of children as a function of group makeup and task ambiguity. *Developmental Psychology, 9,* 124–131.

Costanzo, P., & Shaw, M. (1966). Conformity as a function of age level. *Child Development, 37,* 967–975.

Crockett, L., Losoff, M., & Petersen, A. (1984). Perceptions of the peer group and friendship in early adolescence. *Journal of Early Adolescence, 4,* 155–181.

Dishion, T. J. (2000). Cross-setting consistency in early adolescent psychopathology: Deviant friendships and problem behavior sequelae. *Journal of Personality, 68,* 1109–1126.

Dishion, T. J., McCord, J., & Poulin, F. (1999). When interventions harm: Peer groups and problem behavior. *American Psychologist, 54,* 755–764.

Dishion, T. J., & Medici Skaggs, N. (2000). An ecological analysis of monthly "bursts" in early adolescence substance use. *Applied Developmental Science, 4,* 89–97.

Dishion, T. J., Spracklen, K. M., Andrews, D. W., & Patterson, G. R. (1996). Deviancy training in male adolescent friendships. *Behavior Therapy, 27,* 373–390.

Eder, D., Evans, C. C., & Parker, S. (1995). *School talk: Gender and adolescent culture.* New Brunswick, NJ: Rutgers University Press.

Elder, J., Wildey, M., de Moor, C., & Sallis, J. (1993). The long-term prevention of tobacco use among junior high school students: Classroom and telephone interventions. *American Journal of Public Health, 83,* 1239–1244.

Elliot, D. S., & Menard, S. (1996). Delinquent friends and delinquent behavior: Temporal and developmental patterns. In J. D. Hawkins (Ed.), *Delinquency and crime: Current theories* (pp. 28–67). New York: Cambridge University Press.

Ellis, W. E., & Zarbatany, L. (2007). Peer group status as a moderator of group influence on children's deviant, aggressive, and prosocial behavior. *Child Development, 78,* 1240–1254.

Epstein, J. (1983). The influence of friends on achievement and affective outcomes. In J. Epstein & N. Karweit (Eds.), *Friends in school: Patterns of selection and influence* (pp. 177–200). New York: Academic Press.

Erickson, K. G., Crosnoe, R., & Dornbusch, S. M. (2000). A social process model of adolescent deviance: Combining social control and differential association perspectives. *Journal of Youth and Adolescence, 29,* 395–425.

Estell, D. B. (2007). Aggression, social status, and affiliation in kindergarten children: A preliminary study. *Education and Treatment of Children, 30,* 53–72.

Estell, D. B., Farmer, T. W., Pearl, R., Van Acker, R., & Rodkin, P. C. (2008). Social status and aggressive and disruptive behavior in girls: Individual, group, and classroom influences. *Journal of School Psychology, 46,* 193–212.

Gardner, M., & Steinberg, L. (2005). Peer influence on risk taking, risk preference, and risky decision making in adolescence and adulthood: An experimental study. *Developmental Psychology, 41,* 625–635.

Gardner, T., Dishion, T. J., & Connell, A. (2008). Adolescent self-regulation as resilience: Resistance to antisocial behavior within the deviant peer context. *Journal of Abnormal Child Psychology, 36,* 273–284.

Gorman, A. H., Kim, J., & Schimmelbusch, A. (2002). The attributes adolescents associate with peer popularity and teacher preference. *Journal of School Psychology, 40,* 143–165.

Greenberger, E. (1982). Education and the acquisition of psychosocial maturity. In D. McClelland (Ed.), *The development of social maturity* (pp. 155–189). New York: Irvington.

Guryan, J., Jacobs, B., Klopfer, E., & Groff, J. (2003). Using technology to

explore social networks and mechanisms underlying peer effects in classrooms. *Developmental Psychology, 44*, 355–364.
Hamm, N. H., & Hoving, K. L. (1969). Conformity of children in an ambiguous perceptual situation. *Child Development, 40*, 773–783.
Harton, H. C., & Latané, B. (1997). Social influence and adolescent lifestyle attitudes. *Journal of Research on Adolescence, 7*, 197–220.
Hartup, W. W. (1999). Constraints on peer socialization: Let me count the ways. *Merrill-Palmer Quarterly, 45*, 172–183.
Hartup, W. W. (2005). Peer interaction: What causes what? *Journal of Abnormal Child Psychology, 33*, 387–394.
Harvey, O. J., & Rutherford, J. (1960). Status in the informal group: Influence and influencibility at differing age levels. *Developmental Psychology, 31*, 377–385.
Hawley, P. H. (2002). Social dominance and prosocial and coercive strategies of resource control in preschoolers. *International Journal of Behavioral Development, 26*, 167–176.
Hawley, P. H., Johnson, S. E., Mize, J. A., & McNamara, K. A. (2007). Physical attractiveness in preschoolers: Relationships with power, status, aggression and social skills. *Journal of School Psychology, 45*, 499–521.
Hawley, P. H., Little, T. D., & Pasupathi, M. (2002). Winning friends and influencing peers: Strategies of peer influence in late childhood. *International Journal of Behavioral Development, 26*, 466–474.
Iscoe, I., Williams, M., & Harvey, J. (1963). Modification of children's judgments by a simulated group technique: A normative developmental study. *Child Development, 34*, 963–978.
Juvonen, J., & Ho, A. (2008). Social motives underlying antisocial behavior across middle school grades. *Journal of Youth and Adolescence, 37*, 747–756.
Keenna, K., Loeber, R., Zhang, Q., Stouthamer-Loeber, M., & van Kammen, W. B. (1995). The influence of deviant peers on the development of boys' disruptive and delinquent behavior: A temporal analysis. *Development and Psychopathology, 7*, 715–726.
Kelly, J. A., St. Lawrence, J. S., & Diaz, Y. E. (1991). HIV risk behavior reduction following intervention with key opinion leaders of population. *Journal of Public Health, 81*, 168–171.
Kiesner, J., Cadinu, M., Poulin, F., & Bucci, M. (2002). Group identification in early adolescence: Its relation with peer adjustment and its moderator effect on peer influence. *Child Development, 73*, 196–208.
Killeya-Jones, L.A., Nakajima, R., & Costanzo, P. R. (2007). Peer standing and substance use in early-adolescent grade-level networks: A short-term longitudinal study. *Prevention Science, 8*, 11–23.
Klepp, K., Halper, A., & Perry, C. (1986). The efficacy of peer leaders in drug abuse prevention. *Journal of School Health, 56*, 407–411.
LaFontana, K. M., & Cillessen, A. H. N. (2002). Children's perceptions of popular and unpopular peers: A multimethod assessment. *Developmental Psychology, 38*, 635–647.
Lease, A. M., Kennedy, C. A., & Axelrod, J. L. (2002). Children's social constructions of popularity. *Social Development, 11*, 87–109.

Lease, A. M., Musgrove, K. T., & Axelrod, J. L. (2002). Dimensions of social status in preadolescent peer groups: Likability, popularity, and social dominance. *Social Development, 11,* 508–533.

Luthar, S., & McMahon, T. (1996). Peer reputation among inner-city adolescents: Structure and correlates. *Journal of Research on Adolescence, 6,* 581–603.

Maccoby, E. E. (1990). Gender and relationships: A developmental account. *American Psychologist, 50,* 513–520.

Mayeux, L., Sandstrom, M. J., & Cillessen, A. H. N. (2008). Is being popular a risky proposition? *Journal of Research on Adolescence, 18,* 49–74.

Miller-Johnson, S., & Costanzo, P. R. (2004). If you can't beat 'em ... induce them to join you: Peer-based interventions during adolescence. In J. B. Kupersmidt & K. A. Dodge (Eds.), *Children's peer relations: From development to intervention* (pp. 209–222). Washington, DC: American Psychological Association.

Miller-Johnson, S., Costanzo, P. R., Coie, J. D., Rose, M. R., Browne, D. C., & Johnson, C. (2003). Peer social structure and risk-taking behaviors among African American early adolescents. *Journal of Youth and Adolescence, 32,* 375–384.

Moffitt, T. (1993). Adolescence-limited and life-course-persistent antisocial behavior: A developmental taxonomy. *Psychological Review, 100,* 674–701.

Mounts, N. S., & Steinberg, L. (1995). An ecological analysis of peer influence on adolescent grade point average and drug use. *Developmental Psychology, 31,* 915–922.

Parkhurst, J. T., & Hopmeyer, A. (1998). Sociometric popularity and peer-popularity: Two distinct dimensions of peer status. *Journal of Early Adolescence, 18,* 125–144.

Prinstein, M. J. (2007). Moderators of peer contagion: A longitudinal examination of depression socialization between adolescents and their best friends. *Journal of Clinical Child and Adolescent Psychology, 36,* 159–170.

Prinstein, M. J., & Dodge, K. A. (2008). *Understanding peer influence in children and adolescents.* New York: Guilford Press.

Rodkin, P. C., Farmer, T. W., Pearl, R., & Van Acker, R. (2000). Heterogeneity of popular boys: Antisocial and prosocial configurations. *Developmental Psychology, 36,* 14–24.

Rose, A. J., Swenson, L. P., & Waller, E. M. (2004). Overt and relational aggression and popularity: Developmental differences in concurrent and prospective relations. *Developmental Psychology, 40,* 378–387.

Ryalls, B. O., Gul, R. E., & Ryalls, K. R. (2000). Infant imitation of peer and adult models: Evidence for a peer model advantage. *Merrill-Palmer Quarterly, 46,* 188–202.

Sandstrom, M. J., & Cillessen, A. H. N. (2006). Likable versus popular: Distinct implications for adolescent adjustment. *International Journal of Behavioral Development, 30,* 305–314.

Sandstrom, M. J., & Romano, L. (2007, March). *Popularity and social influence: How status and acceptance influence peers' persuasive ability.* Paper presented at the biennial meeting of Society for Research in Child Development, Boston.

Snyder, J., Schrepferman, L., & McEachern, A. (2008). Peer deviancy training and peer coercion: Dual processes associated with early-onset conduct problems. *Child Development, 79,* 252–268.

Steinberg, L., & Monahan, K. C. (2007). Age differences in resistance to peer influence. *Developmental Psychology, 43,* 1531–1543.

Steinberg, L., & Silverberg, S. (1986). The vicissitudes of autonomy in early adolescence. *Child Development, 57,* 841–851.

Stevens, E., & Prinstein, M. J. (2005). Peer contagion of depressogenic attributional styles among adolescents: A longitudinal study. *Journal of Abnormal Child Psychology, 33,* 25–37.

Stevens, S., Leybas-Amedia, V., Bourdeau, B., McMichael, L., & Nyitray, A. (2006). Blending prevention models: An effective substance use and HIV prevention program for minority youth. *Child and Adolescent Social Work Journal, 23,* 4–23.

Urberg, K. A. (1992). Locus of peer influence: Social crowd and best friend. *Journal of Youth and Adolescence, 21,* 439–450.

Urberg, K. A., Değirmencioğlu, S. M., & Pilgrim, C. (1997). Close friend and group influence on adolescent cigarette smoking and alcohol use. *Developmental Psychology, 33,* 834–844.

Urberg, K. A., Luo, Q., Pilgrim, C., & Değirmencioğlu, S. (2003). A two-stage model of peer influence in adolescent substance use: Individual and relationship-specific differences in susceptibility to influence. *Addictive Behaviors, 28,* 1243–1256.

Utech, D. A., & Hoving, K. L. (1969). Parents and peers as competing influences in the decisions of children of differing ages. *Journal of Social Psychology, 78,* 267–274.

Vaillancourt, T., & Hymel, S. (2006). Aggression and social status: The moderating roles of sex and peer-valued characteristics. *Aggressive Behavior, 32,* 396–408.

Vaughn, B. E., & Langlois, J. H. (1983). Physical attractiveness as a correlate of peer status and social competence in preschool children. *Developmental Psychology, 19,* 561–567.

Walker, M. B., & Andrade, M. G. (1996). Conformity in the Asch Task as a function of age. *Journal of Social Psychology, 136,* 367–372.

Chapter 11

The High Price of High Status
Popularity as a Mechanism of Risk

DAVID SCHWARTZ
ANDREA HOPMEYER GORMAN

    Research on social standing in the peer group has typically emphasized the positive implications of high status with peers (Coie & Dodge, 1983; Coie, Dodge, & Coppotelli, 1982). Children and adolescents who achieve high standing in the peer group are often presumed to be characterized by social competencies that portend desirable adjustment outcomes (Coie, Dodge, & Kupersmidt, 1990; Dodge, Pettit, McClaskey, & Brown, 1986; Eisenberg & Fabes, 1992). High status has also been viewed as an "affordance" for social opportunities, such as friendship formation, that might enhance the development of specific competencies (Bukowski, Pizzamiglio, Newcomb, & Hoza, 1996; Parker & Asher, 1993). Moreover, positive regard from peers could contribute to a child's developing sense of self-esteem and personal efficacy (Schwartz, Gorman, Duong, & Nakamoto, 2008).

    This generally optimistic view of the role of social standing in young people's lives is derived primarily from research conducted with traditional sociometric measures (i.e., social standing operationalized with assessments of acceptance). The picture from research conducted with reputation-based measures of popularity (i.e., scales that focus on social visibility, prestige, and status) has been somewhat less rosy. In fact, a number of researchers have concluded that popular youth may be at risk for problematic outcomes (e.g., Mayeux, Sandstrom, & Cillessen, 2008;

Sandstrom & Cillessen, 2006). A conceptualization of popularity as a potential correlate of maladjustment is also consistent with theory and empirical findings in related areas of inquiry. For example, in the literature on substance abuse, it has long been assumed that popularity and engagement in the peer group play a critically important role in the development of addictions (Alexander, Piazza, Mekos, & Valente, 2001). Similar themes are present in research on other forms of risky behavior, such as early sexual experimentation (Bersamin, Walker, Fisher, & Grube, 2006; Prinstein, Meade, & Cohen, 2003).

Our goal in the current chapter is to consider links between popularity and risk with a critical eye. We begin by identifying some underlying mechanisms that might explain any observed associations between popularity and maladjustment. We then move on to address the available findings with regard to specific classes of problems. In particular, we consider substance abuse, adolescent sexuality, and academic functioning. Our focus on these specific classes of problems reflects current themes in the extant literature.

There is also growing evidence that popularity is predictive of increases in aggressive behavior over time (Cillessen & Mayeux, 2004; Rodkin & Roisman, 2010; Sandstrom & Cillessen, 2006). Our coverage of the findings regarding aggression in the current chapter is somewhat limited because related discussions are offered elsewhere in this volume (Mayeux, Houser, & Dyches, Chapter 4; Pellegrini, Roseth, Van Ryzin, & Solberg, Chapter 6). Still, we emphasize the role of aggression as a moderator variable. As we contend, popularity and aggression interact synergistically as a potent combination in the prediction of risk.

HYPOTHESIZED UNDERLYING PROCESSES

Children and adolescents are likely to view popularity as a very desirable social outcome. Certainly, ethnographic studies suggest that popularity is an organizing goal for many young people by the preadolescent years (Adler & Adler, 1998; Eder, 1985). Indeed, the yearning for status and prestige with peers is commonly depicted in many of today's youth-oriented movies and television programs. To the extent that popularity represents a central objective for some youth, it seems reasonable to wonder about the behaviors that may be adopted as a means of reaching or maintaining status. That is, might some children or adolescents engage in problematic behaviors in an attempt to reach or maintain popularity with peers?

To illustrate our concern, consider the fictionalized case of an early adolescent who we call Ken. During his elementary school years, Ken was regarded as an excellent student and he frequently brought home report cards that made his parents quite proud. After he made the transition to middle school, Ken found himself very focused on becoming popular with his peers. Because the popular students in his new school considered studying to be "uncool," Ken began to disengage from academic pursuits. He spent less and less time on his homework. At the urging of his new friends, he skipped classes and even began "ditching" school. In addition, his teachers were sometimes irritated by Ken's penchant for talking with other students during classroom lectures. Ken did eventually become quite popular with some of his peers, but his grades declined steadily as a result.

The scenario we have just constructed illustrates the potential link between popularity and peer pressure. Here we use the term *peer pressure* to refer to social influences that encourage a young person to conform to particular norms with regard to attitudes, behaviors, and values (Santor, Messervey, & Kusumakar, 2000). These influences might be overt, as in the case of peers cajoling a fellow student to avoid schoolwork. Young people also encounter more indirect social pressures. For example, choices in dress and style often reflect a desire to be consistent with the trends embraced by the larger peer group.

The extent to which peer pressure is influential in shaping behavioral orientations varies across individuals (Urberg, Luo, Pilgrim, & Değirmencioğlu, 2003) and may wax and wane over the course of development (Berndt, 1979; Brown, 1990). In addition, active selection (i.e., the tendency for youth to affiliate with peers with whom they share common proclivities) is often more significant in determining the composition of the peer group than conformity effects (Berndt & Keefe, 1995; Ennett & Bauman, 1994). Nonetheless, these social influences may result in the acquisition of behaviors that adults generally view as undesirable.

We speculate that peer pressure and conformity are likely to play a particularly important role in the social lives of popular youth. Prestige in school peer groups is at least partially dependent on compatibility with the values and behavioral orientations inherent in the larger crowd structures (Brown, Clasen, & Eicher, 1986). Students who exhibit behaviors that are inconsistent with these established norms will be unlikely to achieve high standing with their elite peers. Put succinctly, popularity requires one to "fit in" with high-status peers. Unfortunately, in some social settings, this need to conform can lead to the acquisition of behaviors that are not necessarily adaptive.

Insofar as social prestige does require consistency with the values of the peer group, popular youth could encounter stronger social pressures toward conformity than other youth. We also predict that popular youth who diverge from peer group norms will be particularly likely to experience aversive social sanctions when they engage in behaviors that diverge from peer group norms. Therefore, any tendency toward conformity among popular youth might partially reflect the social demands associated with high standing among elite peers.

An unresolved issue is whether popular adolescents are also more susceptible to peer group influences than other adolescents. Despite our speculation that popular youth will encounter greater pressures to adopt peer conventions than their less visible classmates, we are not yet in a position to make any predictions regarding personal proclivities toward conformity. There have been few direct tests of the relation between social standing and tendencies to comply with peer pressure.

The handful of relevant studies that have been conducted generally focus on social acceptance rather than popularity. A notable example is a study by Allen, Porter, and McFarland (2006). These researchers found that a laboratory assessment of acquiescence to a close friend predicted declines in social status (derived from peer nomination scores that tap friendship and acceptance). Allen et al.'s findings do not shed light on the implications of conformity outside specific dyadic relationships, but at least provide evidence that complying with social pressure is unlikely to play a positive role in determining liking by peers.

Under some conditions, popularity might also afford exposure to peers who represent negative socializing influences. Although there is behavioral heterogeneity among popular youth (Farmer, Estell, Bishop, O'Neal, & Cairns, 2003; Lease, Musgrove, & Axelrod, 2002; Rodkin, Farmer, Pearl, & Van Acker, 2000), high-status social networks can include a relatively large percentage of members who are characterized by aggression or other antisocial behaviors (de Bruyn & Cillessen, 2006). By the early years of adolescence, affiliation with such peers becomes an important etiological factor in the development of problematic behaviors. Antisocial peers might model or reinforce aggression, deceit, and defiance of authority figures (Laird, Pettit, Dodge, & Bates, 1999). Likewise, youth may develop negative attitudes toward school through interactions with these individuals (Schwartz, Gorman, Dodge, Pettit, & Bates, 2008; Vitaro, Brendgen, & Wanner, 2005).

Even when popular cliques and crowds do not include overtly antisocial individuals, popularity could still afford opportunities for youth to observe socially manipulative behaviors or other forms of relational aggression. Particularly during adolescence, relational forms of aggression are closely associated with popularity (Cillessen & Mayeux, 2004). In fact, longitudinal investigations have demonstrated predictive links between relational aggression and popularity (Rose, Swenson, & Waller, 2004).

Let us return to our fictionalized depiction of Ken. Ken had always been a well-behaved child whose general orientation was prosocial in nature. After he became closely identified with the popular crowd during middle school, he was exposed to a number of peers who had sophisticated skills for relational aggression. Ken was able to observe high-status classmates effectively using gossip, exclusion, and socially manipulative behaviors to maintain their positions in the peer group hierarchy. As a result, he began to incorporate these strategies into his own repertoire.

Another possibility is that popularity could provide youth with opportunities for involvement in risky behaviors. As an example, consider potential links between popularity and early sexual experimentation (Prinstein et al., 2003). Research has shown that a predictive factor for the early onset of sexual behavior during adolescence is involvement in a monogamous romantic relationship (Luster & Small, 1994). These findings are notable given evidence that popular adolescents are more likely to have serious girlfriends or boyfriends than their lower status peers (Brown, Mory, & Kinney, 1994; Carlson & Rose, 2007). One "benefit" to the social visibility afforded by popularity might be access to potential partners for dating and sexual exploration.

A related issue is that social reinforcement associated with popularity can also lead to somewhat inflated views of self-worth (Sandstrom & Cillessen, 2010). Of course, an optimistic view of one's own competencies will serve a protective effect against depression and other problems that are rooted in low self-esteem (Schwartz, Gorman, Duong, & Nakamoto, 2008). The flip side is that youth who overestimate their own capacities can feel empowered to engage in maladaptive behaviors (Sandstrom & Herlan, 2007). Overconfidence may lead one to engage in risky behaviors with the assumption that the outcomes will also be desirable.

There are also aspects of popularity that could prove stressful or taxing over time. Popular students at any school are likely to experience considerable pressure to be attractive, cool, and highly visible among their peers (Eder, 1985). An illustration of these demands can be found in the movie "Heathers," a black comedy that depicts rivalries among popular girls attending a public high school. In this movie, the lead character complains with weariness that the other members of her high-status clique are "people I work with—and our job is being popular."

A more mundane issue to consider might be the potential distractions associated with popularity. Ethnographic researchers have described the intricacies involved in the social worlds of popular youth (Adler & Adler, 1998). Popularity appears to be a time-consuming pursuit. As a result, popular youth may wind up spending more time focused on social interactions than studying or preparing in other ways for the next stages of development.

We have conceptualized popularity as a causal mechanism, but a more parsimonious perspective might be that popularity is a "marker" or "lead indicator" of personal attributes that portend later adjustment difficulties. It may be the case that the risks we have discussed reflect underlying characteristics of popular youth rather than the actual experience of being popular. For example, we suspect that personal attributes associated with needs for status and attention will be critical factors in determining negative outcome for some popular youth.

SUBSTANCE USE AND ABUSE

To this point, our discussion has been somewhat abstract, focusing on hypothesized mechanisms. We now move in a more concrete direction and begin to consider specific categories of negative outcomes. We start by examining some of the evidence regarding the role of popularity in problems related to substance use and abuse. This emphasis seems appropriate given existing themes in the literature on cigarette smoking, drinking, and involvement with illicit drugs. Research on the etiology of substance abuse has often highlighted the significance of peer group relationships (e.g., Wills & Cleary, 1999), particularly during adolescence. A central assumption underlying much of the work in this area is that the peer group is a powerful socializing factor (Alexander et al., 2001). Adolescents are presumed to acquire substance abuse behaviors through interactions with close friends and other influential peers at school (Santor et al., 2000; Verkooijen, de Vries, & Nielsen, 2007). This learning process may occur through passive modeling or through a more active process of social pressure. The peer group is also viewed as a potential source of opportunity for involvement with substances. Thus, an adolescent who might not otherwise know how to obtain marijuana could have easy access because of his or her relationships with specific peers.

The role of peers may have emerged as an issue in the substance abuse literature partially because of evidence regarding homophily (i.e., dyadic concordance in behavior, attitudes, and values) among adolescents and their friends. Substance-abusing youth tend to have close friends who engage in comparable behaviors (Urberg, Değirmencioğlu, & Pilgrim, 1997). There is also homogeneity within cliques or friendship networks with regard to cigarette smoking and drinking (Ennett & Bauman, 1994; Ennett, Bauman, & Koch, 1994). Similarities between adolescents and their friends are sometimes hypothesized to reflect observational learning, with adolescents adopting behaviors that are displayed by peer role models (Schwartz, Gorman, Dodge, et al., 2008).

It should be acknowledged that questions regarding the influence of the peer group have generated controversy in the literature. A number of investigators have made the compelling argument that selection effects can take primacy over socialization in determining the composition of peer groups (Caspi, 1993; Urberg et al., 1997, 2003). Adolescents with antisocial proclivities are likely to seek out peers who share similar behaviors and interests (Bullock, Deater-Deckard, & Leve, 2006). Under these conditions, behavioral similarity within friendship networks might simply reflect the tendency of youth to actively construct their social environments. Selection and socialization could also be mutually influential processes (Berndt & Keefe, 1995).

Contradictory perspectives notwithstanding, our focus on the potential risks associated with popularity might lead us to wonder whether high-status youth are particularly likely to be exposed to peers who might model substance use or provide access to illegal drugs. Does social prestige in the peer group increase the probability of interaction with such peers? Insofar as modeling and other related processes play a role in the etiology of substance use problems, will popular youth be especially vulnerable?

One source for information on the peer influences to which popular youth may be exposed comes from research on crowd affiliations. The term "crowd" is generally used to refer to a group of individuals who share similar social reputations. Examples of crowds include "popular/elites," "toughs/druggies," "brains," and "jocks." Empirically, membership in popular or elite crowds is closely associated with traditional peer nomination assessments of popularity (Gorman, Schwartz, Brown, & Frolich, 2009). Identification with a crowd does not imply affiliations between members because youth with similar reputations do not necessarily interact on a regular basis. Still, crowd membership is a critical issue when investigators are concerned about the influence of peer role models. Adolescents who aspire to popular status will likely attend carefully to the attributes of their peers who are seen as members of the elite crowds. Thus, our contention is that these crowd structures will expose popular students to other high-status peers who serve as substance-abusing role models.

The research on crowds does provide evidence that the exemplars of high status in some peer groups may be characterized by substance abuse. Youth who report membership in popular crowds also acknowledge relatively high rates of substance abuse. This pattern is particularly clear in studies that focus on drinking (La Greca, Prinstein, & Fetter, 2001; Verkooijen et al., 2007) and cigarette smoking (Mosbach & Leventhal, 1988). In some school settings, the students who are most respected and admired by their peers are likely to be those who are involved in substance abuse (Becker & Luthar, 2007).

Some additional information might be gleaned from investigations conducted with network analysis techniques (e.g., Ennett et al., 2006). As noted earlier, adolescents tend to be similar to friends with regard to antisocial behaviors such as underage drinking and smoking (i.e., see Urberg et al., 2003). Network centrality also appears to be another important predictive factor, particularly when substance abuse is the norm within a peer group (Ennett et al., 2006). Network centrality is generally operationalized as prominence within a social system and is often conceptualized as an indicator of popularity (Abel, Plumridge, & Graham, 2002). One implication of these findings is that the most visible members of some adolescent cliques are likely to be individuals who are involved in substance use.

To illustrate the processes we are hypothesizing, consider the fictionalized case of an adolescent girl who we call Tamara. Tamara has always been a popular girl and enjoys the resulting social visibility and prestige. In her high school, several of her socially elite peers have begun to smoke cigarettes. Tamara had never had much of an interest in trying cigarettes herself partially because she does not like the smell of tobacco smoke. On the other hand, she does want to fit in with the other members of the high-status crowd. Tamara is also repeatedly offered cigarettes by friends and has ready opportunities to try smoking. By her final year of high school, Tamara becomes a frequent smoker.

Moving beyond this research on crowd identification and clique membership, there are several existing studies in which investigators have attempted to examine associations between high social standing and substance abuse. Alexander et al. (2001) reported correlations between social status and self-reports of cigarette smoking. Interestingly, the observed links were dependent on the level of cigarette smoking within the school. Rates of tobacco use were particularly likely to be elevated for high-status youth in schools where smoking was common.

At least for purposes of the present chapter, a factor complicating interpretation of Alexander et al.'s findings is that their assessment of social standing was based on peer nominations of friendship or liking by peers rather than assessments of prestige and visibility. Alexander et al. used items that appear to correspond more closely to scales assessing social acceptance than popularity (see Cillessen & Marks, Chapter 2, this volume). This issue is notable given evidence that popularity has a stronger association with antisocial outcomes than acceptance (Mayeux et al., 2003).

Similar measurement issues may also be a factor for an important longitudinal study conducted by Allen et al. (2005). These investigators sought to examine associations between high standing in the peer group and antisocial outcomes during the middle years of adolescence. Accordingly, they asked adolescents and their friends to identify peers who were preferred social partners (i.e., classmates with whom the adolescents would like to spend a Saturday night). The resulting index was predictive of increases in alcohol and substance abuse over 2 years. The effects were strongest for those adolescents who reported that their friends positively evaluate misconduct.

A related body of studies has focused on the development of children who are classified as "controversial" in research conducted with sociometric classification techniques. Sociometric researchers have sometimes included a "controversial" category for children who are simultaneously well liked and highly disliked (Coie et al., 1982). Similar to youth with popular social reputations, these youth tend to be characterized by a mixture of negative and positive behavioral features (Parkhurst & Asher, 1992; Wentzel, 1991). Conceptually, the controversial subgroup might correspond closely to popular youth who use aggressive or aversive means to reach high status (Parkhurst & Hopmeyer, 1998). Interestingly, there is some evidence that controversial youth are particularly likely to be involved in risk-taking behaviors, including cigarette smoking (Miller-Johnson et al., 2003)

Insofar as we are aware, there are only three existing studies in which researchers have directly examined links between popularity (as conceptualized in this volume) and substance abuse outcomes. Mayeux et al. (2008) investigated associations between popularity and social acceptance/rejection (assessed via a peer nomination inventory) and self-reports of alcohol use and cigarette smoking over the final 2 years of high school. Popularity was predictive of increases in alcohol use from 10th to 12th grade. On the other hand, the findings for social acceptance/rejection were nonsignificant.

Mayeux et al.'s (2008) analyses also revealed some evidence for reciprocal relations between popularity and substance abuse. For boys, self-reported smoking predicted small increases in popularity over the 2 years of the study. In some settings, adolescents may engage in antisocial behaviors in an effort to enhance their own position within the peer group social hierarchy.

Killeya-Jones, Nakajima, and Costanzo (2007) reported similar findings in a sample of early adolescents. These researchers used a 1-year short-term longitudinal design, with popularity (via peer nominations) and substance abuse (self-reports of drinking or cigarette smoking) assessed in the fall and spring of the school year. Substance abusers in the fall semester had higher popularity scores than youth who abstained, and they tended to keep their high status over the 1-year period.

Insofar as we are aware, the only existing long-term longitudinal study focusing on popularity and substance abuse outcomes was conducted by Sandstrom and Cillessen (2010). Peer nomination assessments of popularity were obtained for 264 adolescents during their initial years of high school. These youth were then followed for several years as they transitioned to early adulthood. Risk behavior was assessed with a self-report questionnaire that included items that tap use/abuse of tobacco, alcohol, and other substances. Popularity in high school had a modest positive association with risky behavior in early adulthood.

Potential ambiguities notwithstanding, the full pattern of findings from these projects does allow for some tentative conclusions. First, there appears to be preliminary support (albeit largely from studies that target social acceptance rather than popularity) for the hypothesis that high status with peers is likely to be particularly problematic when substance use and abuse is a prominent feature of the peer group ecology. The pattern of results also touches on an issue that we return to at multiple points in this chapter. Popularity may be most closely linked to negative outcomes when the peer group is characterized by antisocial values or behaviors. Under such circumstances, popularity will bring social pressures toward the acquisition of negative behaviors as well as opportunities for access to substances. In addition, research on crowds and cliques suggests that the socially elite members of some school peer groups can serve as powerful role models for substance abuse behaviors.

The initial findings regarding the attributes of the peer group might also lead to additional questions regarding the role of behavioral heterogeneity among popular adolescents. Earlier in this chapter, we noted that researchers have identified subclusters of popular youth with levels of antisocial behavior emerging as a critical distinguishing factor. We predict that popularity will have particularly strong links to substance abuse problems for aggressive adolescents. Our expectation is that these youth will be likely to seek prestige or visibility in peer groups that are characterized by antisocial norms that may include involvement with substances.

Longitudinal data are limited, but there is some tentative support for models that incorporate a focus on reciprocal relations between substance abuse and popularity (Mayeux et al., 2008). To understand the nature of the relation between popularity and substance abuse, we need to consider complex transactional relations. Social experience will modify trajectories toward substance abuse outcomes just as substance abuse has implications for an adolescent's standing with peers.

SEXUAL BEHAVIOR

To some extent, the themes that are present in the literature on the etiology of substance abuse are also evident in the research on problematic sexual behaviors. Investigators who have focused on adolescent sexuality have often emphasized the potential deleterious influences of peer relations (Feldman, Rosenthal, Brown, & Canning 1995; Zimmer-Gembeck, Siebenbruner, & Collins, 2004). The role of popularity, in particular, has been frequently discussed (Bersamin et al., 2006). A number of researchers have hypothesized links between popularity and early sexual experimentation (Newcomer, Udry, & Cameron, 1983; Prinstein et al., 2003). Not surprisingly, this work has focused primarily on the middle to late stages of adolescence.

As we hypothesized earlier, one reason that popular youth could become involved in sexual behavior relatively early in development is because of opportunity. Across development, physical intimacy tends to occur within the context of monogamous relationships (Small & Luster, 1994; Zimmer-Gembeck & Collins, 2008). Reflecting their high social profile in the school peer group, popular students are more likely to have a boyfriend or girlfriend than other students (Carlson & Rose, 2007). Accordingly, in contrast to some of their less visible peers, they may be more apt to find themselves in social situations in which sexual interactions are possible. Insofar as popular adolescents are embedded in peer groups where dating is the norm, they could also establish friendships with classmates who are sexually active. These peers could serve as powerful role models and might provide access to information. Likewise, some popular youth may feel pressured to become involved in such behaviors as a way of achieving status.

Consider the fictionalized case of a popular adolescent who we call Steve. Steve and his friends have been eagerly looking forward to the prom. Steve is planning to take his girlfriend, whom he has been dating for most of his senior year. His girlfriend is an attractive classmate who is also quite popular at their school. Their relationship has grown increasingly close during this period and is now beginning to move in a physical direction. Steve has been encouraged to take the next step by his popular friends, who frequently brag about their own sexual interactions with their girlfriends. In fact, Steve sometimes feels left out because he has not engaged in the same level of activity as the other boys in his clique.

Along with these social mechanisms, popularity could have an impact on adolescent sexual behavior through the mediation of other problematic behaviors. We have previously highlighted potential links between social prestige and substance abuse. The research on risky sexual behavior has often implicated the role of drugs and alcohol. As might be expected, adolescents tend to make bad decisions about sexual behavior when under the influence of substances (Zimmer-Gembeck & Collins, 2008). Substance abuse can also be a manifestation of a larger antisocial lifestyle that incorporates attributes such as impulsiveness or sensation seeking (Mâsse & Tremblay, 1997). Sexual acting out could be one product of such attributes.

We are essentially proposing partially distinct sets of mechanisms that might link popularity to sexual activity. One set of underlying processes is hypothesized to reflect opportunity and social pressures. A second group of factors may be more closely tied to substance abuse or other antisocial proclivities (Capaldi, Crosby, & Stoolmiller, 1996) that will likely characterize a subgroup of popular youth (de Bruyn & Cillessen, 2006; Farmer et al., 2003; Lease et al., 2002; Rodkin et al., 2000). This focus on multiple processes is consistent with recent themes in research on adolescent sexuality that emphasize diversity in the causal pathways (for a review, see Zimmer-Gembeck & Helfand, 2008).

These complexities notwithstanding, there are a number of existing studies that offer insight into the potential role of popularity in adolescent sexual behavior. Because behavioral compatibility with peers is an organizing issue for popular youth, we might start by considering research on links between sexual activity and the composition of adolescents' friendship networks. Researchers have reported consistent evidence that adolescents' attitudes toward sexuality often mirror those of their friends. Adolescents tend to remain abstinent when their friends disapprove of premarital sex (Silver & Bauman, 2006). Conversely, adolescents who affiliate with antisocial peers are relatively likely to engage in early sexual activity (French & Dishion, 2003). We acknowledge ongoing debate regarding selection versus socialization. Nonetheless, these findings might indicate that sexual experimentation is responsive to social influences in the peer group to which popular youth may be especially vulnerable.

Researchers have also attempted to examine direct associations between social status and different aspects of sexual behavior. However, the initial focus in the literature was on social acceptance rather than popularity. For example, Feldman et al. (1995) followed boys for a 4-year period, from 6th through 10th grade. Social acceptance in 6th grade was predictive of total number of sexual partners and dating activity in 10th grade. Path analyses also demonstrated that dating activity mediates associations between acceptance and number of sexual partners. Likewise, Zimmer-Gembeck and colleagues (2004) conducted a longer term study, following 155 participants from middle childhood through early adulthood (age 19). Sixth-grade peer competence was obtained via teacher ratings that included items assessing both acceptance and social influence (i.e., "others respect him/her"). These investigators reported a modest indirect relation, with 6th-grade peer competence predicting alcohol use and total number of sexual partners.

During early adolescence, controversial social status (which we cautiously view as a potential proxy for popularity) may be another correlate of sexual behavior. Miller-Johnson et al. (2003) obtained self-reports of sexual activity for 647 African American adolescents (approximate mean age, 13 years). Sociometric status groups were then determined using scores from a peer nomination inventory. A relatively high percentage (44%) of the controversial adolescents acknowledged that they had engaged in sexual intercourse in the 3-month period before data collection.

Popularity has been examined as a direct predictor or correlate of sexual activity in only a small number of studies. Prinstein et al. (2003) investigated correlates of adolescents' (mean age, 16.3 years) self-reports of oral sex, intercourse, and number of sexual partners. Adolescents who acknowledged experiences with oral sex and intercourse had relatively high popularity scores (via peer nominations). Interestingly, there was also a negative correlation between popularity and total number of partners. Thus, the full pattern of findings seems to suggest that popularity is linked to sexual activity but that this activity tends to occur within a small number of relationships. These results are also consistent with the suggestion that popular adolescents are especially likely to have a serious girlfriend or boyfriend (Carlson & Rose, 2007).

Mayeux et al. (2008) built on findings by Prinstein et al. (2003)

examining associations between peer nomination scores for popularity and self-reported sexual intercourse over the final 2 years of high school. The results of their path analyses indicated that popularity was predictive of increases in sexual activity over this period. On the other hand, these investigators did not find a similar pattern of associations in analyses conducted with social preference as the predictor variable. Mayeux et al.'s findings seem to suggest that popularity is the dimension of social status that is most closely associated with sexual behavior.

The Prinstein et al. (2003) and Mayeux et al. (2008) studies provide evidence of a link between popularity and sexual behavior during the middle years of adolescence. From a risk perspective, however, these links are not necessarily of marked concern because sexuality can be viewed as a central aspect of a normative adjustment. A number of theorists have conceptualized negotiation of intimacy and sexuality as salient developmental tasks of late adolescence and early adulthood (Zimmer-Gembeck & Helfand, 2008). Thus, to identify maladaptive trajectories, our focus should not be on the potential implications of popularity for all sexual behavior. Rather, we must seek to understand problematic behaviors such as sexual experimentation at especially young ages, physical intimacies under potentially risky conditions (i.e., unprotected sex or sex with multiple partners), and teenage pregnancy.

A conceptualization of sexuality as normative might suggest a need to consider critical moderating variables that could determine the potential developmental implications of the relevant behaviors. In particular, the age of onset is likely to be a very important factor in determining the meaning of sexual behavior for development. Youth who become sexually active at early stages of adolescence are especially likely to experience psychosocial maladjustment (Bingham & Crockett, 1996). Their sexual behavior is also likely to be unplanned and may have unsafe features (e.g., lack of contraception, multiple partners; Zimmer-Gembeck & Helfand, 2008).

One problematic outcome of sexual behavior that may be of particular concern is adolescent pregnancy (Coley & Chase-Lansdale, 1998; Miller-Johnson et al., 1999). The preliminary findings offer some evidence that popular adolescents are relatively likely to be involved in physical intimacies. Additionally, some popular youth are characterized by attributes (i.e., impulsiveness) that might exacerbate risk for unplanned pregnancies. For these reasons, it does seem logical to wonder about potential links between popularity and adolescent pregnancy. Unfortunately, such concerns may be well founded. Underwood, Kupersmidt, and Coie (1996) used a longitudinal design to examine predictive associations between sociometric status during middle childhood and childbearing in late adolescence. Although these investigators did not include an assessment of popularity in their data collection, they did identify controversial youth using a peer nomination inventory. Underwood et al. used survival analysis to demonstrate that controversial status during childhood was predictive of childbearing later in development.

Underwood et al.'s (1996) findings are intriguing but have not been replicated in subsequent studies. Most notably, Miller-Johnson et al. (1999) conducted a longitudinal study with a sample drawn from the same community as in Underwood et al. (1996). These investigators did not find any evidence that controversial girls are at high risk for childbearing.

Other research teams have also reported seemingly contradictory findings. Xie, Cairns, and Cairns (2001) followed 475 participants from seventh grade to early adulthood. Youth who were characterized by aggression, low levels of popularity, and poor academic functioning tended to emerge as either teen fathers or teen mothers. Measurement differences across studies may account for some variability in results. The assessment used by Xie et al. included social acceptance items ("has friends") as well as popularity items, and their index was also derived from teacher ratings (vs. peer nomination scores). Nonetheless, Xie et al.'s findings seem to suggest that it is socially marginalized youth rather than high-status youth who are at greatest risk.

A potential interpretation of the full pattern of results across studies might be that there are distinct social pathways to maladaptive outcomes such as adolescent childbearing. For unpopular adolescents, the predictive mechanisms could be related to the stress associated with social ostracism. For more high-status youth, the risk processes that we have discussed throughout this chapter may be more relevant.

As this discussion illustrates, much remains to be learned about the implications of popularity for sexual behavior. At this point, there is preliminary evidence that popular youth are more likely to be involved in sexual experimentation during the middle years of adolescence than their lower status peers. We believe that further research will likely confirm this pattern in a more conclusive manner. Nonetheless, we are not yet in a position to draw any conclusions regarding central issues such as the role that social status might play in determining age of onset for sexual behavior or the relation between popularity and involvement in unsafe sexual practices. It is also too early for us to reach any conclusions regarding specific problematic outcomes such as adolescent childbearing. For now, we urge future popularity researchers to consider normative trajectories in the development of intimacy and sexuality.

ACADEMIC DIFFICULTIES

We move on now to consider potential links between popularity and deficient academic performance. Associations between social standing in the school peer group and academic functioning in the classroom have been the subject of considerable empirical attention (Schwartz, Gorman, Nakamoto, & Toblin, 2005; Wentzel, 1991). This emphasis seems warranted given that the school environment is a critical context for peer relationships. During childhood and adolescence, a large percentage of a young person's interactions with peers occurs within school walls.

Spurred by research conducted with acceptance as the primary predictor construct, investigators initially described links between high social status and achievement during the elementary school years (Wentzel & Caldwell, 1997). The effect sizes in the relevant studies are typically small to medium in magnitude but are notably large in some cultural contexts (Chen, Rubin, & Li, 1997). It is not yet clear whether these associations persist through the later stages of adolescence, although there is some evidence for positive relations between social acceptance and achievement during the middle school years (Wentzel, 1991). Other dimensions of adjustment with peers, such as friendship, also seem to be predictive of academic competence in the classroom (Wentzel & Caldwell, 1997).

The implications of popularity for academic functioning may be less positive, at least for a subgroup of students. Studies conducted with cluster analysis techniques have consistently identified popular youth who are characterized by negative attitudes toward school and/or poor achievement (Farmer et al., 2003; Rodkin et al., 2000). These youth tend to be high in aggression and other antisocial attributes. Conversely, popular youth with more prosocial dispositions are less likely to exhibit problematic academic adjustment (de Bruyn & Cillessen, 2006). Taken together, these findings seem to suggest that popularity is linked to academic difficulties, but the associations hold only for students who are also concurrently aggressive.

Longitudinal research has also provided evidence that aggression and popularity are a problematic combination. Schwartz, Gorman, Nakamoto, and McKay (2006) followed high school students for four consecutive semesters, and assessed popularity via peer ratings. Increases in popularity were associated with both decreased grade point averages (GPAs) and increased unexplained absences from school. Consistent with the earlier cluster analysis studies (Lease et al., 2002; Rodkin et al., 2000), these effects held only for adolescents who were also experiencing increases in aggression. At lower levels of aggression, popularity was not linked to academic difficulties.

Another relevant line of evidence comes from research on sociometrically controversial children. Recall that these children are simultaneously well liked and highly disliked and also tend to be characterized by a mixture of positive and negative behavioral features. In other words, controversial children seem to have social profiles that are consistent with those of youth who are aggressive and popular. The findings with regard to this interesting subgroup are somewhat limited, but Wentzel (2003) found that controversial status in sixth grade was negatively correlated with GPA in eighth grade.

The mechanisms underlying the academic difficulties experienced by youth who are concurrently aggressive and popular are not yet fully clear. We suspect that one critical factor is conformity. Earlier in this chapter, we suggested that popularity would require compatibility with the dominant norms of the peer group. Because aggressive youth often do not have very positive attitudes toward school (Vitaro et al., 2005), status in aggressive cliques or crowds could incorporate social pressures toward academic disengagement. For these reasons, a student who is focused on achieving popularity with aggressive classmates may experience subsequent declines in academic engagement.

Ethnographic perspectives have offered some support for our focus on conformity as a potential etiological mechanism. Adler and Adler (1998) discussed the implications of high achievement for preadolescents. These researchers described a "machismo culture" among boys attending an elementary school. Doing poorly in school was seen as a manifestation of being tough or cool and was a necessary component of popularity.

The hypothesis that the social pressures accompanying popularity could exert a pernicious influence on classroom performance has also been prominent in theoretical perspectives on the academic difficulties experienced by vulnerable adolescents. In their influential review, Steinberg, Dorbusch, and Brown (1992) discussed academic difficulties experienced by minority adolescents attending urban schools. These researchers suggested that popularity and achievement were essentially incompatible for inner-city youth because of negative peer group attitudes toward school. Their central premise was that engagement in school would bring social sanctions from elite peers.

Steinberg et al. were concerned primarily with the determinants of academic functioning for vulnerable adolescents attending school in economically distressed neighborhoods. We contend that this perspective has wider implications. Peer values toward achievement can have a significant impact on students' academic engagement in a wide variety of school settings (Becker & Luthar, 2002; Juvonen, 1996; Juvonen & Murdock, 1995). We expect popularity to pose a significant threat to classroom performance in any social context where the norms of the elite peers do not support an academic orientation.

To demonstrate how the social context might emerge as a pivotal factor, consider the academic adjustment of popular youth in two different high school environments. The first school has received some attention from state authorities because of disappointing achievement test scores and rising dropout rates. The students at this school are often characterized by dismissive attitudes regarding the role of education in their lives. Not surprisingly, the most popular students tend to view studying and schoolwork as "nerdy" pursuits that might warrant social ostracism. In contrast, the second school is widely regarded as one of the best in the region, with nearly all of the attending students going on to pursue college educations. The student body at this school is highly engaged in learning, and the peer group ethos is one that promotes positive attitudes toward teachers and staff. Indeed, many of the highest achieving youth at this school are also among the most popular. In the first of the two schools described, popularity and achievement will likely be quite incompatible. For these students, an emphasis on academics would run counter to the dominant norms of the peer group. On the other hand, students attending the second school could focus on classroom performance while retaining a behavioral orientation that is compatible with their peers.

Regardless of the nature of the context, we would not expect the implications of popularity for academic adjustment to be constant across development. Our assumption is that peer group influences on academic functioning will become more pronounced as the socializing influence of peers begins to approach that of parents (Berndt, 1979). The reorganization in school structure that occurs with the transition to secondary school could also be a determining factor. Stratification by achievement levels may be more readily apparent as students select different tracks (i.e., college preparation vs. vocational training). Adler and Adler (1998) offered similar hypotheses, suggesting that popular youth might encounter progressively stronger social pressures against academic engagement as they transition to adolescence.

Before we conclude this section of our chapter, we once again caution against making strong assumptions regarding causality. There is preliminary evidence that popular–aggressive youth tend to be characterized by poor achievement, but the underlying processes have yet to be examined. We have suggested that the social pressures faced by popular students (particularly those who seek status with aggressive or antisocial peers) may lead to disengagement from school. A more parsimonious hypothesis might be that popularity and aggression are markers of child attributes that interfere with adjustment at school (e.g., disengagement from adult caregivers and an orientation toward peers; see Fuligni, Eccles, Barber, & Clements, 2001). Clearly, further research will be needed before the underlying processes are fully understood.

CONCLUDING REMARKS AND FUTURE DIRECTIONS

Reflecting the current state of the literature, we focused our review on popularity as a predictor of substance abuse, sexual experimentation, and academic difficulties. This directed strategy should not be taken to suggest that popularity does not have a role in other forms of maladjustment. For example, perspectives on the development of a variety of nonaggressive antisocial behaviors (e.g., status offense, shoplifting, lying, manipulation) have often highlighted the potential deleterious effects of peer influences (Moffitt, 1993). As the research on popularity continues to evolve, new evidence may emerge regarding a wider set of outcomes.

In a related vein, our attempts to identify potential mechanisms of risks have emphasized compatibility with peer group norms. We hypothesized that popular youth will be particularly likely to experience pressures to conform and that they may engage in maladaptive behaviors as a result. We also described other related difficulties, such as exposure to maladaptive role models and increased opportunity for involvement in problematic behaviors. Although we view these factors as having a critical role in trajectories toward negative outcomes, there are other potentially problematic aspects of the social lives of popular youth that should also be considered. In our view, processes that are likely to be more closely linked to internalized distress have been underinvestigated. For some popular youth, pressures to be attractive, visible, and cool could exert a toxic influence on a developing self-image (de Bruyn & van den Boom, 2005; Wang, Houshyar, & Prinstein, 2006).

Regardless of the specific mechanisms, the pathways linking popularity to negative outcomes will be moderated by youths' own behavioral orientation. Much remains to be learned, but the preliminary findings provide convincing evidence that popularity poses a special risk for those youth who are also highly aggressive or characterized by antisocial attributes. For these young people, substance abuse, sexual experimentation, and other potentially hazardous behaviors may be manifestations of the dynamics of high status.

Paradoxically, aggression and popularity could also combine to predict psychological resources (e.g., self-confidence) that serve a protective effect against some classes of problems. Consistent with this suggestion, Sandstrom and Cillessen (2010) found low levels of depression among boys who are both highly popular and relationally aggressive. There appear to be multiple processes at work, and the final picture will need to move well beyond simple main effect models.

We also contend that the implications of popularity cannot be fully understood without careful consideration for the nature of the social context. By social context, we refer to both molecular aspects of the proximal social systems (i.e., peer group attitudes toward achievement) and the wider sociocultural environment (Schwartz et al., 2010). The most efficient explanatory models will need to take into account a number of features related to the larger social setting.

To summarize, popularity appears to be a double-edged sword during childhood and adolescence. Understandably, young people are often motivated to seek high status with their peers. The resulting social prestige and visibility will bring opportunities for friendship and dating as well as potential enhancement to self-esteem. The cost of popularity, however, may be increased exposure to problematic social pressures and influences. A balanced perspective on popularity will need to incorporate an awareness of both the risks and benefits.

REFERENCES

Abel, G., Plumridge, L., & Graham, P. (2002). Peers, networks or relationships: Strategies for understanding social dynamics as determinants of smoking behaviour. *Drugs: Education, Prevention and Policy, 9,* 325–338.

Adler, P. A., & Adler, P. (1998). *Peer power: Preadolescent culture and identity.* New Brunswick, NJ: Rutgers University Press.

Alexander, C., Piazza, M., Mekos, D., & Valente, T. (2001). Peers, schools, and adolescent cigarette smoking. *Journal of Adolescent Health, 29,* 22–30.

Allen, J. P., Porter, M. R., & McFarland, F. C. (2006). Leaders and followers in adolescent close friendships: Susceptibility to peer influence as a predictor of risky behavior, friendship instability, and depression. *Development and Psychopathology, 18,* 155–172.

Allen, J. P., Porter, M. R., McFarland, F. C., Marsh, P., & McElhaney, K. B. (2005). The two faces of adolescents' success with peers: Adolescent popularity, social adaptation, and deviant behavior. *Child Development,76*(3), 747–760.

Becker, B. E., & Luthar, S. S. (2002). Social-emotional factors affecting achievement outcomes among disadvantaged students: Closing the achievement gap. *Educational Psychologist, 37,* 197–214.

Becker, B. E., & Luthar, S. S. (2007). Peer-perceived admiration and social preference: Contextual correlates of positive peer regard among suburban and urban adolescents. *Journal of Research on Adolescence, 17,* 117–144.

Berndt, T. J. (1979). Developmental changes in conformity to peers and parents. *Developmental Psychology, 15,* 608–616.

Berndt, T. J., & Keefe, K. (1995). Friends' influence on adolescents' adjustment to school. *Child Development, 66,* 1312–1329.

Bersamin, M. M., Walker, S., Fisher, D. A., & Grube, J. W. (2006). Correlates of oral sex and vaginal intercourse in early and middle adolescence. *Journal of Research on Adolescence, 16,* 59–68.

Bingham, C. R., & Crockett, L. J. (1996). Longitudinal adjustment patterns of boys and girls experiencing early, middle, and late sexual intercourse. *Developmental Psychology, 32,* 647–658.

Brown, B. B. (1990). Peer groups and peer cultures. In S. S. Feldman & G. R. Elliot (Eds.), *At the threshold: The developing adolescent* (pp. 171–196). Cambridge, MA: Harvard University Press.

Brown, B. B., Clasen, D. R., & Eicher, S. A. (1986). Perceptions of peer pressure, peer conformity dispositions, and self-reported behavior among adolescents. *Developmental Psychology, 22,* 521–530.

Brown, B. B., Mory, M. S., & Kinney, D. (1994). Casting adolescent crowds in a relational perspective: Caricature, channel, and context. In R. Montemayor, G. R. Adams, & T. P. Gullotta (Eds.), *Personal relationships during adolescence* (pp. 123–167). Thousand Oaks, CA: Sage.

Bukowski, W. M., Pizzamiglio, M. T., Newcomb, A. F., & Hoza, B. (1996). Popularity as an affordance for friendship: The link between group and dyadic experience. *Social Development, 5,* 189–202.

Bullock, B. M., Deater-Deckard, K., & Leve, L. D. (2006). Deviant peer affiliation and problem behavior: A test of genetic and environmental influences. *Journal of Abnormal Child Psychology, 34,* 29–41.

Capaldi, D. M., Crosby, L., & Stoolmiller, M. (1996). Predicting the timing of first sexual intercourse for at-risk adolescent males. *Child Development, 67,* 344–359.

Carlson, W., & Rose, A. J. (2007). The role of reciprocity in romantic relationships in middle childhood and early adolescence. *Merrill-Palmer Quarterly, 53,* 262–290.

Caspi, A. (1993). Why maladaptive behaviors persist: Sources of continuity and change across the life course. In D. C. Funder, R. D. Parke, C. Tomlinson-Keasey, & K. Widaman (Eds.), *Studying lives through time: Personality and development* (pp. 343–376). Washington, DC: American Psychological Association.

Chen, X., Rubin, K. H., & Li, D. (1997). Relation between academic achievement and social adjustment: Evidence from Chinese children. *Developmental Psychology, 33,* 518–525.

Cillessen, A. H. N., & Mayeux, L. (2004). From censure to reinforcement: Developmental changes in the association between aggression and social status. *Child Development, 75,* 147–163.

Coie, J. D., & Dodge, K. A. (1983). Continuities and changes in children's social status: A five-year longitudinal study. *Merrill-Palmer Quarterly, 29,* 261–282.

Coie, J. D., Dodge, K. A., & Coppotelli, H. (1982). Dimensions and types of social status: A cross-age perspective. *Developmental Psychology, 18,* 557–570.

Coie, J. D., Dodge, K. A., & Kupersmidt, J. B. (1990). Peer group behavior and social status. In S. R. Asher & J. D. Coie (Eds.), *Peer rejection in childhood* (pp. 17–59). New York: Cambridge University Press.

Coley, R. L., & Chase-Lansdale, P. L. (1998). Adolescent pregnancy and parenthood: Recent evidence and future directions. *American Psychologist, 53,* 152–166.

de Bruyn, E. H., & Cillessen, A. H. N. (2006). Heterogeneity of girls' consensual popularity: Academic and interpersonal behavioral profiles. *Journal of Youth and Adolescence, 35,* 435–445.

de Bruyn, E. H., & van den Boom, D. C. (2005). Interpersonal behavior, peer popularity, and self-esteem in early adolescence. *Social Development, 14,* 555–573.

Dodge, K. A., Pettit, G. S., McClaskey, C. L., & Brown, M. M. (1986). Social competence in children. *Monographs of the Society for Research in Child Development, 51,* 1–85.

Eder, D. (1985). The cycle of popularity: Interpersonal relations among female adolescents. *Sociology of Education, 58,* 154–165.

Eisenberg, N., & Fabes, R. A. (1992). Emotion, regulation, and the development of social competence. In M. S. Clark (Ed.), *Emotion and social behavior* (pp. 119–150). Thousand Oaks, CA: Sage.

Ennett, S. T., & Bauman, K. E. (1994). The contribution of influence and selection to adolescent peer group homogeneity: The case of adolescent cigarette smoking. *Journal of Personality and Social Psychology, 67,* 653–663.

Ennett, S. T., Bauman, K. E., & Koch, G. G. (1994). Variability in cigarette smoking within and between adolescent friendship cliques. *Addictive Behaviors, 19,* 295–305.

Ennett, S. T., Bauman, K. E., Hussong, A., Faris, R., Foshee, V. A., Cai, L., & DuRant, R. H. (2006). The peer context of adolescent substance use: Findings from social network analysis. *Journal of Research on Adolescence, 16,* 159–186.

Farmer, T. W., Estell, D. B., Bishop, J. L., O'Neal, K. K., & Cairns, B. D. (2003). Rejected bullies or popular leaders? The social relations of aggressive subtypes of rural African American early adolescents. *Developmental Psychology, 39,* 992–1004.

Feldman, S. S., Rosenthal, D. R., Brown, N. L., & Canning, R. D. (1995). Predicting sexual experience in adolescent boys from peer rejection and acceptance during childhood. *Journal of Research on Adolescence, 5,* 387–411.

French, D. C., & Dishion, T. (2003). Predictors of early initiation of sexual intercourse among high-risk adolescents. *Journal of Early Adolescence, 23,* 295–315.

Fuligni, A. J., Eccles, J. S., Barber, B. L., & Clements, P. (2001). Early adolescent peer orientation and adjustment during high school. *Developmental Psychology, 37,* 28–36.

Gorman, A. H., Schwartz, D., Brown, B. B., & Frolich, M. (2009, March). *Are you a girly-girl or a schoolgirl?: Crowd affiliation, status and academic adjustment in early adolescence.* Paper presented at the biennial meeting of the Society for Research in Child Development, Denver, CO.

Juvonen, J. (1996). Self-presentation tactics promoting teacher and peer approval: The function of excuses and other clever explanations. In J. Juvonen & K. R. Wentzel (Eds.), *Social motivation: Understanding children's school adjustment* (pp. 43–65). New York: Cambridge University Press.

Juvonen, J., & Murdock, T. B. (1995). Grade-level differences in the social value of effort: Implications for self-presentation tactics of early adolescents. *Child Development, 66,* 1694–1705.

Killeya-Jones, L. A., Nakajima, R., & Costanzo, P. R. (2007). Peer standing and substance use in early-adolescent grade-level networks: A short-term longitudinal study. *Prevention Science, 8,* 11–23.

La Greca, A. M., Prinstein, M. J., & Fetter, M. D. (2001). Adolescent peer crowd affiliation: Linkages with health-risk behaviors and close friendships. *Journal of Pediatric Psychology, 26,* 131–143.

Laird, R. D., Pettit, G. S., Dodge, K. A., & Bates, J. E. (1999). Best friendships, group relationships, and antisocial behavior in early adolescence. *Journal of Early Adolescence, 19,* 413–437.

Lease, A. M., Musgrove, K. T., & Axelrod, J. L. (2002). Dimensions of social status in preadolescent peer groups: Likability, perceived popularity, and social dominance. *Social Development, 11,* 508–533.

Luster, T., & Small, S. A. (1994). Factors associated with sexual risk-taking behaviors among adolescents. *Journal of Marriage and the Family, 56,* 622–632.

Mâsse, L. C., & Tremblay, R. E. (1997). Behavior of boys in kindergarten and the onset of substance use during adolescence. *Archives of General Psychiatry, 54,* 52–68.

Mayeux, L., Sandstrom, M. J., & Cillessen, A. H. N. (2008). Is being popular a risky proposition? *Journal of Research on Adolescence, 18,* 49–74.

Miller-Johnson, S., Costanzo, P. R., Coie, J. D., Rose, M. R., Browne, D. C., & Johnson, C. (2003). Peer social structure and risk-taking behaviors among African American early adolescents. *Journal of Youth and Adolescence, 32,* 375–384.

Miller-Johnson, S., Winn, D., Coie, J., Maumary-Gremaud, A., Hyman, C., Terry, R., et al. (1999). Motherhood during the teen years: A developmental perspective on risk factors for childbearing. *Development and Psychopathology, 11,* 85–100.

Moffitt, T.E. (1993). Adolescence-limited and life-course-persistent antisocial behavior: A developmental taxonomy. *Psychological Review, 100,* 674–701.

Mosbach, P., & Leventhal, H. (1988). Peer group identification and smoking: Implications for intervention. *Journal of Abnormal Psychology, 97*, 238–245.

Newcomer, S. F., Udry, J. R., & Cameron, F. (1983). Adolescent sexual behavior and popularity. *Adolescence, 18*, 515–522.

Parker, J. G., & Asher, S. R. (1993). Friendship and friendship quality in middle childhood: Links with peer group acceptance and feelings of loneliness and social dissatisfaction. *Developmental Psychology, 29*, 611–621.

Parkhurst, J. T., & Asher, S. R. (1992). Peer rejection in middle school: Subgroup differences in behavior, loneliness, and interpersonal concerns. *Developmental Psychology, 28*, 231–241.

Parkhurst, J. T., & Hopmeyer, A. (1998). Sociometric popularity and peer-perceived popularity: Two distinct dimensions of peer status. *Journal of Early Adolescence, 18*, 125–144.

Prinstein, M. J., Meade, C. S., & Cohen, G. L. (2003). Adolescent oral sex, peer popularity, and perceptions of best friends' sexual behavior. *Journal of Pediatric Psychology, 28*, 243–249.

Rodkin, P. C., Farmer, T. W., Pearl, R., & Van Acker, R. (2000). Heterogeneity of popular boys: Antisocial and prosocial configurations. *Developmental Psychology, 36*, 14–24.

Rodkin, P. C., & Roisman, G. I. (2010). Antecedents and correlates of the popular-aggressive phenomenon in elementary school. *Child Development, 81*, 837–850.

Rose, A. J., Swenson, L. P., & Waller, E. M. (2004). Overt and relational aggression and perceived popularity: Developmental differences in concurrent and prospective relations. *Developmental Psychology, 40*, 378–387.

Sandstrom, M. J., & Cillessen, A. H. N. (2006). Likeable vs. popular: Distinct implications for adolescent adjustment. *International Journal of Behavioral Development, 30*, 305–314.

Sandstrom, M. J., & Cillessen, A. H. N. (2010). Life after high school: Adjustment of popular teens in emerging adulthood. *Merrill-Palmer Quarterly, 56*, 474–499.

Sandstom, M., & Herlan, R. (2007). Threatened egotism or confirmed inadequacy? How children's perceptions of social status influence aggressive behavior toward peers. *Journal of Social and Clinical Psychology, 26*, 272–299.

Santor, D. A., Messervey, D., & Kusumakar, V. (2000). Measuring peer pressure, popularity, and conformity in adolescent boys and girls: Predicting school performance, sexual attitudes, and substance abuse. *Journal of Youth and Adolescence, 29*, 163–182.

Schwartz, D., Gorman, A. H., Dodge, K. A., Pettit, G. S., & Bates, J. E. (2008). Friendships with peers who are low or high in aggression as moderators of the link between peer victimization and declines in academic functioning. *Journal of Abnormal Child Psychology, 36*, 719–730.

Schwartz, D., Gorman, A. H., Duong, M. T., & Nakamoto, J. (2008). Peer relationships and academic achievement as interacting predictors of depressive symptoms during middle childhood. *Journal of Abnormal Psychology, 117,* 289–299.

Schwartz, D., Gorman, A. H., Nakamoto, J., & McKay, T. (2006). Popularity, social acceptance, and aggression in adolescent peer groups: Links with academic performance and school attendance. *Developmental Psychology, 42,* 1116–1127.

Schwartz, D., Gorman, A. H., Nakamoto, J., & Toblin, R. L. (2005). Victimization in the peer group and children's academic functioning. *Journal of Educational Psychology, 97,* 425–435.

Schwartz, D , Tom, S., Chang, L. Xu, Y., Duong, M. T., & Kelly, B. M. (2010). Popularity and acceptance as distinct dimensions of social standing for Chinese children in Hong Kong. *Social Development, 19,* 681–697.

Silver, E. J., & Bauman, L. J. (2006). The association of sexual experience with attitudes, beliefs, and risk behaviors of inner-city adolescents. *Journal of Research on Adolescence, 16,* 29–45.

Small, S. A., & Luster, T. (1994). Adolescent sexual activity: An ecological, risk-factor approach. *Journal of Marriage and the Family, 56,* 181–192.

Steinberg, L., Dornbusch, S. M., & Brown, B. B. (1992). Ethnic differences in adolescent achievement: An ecological perspective. *American Psychologist, 47,* 723–729.

Underwood, M. K., Kupersmidt, J. B., & Coie, J. D. (1996). Childhood peer sociometric status and aggression as predictors of adolescent childbearing. *Journal of Research on Adolescence, 6,* 201–223.

Urberg, K. A., Değirmencioğlu, S. M., & Pilgrim, C. (1997). Close friend and group influence on adolescent cigarette smoking and alcohol use. *Developmental Psychology, 33,* 834–844.

Urberg, K. A., Luo, Q., Pilgrim, C., & Değirmencioğlu, S. M. (2003). A two-stage model of peer influence in adolescent substance use: Individual and relationship-specific differences in susceptibility to influence. *Addictive Behaviors, 28,* 1243–1256.

Verkooijen, K. T., de Vries, N. K., & Nielsen, G. A. (2007). Youth crowds and substance use: The impact of perceived group norm and multiple group identification. *Psychology of Addictive Behaviors, 21,* 55–61.

Vitaro, F., Brendgen, M., & Wanner, B. (2005). Patterns of affiliation with delinquent friends during late childhood and early adolescence: Correlates and consequences. *Social Development, 14,* 82–108.

Wang, S. S., Houshyar, S., & Prinstein, M. J. (2006). Adolescent girls' and boys' weight-related health behaviors and cognitions: Associations with reputation- and preference-based peer status. *Health Psychology, 25,* 658–663.

Wentzel, K. R. (1991). Relations between social competence and academic achievement in early adolescence. *Child Development, 62,* 1066–1078.

Wentzel, K. R. (2003). Sociometric status and adjustment in middle school: A longitudinal study. *Journal of Early Adolescence, 23,* 5–28.

Wentzel, K. R., & Caldwell, K. (1997). Friendships, peer acceptance, and group membership: Relations to academic achievement in middle school. *Child Development, 68,* 1198–1209.

Wills, T. A., & Cleary, S. D. (1999). Peer and adolescent substance use among 6th-9th graders: Latent growth analyses of influence versus selection mechanisms. *Health Psychology, 18,* 453–463.

Xie, H., Cairns, B. D., & Cairns, R. B. (2001). Predicting teen motherhood and teen fatherhood: Individual characteristics and peer affiliations. *Social Development, 10,* 488–511.

Zimmer-Gembeck, M. J., & Collins, W. A. (2008). Gender, mature appearance, alcohol use, and dating as correlates of sexual partner accumulation from ages 16–26 years. *Journal of Adolescent Health, 42,* 564–572.

Zimmer-Gembeck, M. J., & Helfand, M. (2008). Ten years of longitudinal research on U.S. adolescent sexual behavior: Developmental correlates of sexual intercourse, and the importance of age, gender and ethnic background. *Developmental Review, 28,* 153–224.

Zimmer-Gembeck, M. J., Siebenbruner, J., & Collins, W. A. (2004). A prospective study of intraindividual and peer influences on adolescents' heterosexual romantic and sexual behavior. *Archives of Sexual Behavior, 33,* 381–394.

Part V
INTEGRATION

Chapter 12

Toward a Theory of Popularity

Antonius H. N. Cillessen

Over 20 years ago, Coie (1990) published this influential work, "Toward a Theory of Peer Rejection," which was the concluding chapter of a book devoted entirely to peer rejection (Asher & Coie, 1990). In this chapter, Coie presented a four-stage model of the factors that precede, cause, and maintain rejection and the consequences associated with it.

The current chapter carries a similar title and concludes a book on popularity. However, the contributions of this chapter may be more modest than those of Coie's (1990). First, why would one study children or adolescents who are already successful in the peer group? Do rejected or ostracized youth not have a higher priority? Second, the ideas about popularity in this chapter may not flourish over the next 20 years as the ideas about peer rejection have. The current chapter is an attempt toward a model of popularity, but it is not the final model. Third, the current chapter is less original, because it was clearly inspired by Coie's.

So what is the value of the study of popularity for the field of peer relationships or developmental psychology more generally? Why not stick with the study of peer group difficulties, maladjustment, and psychopathology? The answers to these questions come from peer relationships researchers themselves who, while continuing to focus on rejection, have also increasingly studied popularity over the past 10 years.

Four reasons can be identified for the extension of research from rejection to popularity. First, popular youth can be seen as models of adequate social functioning and social skills from whom much can be learned about the nature of social competence. Second, popular students in schools are sometimes the instigators or maintainers of peer rejection, as shown by research on popular bullies and the association between popularity and aggression. Third, popular children, and particularly adolescents, are subject to risks of their own, including deviancy and health risk behaviors. Fourth, the risks associated with adolescent popularity may spread in the peer group to others who are susceptible to their influence. For each of these reasons, the study of child and adolescent popularity is a valuable addition to the study of peer relationships. The chapters in this volume attest to this in multiple ways.

This chapter has four sections. The first reviews main points about the nature of popularity from the previous chapters. This sets the stage for the next two sections, which present a model for the development of popularity. The second section focuses on the emergence and maintenance of popularity in peer groups such as classrooms or grades over relatively short periods of time. The third section places popularity in a broader developmental time frame from early childhood to emerging adulthood. Among other things, this section addresses developmental precursors of the ability to become popular and long-term outcomes of popularity once it has been achieved. The fourth, and final, section is a conclusion.

The model of the development of popularity presented in this chapter differs in one way from Coie's (1990) model of the development of rejection. In Coie's model, the developmental precursors of rejection and its emergence, maintenance, and consequences were placed on one progressing time line. This approach was justified because the literature had clearly shown that peer rejection is connected to maladjustment across the broader developmental time frame, as indicated by negative developmental antecedents and negative later consequences.

The model of popularity presented in this chapter includes a sharper distinction between the "local" and relatively short-term emergence and maintenance of popularity at the specific level of groups and the broader and longer term developmental trajectory of popularity. The rationale for this sharper distinction is that popularity at the local level (e.g., the high school peer group) is not always translated into social success in a broader developmental perspective. Conversely, a lack of popularity during a part of adolescence is not always accompanied by a lack of adjustment either earlier or later in development. In this conceptualization, it is, of course, essential to consider how the two trajectories, short term and long term, are connected.

THE NATURE OF POPULARITY

This section reviews the nature of popularity as described in the previous chapters. One challenge for defining a model of popularity is that being likeable and being seen as popular are not one and the same. In the Coie (1990) chapter and in much of the Asher and Coie (1990) book, popularity was identified with being well liked and prosocial in the peer group, associated with positive outcomes and social success. The terms *accepted* and *popular* were used interchangeably as the opposites of rejection, which was equated with unpopularity.

This approach to popularity was also present in our own initial research. For example, Cillessen (1991) conducted a quasi-experimental study with boys in small groups. In individual interviews before and after they played together, the boys made primarily positive attributions about their popular peers, almost irrespective of how they actually behaved. To replicate such positive stereotypes of popularity experimentally, LaFontana and Cillessen (1998) conducted similar interviews with early adolescents. Somewhat surprisingly, the results were quite different. Early adolescents made more negative attributions about peers who had been described to them as "popular" than about neutral peers and their attributions about popular peers were a mixture of positive and negative evaluations.

Two facts explain this contrast. First, Cillessen (1991) defined popularity as being well liked in the peer group (liked by many, disliked by few), whereas LaFontana and Cillessen (1998) primed early adolescents with the label "popular" to describe a hypothetical popular peer, without providing information about likeability. Second, Cillessen (1991) studied elementary school children, whereas LaFontana and Cillessen (1998) studied early adolescents.

LaFontana and Cillessen's (1998) study coincided with one by Parkhurst and Hopmeyer (1998), in which the authors defined *sociometric popularity* as being liked in the peer group and *perceived popularity* as being seen as popular. By juxtaposing these two meanings of popularity, Parkhurst and Hopmeyer (1998) brought together the developmental psychology and sociology of education literatures, in which the two meanings had been considered separately.

The research that followed has led to a consensus that likeability and popularity are separate dimensions of the peer group. This means that the term *popularity* is used in a narrow sense, separate from likeability, and not broadly to refer to both. This book advocates this narrow use of terminology in which "likeability" replaces *sociometric popularity* and "popularity" replaces *perceived popularity*. One advantage of this system is an obvious close match between terminology and measurement. It is only logical to use *likeability* for scores derived from liking nominations or ratings (such as acceptance and preference scores) and *popularity* for scores derived from assessments of popularity by peers.

The previous chapters described five sources of evidence for the distinction between popularity and likeability. First, popularity and likeability are moderately correlated. Although the correlations vary across studies and age groups, they indicate discriminant validity. Second, popularity and likeability differ in stability. Popularity is more stable than likeability, even across school transitions when peer groups change. Children and adolescents vary in who they like over the course of a school year and from year to year. They vary less in who they see as popular in their peer groups. Third, likeability and popularity have different profiles of social behavior. The profile of likeability is primarily prosocial; the profile of popularity is a mixture of prosocial and aggressive behaviors. Fourth, popularity and likeability play different roles in processes of peer influence. The locus of peer influence resides more with popular peers than with likeable peers. Fifth, popularity and likeability have different associations with adjustment outcomes. Likeability is associated with prosocial outcomes such as academic achievement; popularity is also associated with antisocial outcomes such as health risk behaviors.

If popularity is not likeability, then what is it? As described consistently in this volume, popularity in the child and adolescent peer group is a dimension of prestige and visibility. When children or adolescents nominate the most popular peers in their classroom or grade, they name who is highly visible and who they see as prestigious. Although visibility can be determined relatively objectively, prestige is more subjective. With prestige and visibility come dominant behaviors, either as a cause or as a consequence (Pellegrini, Roseth, Van Ryzin, & Solberg, Chapter 6, this volume). With prestige, visibility, and dominance come power and influence (Sandstrom, Chapter 10, this volume). By describing popularity as visibility, it bears resemblance to the social impact dimension of the traditional sociometric system (Clifford, 1963), although it is not identical, because impact does not have the evaluative component of prestige that popularity has. Popularity implies impact, but impact does not imply popularity. The difference is also seen empirically. Impact has very poor stability in longitudinal studies, whereas the stability of popularity is high.

The mixed behavioral profile of popularity emphasizes that it should be seen as an interaction between opposites. Study after study shows popularity as a mixture of prosocial and antisocial traits and behaviors. This is also seen in the combination of peer-valued characteristics and aggressive and manipulative behaviors that characterize popularity (Vaillancourt & Hymel, 2006). Being dominant, which may include using overt or relation aggression, in the context of compensatory prosocial behaviors or valuable traits, is an essential defining part of the nature of popularity in the child and adolescent peer group.

Given the analogy to social impact, it is not surprising that there is a connection between popularity and controversial status in the traditional sociometric system. After all, controversial status is defined by a high impact score. The meta-analysis by Newcomb, Bukowski, and Pattee (1993) showed that controversial students score high on broadband categories of both aggression *and* peer sociability. It also showed that the effect size of aggression for controversial status was even higher than for rejected status. Of course, the broadband category of aggression did not indicate the type of aggression involved. One hypothesis in this regard is that the aggression displayed by controversial youth is predominantly proactive and relational in nature, whereas the aggression displayed by rejected youth is primarily reactive and overt. This would make controversial students look like popular students behaviorally, a similarity that fits perfectly with the fact that popular students are liked by some but disliked by others. Parkhurst and Hopmeyer (1998) already found evidence for the connection between popularity and controversial status.

Popularity has a complex connection to peer influence. Given the key elements of popularity as impact and an interaction between dominant behaviors and desirable characteristics, it is not surprising that popular peers have influence. The *popularity effect* is the influence that popular peers have over others. Sandstrom (Chapter 10, this volume) described what is known about this effect. The popularity effect leads to the *popularity risk hypothesis,* or the idea that certain risks are associated with being popular. Schwartz and Gorman (Chapter 11, this volume) described what is known about the concurrent and later risks of popularity.

The popularity effect and the popularity risk hypothesis are two sides of the same coin. Popular peers can influence others because of their position of high status and their skills (Sandstrom, Chapter 10, this volume). However, being in a position of high status often comes with the desire to maintain it (e.g., Eder, 1985; Merten, 1997). As a result, popular peers not only influence others but are also susceptible to influence from others (Lansu, Cillessen, & Karremans, 2010). To maintain their position of prominence, they adopt behaviors that carry high status in the peer group; some of these behaviors are deviant from the mainstream but highly status enhancing, such as alcohol or drug use (Mayeux, Sandstrom, & Cillessen, 2008; Miller-Johnson et al., 2003).

Further, maintaining a position of prominence and influence is hard work and may fail. That may be why stress and depression are also among the risks of popularity (Sandstrom & Cillessen, 2010). Finally, those who engage in status-maintaining aggression and manipulation are at risk of reciprocation, because aggression is a highly reciprocal behavior. This places popular students at risk for victimization, especially when the power balance in the peer group tips into a direction that is unfavorable for them (see Eder, 1985; Merten, 1997). In summary, although popularity means impact and influence, the nature of popularity also implies various risks.

In addition to separating likeability and popularity as continuous dimensions, the heterogeneity of high status has also been shown categorically. In an analogy to earlier research on subtypes of rejection (see, e.g., Bierman & Wargo, 1995; Cillessen, van IJzendoorn, van Lieshout, & Hartup, 1992), researchers have identified subtypes of popular children. Rodkin, Farmer, Pearl, and Van Acker (2000) identified two subgroups of popular boys, one described as "toughs" (popular and aggressive) and the other as "models" (popular and prosocial). Similarly, de Bruyn and Cillessen (2006) identified two subgroups of popular girls, one described as "popular and studious" (like the models in Rodkin et al.) and the other described as "popular and getting in trouble" (like the toughs). In the older terminology, one of the groups of each gender could be labeled sociometrically popular and the other perceived popular. In the new terminology of this book, the first group is described as popular and likeable and the second as popular but not necessarily liked. It is important to point out that neither the continuous approach nor the categorical approach is "better": they are complementary views of the same underlying heterogeneity of high status in the peer group.

SHORT-TERM DYNAMICS OF POPULARITY: EMERGENCE AND MAINTENANCE IN PEER GROUPS

Coie (1990) distinguished the emergence of peer rejection from the maintenance of peer rejection. The same distinction can be made for popularity: a phase in which popularity is acquired and a phase in which it is maintained or stabilized. Different factors may play a role in each phase. We identify four factors that may play a role in the acquisition of popular status and four factors that may play a role in its maintenance. Together, they describe the process of becoming popular and staying popular. As Coie indicated, a hard line between the emergence and maintenance stages of status is sometimes difficult to draw, and the factors that play a primary role in one stage can play a secondary role in the other as well. The same principle applies to the factors involved in gaining and maintaining popularity.

Emergence

Four factors may play a role in the acquisition of popularity: social attention-holding power, motivation, behavioral skills, and psychobiological factors. These factors are considered to be important preconditions for popularity but not sufficient for its maintenance.

Social Attention-Holding Power

Because popularity implies visibility (and prestige), a first requirement to achieve popularity is the ability to attract attention from others. An effective way to do so is through physical attractiveness, looking good, or dressing well. Another way is through achievements that make a student stand out in school (e.g., academic, athletic). Behavioral ways of capturing attention involve leadership: being the first to answer questions in the classroom, being dominant in play or group discussions, and taking the lead in school activities. In line with the association between bullying and popularity, another way to become the center of attention is by being a ringleader bully in the overt or relational manipulation of other students (e.g., Caravita & Cillessen, 2010). A common element among these options is that they attract the attention of a broad representation of the peer group and put the spotlight on the potentially popular student. Grabbing attention is not the same as holding attention, but it is an important first step on the road to popularity.

In their evolutionary research on social comparison and self-esteem, Gilbert, Price, and Allan (1995) described two ways in which people can display status in groups: the "attracting" display and the threat display. According to Gilbert et al., these two displays correspond to two forms of social power: *social attention-holding power* and *resource-holding power* (see also de Bruyn & Cillessen, 2010). Social attention-holding power is the ability to attract attention from others and is part of the emergence stage of popularity. The just-mentioned variables fall in this category.

This category also includes what have been called *peer-valued char-*

acteristics, possessions or traits that a peer group values (Vaillancourt & Hymel, 2006). Vaillancourt and Hymel identified a number of attributes that peer groups admire and strongly predispose youth to achieve social power. The attributes of being funny, attractive, and well dressed impress peers and draw them near, possibly setting off a self-perpetuating cycle of attention and increasingly positive social self-perceptions over time. Attributes such as athletic ability may also allow adolescents to garner attention from peers in positive ways that lead to status over time.

Motivation

Motivation researchers have distinguished two basic goals of people in interpersonal relationships. Bakan (1966) made the distinction between agentic and communion orientation. Individuals high in *agency* are independent, autonomous, and leaders. Individuals high in *communion* are connected to others, included in groups, and serve group goals. McAdams (1985) said that people's interpersonal relationships are shaped by the tendencies "to feel close to others and to have impact on others" (p. 85) and labeled these the *intimacy motive* and the *power motive,* respectively. McClelland (1985) named these tendencies the *need for affiliation* and the *need for power and dominance.* It can be hypothesized that an agentic orientation is needed to become popular in the peer group, whereas a communal orientation is needed for likeability. If this is the case, popularity should correlate with agentic, power, and dominance goals and likeability with communal, intimacy, and affiliation goals. Consistent with this hypothesis, Caravita and Cillessen (2010) found unique associations of popularity with agentic goals and of likeability with communal goals. Of course, these correlations do not prove a causal effect from agentic, power, or dominance goals to popularity; the causal arrow may also run in the opposite direction. Cross-lagged panel analyses of both types of goals and both types of status in a longitudinal study will shed light on this issue.

LaFontana and Cillessen (2010) took a slightly different approach to the issue of motivation by measuring the degree to which youth prioritize being popular with peers over other concerns (friendship, romance, altruism, rule compliance, and achievements). They found a curvilinear trend of the priority of popularity across development that peaked between the ages of 12 and 16 years. In a follow-up study using the same measure, Cillessen, de Bruyn, and LaFontana (2009) demonstrated that prioritizing popularity is more than an abstract motivation and may cause the very behaviors that characterize popular students. They found that early adolescents who are popular *and* prioritize being popular were the most aggressive and manipulative in the peer group. This finding suggests that motivation plays a role in achieving high status. The motivation to be popular increased the level of the behaviors that predict popularity.

Behavioral Skills

Evidence for behavioral determinants of status can come from two types of studies: observational studies in contrived playgroups, using designs such as the peer entry situation, and longitudinal sociometric studies, especially those that include transitions to new peer groups in new schools. As indicated by Aikins and Litwack (Chapter 7, this volume), observational studies have primarily addressed the predictors of likeability, not popularity. It can be assumed that some of the causes of acceptance into new groups, such as the ability to "hover" and size up the norms and ongoing flow of interaction in a group before participating, might also predict popularity. However, because of the lack of observational studies of the emergence of popularity in new groups, this is not yet known conclusively.

Longitudinal sociometric studies have looked at popularity and also controlled for its possible overlap with likeability (e.g., Cillessen & Mayeux, 2004; Rose, Swenson, & Waller, 2004). These studies have focused primarily on the role of aggression in the acquisition of popularity and indicate that the successful use of overt and relational aggression can be highly useful in achieving popularity (see also Cillessen & Rose, 2005).

As discussed by Mayeux, Houser, and Dyches (Chapter 4, this volume), many studies have examined the unique correlates of likeability and popularity in cross-sectional analyses. These studies show consistently that likeability is correlated with prosocial traits and behaviors, whereas popularity is correlated with a mixture of prosocial and antisocial behaviors. One finding that stands out in this research is the opposite association of overt and relational aggression with likeability and popularity. Both forms of aggression are typically negatively correlated with likeability but positively with popularity. The contrast is particularly noticed for relational aggression and especially in early adolescent samples.

Two longitudinal studies on the association between popularity and relational aggression (Cillessen & Mayeux, 2004; Rose et al., 2004) demonstrated that early relational aggression predicted later popularity. In the Cillessen and Mayeux (2004) study, this was the case across the transition to a new peer group. These findings strongly suggest that relational aggression plays a role in the acquisition of peer group popularity.

Adolescents who were relationally aggressive earlier were able to achieve popularity later, even among new peers.

These findings for relational aggression suggest that the ability to manipulate relationships is a behavioral skill that plays a role in the acquisition of popularity. Even though relational aggression is harmful to others, it also requires a certain amount of skill. A child or adolescent who engages in relationally aggressive behaviors needs to have a fairly sophisticated understanding of how relationships work in order to be able to manipulate them. In addition, relational aggression requires a network of relationships in order to be successful. One cannot have a network of relationships without other social skills and competencies. These facts help us understand why relational aggression may help youth to win status in the peer group.

As Mayeux and colleagues also demonstrate (Chapter 4, this volume), other behaviors that are not (relationally) aggressive are also correlated with popularity. These behaviors, most derived from peer nominations, include leadership, bossiness, and various types of prosocial behaviors. However, it is difficult to tell from the design of the studies that report them what their role is in the acquisition of popularity. The same cross-lagged analyses that have been conducted for relational aggression have not yet been conducted for these other behaviors. Thus, new studies should examine the cross-lagged associations of various prosocial behaviors with popularity, ideally in new peer groups and across school transitions, to determine their role in the emergence of popularity. There is an even higher need for observational studies similar to those conducted in the 1980s and 1990s to study rejection, which included repeated play sessions of familiar and unfamiliar peer groups over time combined with preplay classroom sociometrics and postplay playgroup assessments of status (e.g., Coie & Kupersmidt, 1983; Dodge, 1983). Such studies are needed to understand the behavioral determinants of popularity beyond relational aggression.

Psychobiological Factors

In an effort to study the psychobiology of peer relations, research has begun to examine psychobiological factors associated with popularity (Peters, Cillessen, Riksen-Walraven, Haselager, & de Weerth, 2010). Regarding the psychobiological underpinnings of high status, it can be hypothesized that a certain level of stress resistance is needed to become popular. Students who are too sensitive to the needs of others are unlikely to achieve popularity. The requirements of high status include the ability to stay calm and collected when making unpopular decisions or engaging in manipulative behaviors that harm others. Resistance to stress is often determined by measuring the stress hormone cortisol. Indeed, Peters, Cillessen, Riksen-Walraven, Haselager, et al. (2010) found that popularity, especially when combined with aggression, is related to unique aspects of the diurnal cortisol curve. This finding suggests that, in addition to valued characteristics, motivational factors, and behavioral skills, a certain biological preparedness, especially in terms of resistance to stress, may be needed to achieve high status or popularity in the peer group. Because almost nothing is known about the psychobiology of child and adolescent peer relationships in general, this is a growing area of future research.

Maintenance

Gaining popularity is not the same as maintaining popularity. In addition to the four factors that play a role in becoming popular, four others may play a role in staying popular: resource-holding power, self-awareness, social-cognitive skills, and flexible adjustment to groups.

Resource-Holding Power

Gilbert and colleagues (1995) defined resource-holding power as "an intervening process which allows an estimate of fighting capacity and the probability of making a successful challenge or successfully defending against other challengers" (p. 152). A core element of Gilbert et al.'s definition of resource-holding power is what they call *fighting/winning capacity*. According to these researchers, individuals in groups go through a social comparison process in which they compare their own ability to hold on to valuable resources with that of others. If they see others as weaker than themselves, they challenge them. If they see others as stronger than themselves, they submit. According to Gilbert et al., winning capacity is determined by "size, strength, skill, previous success, ... allies and other factors" (p. 152). Thus, it seems that one important factor in maintaining high status in the peer group is having and perceiving the ability to stay at the top relative to others.

Self-Awareness

The accuracy of self-perceptions of status has been a topic of interest for peer relationships researchers for some time (e.g., Bellmore & Cillessen,

2003, 2006). Building on this theme, Mayeux and Cillessen (2008) assessed adolescents' self-perceived popularity, how it relates to actual popularity, and how the combination of actual and self-perceived popularity might influence subsequent status and behavior in the peer group. They found that self-perceptions moderated the link between popularity and overt and relational aggression among ninth graders: students who were both popular and saw themselves as popular were the most aggressive, both overtly and relationally. Further, the combination of peer- and self-perceived popularity predicted increasing aggression across the 4 years of high school. Adolescents who were popular and knew it were the most likely to engage in the sort of aggressive behaviors that predict popularity. These findings suggest that an awareness of one's popularity in the peer group plays a role in the continuation of it. Students who saw themselves as popular seemed motivated to engage in the behaviors that predict continued popularity.

The participants in the Mayeux and Cillessen (2008) study were in high school. It is not known if the same phenomenon occurs at earlier ages, for example in middle school. As the available findings on the factors that play a role in the emergence and maintenance of popularity indicate, there are still gaps in our knowledge that need to be addressed in future studies.

Social-Cognitive Skills

Are sophisticated social-cognitive skills involved in popularity? Popularity researchers often suggest that they are, despite limited direct evidence for a correlation between popularity and social-cognitive skills. Most of our assumptions about the role of social-cognitive skills stems from the strong association between relational aggression and popularity. Because relational aggression is thought to require a significant degree of social savoir faire in order to enact successfully (see Sutton, Smith, & Swettenham, 1999), and indeed is correlated with social intelligence (Andreou, 2006), researchers have often suggested that one hallmark of popularity may be particularly high levels of social intelligence or social savvy. Although more conclusive data are still lacking on the correlation between social-cognitive skills and popularity, it can be hypothesized that advanced social-cognitive skills play a particularly important role in the maintenance of popularity. An advanced understanding of relationships and the ability to forecast the effect of one's actions on relationships are expected to be essential to maintain a position of high status in the peer group.

Researchers interested in the effects of relational aggression on popularity have started to look at moderators of this association. Puckett, Wargo Aikins, and Cillessen (2008) conducted one such study in which they examined data across two longitudinal waves enabling the examination of unique predictive effects. They were interested in the degree to which the effect of relational aggression on later popularity was moderated by adolescents' beliefs in their own ability to be socially successful and efficacious in the peer group (social self-efficacy). The results showed that (self-perceived) social and relational skills uniquely predicted later popularity beyond the effects of earlier popularity and also moderated the effect of earlier relational aggression on later popularity. These findings indicate that social and relational skills play a role in the maintenance of popularity through relational aggression. Whether these results also hold for social and relational skills that are not self-perceived is still to be determined.

Flexible Adjustment

The final hypothesis regarding the factors involved in the maintenance of popularity regards youth's ability to adjust themselves flexibly to changing group norms and goals. Norms and goals differ between peer groups, change within groups over time, and change with development. Given these changes, popularity does not benefit from a rigid adherence to values that led to popularity in the past. Research has shown that accepted children "hover" around in a new peer group to read the norms of the group and then adjust their behavior to it (see Putallaz & Wasserman, 1990). Popular youth may do something similar. The difference may be that they play a stronger role in determining group norms once they are a member. They may then read a group sufficiently accurately to know when a change of group goals and norms is possible and then take the lead in making such changes.

A construct that captures this idea of flexible adjustment is *ego resilience*, defined as the ability to respond flexibly to problem situations and to persist in solving them (Block, 2002). Indeed, in one study, ego resilience at age 5 predicted popularity at age 9 (Peters, Cillessen, Riksen-Walraven, & Haselager, 2010). However, further research on the role of this construct in the maintenance of popularity is needed.

Dual-Component Model of Social Competence

As indicated, there may be some overlap between the factors that predict the emergence of popularity and those that predict the maintenance of popularity. For example, the behavioral skills involved in acquiring popularity may also play a role in maintaining it. The social-cognitive skills involved in maintaining popularity may also play a role in acquiring it.

One way to combine the acquisition and maintenance of popularity is to think of both as a form of social competence. The nature of social competence is a much-debated issue. General definitions refer to adequacy, effectiveness, or success in interactions with peers. Beyond these abstract definitions, one common operational definition of social competence has been in terms of peer acceptance (Rose-Krasnor, 1997). Indeed, peer acceptance correlates with many prosocial behaviors and skills. However, the distinction between acceptance and popularity suggests that a one-dimensional view of social competence as represented by peer acceptance only is incomplete. The heterogeneity of popularity suggests that there is not one way to be socially competent with peers, but two. Cillessen and Bellmore (2011) theorized that likeability and popularity reflect two different ways of being competent or successful in interactions with others.

The first form of social competence refers to youth's abilities to be prosocial and cooperative, perceive others accurately, take their perspective, and properly read and understand their emotions. Prosocial behavior, interpersonal perception accuracy, perspective taking, and emotion understanding enable children and adolescents to be empathic, understanding, and supportive and to respond to the needs of peers. Children and adolescents who possess these skills behave in ways that make them well liked. They do not need force to express or assert themselves; hence, aggression or dominant behaviors are not part of their behavioral repertoire.

The second form of social competence refers to youth's abilities to be interpersonally effective and to achieve goals in social situations, either for themselves or the group, in principle through playing by the rules but if needed through convincing argumentation, coercion and forcefulness, strong self-assertions, or intelligent manipulation. A child or adolescent who excels in this domain may not be the most interpersonally sensitive, but is a well-connected leader who can achieve goals in effective ways that may be seen as domineering, aggressive, or manipulative by some but as assertive, socially savvy, and effective by others. Those who possess these skills behave in ways that make them visible, prestigious, and central in the peer group; hence, they are seen as popular but not necessarily well liked. They may use force to assert themselves; therefore, certain forms of aggression or dominant behaviors are in their behavioral repertoire.

In an application of this framework, de Bruyn, Cillessen, and Wissink (2010) considered both forms of social competence protective against victimization. Students who are well liked provide few reasons to elicit bullying from peers. The popular student is too dominant or well connected to become a victim. Therefore, negative associations were expected of likeability and popularity with victimization. These expectations were confirmed.

Contrasting associations were expected for bullying. Likeability, indicating the prosocial and interpersonally sensitive dimension of social competence, was expected to be negatively related to bullying. Popularity, a marker of the interpersonally effective but not necessarily sensitive component of social competence, was expected to be positively related to bullying. Youth who are primarily effective in achieving personal or group goals may sometimes resort to aggression and peer group manipulation to do so. These expectations were also confirmed. Indeed, de Bruyn et al. (2010) found negative associations between likeability and bullying but positive associations between popularity and bullying.

The view that dominance and aggression may be associated with social competence is not without controversy. On the one hand are researchers who, from various theoretical perspectives, point to the benefits associated with certain forms of aggression and to the fact that highly successful individuals (e.g., those who control resources) often use aggression or a combination of prosocial and aggressive tactics. This is perfectly consistent with the behavioral correlates profile of popularity. On the other hand are researchers who argue that any form of aggression is in the end always maladaptive and dysfunctional and a sign of underlying psychopathology, even when there are short-terms gains associated with it. This is not an either–or issue, but there seems to be some truth to both perspectives. The data on the concurrent behavioral correlates of likeability and popularity reviewed previously clearly and consistently show positive correlations of aggression, especially relational aggression, with popularity and indicate that relational aggression can be used to win prestige in the peer group. However, the long-term consequences of popularity indicate that there are also costs associated with it.

LONG-TERM DYNAMICS OF POPULARITY: DEVELOPMENTAL ANTECEDENTS AND CONSEQUENCES

Not surprisingly, much of what is known about popularity comes from studies with adolescents. After all, adolescence is the age when youth are highly sensitive about their image and the impressions they make on others and hence popularity is an important concern (LaFontana & Cillessen, 2010a). The fact that popularity is particularly distinct from likeability in adolescence (Cillessen & Mayeux, 2004) has further reinforced the research focus on adolescents. Although adolescence may be the "focal point" of popularity when it is prioritized the most and when its distinction with likeability is the largest, the impact of popularity is not limited to adolescence. Therefore, it should be considered in a broader developmental perspective. This section does just that by addressing the precursors and outcomes of popularity across development from early childhood to emerging adulthood.

Antecedents

Almost nothing is known about the roots of popularity, its developmental precursors, and childhood antecedents. So little prospective longitudinal research has been conducted on the development of popular status that most of our hypotheses are just that—educated guesses based on indirect associations in the literature. Little is known about the more distal predictors of popularity, such as early childhood behaviors or strengths. There are some exceptions.

Rodkin and Roisman (2010) used data from the National Institute of Child Health and Human Development Study of Early Child Care and Youth Development to examine early childhood predictors of popularity and found significant antecedents in children's day care experiences. Children were classified as popular–aggressive, popular–nonaggressive, aggressive–nonpopular, or nonpopular–nonaggressive using teacher ratings aggregated over grades 3 to 6. The study showed that children who were both popular and aggressive spent more hours per week in nonmaternal child care before they transitioned to grade school. This indicates that certain roots of popularity in elementary school can already be found in children's early socialization experiences with peers before elementary school.

Peters, Cillessen, Riksen-Walraven, and Haselager (2010) examined the developmental precursors in early childhood and preschool of likeability and popularity in early adolescence. The study used data collected at 15 months, 5 years, and 9 to 10 years of age. At 15 months, two dimensions of parent–child interaction were observed. *Effective guidance* is marked by effective structure and limit setting, high quality of instructions, and supportive presence by parents and by compliance and low avoidance by the child. *Negative interaction* is marked by hostility and lack of respect and support from parents and by child negativity and the absence of positive affect. At 5 years, preschool teachers judged children's ego resilience and ego control using the California Child Q-Sort (Block, 2002). *Ego resilience* is the child's capacity to respond flexibly but persistently to challenging social situations. *Ego control* is the child's capacity to regulate emotions without being excessively inhibited (overcontrol) or impulsive (undercontrol). At 9 to 10 years, popularity and preference were assessed in the participants' classrooms with peer nominations.

Causal models examined the associations. From 15 months to 5 years, effective guidance predicted ego resilience for girls, whereas negative interactions predicted ego undercontrol for boys. From 5 years to 9 to 10 years, ego resilience predicted social preference for both genders. The prediction of popularity varied by gender: It was predicted by earlier ego resilience for girls but by earlier ego undercontrol for boys. This suggests that popularity depends on a dominant or forceful presence for boys but on more subtle aspects of social interaction for girls.

The results from these studies reveal fascinating developmental pathways to adolescent popularity, rooted in earlier relationships with parents and peers. In addition to being substantively important for developmental theory, their unique antecedents validate the distinction between popularity and likeability. However, more longitudinal data are needed to replicate and extend these results. Toward that purpose, and consistent with the recommendations of Cillessen and Marks (Chapter 2, this volume), new data collections from ongoing longitudinal studies should include peer nominations of all four sociometric criteria: acceptance (liked most), rejection (liked least), popularity (most popular), and unpopularity (least popular).

Consequences

In 1990, Coie wrote: "Not as much attention has been given to the long-term consequences of popularity as has been given to rejection. We do know that popularity is associated with social skill and is not just a consequence of superficial characteristics, so it seems reasonable to suppose that positive peer status may be a predictor of future well-being" (p. 390). The first part of this statement is still true today. We still know relatively little about the long-term consequences of popularity. From the few studies that are available, we know that the second part of Coie's statement depends on how one defines positive peer status. If it is defined as likeability, the hypothesis may hold true. If it is defined as popularity, there are positive consequences as well as risks. In this volume, Sandstrom (Chapter 10) and Schwartz and Gorman (Chapter 11) have reviewed the later successes and risks of popularity. To the degree that popularity is followed by later successes, it serves as a model that will shed further light on the development of social competence. To the extent that popularity is associated with risks, these risks should be understood for prevention and intervention efforts.

In either case, important questions still need to be asked about popularity after adolescence. Is popularity a valid construct in the peer groups of emerging adults? What happens to the popularity–likeability distinction after high school? Will both dimensions again be more highly correlated in emerging adulthood as they were at the end of elementary school? What happens to popular peers after high school? How do they adjust? Answers to some of these questions are arising from different studies.

In a sociometric study with emerging adults, Lansu and Cillessen (2010) found that popularity and likeability continue to have differential profiles after high school. As at earlier ages, popularity correlated positively with dominant leadership and relational aggression, while these correlations were negative for likeability. This suggests that popularity and likeability continue to be separate dimensions in emerging adulthood.

Sandstrom and Cillessen (2006) examined the associations of popularity with adjustment over time from grade 5 to grade 8. Popularity in grade 5 was associated with higher levels of externalizing problems 3 years later but also with fewer internalizing symptoms over time for boys. Mayeux et al. (2008) examined the associations of popularity with later risk behaviors (smoking, alcohol use, and sexual activity) in high school. Popularity in grade 10, unlike social acceptance, predicted increased alcohol use and sexual activity in grade 12 for both boys and girls. A reciprocal relationship was found for boys, in which smoking in grade 10 also predicted gains in popularity over time. The results also suggested that gains in popularity may lead to subsequent losses in peer acceptance.

Sandstrom and Cillessen (2010) examined the adjustment consequences of popularity beyond high school as well as the moderating role of relational aggression in this process. Popularity and relational aggression were measured with peer nominations in each grade of high school. For 3 years after graduation from high school, adjustment was assessed with self-report measures of depression, psychopathology, workplace victimization, and health risk behaviors such as substance use. Popularity in high school predicted more risk behaviors after high school. Low popularity combined with high relational aggression also predicted adjustment problems after high school for boys. For girls, relational aggression in high school predicted lower levels of depression but higher levels of workplace victimization after high school.

The results from this study led to the hypothesis of *two pathways of popularity*. According to this hypothesis, there are two divergent pathways of adolescent popularity: one that leads from high school popularity to continued success after high school and another in which success is limited to the social ecology of high school and disappears when high school is left behind. An important question is what distinguishes these two developmental trajectories and what determines whether a popular high school student will stay on one course or fall back on the other.

As explained by Schwartz and Gorman (Chapter 11, this volume), popularity predicts academic adjustment problems, particularly for adolescents who are aggressive. Increases in popularity over time are associated with increases in absenteeism and decreases in grade point average. Although adolescents' academic attitudes were not assessed, these findings beg the question of whether youth begin to devalue academic excellence once they have achieved some level of popularity. Popular adolescents may believe that academic excellence cannot coexist with their status, or that being academically oriented will cause them to lose face. For some popular adolescents, the desire to maintain social power may be far more important than keeping up their grades.

Together, these studies indicate that popularity is associated with several risk behaviors and negative consequences in adolescence and beyond. The same risks do not seem to apply to accepted youth. The fact that popularity has more negative consequences than peer acceptance is consistent with the idea that they reflect different underlying competencies. However, the causal models that link popularity with adjustment need to be delineated more precisely.

In the literature on peer rejection, Parker and Asher (1987) made a distinction between the incidental effects and the causal effects of peer rejection. Rejection is an incidental effect when it is merely the result of an already existing underlying disorder. In this case, peer rejection is also called a marker variable of the underlying disorder. Rejection has a causal effect when it makes an independent and unique contribution to (concurrent or later) adjustment, beyond being merely a marker of already existing adjustment or disorder.

The distinction between incidental and causal effects can also be applied to popularity. In the incidental view, popularity is the result of already existing underlying skills and competencies. In the causal view, being popular in the peer group has further unique effects on later skills, competencies, and adjustment beyond already existing ones. The emerging data on the association between popularity and later adjustment (e.g., Sandstrom & Cillessen, 2010) are beginning to support a causal view of popularity. The causal view of popularity is also closely connected to developmental theory, stating that peer contact serves essential roles in development (e.g., Hartup, 1996). However, further modeling of longitudinal data is needed to carefully parse out the causal and incidental effects of popularity.

Not all hypotheses about the future of popularity have to focus on risk. In the leadership literature, a common distinction is between *relationship leadership* and *task leadership* (Forsyth, 2010). The first is supportive, employee centered, and focused on group maintenance. The second is work facilitative, production centered, and goal oriented. Relationship leaders sound like communal high-status peers and task leaders like agentic high-status peers. It can be hypothesized that child or adolescent likeability uniquely predicts later relational leadership, whereas popularity might uniquely predict later task leadership in emerging adulthood.

Another observation relates to the domain of agentic leadership and popularity and the role of gender in it. In our longitudinal study (Cillessen & Mayeux, 2004), we noticed that the correlation between popularity and likeability decreased almost linearly from year to year in adolescence (see also Cillessen & Borch, 2006) but with a remarkable gender difference. For both boys and girls, the correlation was about .70 by the end of elementary school. For boys, it then decreased to about .40 by the end of high school. For girls, it decreased more sharply to zero by the beginning of high school and then crossed over to a negative value for the remainder of high school.

What explains this incompatibility between likeability and popularity for adolescent girls? Apparently, whereas adolescent males can be both popular and liked, it is more difficult for adolescent girls to combine both roles. Being highly visible and likeable at the same time in the adolescent peer group seems more challenging for girls than boys. An explanation for this phenomenon may come from the connection between popularity and being agentic (Caravita & Cillessen, 2010) and from gender differences in the evaluation of agency. Rudman and Glick (1999) have shown that agentic women are perceived more negatively than agentic men. Their research indicates that adult women who are agentic leaders pay a price by how they are seen by others. The negative correlation between popularity and likeability for high school girls may show the beginnings of this phenomenon in the adolescent peer group.

Linking Short-Term Group Dynamics to Long-Term Developmental Dynamics

A challenge for this model of popularity is to link the short-term group dynamics of popularity to the long-term developmental dynamics. It seems important not to place the short-term and long-term dynamics of popularity on one linear time line as was appropriate in the four-stage model of rejection (Coie, 1990). In the case of rejection, both the short-term and long-term trajectories are characterized by behavior problems and competence deficiencies; there seems to be great continuity among problematic developments both short term and long term. This is different for popularity. Popularity is not uniformly prosocial or antisocial but is both. As a result, there are developmental continuities and discontinuities. For example, Peters, Cillessen, Riksen-Walraven, and Haselager (2010) showed that popularity has roots in negative interactions with parents for boys, which may indicate that popular boys had high activity levels when they were young. Their aversive interactions with parents predicted later popularity, which may then predict task leadership in emerging adulthood. Thus, there may be one developmental trajectory of popularity with negative early roots, positive long-term outcomes, and in between emergent and maintenance stages with both positive and negative elements.

Consequently, the short-term adolescent and long-term developmental trajectories of popularity should be considered separately, as two levels of a multilevel model. For one dependent variable, both trajectories will have their own intercepts and linear (and possibly nonlinear) slopes. Hypotheses are then needed to link the intercepts and slopes of the short-term group dynamic trajectory to the long-term developmental trajectory. This will require not only strong hypotheses but, most importantly, sufficient longitudinal data to test them.

Although this perspective is challenging, it seems important. If the study of popularity has taught us one thing, we warn against an oversimplified model that puts all of popularity on one overall positive and prosocial trajectory. The study of popularity, from Eder's (1985) qualitative descriptions of relationally aggressive popular girls to Mayeux et al.'s (2008) associations of popularity with health risk behaviors, has shown us too many twists and turns to place popularity only on one continuous trajectory of prosocial development and adjustment.

CONCLUSION

Much has been learned about popularity in recent years. The field of child and adolescent peer relations has moved from a primary focus on peer rejection to one that also includes popularity. An important conceptual and empirical contribution was demonstrated by making explicit the distinction between likeability and popularity, a measure of prestige and visibility, dominance and influence. Research has confirmed that these are distinct constructs with unique behavioral correlates and unique implications for adolescent development and beyond. In spite of these advances, numerous gaps exist in our knowledge of high status in the peer group. Next, four critical needs are identified to be addressed in future research.

First, more needs to be known about the correlates that validate the distinction between likeability and popularity. So far, research on correlates has focused primarily on social behaviors and health outcomes. Research on concurrent behavioral correlates has primarily shown important differences in aggressive behaviors. The proposed dual-component model of social competence specifies distinctions between likeability and popularity in a variety of other domains. Other skills implied by the model include social-cognitive skills and emotion regulation and understanding skills. Their unique associations with both forms of popularity should be considered. Personality variables should also be considered, specifically traits that indicate manipulative skills or orientations, such as Machiavellianism and narcissism. For example, there is preliminary evidence that the combination of relational aggression and Machiavellianism is a particularly strong predictor of popularity among high school girls (Mayeux, 2009). Certain personality constructs might predispose children or adolescents to value or pursue status-related goals. Studies should be conducted to determine the unique associations of popularity and likeability with dependent variables in these yet unexplored domains. Developmental and gender differences should be considered at the same time.

Second, more needs to be known about the consequences of popularity and the divergent pathways of popular youth after they leave high school. Although research has shown associations of popularity with risk and maladjustment, not all popular youth are expected to be at risk in or after high school. Consistent with the hypothesis of two pathways of popularity presented previously, new studies should determine what distinguishes popular youth who continue to excel in relationships, adjustment, education, and careers after they leave structured education from those who fail in these domains after they leave high school. One obvious hypothesis is that youth who are both liked and popular are the most likely to succeed later in life; this hypothesis has also not yet been examined.

Third, more needs to be known about the unique developmental precursors of peer acceptance and popularity. What other childhood variables uniquely predict adolescent popularity? Building on the results of Peters, Cillessen, Riksen-Walraven, and Haselager (2010) and Rodkin and Roisman (2010), other early peer experiences may be highly predictive of later likeability and popularity. Early predictors may also be found in children's psychobiological functioning that is connected to temperament and family variables, as emerging data on the psychobiology of peer relations suggest (e.g., Peters, Cillessen, Riksen-Walraven, Haselager, et al., 2010). Understanding the early childhood predictors of child and adolescent popularity is critical to make a developmental theory of popularity more complete and, in that process, contribute to theorizing about the developmental significance of peer relationships more generally.

Fourth, a cross-cultural perspective is needed. Relatively little is known about popularity among youth in non-Western societies. Fortunately, popularity research is on the way in numerous other countries and cultures. This research is important because it has often been questioned whether popularity, along with its stereotypical associations, is primarily a North American phenomenon or limited to Western societies. In contrast, it seems logical to assume that the stratification of the peer group is a universal phenomenon governed by fundamental processes and principles. Data from other countries and cultures will make it possible to determine to what degree popularity is indeed culturally specific or universal.

The chapters in this volume examined popularity in the peer system, and this chapter integrates what was learned from preceding ones. It was observed that popularity is distinct from likeability, and that this distinction has analogies to other distinctions in psychology. The nature of popularity is impact, an interaction between antagonistic behaviors and valuable characteristics, and hence controversial. Popularity has a complex connection with peer influence. Popular peers are able to engage others in risk behaviors but are also susceptible to risks themselves. Two developmental pathways of adolescent popularity were hypothesized: one with a prosperous future, another less fortunate. To understand the development of popularity and likeability more fully, an underlying model of social competence was proposed. This model highlights that popularity is not an adolescence-limited phenomenon. Instead, it is a key phenomenon at a key stage in development but embedded in a broader developmental perspective that includes childhood precursors and later consequences.

This chapter opened with the question of whether popularity should be studied at all. Collectively, the chapters in this volume show that understanding popularity is important for developmental researchers concerned about peer relations. Peer group status in general and popularity specifically are associated with numerous critical aspects of development, such as the growth of social competence in childhood and adolescence, the occurrence of health risk behaviors among youth, successful relationship development, school and career achievement, and developmental psychopathology. For all these reasons, the study of popularity will remain an important endeavor for years to come.

REFERENCES

Andreou, E. (2006). Social preference, perceived popularity and social intelligence: Relations to overt and relational aggression. *School Psychology International, 27,* 339–351.

Asher, S. R., & Coie, J. D. (Eds.). (1990). *Peer rejection in childhood.* New York: Cambridge University Press.

Bakan, D. (1966). *The duality of human existence.* Chicago: Rand McNally.

Bellmore, A. D., & Cillessen, A. H. N. (2003). Children's meta-perceptions and meta-accuracy of acceptance and rejection by same-sex and other-sex peers. *Personal Relationships, 10,* 217–234.

Bellmore, A. D., & Cillessen, A. H. N. (2006). Reciprocal influences of victimization, perceived social preference, and self-concept in adolescence. *Self and Identity, 5,* 209–229.

Bierman, K. L., & Wargo, J. B. (1995). Predicting the longitudinal course associated with aggressive-rejected, aggressive (nonrejected), and rejected (nonaggressive) status. *Development and Psychopathology, 7,* 669–682.

Block, J. (2002). *Personality as an affect-processing system.* Mahwah, NJ: Erlbaum.

Caravita, S. C. S., & Cillessen, A. H. N. (2010). *Agentic or communal?: Effects of interpersonal goals on popularity and bullying in middle childhood and early adolescence.* Unpublished manuscript, Department of Psychology, Catholic University of Milan, Milan, Italy.

Cillessen, A. H. N. (1991). *The self-perpetuating nature of children's peer relationships.* Kampen, The Netherlands: Mondiss.

Cillessen, A. H. N., & Bellmore, A. D. (2011). Social skills and social competence in interactions with peers. In P. K. Smith & C. H. Hart (Eds.), *The Wiley-Blackwell handbook of childhood social development* (2nd ed., pp. 393–412). Malden, MA: Blackwell.

Cillessen, A. H. N., & Borch, C. (2006). Developmental trajectories of adolescent popularity: A growth curve modelling analysis. *Journal of Adolescence, 29,* 935–959.

Cillessen, A. H. N., & Mayeux, L. (2004). From censure to reinforcement: Developmental changes in the association between aggression and social status. *Child Development, 75,* 147–163.

Cillessen, A. H. N., de Bruyn, E. H., & LaFontana, K. M. (2009, April). *Behavioral effects of prioritizing popularity.* Paper presented at the biennial meeting of the Society for Research in Child Development, Denver, CO.

Cillessen, A. H. N., & Rose, A. J. (2005). Understanding popularity in the peer system. *Current Directions in Psychological Science, 14,* 102–105.

Cillessen, A. H. N., van IJzendoorn, H. W., van Lieshout, C. F. M., & Hartup, W. W. (1992). Heterogeneity among peer rejected boys: Subtypes and stabilities. *Child Development, 63,* 893–905.

Clifford, E. (1963). Social visibility. *Child Development, 34,* 799–808.

Coie, J. D. (1990). Toward a theory of peer rejection. In S. R. Asher & J. D. Coie (Eds.), *Peer rejection in childhood* (pp. 365–401). New York: Cambridge University Press.

Coie, J. D., & Kupersmidt, J. B. (1983). A behavioral analysis of emerging social status in boys' groups. *Child Development, 54,* 1400–1416.

de Bruyn, E. H., & Cillessen, A. H. N. (2006). Heterogeneity of girls' consensual popularity: Academic and interpersonal behavioral profiles. *Journal of Youth and Adolescence, 35,* 435–445.

de Bruyn, E. H., & Cillessen, A. H. N. (2010). *Peer group hierarchies and the emergence of sexual activity in early adolescence.* Unpublished manuscript, Department of Education, University of Amsterdam, Amsterdam, The Netherlands.

de Bruyn, E. H., Cillessen, A. H. N., & Wissink, I. B. (2010). Associations of peer acceptance and perceived popularity with bullying and victimization in early adolescence. *Journal of Early Adolescence, 30,* 543–566.

Dodge, K. A. (1983). Behavioral antecedents of peer social status. *Child Development, 54,* 1386–1399.

Eder, D. (1985). The cycle of popularity: Interpersonal relations among female adolescents. *Sociology of Education, 58,* 154–165.

Forsyth, D. R. (2010). *Group dynamics* (5th ed.). Belmont, CA: Wadsworth.

Gilbert, P., Price, J., & Allan, S. (1995). Social comparison, social attractiveness, and evolution: How might they be related? *New Ideas in Psychology, 13,* 149–165.

Hartup, W. W. (1996). The company they keep: Friendships and their developmental significance. *Child Development, 67,* 1–13.

LaFontana, K. M., & Cillessen, A. H. N. (1998). The nature of children's stereotypes of popularity. *Social Development, 7,* 301–320.

LaFontana, K. M., & Cillessen, A. H. N. (2010). Developmental changes in the priority of perceived status in childhood and adolescence. *Social Development, 19,* 130–147.

Lansu, T. A. M., & Cillessen, A. H. N. (2010). *Peer status in emerging adulthood: Associations of popularity and preference with social roles and behavior.* Unpublished manuscript, Behavioural Science Institute, Radboud University, Nijmegen, The Netherlands.

Lansu, T. A. M., Cillessen, A. H. N., & Karremans, J. C. (2010). *The popularity effect: Impact of popularity on imitation and choice.* Unpublished manuscript, Behavioural Science Institute, Radboud University, Nijmegen, The Netherlands.

Mayeux, L. (2009, April). *Machiavelli goes to high school: Machiavellianism moderates the aggression-status link in late adolescence.* Paper presented at the biennial meeting of the Society for Research in Child Development, Denver, CO.

Mayeux, L., & Cillessen, A. H. N. (2008). It's not just being popular, it's knowing it, too: The role of self-perceptions of status in the associations between peer status and aggression. *Social Development, 17,* 881–888.

Mayeux, L., Sandstrom, M. J., & Cillessen, A. H. N. (2008). Is being popular a risky proposition? *Journal of Research on Adolescence, 18,* 49–74.

McAdams, D. P. (1985). Motivation and friendship. In S. Duck & D. Perlman (Eds.), *Understanding personal relationships* (pp. 85–105). London: Sage.

McClelland, D. C. (1985). *Human motivation.* Cambridge, UK: Cambridge University Press.

Merten, D. E. (1997). The meaning of meanness: Popularity, competition, and conflict among junior high school girls. *Sociology of Education, 70,* 175–191.

Miller-Johnson, S., Costanzo, P. R., Coie, J. D., Rose, M. R., Browne, D. C., & Johnson, C. (2003). Peer social structure and risk-taking behaviors among African American early adolescents. *Journal of Youth and Adolescence, 32,* 375–384.

Newcomb, A. F., Bukowski, W. M., & Pattee, L. (1993). Children's peer relations: A meta-analytic review of popular, rejected, neglected, controversial, and average sociometric status. *Psychological Bulletin, 113,* 99–128.

Parker, J. G., & Asher, S. R. (1987). Peer relations and later personal adjustment: Are low-accepted children "at risk"? *Psychological Bulletin, 102,* 357–389.

Parkhurst, J. T., & Hopmeyer, A. (1998). Sociometric popularity and peer-perceived popularity: Two distinct dimensions of peer status. *Journal of Early Adolescence, 18,* 135–144.

Peters, E., Cillessen, A. H. N., Riksen-Walraven, J. M., & Haselager, G. J. T. (2010, March). *Developmental precursors of sociometric and perceived popularity in early adolescence.* Paper presented at the biennial meeting of the Society for Research on Adolescence, Philadelphia, PA.

Peters, E., Cillessen, A. H. N., Riksen-Walraven, J. M., Haselager, G. J. T., & de Weerth, C. (2010). *Aggression and diurnal cortisol: The moderating role of peer status.* Unpublished manuscript, Behavioural Science Institute, Radboud University, Nijmegen, The Netherlands.

Puckett, M. B., Wargo Aikins, J., & Cillessen, A. H. N. (2008). Moderators of the association between relational aggression and perceived popularity. *Aggressive Behavior, 34,* 563–576.

Putallaz, M., & Wasserman, A. (1990). Children's entry behavior. In S. R. Asher & J. D. Coie (Eds.), *Peer rejection in childhood* (pp. 60–89). New York: Cambridge University Press.

Rodkin, P. C., Farmer, T. W., Pearl, R., & Van Acker, R. (2000). Heterogeneity of popular boys: Antisocial and prosocial configurations. *Developmental Psychology, 36*, 14–24.

Rodkin, P. C., & Roisman, G. I. (2010). Antecedents and correlates of the popular-aggressive phenomenon in elementary school. *Child Development, 81*, 838–852.

Rose, A. J., Swenson, L. P., & Waller, E. M. (2004). Overt and relational aggression and perceived popularity: Developmental differences in concurrent and prospective relations. *Developmental Psychology, 40*, 378–387.

Rose-Krasnor, L. (1997). The nature of social competence: A theoretical review. *Social Development, 6*, 111–135.

Rudman, L. A., & Glick, P. (1999). Feminized management and backlash toward agentic women: The hidden costs to women of a kinder, gentler image of middle managers. *Journal of Personality and Social Psychology, 77*, 1004–1010.

Sandstrom, M. J., & Cillessen, A. H. N. (2006). Likable versus popular: Distinct implications for adolescent adjustment. *International Journal of Behavioral Development, 30*, 305–314.

Sandstrom, M. J., & Cillessen, A. H. N. (2010). Life after high school: Adjustment of popular teens in emerging adulthood. *Merrill-Palmer Quarterly, 56*, 474–499.

Sutton, J., Smith, P. K., & Swettenham, J. (1999). Social cognition and bullying: Social inadequacy or skilled manipulation? *British Journal of Developmental Psychology, 17*, 435–450.

Vaillancourt, T., & Hymel, S. (2006). Aggression and social status: The moderating roles of sex and peer-valued characteristics. *Aggressive Behavior, 32*, 396–408.

Index

Academic competence. *see also* Costs of
    popularity
  acceptance and, 88–90
  costs of popularity and, 260–263
  ethnicity and, 200–202, 206
  gender and, 109–110, 116
  group organization and, 170
  influence processes and, 230–231
  social competence and, 152–153
Acceptance
  aggression and, 83–88
  alternative peer (sociometric) measures, 35
  behavioral and academic risk and, 88–90
  compared to popularity, 15
  developmental trajectories, 149–152
  emotional adjustment and, 94–96
  ethnicity and, 196–198
  friendships and, 92–94
  historical perspective and, 29
  influence processes and, 224–225
  measurement of popularity and, 27–29, 31
  overview, 79–81, 96–99
  romantic relationships and, 93–94
  social behaviors associated with, 90–92
  social competence and, 143, 155–156
  social-cognitive factors and, 94–96, 144–147
  stability, change and overlap between
    popularity and, 81–83
  word meaning and, 8–9
Acculturation, 207. *see also* Ethnicity
Activity participation
  ethnicity and, 209–210
  gender and, 105, 110
  paths to popularity and, 65
Adjustment, emotional, 94–95, 290–291
Adolescence
  definition of popularity during, 30
  developmental trajectories, 149–152
  peer groups and, 182–185
Affiliation
  gender and, 107–108
  outgroup membership and, 172–173

paths to popularity and, 68–69, 107–108
social dominance and, 128–131
stability of group membership and, 188
status striving and, 180
Affluence, 105, 109. *see also* Socioeconomic
    status (SES)
Age
  measurement of popularity and, 44, 45
  social competence and, 149–152
  status-aggression link and, 86–88
Agency, 280–281
Aggression. *see also* Meanness; Relational
    aggression; Social dominance
  academic competence and, 110, 116,
    260–261
  collective aspects of popularity and, 70–
    71
  contest versus scramble competition and,
    131–133
  costs of popularity and, 246, 249, 264
  developmental trajectories, 150
  emotional adjustment and, 96
  ethnicity and, 199–200, 203
  forms of, 127–128
  gender and, 44–45, 104, 106–107, 110,
    112–114, 115–116
  individualism and, 18
  influence processes and, 227, 231–232,
    237
  measurement of popularity and, 44–45,
    49–50
  moderators of the link with popularity,
    86–88
  peer contagion and, 223
  peer groups and, 176–182, 183
  school transitions and, 133–134
  social competence and, 152–154, 287
  status and, 83–88
  within-group aggression, 126
Alcohol use. *see* Drinking
Alternative peer measures, 34–37
Ambivalence from peers, 105–106

Index

Antisocial behavior. *see also* Aggression
 costs of popularity and, 248–249, 252
 gender and, 115–116
 influence processes and, 227
 nature of popularity and, 276–277
 sexual behavior and, 256–257
 social competence and, 153–154
Appearance. *see* Attractiveness
Assertiveness, 142, 145
Assessment, cultural, 186
Assimilation, 10
Attention from others, 279–280
Attracted-pairs method, 130
Attractiveness
 collective aspects of popularity and, 71
 developmental trajectories, 150
 fashion and, 105
 gender and, 105, 106, 108–109
 influence processes and, 231–232
 overview, 26
Attributes of popularity, 64–67
Autonomy, 166–167
Average status, 82. *see also* Status

Behavior. *see also* Antisocial behavior; Prosocial behavior
 emergence and maintenance of popularity and, 281–282
 ethnicity and, 208
 influence processes and, 228–232, 233–234
 peer contagion and, 222–224
 social competence and, 141–143, 152–154
Behavioral risks. *see also* Aggression; Costs of popularity; Drinking; Sexual behavior; Smoking
 acceptance and, 88–92
 costs of popularity and, 249
 ethnicity and, 206
Best-friendships, 93. *see also* Friendships
Bistrategic resource controllers, 129, 146–147
Boys, culture of. *see also* Gender
 overview, 103–104, 118–120
 paths to popularity and, 104–114
 social competence and, 142–143
Bullying. *see also* Aggression; Relational aggression
 acceptance and, 90–92
 ethnicity and, 203
 influence processes and, 227, 231–232
 peer groups and, 178–179
 social dominance and, 127–128
Burnouts. *see also* Outgroup membership

Causal models
 developmental trajectories and, 152
 overview, 291–292
 predictors of popularity and, 288–289
Change, 81–83
Cheerleading, 65, 105

Childhood, 30, 149–152
Cigarette smoking. *see* Smoking
Class-based structure, 20
Cliques
 collective aspects of popularity and, 70–72
 costs of popularity and, 252–253
 dynamics of, 173–182
 operational principles and, 171–173
 overview, 169–171. *see also* Peer groups
 preserving popularity and, 67–70
 stability of membership in, 188
Coercive strategies, 146
Cohesion, 11–12
Collective aspects of popularity, 70–72
Collectivism, 18
Communication skills, 106, 280–281
Competence perceptions, 144
Competitive encounters, 129–131, 131–133
Conflict resolution, 129–131
Conformity, 220–221, 247–248. *see also* Influence processes
Consensual popularity, 30
Construct validity, 45–46
Contagion, peer. *see* Peer contagion
Contest competition, 131–133. *see also* Competitive encounters
Contextual approach, 18–19
Contextual moderators, 235–236
Controlling strategies, 145
Controversial status
 academic competence and, 261
 overview, 82, 253, 277
 sexual behavior and, 257
Cooperation, 84
Costs of popularity. *see also* Academic competence; Behavioral risks; Status
 academic competence and, 260–263
 developmental trajectories and, 287–293
 ethnographic studies and, 72–74
 overview, 16, 245–246, 263–264, 274
 sexual behavior, 255–259
 underlying processes, 246–250
Cross-cultural perspective, 295–296
Cross-sex nominations, 40
Crowds. *see also* Groups; Peer groups
 costs of popularity and, 251–253
 dynamics of, 173–182
 overview, 169–171
 stability of membership in, 188
Cultural assessment, 186
Cultural perspectives, 185–186, 295–296. *see also* Ethnicity
Culture of boys and girls. *see also* Gender
 costs of popularity and, 292
 overview, 103–104, 118–120
 paths to popularity and, 104–114
 social competence and, 142–143
Cycle of popularity
 gender and, 107–108, 118
 likability and, 118

Cycle of popularity (continued)
  overview, 68–69
  status striving and, 180

Defending behaviors, 90–92
Definition of popularity, 5–10
Demographic factors, 86–88
Depressive symptoms, 95–96, 264
Developmental trajectories
  influence processes and, 236–237
  overview, 287–293
  social competence and, 149–152
  status and, 182–185
Differentiation, 10
Discriminant validity, 43–45
Discrimination, peer, 198–199, 206
Dominance-based popularity. see also Social dominance
  motivation and, 280–281
  overview, 79–81
  social competence and, 287
Drinking. see also Substance use
  acceptance and, 88–90
  costs of popularity and, 72, 250–255
  influence processes and, 230–231
Dual-component model of social competence, 285–287
Dyadic relationships, 179–182

Effective guidance, 288–289
Effects of popularity, 19–21
Ego control, 289
Ego resilience, 289
Emergence, 278–287. see also Paths to popularity
Emotion regulation, 147–148
Emotional functioning, 94–96, 147–149, 290–291
Empathy, 96
Ethnicity
  group differences or similarities, 195–202
  overview, 193–195, 202–210, 210
  peer groups and, 186
  research and, 202–210
Ethnographic studies. see also Measurement of popularity; Research programs
  academic competence and, 261
  aggression and, 115–116
  dynamics of popularity, 64–74
  ethnicity and, 199–202
  gender and, 104–108, 115–116
  overview, 57–58, 74–75
  rationale and practices, 58–62
  research roles in, 62–64
Exclusiveness, 110–112
Extracurricular activities. see Activity participation

Fashion, 105, 106, 108–109
Features of popularity, 18–19

Flexibility, 285
Four-stage model, 273–274
Friendliness, 143
Friendships
  acceptance and, 92–94
  ethnicity and, 205
  gender and, 104
  quality of, 92–93

Game theory, 129, 135
Gender. see also Culture of boys and girls
  acceptance and, 81–83, 95, 96
  attributes of popularity and, 65–66
  contest versus scramble competition and, 132–133
  correlates and predictors of popularity and, 104–114
  costs of popularity and, 292
  friendships and, 93
  group organization and, 170
  influence processes and, 226, 233
  likability and, 117–118
  measurement of popularity and, 40, 44–45
  overview, 103–104, 118–120
  psychosocial outcomes associated with popularity and, 114–118
  social competence and, 142–143
  status-aggression link and, 86–88
Girls, culture of. see also Gender
  costs of popularity and, 292
  overview, 103–104, 118–120
  paths to popularity and, 104–114
  social competence and, 142–143
Good-natured personality, 114
Grades. see Academic competence
Group, peer. see Peer groups
Group classification, 34
Group formation, 133–134
Groups
  dynamics of, 173–182
  ethnicity and, 195–202, 209–210
  organization of, 169–171
  overview. see also Peer groups
  popularity concept overview and, 10–14

Hierarchical needs, 20
Hierarchies, social
  ethnicity and, 208
  group organization and, 170–171
  social dominance and, 125–127
High status. see Status
Historical perspective, 29
Homogeneity, 11–12
Humor, 106, 114

Identity, 205–206, 251–253
Impact (social), 27–29, 49
Impression management, 71–72
Incidental models, 152, 291–292
Individual-differences moderators, 232–234

Individualism, 18
Individuals, 10–14
Influence processes
    developmental trajectories and, 236–237
    mechanisms of, 228–232
    moderators of, 232–236
    overview, 219–224, 237–239, 246–250
    popularity effect and, 277
    power and, 224–225
    research and, 225–228, 238–239
Institutional expectations, 71–72
Instrumental relational aggression, 111–112. see also Relational aggression
Intergroup interactions, 176–182
Interitem reliability, 42
Internalizing symptoms, 96, 116–117
Interpersonal skills, 106, 119. see also Social competence; Social skills
Interrater reliability, 42
Interviews, open-ended, 61–62
Intimacy motive, 280–281

Judgmental popularity, 30

Leadership
    acceptance and, 97
    aggression and, 84
    costs of popularity and, 292
Likability. see also Sociometric popularity
    alternative peer (sociometric) measures, 35
    costs of popularity and, 292
    gender and, 117–118
    motivation and, 280–281
    overview, 25–26, 275–276, 278, 294–295
Limited nominations, 40–41
Longitudinal research. see also Research programs
    academic competence and, 116, 260–261
    acceptance and, 81–82
    aggression and, 83–84, 112–113
    costs of popularity and, 253
    developmental trajectories, 149–152
    influence processes and, 231
    preserving popularity and, 70
    relational aggression and, 281–282
Losing popularity. see also Preserving popularity
    aggression and, 86
    collective aspects of popularity and, 70–71
    ethnographic studies and, 67–70

Machiavellianism, 294
Maintaining popularity status. see Preserving popularity
Majority status, 202–203. see also Status
Manchester Youth Study, 84
Manipulation
    acceptance and, 85
    emergence and maintenance of popularity and, 283

gender and, 44–45, 110–112
    measurement of popularity and, 44–45
Mean Girls (2002), 72
Meanness. see also Aggression; Relational aggression
    collective aspects of popularity and, 70–71
    costs of popularity and, 72
    gender and, 106
    paths to popularity and, 69
    peer groups and, 176–182
Measurement of popularity. see also Ethnographic studies
    alternative measures of popularity, 46–49
    ethnicity and, 203–205
    methodological issues, 37–41
    overview, 25–26, 31–37, 49–50
    psychometric properties of, 42–46
    terminological clarification and, 29–31
    types of popularity and, 27–29
Minority status, 202–203. see also Status
Motivation, 280–281
Multiethnic youth, 204–205. see also Ethnicity
Multiple-group membership, 204–205

Nationality. see Ethnicity
Nature of popularity, 275–278
Negative interaction, 288–289
Negative nominations, 38–40
Neglected status, 82
Nominations, popularity, 32

Observations, 48–49, 60–61
Open-ended interviews, 61–62
Operational principles, 171–173
Organizational changes, 169–171
Others, 10–14
Outgroup membership. see also Peer groups
    aggression and, 178–179
    ethnic discrimination and, 198–199
    overview, 172–173
    status and, 181–182
Overconfidence, 249
Overt aggression, 112–114. see also Aggression

Parent–child interactions, 288–289
Parenting styles, 233, 288–289
Paths to popularity. see also Predictors of popularity; Wannabes
    costs of popularity and, 291
    emergence and maintenance and, 278–287
    ethnicity and, 199–202, 206
    ethnographic studies and, 64–67
    gender and, 104–114
    influence processes and, 232–236
    overview, 294–296
    predictors of popularity and, 104–114, 288–289

Index

Paths to popularity (*continued*)
  preserving popularity and, 67–70
  social impetus for popularity, 166–168
Peer contagion, 222–224
Peer discrimination, 198–199, 206
Peer groups. *see also* Cliques; Groups; Status
  cultural perspectives and, 185–186
  developmental trajectories, 182–185
  dynamics of, 173–182
  ethnicity and, 195–202, 209–210
  influence processes and, 220–224, 233–234
  organizational and operational principles of, 168–173
  overview, 165–166
  research and, 187–189
  social impetus for popularity, 166–168
  status and, 182–185
Peer pressure, 221–222, 247–248. *see also* Influence processes
Peer relations
  developmental trajectories, 150
  popularity concept overview and, 3–5
  social competence and, 140–141
Peer-perceived popularity, 79–81
Peer-valued characteristics
  gender and, 117–118
  overview, 279–280
  status-aggression link and, 87
Perceived popularity
  acceptance and, 91–92
  friendships and, 92–93
  overview, 30, 49, 276
  status-aggression link and, 87–88
Personality
  emergence and maintenance of popularity and, 282–283
  overview, 294
  status-aggression link and, 86–88
Person-centered analyses, 128
Physical aggression. *see* Aggression
Physical appearance. *see* Attractiveness
Political sphere, 12–13
Popularity effect, 277–278. *see also* Influence processes
Popularity overview, 3–5, 10–14, 21–22, 26–27, 275–278, 293–296
  developmental trajectories and, 287–293
  ethnographic studies and, 59
  measurement of popularity and, 37–38, 49
  as a social construct, 17–22
  theory of popularity, 273–274, 275–278
  types of popularity, 27–29
  what is popularity good for, 14–17
  word meaning and, 5–10
Popularity risk hypothesis, 277–278. *see also* Costs of popularity
Popularity-preference correlations, 43–45
Popular-prosocial subtype of popularity, 89, 91–92
Populism, 12–13

Populistic subtype of popularity, 89, 91–92
Positive nominations, 38–40
Post-conflict-matched control method, 130
Power
  aggression and, 85–86
  ethnicity and, 193
  motivation and, 280–281
  overview, 16–17
  social competence and, 143
Predictors of popularity, 104–114, 288–289. *see also* Paths to popularity
Preference (social)
  acceptance and, 82–83
  alternative peer (sociometric) measures, 35
  measurement of popularity and, 27–29, 43, 43–45, 49
  preserving popularity and, 82–83
Pregnancy during adolescence, 258–259. *see also* Sexual behavior
Preserving popularity. *see also* Losing popularity; Stability
  acceptance and, 81–83
  aggression and, 86
  collective aspects of popularity and, 70–71
  ethnographic studies and, 67–70
  overview, 278–287
Pressure, peer. *see* Peer pressure
Prestige, 276
Proactive aggression, 127–128. *see also* Aggression
Prosocial behavior. *see also* Social competence
  acceptance and, 144–147
  developmental trajectories, 149–152
  gender and, 104, 108
  nature of popularity and, 276–277
  overview, 140–141, 141–143
  social dominance and, 129
Psychobiological factors, 282–283
Psychosocial outcomes, 114–118
Pubertal development, 166–167

Qualitative research, 31–32, 224. *see also* Research programs
Quantitative research, 32–34, 108–114. *see also* Research programs
Queen bees, 97–98

Race. *see* Ethnicity
Ratings, popularity, 32–33
Reactive aggression, 127. *see also* Aggression
Rebellious behavior, 231–232. *see also* Aggression
Reciprocal models, 151–152
Reconciliations, 129–131
Rejection
  aggression and, 86
  developmental trajectories and, 151–152
  emotional adjustment and, 94–96
  gender differences and, 44–45

measurement of popularity and, 27–29, 49, 50
overview, 82, 278
social competence and, 145
word meaning and, 8–9
Relational aggression. *see also* Aggression; Meanness
  costs of popularity and, 249, 264
  emergence and maintenance of popularity and, 281–282
  emotional adjustment and, 96
  function of, 111
  gender and, 44–45, 104, 110–112, 115–116, 132–133
  measurement of popularity and, 44–45
  moderators of the link with popularity, 86–88
  peer groups and, 176–182
  status and, 83–88
Relational moderators, 234–235
Relationship leadership, 292. *see also* Leadership
Relationships
  acceptance and, 92–94
  collective aspects of popularity and, 71
  influence processes and, 234–235
  romantic relationships, 71, 93–94, 230–231
Reliability, 42–43
Reputational popularity, 30, 79–81, 82–83
Research programs. *see also* Ethnographic studies; Longitudinal research
  ethnicity and, 202–210
  influence processes and, 225–228, 238–239
  measurement of popularity and, 31–37
  overview, 17–18
  peer groups and, 187–189
Research roles, 62–64
Resources
  influence processes and, 229
  preserving popularity and, 283
  social dominance and, 134
  socioeconomic status (SES) and, 19–20
Risks, behavioral. *see* Behavioral risks
Romantic relationships. *see also* Sexual behavior
  acceptance and, 93–94
  collective aspects of popularity and, 71
  influence processes and, 230–231

Same-sex nominations, 40
School transitions
  operational principles and, 171–172
  peer groups and, 183
  social dominance and, 133–134
Scramble competition, 131–133. *see also* Competitive encounters
Secularization, 19–20
Seeking popularity. *see* Wannabes
Segregation, 209–210

Self, 10–14
Self-awareness. *see* Self-perceptions
Self-blame, 203
Self-concept, 144
Self-control, 142
Self-disclosure, 104
Self-efficacy, 84
Self-esteem, 206
Self-other dialectic, 10–14
Self-perceptions
  acceptance and, 95, 144
  measurement of popularity and, 46–47
  preserving popularity and, 283–284
  status-aggression link and, 87–88
Self-presentation, 150
Self-ratings, 46–47
Self-worth, 249
Sensitivity, 282–283
Sex-typed interpersonal style, 119. *see also* Gender
Sexual behavior. *see also* Romantic relationships
  acceptance and, 88–90
  costs of popularity and, 72, 255–259, 263–264
  influence processes and, 230–231
Smoking. *see also* Substance use
  costs of popularity and, 72, 250–255
  influence processes and, 230–231
Sociability, 84, 142
Social acceptance. *see* Acceptance
Social adjustment, 172–173
Social aggression, 104. *see also* Aggression; Relational aggression
Social anxiety, 96
Social behavior, 45–46
Social competence. *see also* Prosocial behavior; Social skills
  behavioral components of, 141–143, 152–154
  developmental trajectories, 149–152
  dual-component model of, 285–287
  emotional functioning and, 147–149
  overview, 140–141, 155–156
  reconceptualization of, 154–155
  underlying processes, 144–149
Social context, 261–262, 264
Social dominance. *see also* Aggression; Dominance-based popularity
  affiliation and, 128–131
  competition and, 129–133
  contest versus scramble competition, 131–133
  forms of aggression and, 127–128
  overview, 123–127, 134–135
  school transitions and, 133–134
Social goals, 94–95, 145
Social influence processes. *see* Influence processes

Social information processing, 123–124, 144–147
Social intelligence, 94, 145–146
Social network centrality, 35–36, 84–85, 188
Social reinforcement, 249
Social skills, 108, 141–143. see also Interpersonal skills; Social competence
Social standing. see Status
Social support, 206
Social-cognitive factors
  acceptance and, 94–96
  preserving popularity and, 284–285
  social competence and, 144–147
  status-aggression link and, 86–88
Social-cognitive mapping technique, 169–170
Socialization, 119, 176–177
Socioeconomic status (SES)
  collective aspects of popularity and, 71–72
  fashion and, 105
  gender and, 105, 109
  overview, 19–20
Sociological constructs, 15–16
Sociometric methods. see also Measurement of popularity
  alternative peer (sociometric) measures, 34–37
  overview, 27–28
  peer groups and, 165–166, 188
  psychometric properties of, 42–46
  voter population and, 33–34
Sociometric popularity. see also Likability
  academic competence and, 261
  overview, 30, 49–50, 79–81, 275
Sports participation, 65, 110
Stability. see also Losing popularity; Preserving popularity
  acceptance and, 81–83, 97–98
  measurement of popularity and, 43
  peer groups and, 188
Status. see also Costs of popularity; Peer groups
  academic competence and, 260–263
  acceptance and, 79–81
  affiliation and, 128–131
  aggression and, 83–88, 124
  behavioral and academic risk and, 88–90
  developmental trajectories, 182–185
  emergence and maintenance of popularity and, 278–287
  ethnicity and, 195–202, 202–203
  gender and, 105–106
  group organization and, 170–171
  influence processes and, 225–228
  overview, 15–16, 16–17, 165–166, 245–246, 263–264
  peer groups and, 180–182
  sexual behavior and, 255–259
  social behaviors associated with, 90–92
  social competence and, 140–141
  substance use and, 250–255
  underlying processes, 246–250
Status striving. see also Paths to popularity
  acceptance and, 97–98
  overview, 73–74
  peer groups and, 180
  social competence and, 154–155
Stereotypes, 209–210
Strategic relational aggression, 111–112. see also Relational aggression
Stress, 282–283
Substance use. see also Drinking; Smoking
  acceptance and, 88–90
  costs of popularity and, 250–255, 263–264
  sexual behavior and, 256

Task leadership, 292. see also Leadership
Teacher ratings, 47–48
Teachers, 63–64
Teen pregnancy, 258–259. see also Sexual behavior
Test-retest reliability, 42–43
"The Adolescent Society" (Coleman, 1961), 31
Theory of popularity, 273–274, 275–278. see also Popularity overview
Toughness, 112–114, 129. see also Aggression
Transactional model, 151–152, 152
Transitions, school
  operational principles and, 171–172
  peer groups and, 183
  social dominance and, 133–134
Two pathways of popularity model, 291
Two-culture model, 103–104, 118–120. see also Gender
Types of popularity, 27–29

Unlimited nominations, 40–41
Unpopulars, 181–182. see also Outgroup membership

Verbal aggression, 176–182. see also Aggression; Relational aggression
Victimization, peer, 203. see also Aggression
Visibility, 125, 193, 276
Void of vagueness concept, 7–8
Voter population, 33–34

Wannabes. see also Paths to popularity
  acceptance and, 97–98
  overview, 73–74
  peer groups and, 180
  social competence and, 154–155
Within-group aggression, 126. see also Aggression; Peer groups
Word meaning, 5–10